THE FUTURE OF

Erotic Fantasy Art

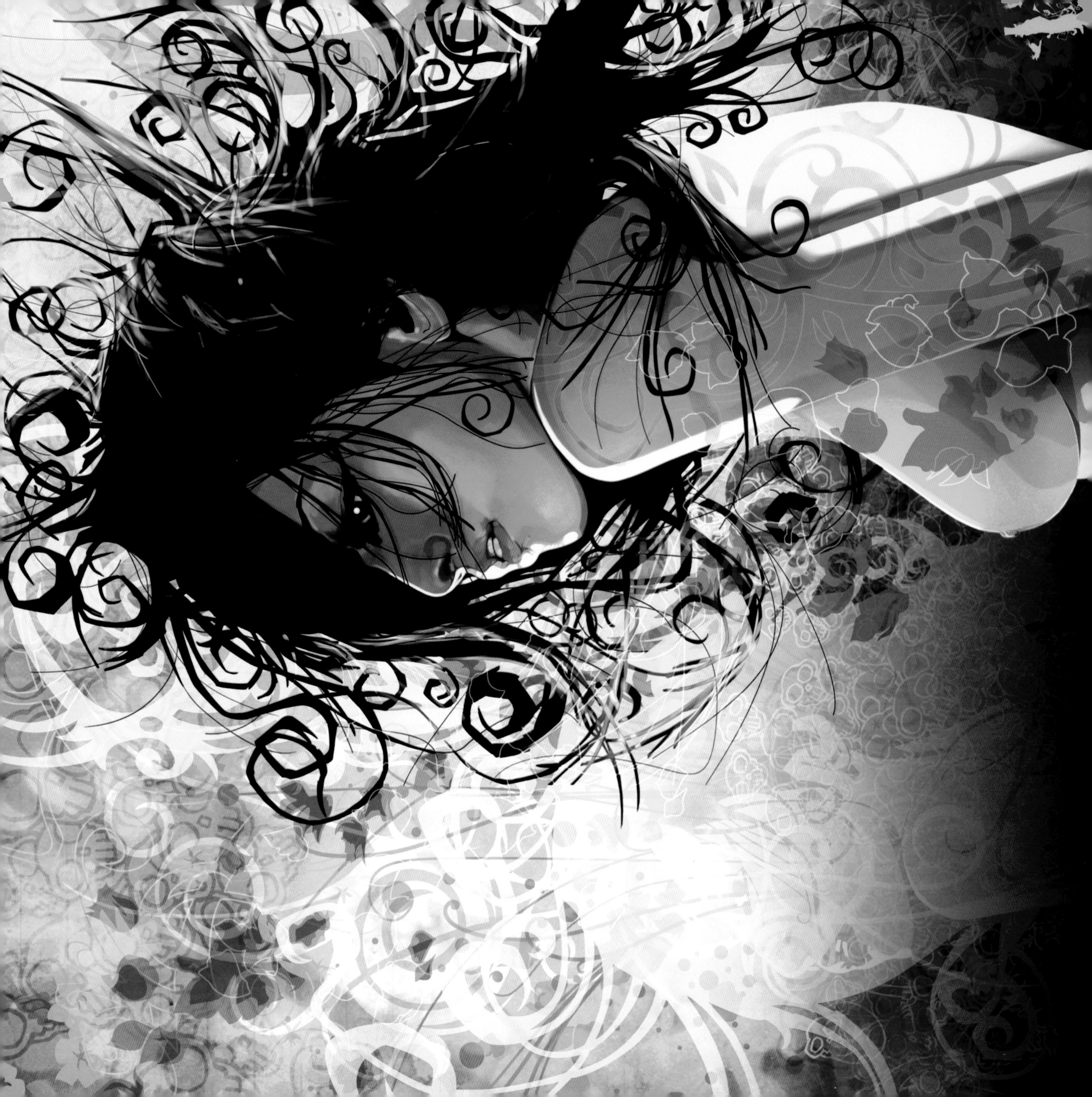

THE FUTURE OF Erotic Fantasy Art

PAUL PEART-SMITH

HARPER
DESIGN

An Imprint of HarperCollinsPublishers

THE FUTURE OF EROTIC FANTASY ART

HarperCollins books may be purchased for educational, business, or sales promotional use. For information, please write: Special Markets Department, HarperCollins*Publishers*, 10 East 53rd Street, New York, NY 10022.

First published in the United States and Canada in 2011 by:
Harper Design
An *Imprint of* HarperCollins*Publishers*
10 East 53rd Street
New York, NY 10022
Tel: (212) 207-7000
Fax: (212) 207-7654
harperdesign@harpercollins.com
www.harpercollins.com

Distributed throughout the United States and Canada by:
HarperCollins*Publishers*
10 East 53rd Street
New York, NY 10022
Fax: (212) 207-7654

This book was conceived, designed, and produced by
I L E X
210 High Street
Lewes
East Sussex BN7 2NS
www.ilex-press.com

Publisher: Alastair Campbell
Creative Director: Peter Bridgewater
Managing Editor: Nick Jones
Editor: Ellie Wilson
Commissioning Editor: Tim Pilcher
Art Director: Julie Weir
Designer: Simon Goggin

Library of Congress Control Number: 2011932827

ISBN: 978-0-062082-86-2

Printed in China
First Printing, 2011
Color Origination by Ivy Press Reprographics

Introductory images:
p. 2 *Fallen Angel* by Steve Sampson
p. 4 – 5 *The Hunted* by Vince Natale
p. 6 *Penthesilea* by Chris Achilléos
p. 8 *Fishgirl* by Chris Achilléos
p. 9 *First Lady* by Chris Achilléos
p. 10 *Zainib* by Felipe Machado Franco

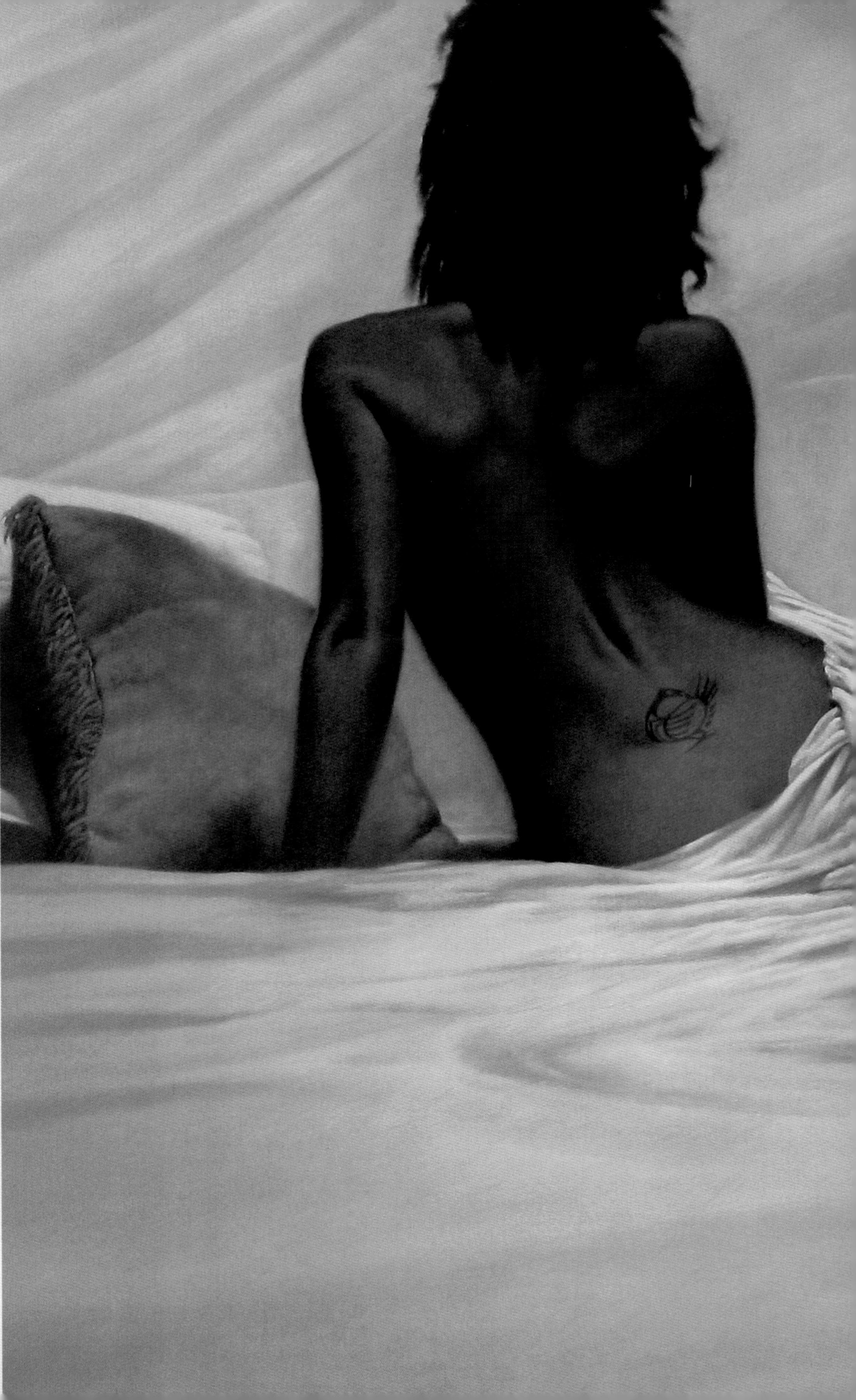

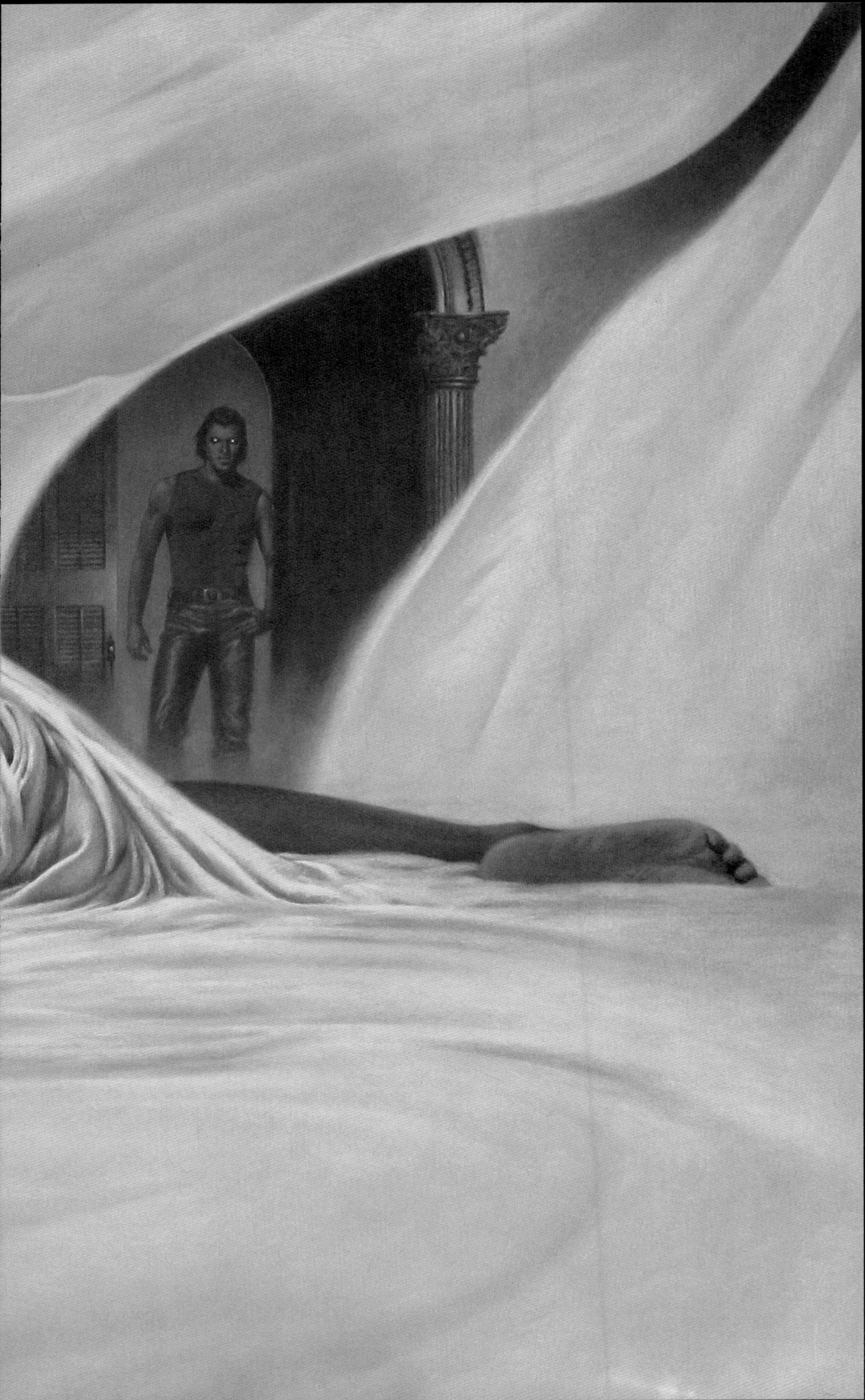

Contents

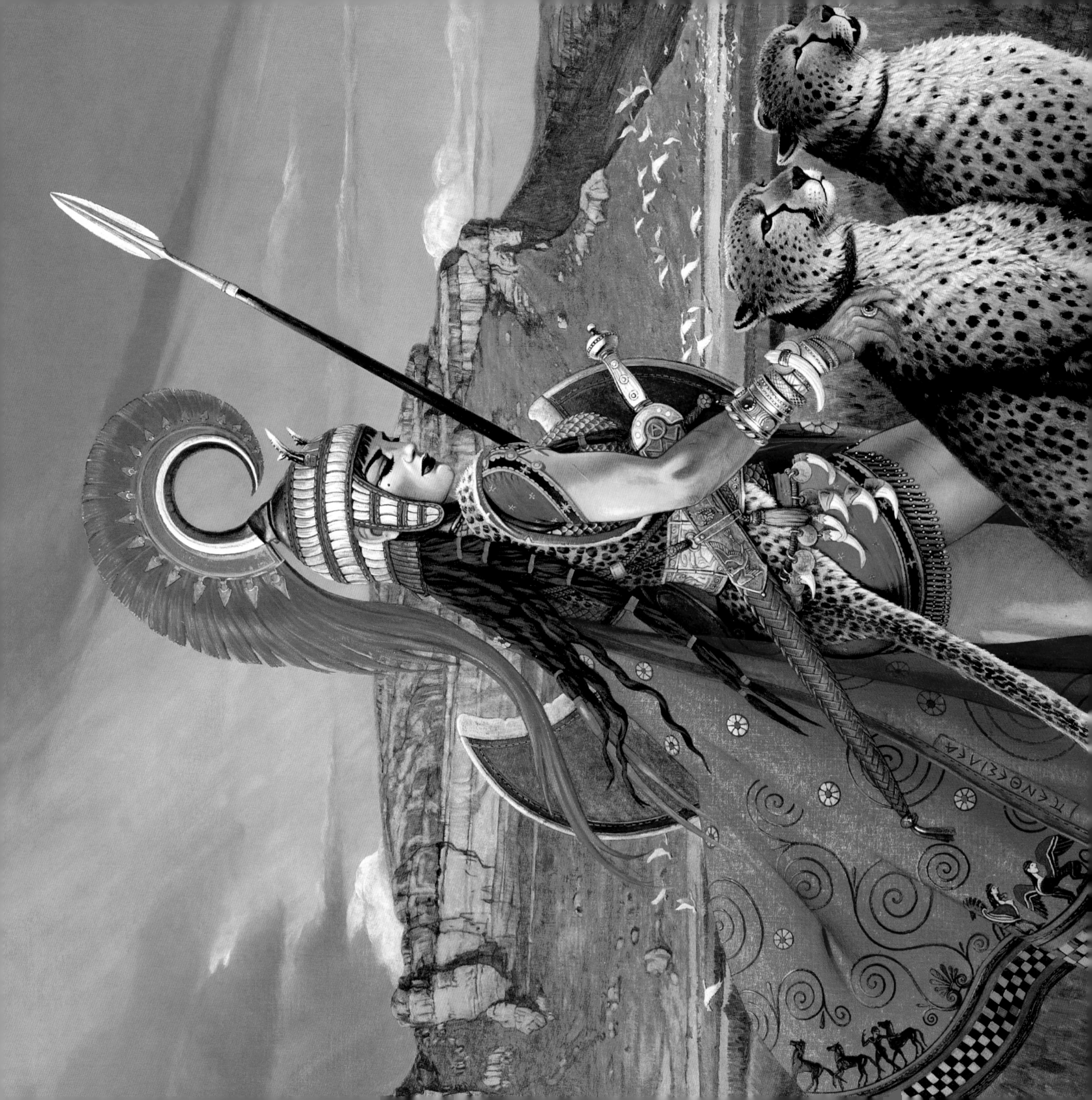

Foreword

What is the art of erotic fantasy?

I suppose it's painting the human form—mainly the female—in a pose or composition that is exciting and even arousing to the viewer.

I can't really say whether I had that in mind when I was working on my "erotic pictures." Perhaps I did, but that was probably coincidental. I want to make it clear here, that, as an artist, I love and worship the female figure. I love the curves, the symmetry, the texture . . . I could go on and on, but I mustn't get too excited! All this is why I choose to paint the female form in its perfection, again and again.

My early work in the genre was inspired by the Greek myths and the classical and Celtic worlds, and most of my current work continues to be inspired by this. For an Amazon, I would pose a female figure and clothe it in armor and weapons that were usually worn by the male figure. In other words, I was simply resurrecting the Amazons of ancient Greek tales. The stuff that I am made of! As an example, see *First Lady* (p. 9), which I painted in 1973.

I also depicted the half-creature/half-females from the ancient myths, such as the Gorgons, the sirens, and the shape-shifting Gods. Good examples of these are my *Fishgirl* (1976; p. 8) and *Seduction* (1977) paintings—two very controversial and influential pieces. These pictures have been described as erotic fantasy, in that they juxtapose the beauty of the human form with mythical creations.

Thinking about some of my earlier work, mostly for *Men Only* magazine in the 1970s and early '80s, the images are quite "erotic," such as *Foam* (1980), as it was commissioned by a skin-mag who expected nothing less! However, my main aim

for that work was to paint the female form in an exotic, weird, and (hopefully) new way—and yet still have it relate to the story it was illustrating in the magazine.

The execution of such paintings was to underpaint with the airbrush and then to hand paint with brushes, carefully and painstakingly adding texture and light. Days or weeks of work could easily be ruined with a slip of a brush, and the dreaded deadline missed, resulting in no pay and the loss of a client.

I look around today and see the proliferation of contemporary imagery done mostly by the digital generation, who execute their work with unbelievable slinkiness. I must confess, that they look amazing whether printed or onscreen.

For me, a traditional-media artist, it is the act of painting that matters. You can't beat gazing at a painting and admiring the skill and craftsmanship of the artist that has created it.

My more recent work has evolved to a more historical, costume-orientated, and symbolistic approach. The female figure is still there, but the airbrush is hardly used. It's far more likely that I'd be using oils on canvas, something I could not entertain when tight deadlines were involved.

I like people to always look at my pictures with the title in mind, as most of my more recent images have a story to tell. I feel that a picture—including an erotic one with an aim to arouse—has to say something to the viewer, it has to communicate in more than just an aesthetic way. Hopefully, you'll be drawn into the fantasy worlds captured within the images of this collection; the following artworks represent the visions of leading erotic fantasy artists today.

Chris Achilléos

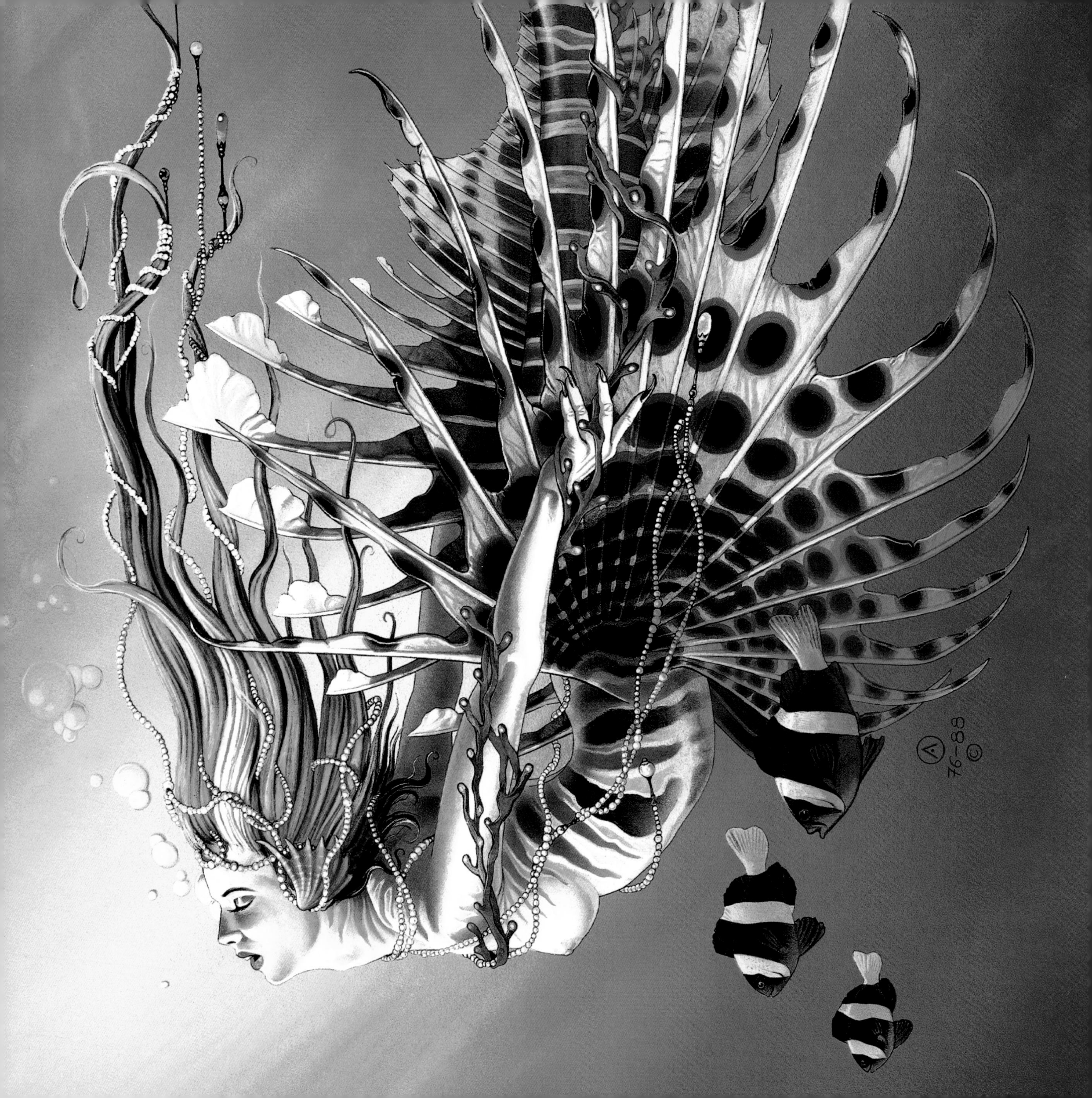
76-88
©

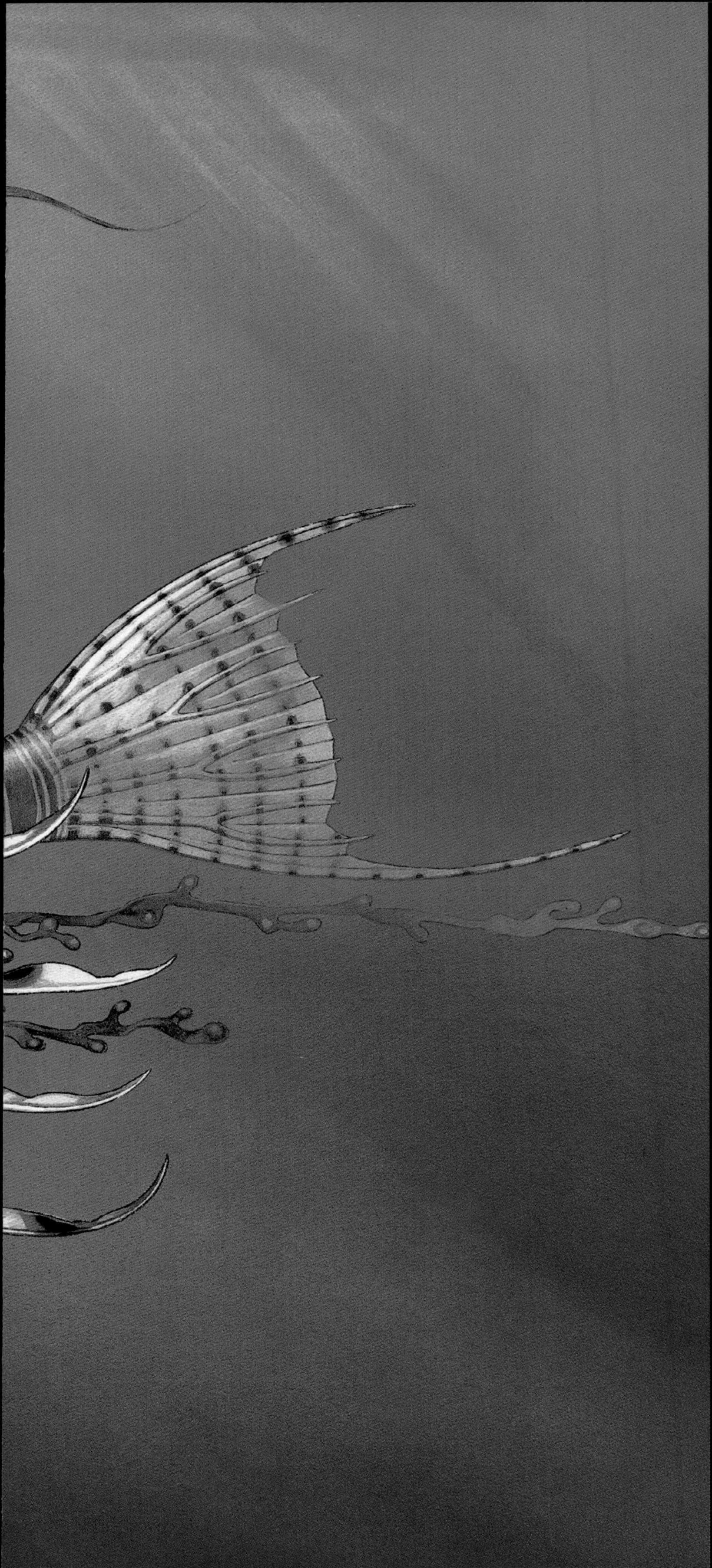

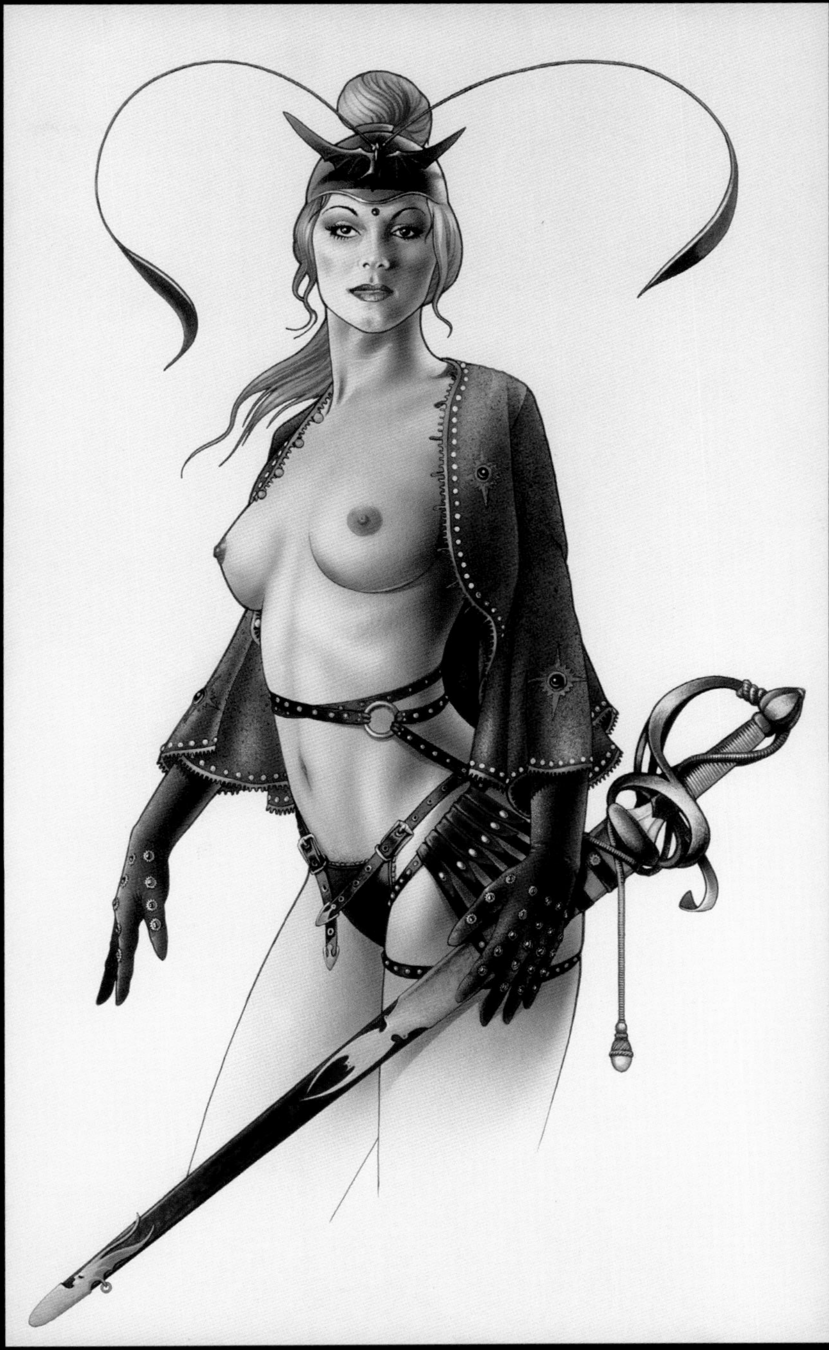

Chris Achilléos, artist and illustrator, has created some of the best-loved fantasy and glamour art of the past thirty years. His work ranges from Taarna, the famous Heavy Metal *heroine, through classic* Conan *covers and Amazonian women to his more recent fetish paintings, all the time experimenting with new techniques and different materials.*

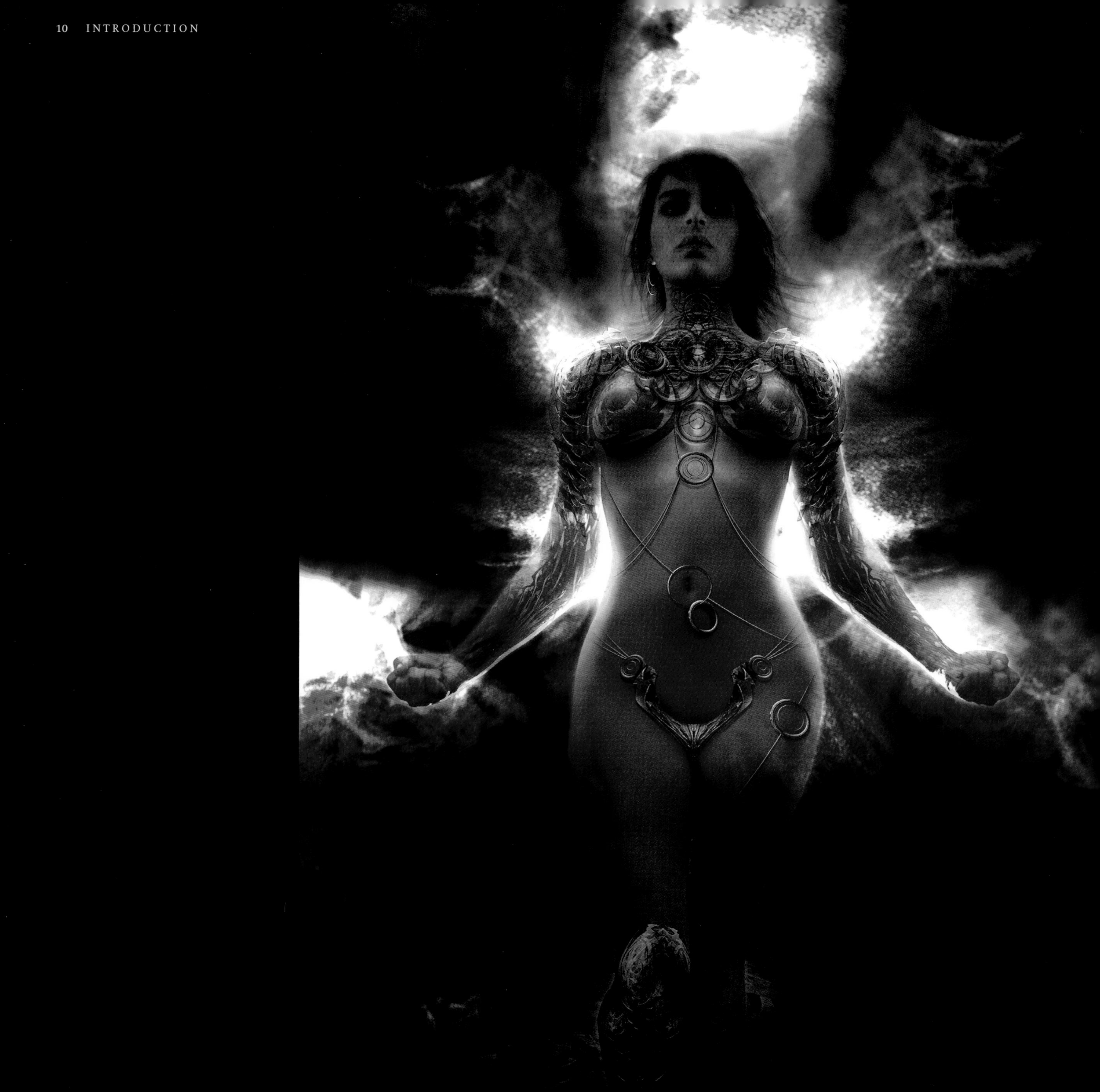

Introduction

Welcome to this titillating collection of sensual art, celebrating the genre of *Erotic Fantasy*.

I've been working as a comics artist, designer, and illustrator for 20 years, drawing demons, mutants, cyborgs, mutant cyborgs, demon mutant cyborgs, monsters, dinosaurs, monster dinosaurs—you get the idea.

When I began my research into the world of erotic fantasy art to compile this book, it triggered the realization that in all those years I had never drawn a sexual act or organ. Incredibly, whenever I picked up a pencil or brush, creating images of heroic bodies in skin-tight suits, I would completely stash my sexual impulses away.

Sex is supernatural. And therein lies the joy of it. Sex cannot be scientifically contained, quantified as a mere exchange of bodily fluids. Sex is passionate. We want the energy, the feeling of possession that is the essence of lust, as powerful as any ethereal host. In this book you will find succubae, mermaids, vampires, and all varieties of temptresses; creatures of passion, symbols of desire. Here, the artists present images that capture the imaginative nature of eroticism.

In 1781, the Swiss painter John Henry Fuseli exhibited a painting which was to influence artists the world over,

forming the basis of the book you now hold. *The Nightmare* portrayed a pallid woman reclining on a bed in a dark room. The look on her face is ambiguous, we don't know whether she is in turmoil or the throes of pleasure. The demonic figure of an incubus squats on her stomach and the duo are watched by an unusual voyeur creeping from behind a curtain, a dark horse with eerie, white eyes. It is believed that the creatures are the manifestations of the woman's erotic nightmare.

The painting was a sensation amongst its first audiences—partly due to the provocative pose of the sleeping woman and the myths surrounding incubi—and word quickly spread throughout Europe about the power of its enigmatic horror. I've seen this piece many times, and I can't help but think that Fuseli's choice of an attractive woman in a nightdress as the painting's protagonist was to provoke the notorious 18th-century reputation it duly garnered. It's a killer combination that continues to have impact with repeated viewings.

The artists in this book are descendants of Fuseli. They represent some of the best examples of contemporary fantasy illustration, infused with the surreal and the outlandish. Much of it is digital, and yet still sensual, successfully capturing the excitement and danger of arousal. These creators remind me that artistic expression is an honest and direct response to life as it is felt, in our head, our guts, and our lower regions.

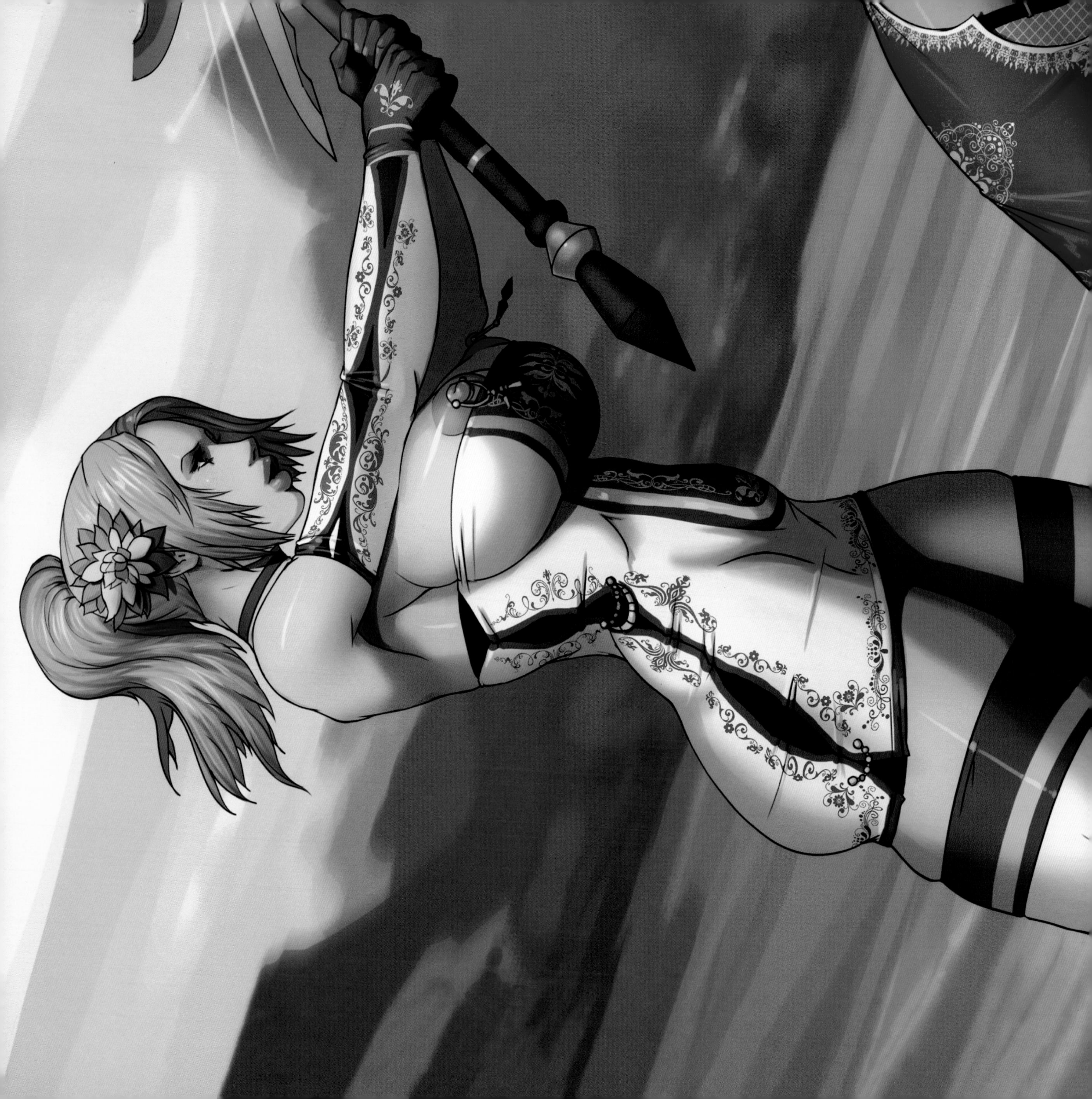

CHAPTER 1

WE CAN BE HEROES

▼ **Mage vs Warrior**
Dmitry Sergeev
Adobe Photoshop
http://dmitrys.deviantart.com

Sergeev captures a real sense of movement in his snapshot of a battle scene between a mage and a warrior through his use of a low perspective and blurred background. "For this image I wanted to depict a dynamic fighting scene with a naughty twist—especially in the clothes department. The costumes are inspired by many MMORPGs, although I dont actually play them myself."

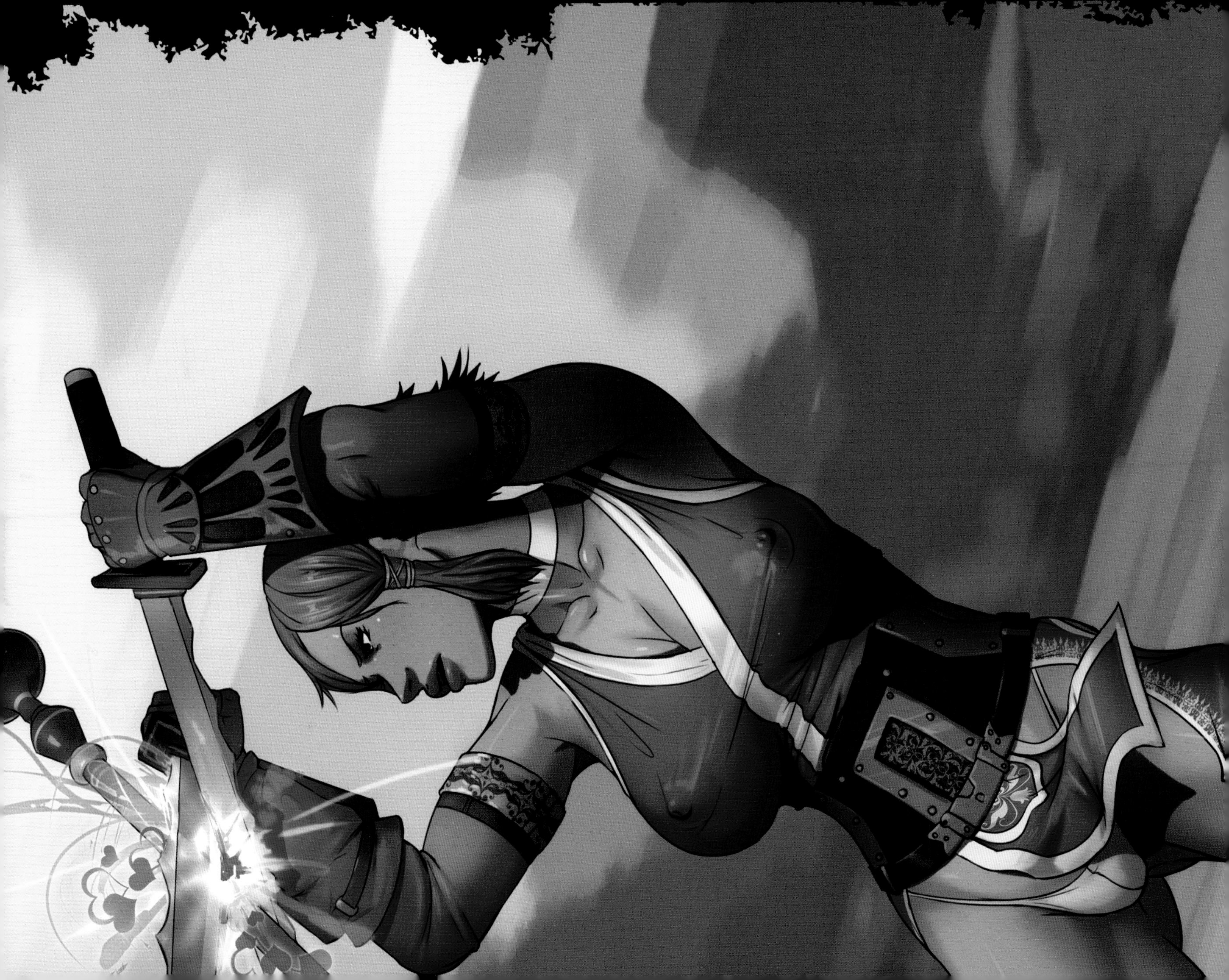

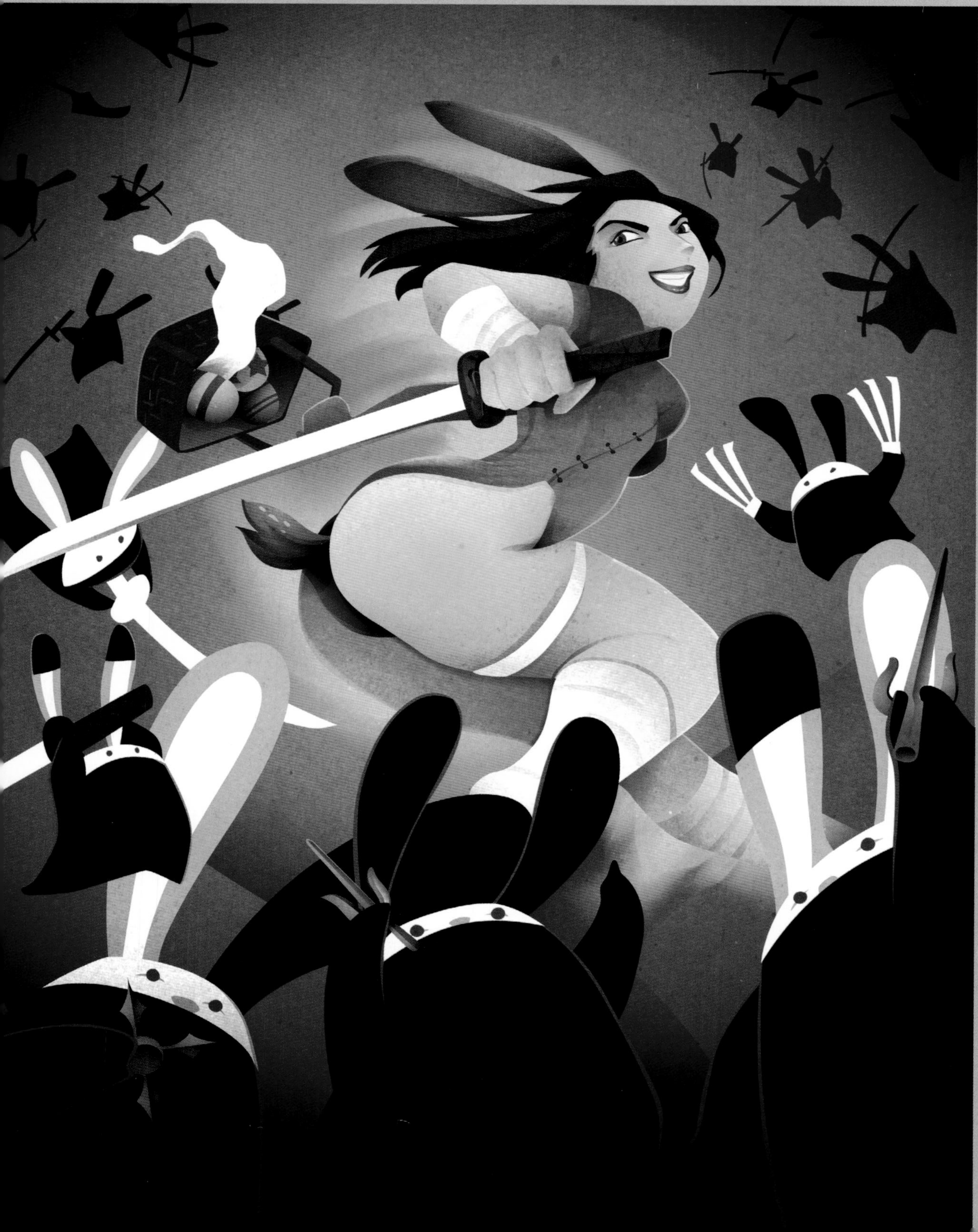

◀ **Ninja Bunny**
Charlene Chua
Adobe Illustrator
and Adobe Photoshop
www.charlenechua.com

"I've always liked bunnies, and one day, while trying to think of an Easter image, I thought it would be cute to do ninja bunnies. I like drawing girls too, so I thought it would be interesting to pair a sexy-looking girl with some cute, abstracted ninja rabbits to see what would happen. At the time, I was experimenting with trying to get more movement in my images through blurs and depth, which I think comes across quite well in this picture."

▶ **Drow**
Charlene Chua
Adobe Illustrator
and Adobe Photoshop
www.charlenechua.com

"This is a piece that I did after picking up Illustrator (I originally started working in Macromedia FreeHand). I have been an admirer of fantasy art since I was a kid, although I had resigned myself to not doing fantasy artwork because at the time, it seemed like everything needed to be painted and I am a terrible painter. My style and sense of anatomy are also nowhere close to that of the great fantasy painters. I did this as an experiment, to see how a fantasy subject would look in my style."

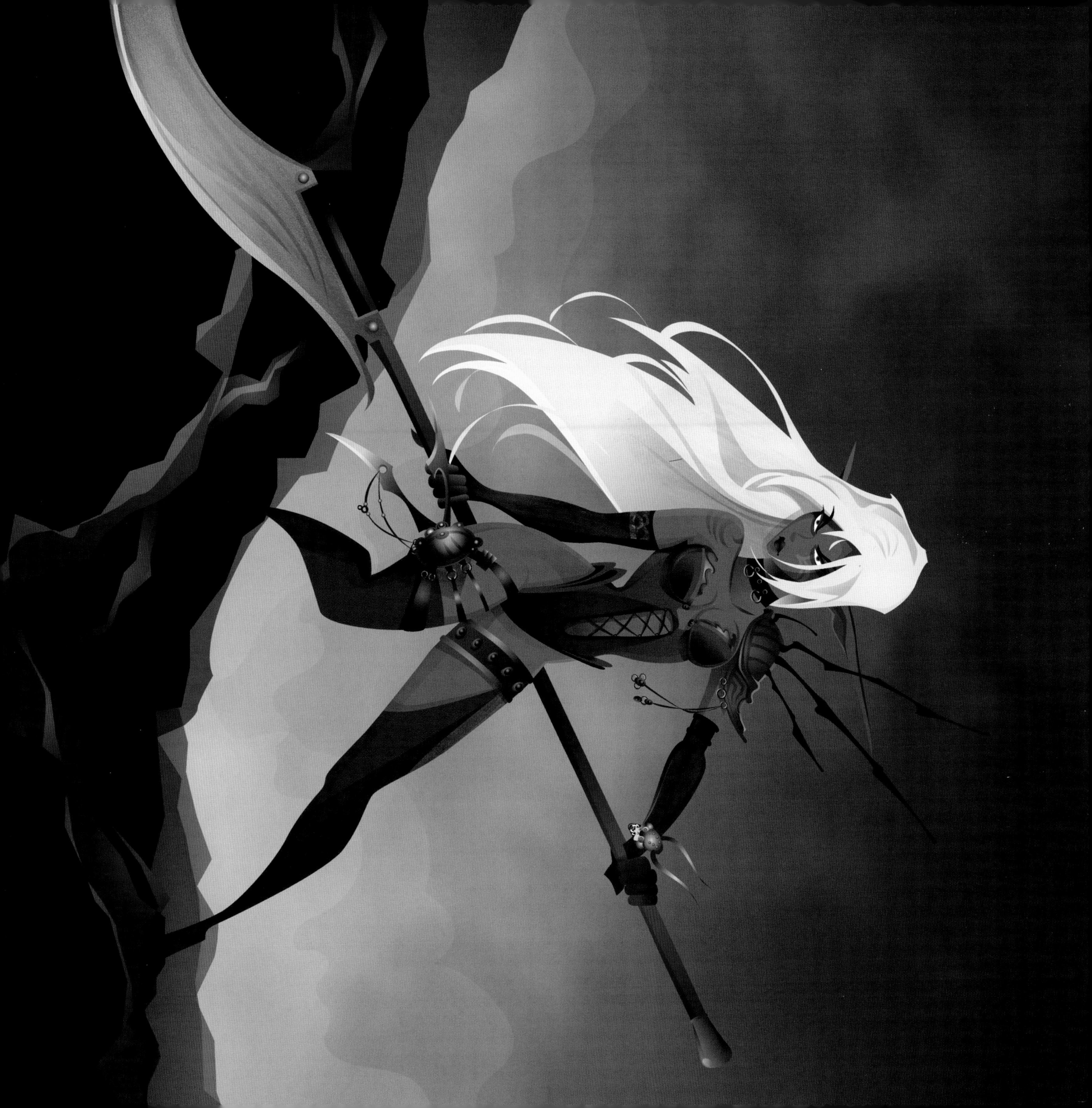

▶ **Erotic Thoughts**
Scott Koznar
Poser, Bryce, and
Adobe Photoshop
http://weenie2.deviantart.com

"Erotic Thoughts *is one of my latest 'Gargirl' works. I used the Aiko 3 base figure with a Sylfie Face morph. A 'morph' is a set of figure controls that, when applied, change the face, body, or any other part of a figure it is matched to. Sylfie is my favorite Aiko 3 morph figure as it creates a young, cutesy female character. The topless suit she is wearing is a Hex bodysuit figure with a demonic tail. This character is a wingless Gargirl known as a 'Lamara.' Her origin is far south of the Czech Republic in the upper desert regions of Northern Africa. Although they cannot fly and are mainly confined to the ground and trees, they are the fastest and most agile of any of the Gargirl species."*

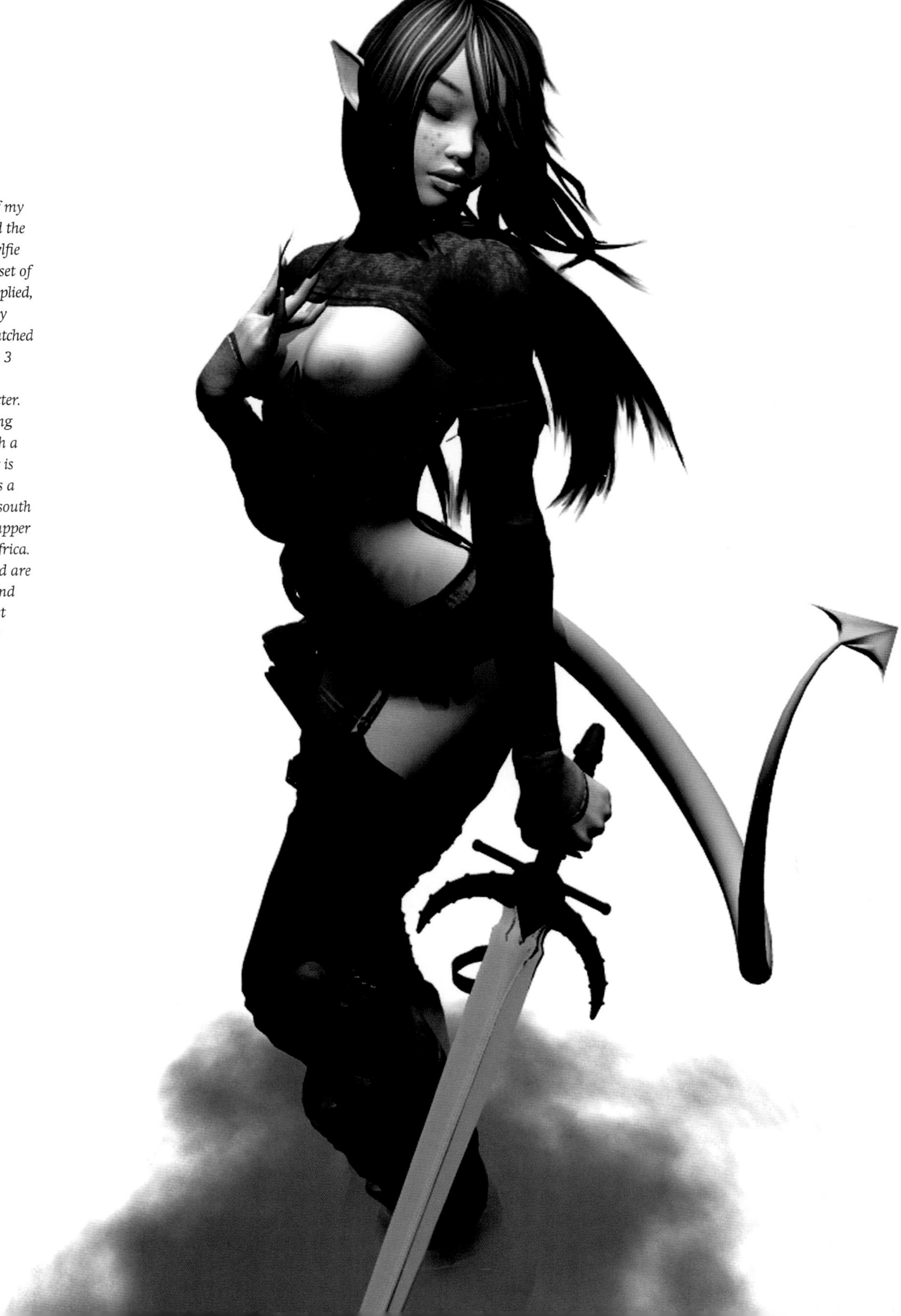

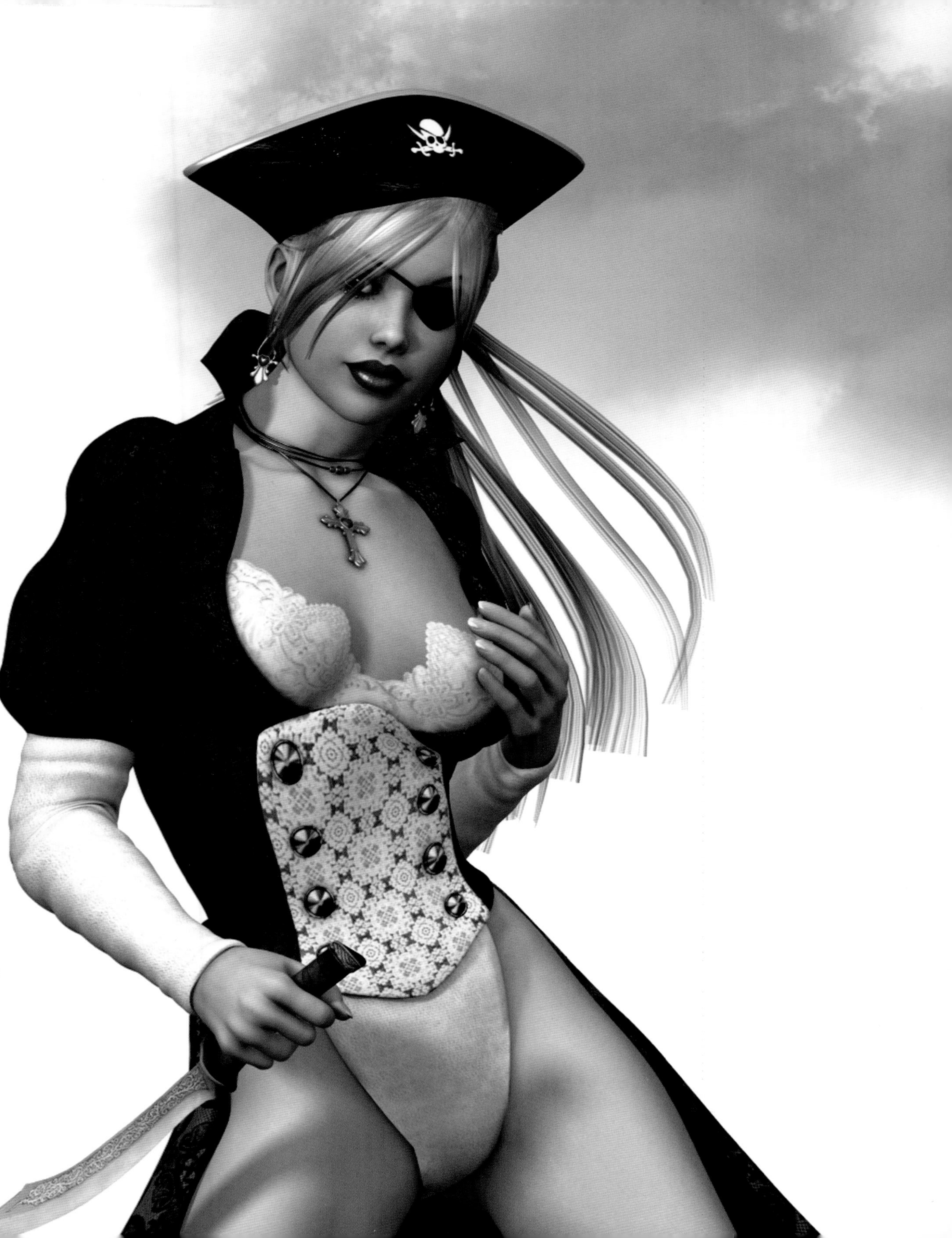

▶ **Woman and Pirate**
Jane Dahl Jensen
Poser Pro and Adobe Photoshop
http://janedj.deviantart.com

This piece is all about attitude. The glamorous captain confronts us, daring us to argue that her obvious femininity makes her unfit to command her ship. As with all of Jane Dahl Jensen's work, it is the details that delight: the minute rendering of the materials in her costume and blade, the rendering of the silky material of her hat, the tiny jewel in her crucifix.

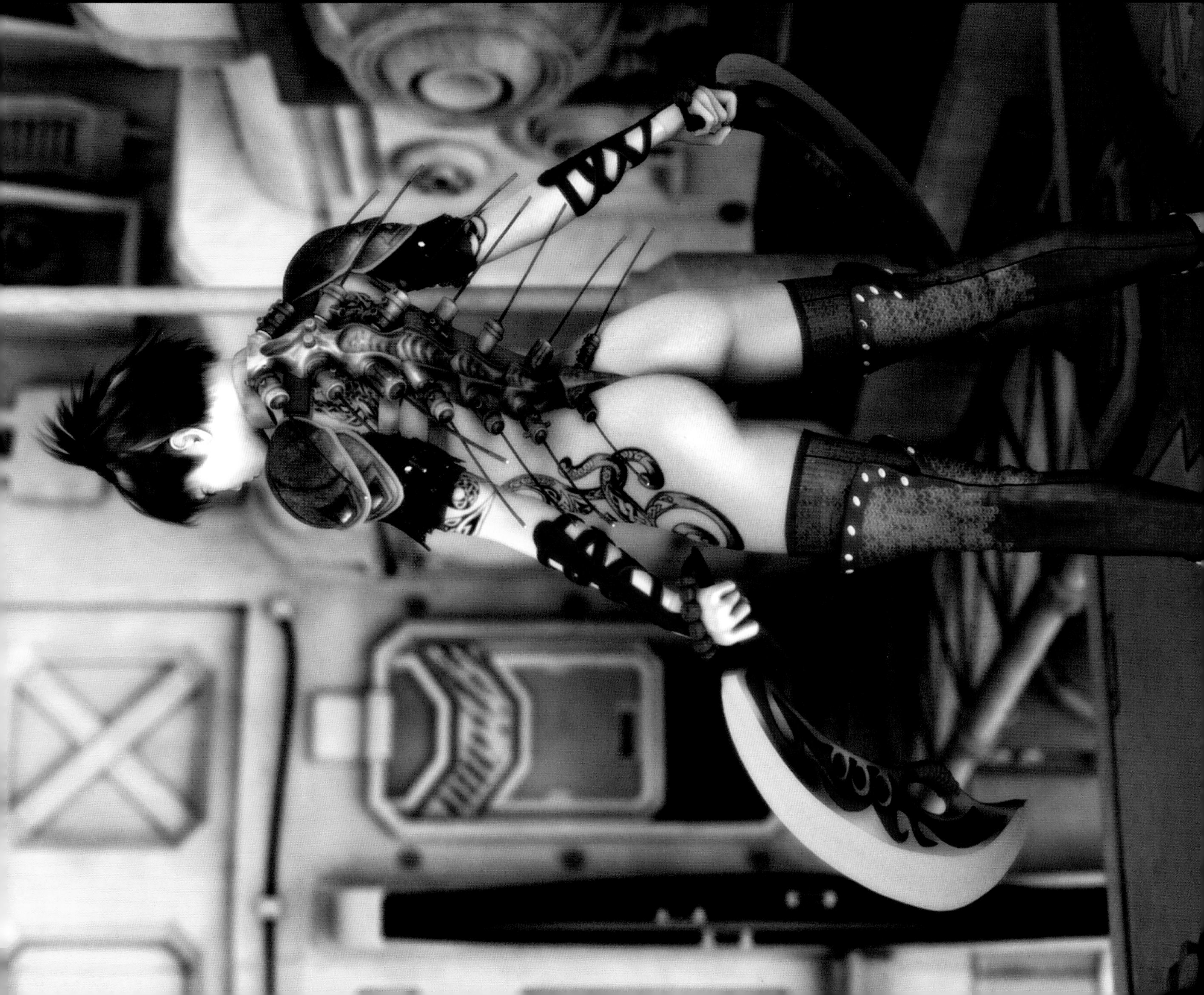

CyberValkyrie
I.L. Jackson
DAZ Studio 3 Advanced and GIMP
http://darklorddc.deviantart.com

"When I was a young boy, my mother was a science fiction fanatic. She even helped me roll up my first Dungeons & Dragons *character. One day, hidden in a big chest under all her* Star Trek *books and* D&D *supplements, I came across a stack of magazines called* Heavy Metal. *I was blown away by the cover art, which always seemed to depict some science fiction or fantasy babe in beautiful, revealing colors. This piece was done in memory of all those summer afternoons spent thumbing through page after page of torrid stories of heroes and heroines who always managed to get laid after defeating the bad guys."*

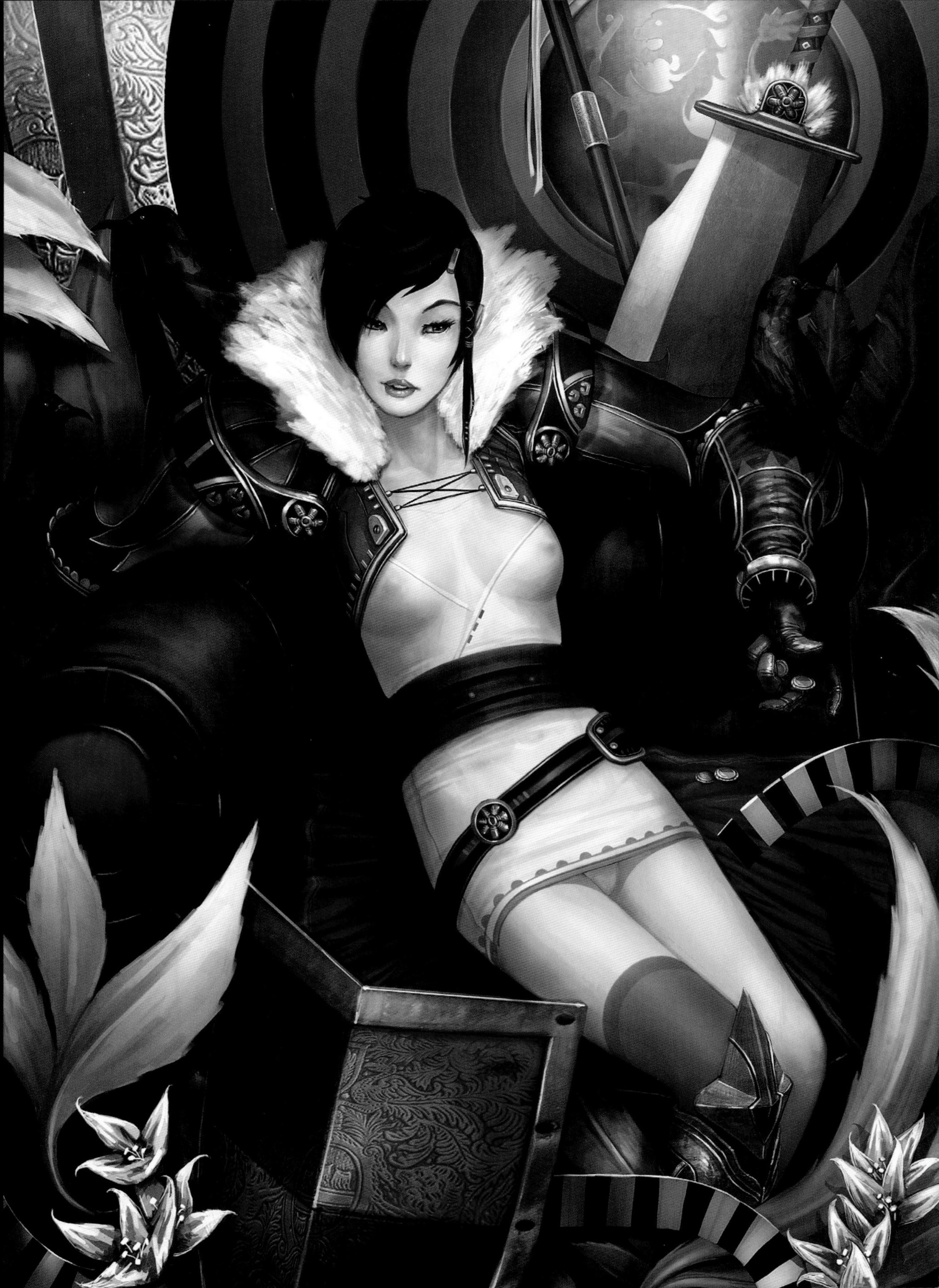

Red Knight
DCWJ
Adobe Photoshop
www.dcwj.deviantart.com

"For this piece I wanted to depict a female knight sitting in her room. For the background, I added some graphic elements to frame her, and strove to blend these elements with her so that it would look more natural."

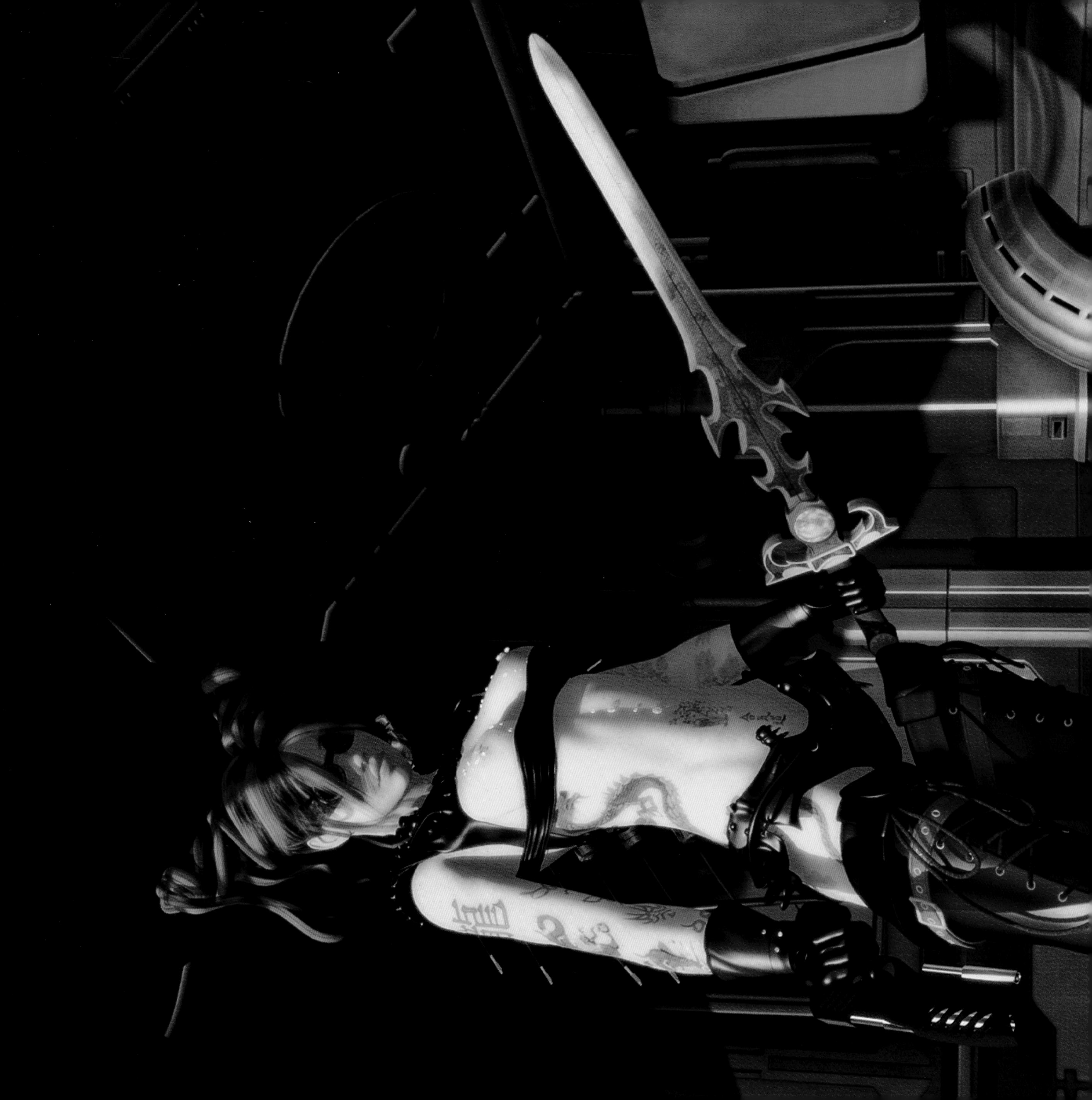

◀ **The Space Pirate**
I.L. Jackson
DAZ Studio 3 Advanced and GIMP
http://darklorddc.deviantart.com

"The only thing cooler than pirates is probably hot, female, half-naked pirates from the future. Or perhaps ninjas. My only real goal with this piece was to load her down with accessories to make her as counterculture as possible. Even after all that effort spent accessorizing, I somehow forgot to give her earrings."

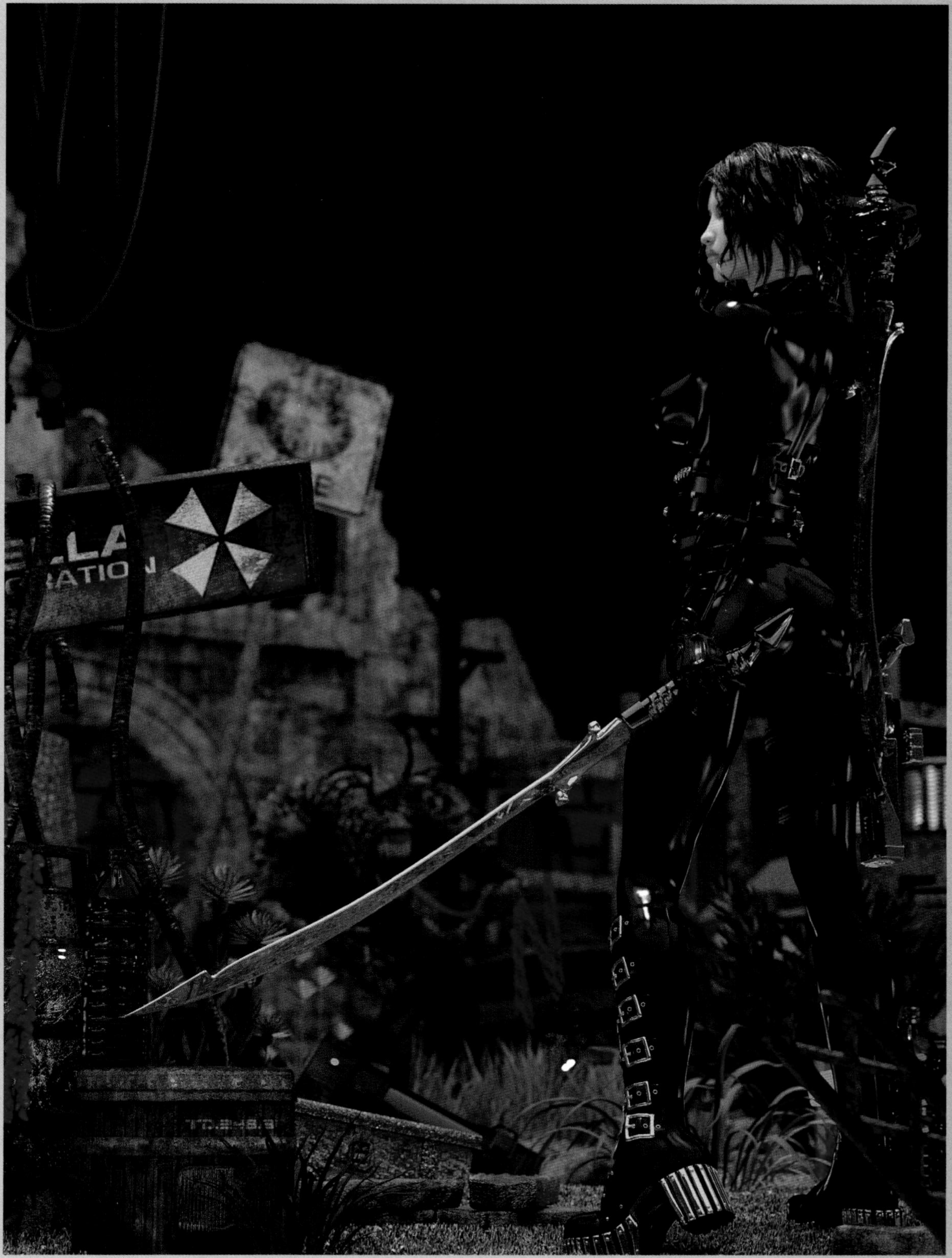

LA
RATION

▶ **Biohazard Evolution**
JeanneDark
ZBrush, Adobe Photoshop, Poser, and Maxwell
http://jeannethedark.daportfolio.com

"I used one of the 360° panoramic HDRI sets as the main light source that I created with a photographer to make this picture. It was taken at night with a lot of street lights on, which resulted in a very nice yellowish ground that is responsible for the 'wasteland charm' on this artwork. Using the panoramic photo had a very nice effect on the latex reflections on the monster-hunter's bodysuit, making it look a little more realistic without too much effort. Movies and games like Underworld *and* Resident Evil *were the main inspiration behind this. The mix of the shiny fetish-look and a very tough huntress really left an impression on me."*

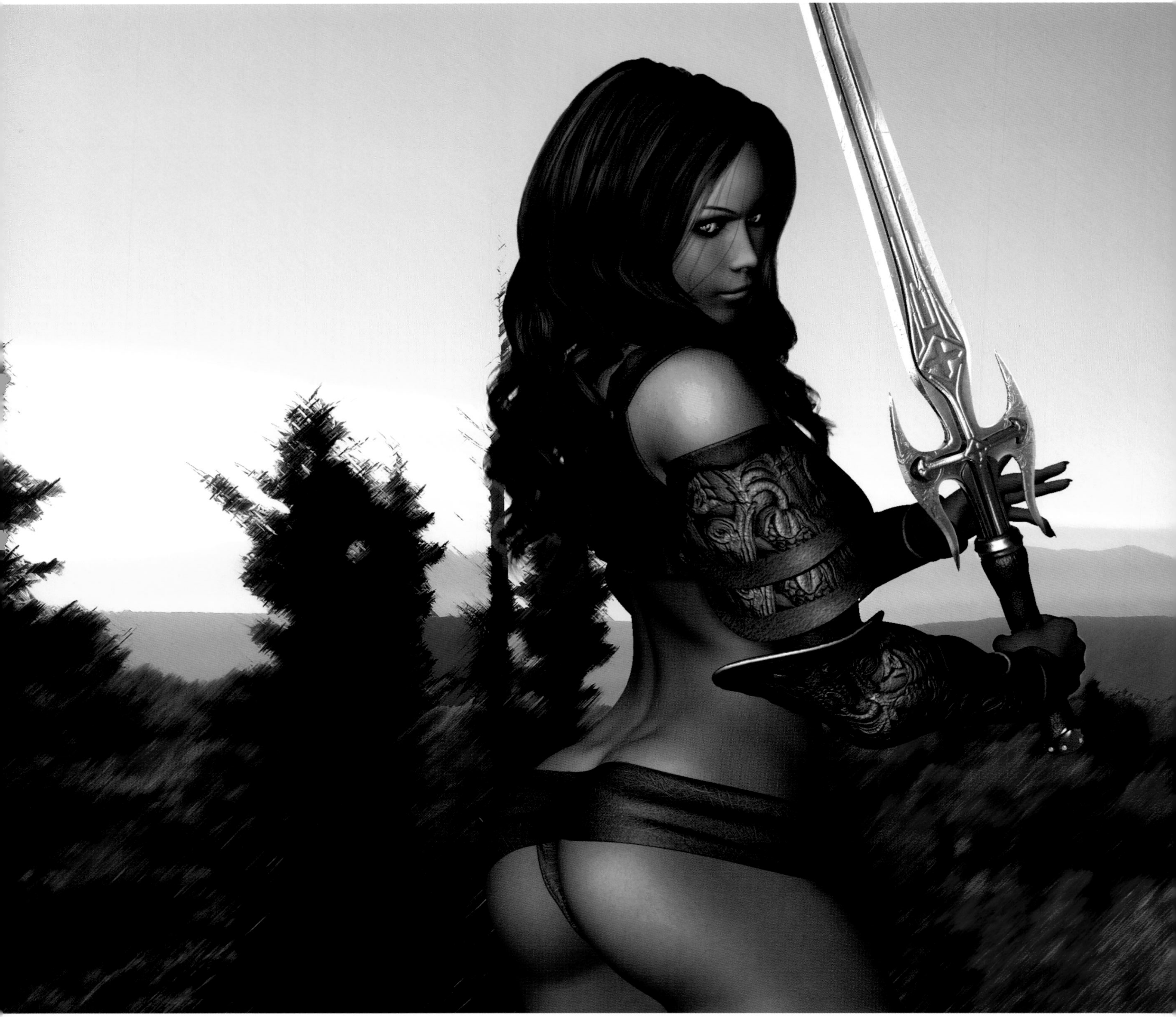

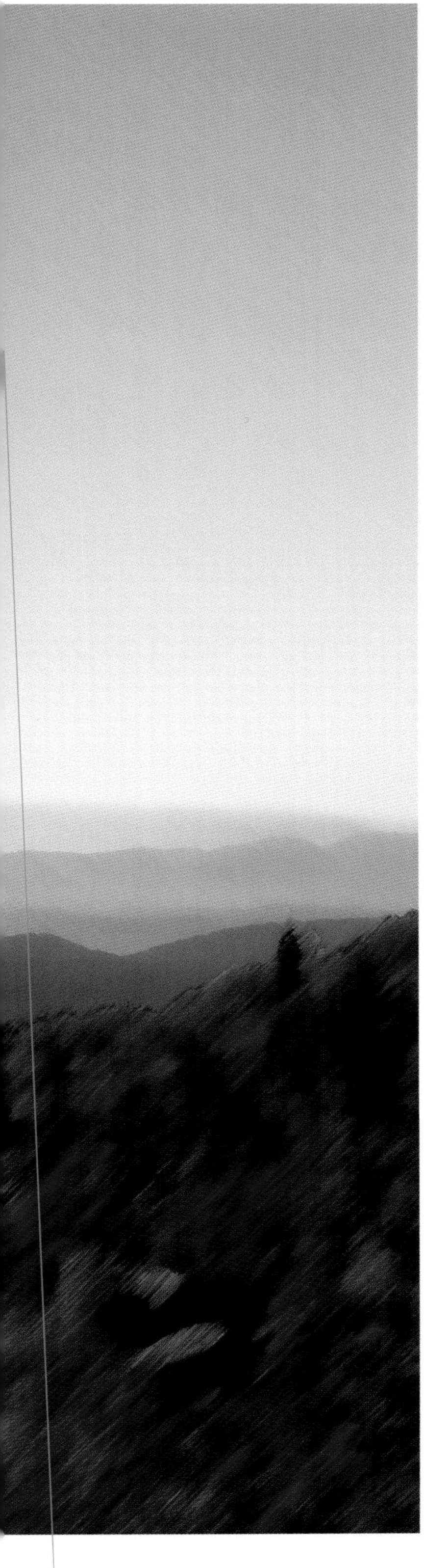

◀ **Cullie**
Aaron Birch "Lunariis"
Poser Pro and Adobe Photoshop
http://lunariis.deviantart.com
www.treeworx.org

"Something I enjoy doing more than anything else is creating the vision my clients have in their minds and putting it before them. Cullie *was a commissioned piece. I enjoyed creating it as it was different to all of the elves and such that I typically make. The process of creating a commission is as follows: the client sends me simple screenshots from whatever game he or she is playing. He or she then sends me a background story and character motivations, and describes every little detail of the character's physicality and personality. I take it from there, doing my best to literally create what my client has in his or her mind. This was one of my successes."*

▶ **Maiden of War**
Tariq Raheem
Adobe Photoshop
and Corel Painter
www.tariqart.net

"I created this image straight after watching the Star Trek *movie. The Romulans with their crazy cool tribal tatts and bad-ass attitude compelled me to create this armor-clad 'battle babe.' Set against a fiery backdrop of war and destruction, she could be a mighty warrior princess of the ancient clan that scorched a planet and ran it red with blood. I wanted a warm color palette with red setting the tone. The blades were designed to complement the spiky organic tattoos as well the intricate engravings on the armor."*

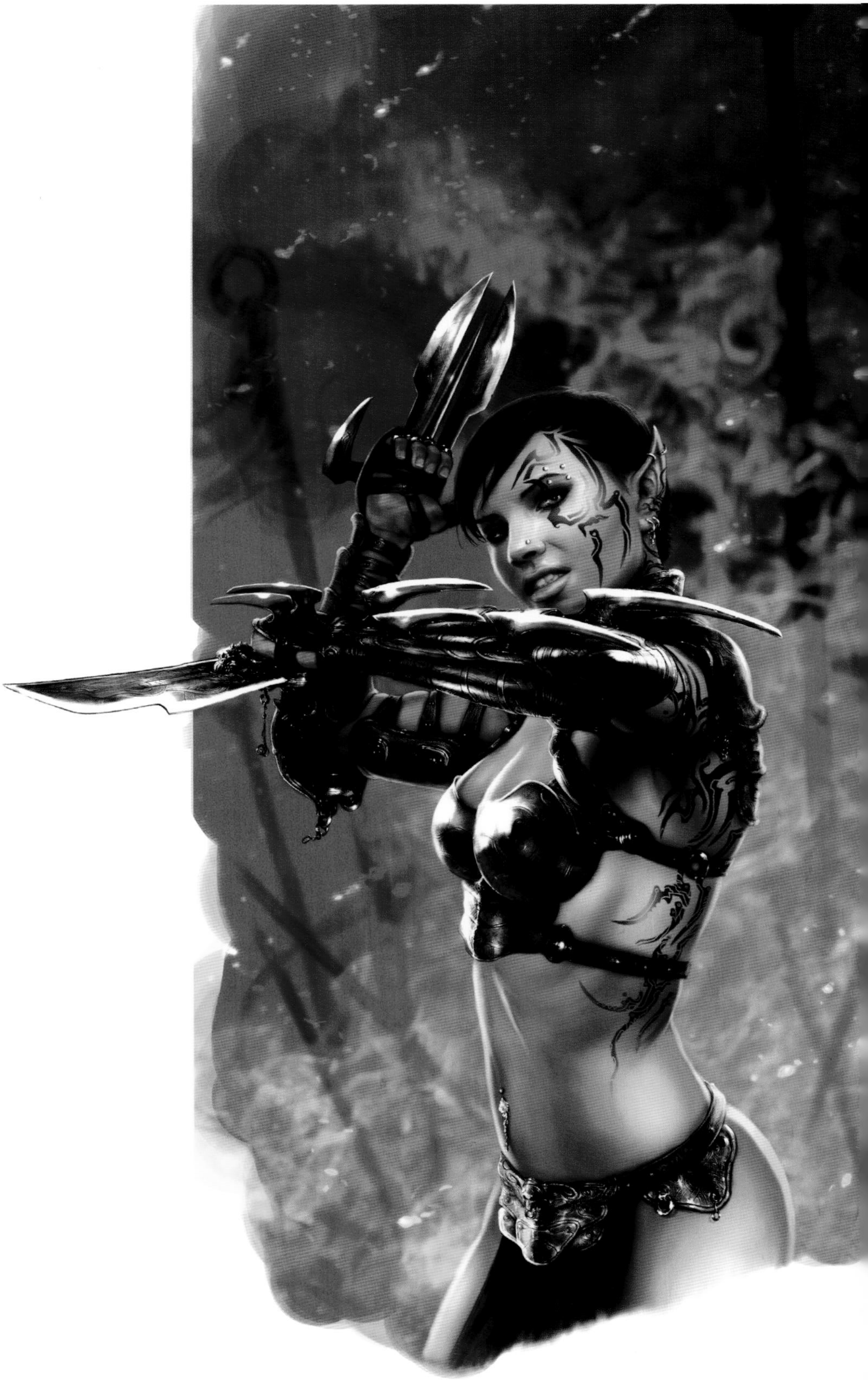

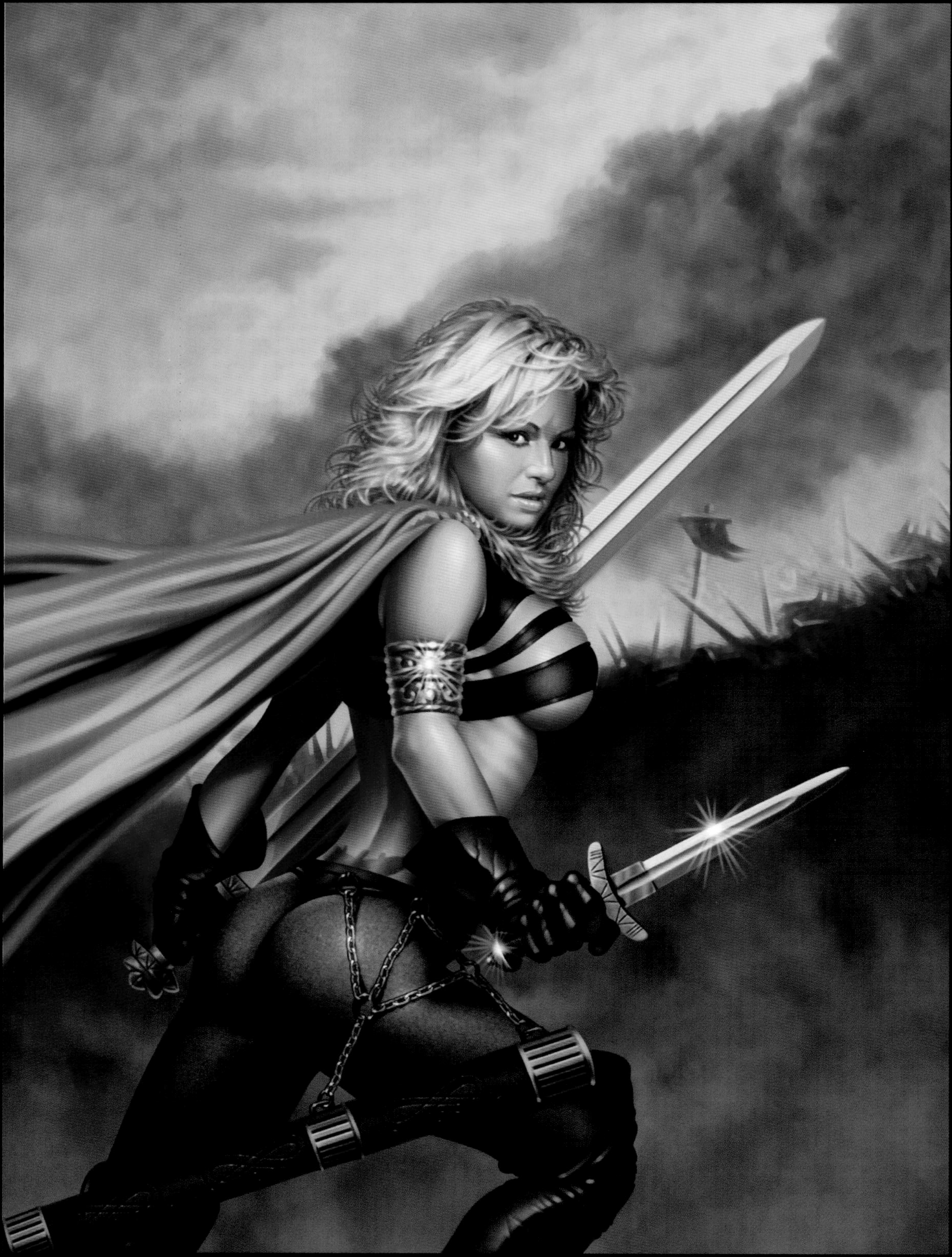

It's Time For Heroes
Lorenzo Di Mauro
Adobe Photoshop
and Corel Painter
www.lorenzodimauro.com
http://lorenzoart.blogspot.com

"For this painting of a fantasy warrior girl, I first did a rough sketch of the pose and the background. Then I collected a few image references for the outfit and weapons. As a reference for the girl, I used a photo of a model, showing a wonderful, intense expression and wearing a very sexy outfit. I changed the clothing and the pose according to the original pencil sketch."

The Witch Queen
Tariq Raheem
Adobe Photoshop
and Corel Painter
www.tariqart.net

"This was initially a commission piece done for a friend/model who wanted something different in her portfolio. I had re-watched The 13th Warrior and wanted to create a sexy version of the Wendol Witch. Instead of the mud-and-bone costumes I decided to go with body-hugging armor and intricate tattoos. I wanted to create an ominous feel with the red mist and fire lanterns, and with her looking directly at the viewer, almost as if YOU are the sacrifice. The big knife helps too."

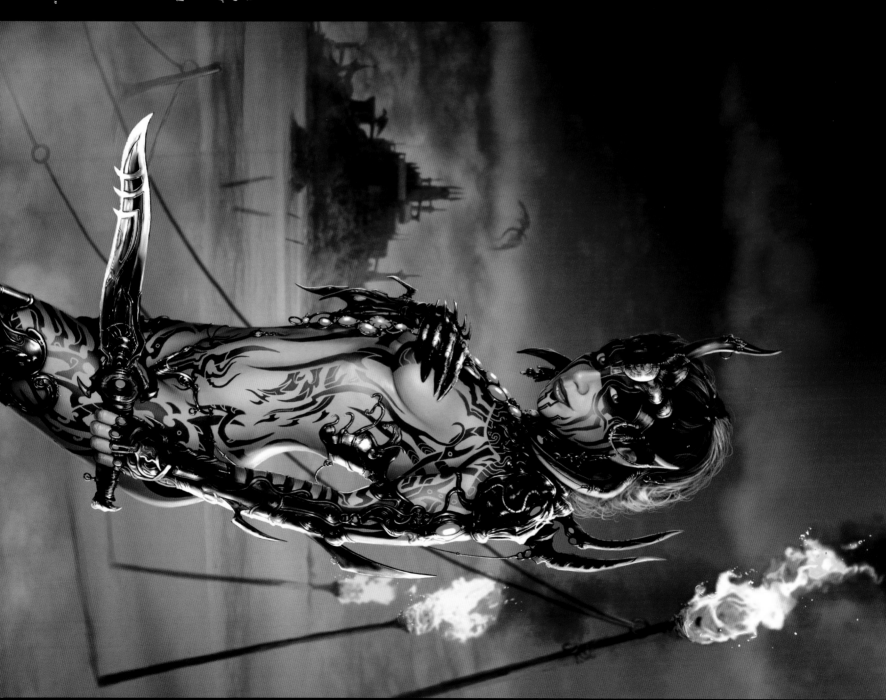

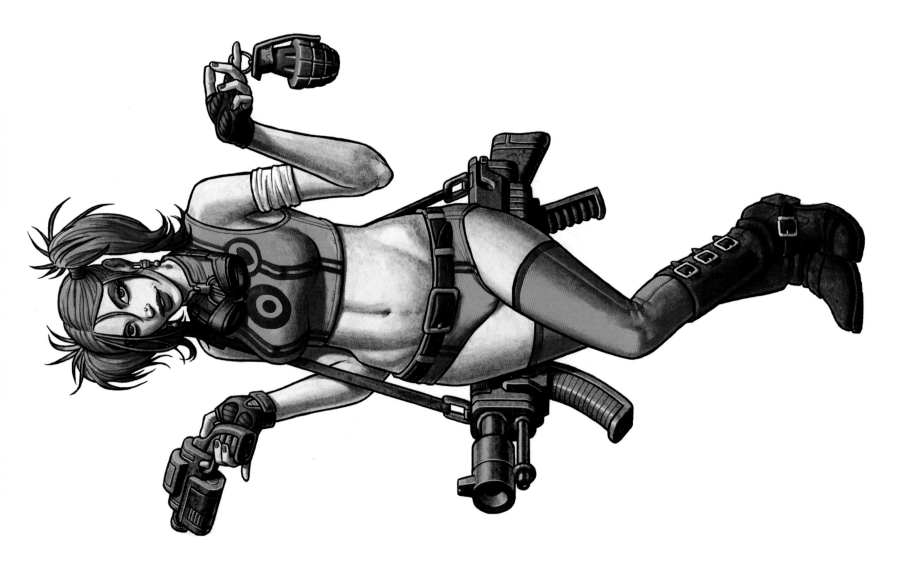

▲ **Boom!**
Paul McCaffrey
Pen, acrylics,
and Adobe Photoshop
www.coroflot.com/paul_mccaffrey

*"Cute but deadly. I drew the
line artwork for this nameless,
futuristic bounty hunter by
hand, photocopied it, and
colored it using acrylic inks.
Inevitably, it was scanned into
Photoshop and went through
a fair amount of tweaking—
probably more because I could
than because I really needed to.
As for influences, I'm not a huge
fan of manga but I guess it
worked its way in there
somewhere along the line,
and Tank Girl was probably
in the back of my mind, too."*

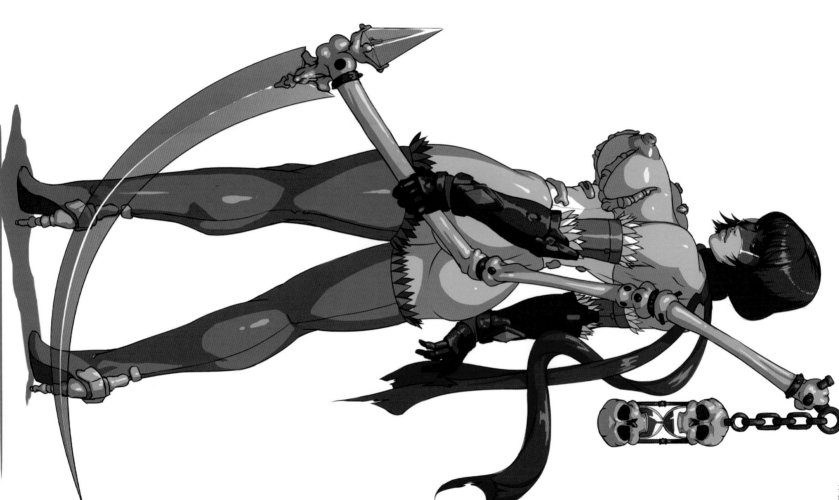

Baba Yaga
Dmitry Sergeev
Adobe Photoshop
http://dmitrys.deviantart.com

"This is a character redesign for Baba Yaga, an antagonist/ wise woman (depending on the story) from Slavic folk tales. She is usually associated with death and deception, and often portrayed as an ugly old woman. As much as I love drawing ugly old women, this time I drew Baba Yaga as busty death-dealing lady."

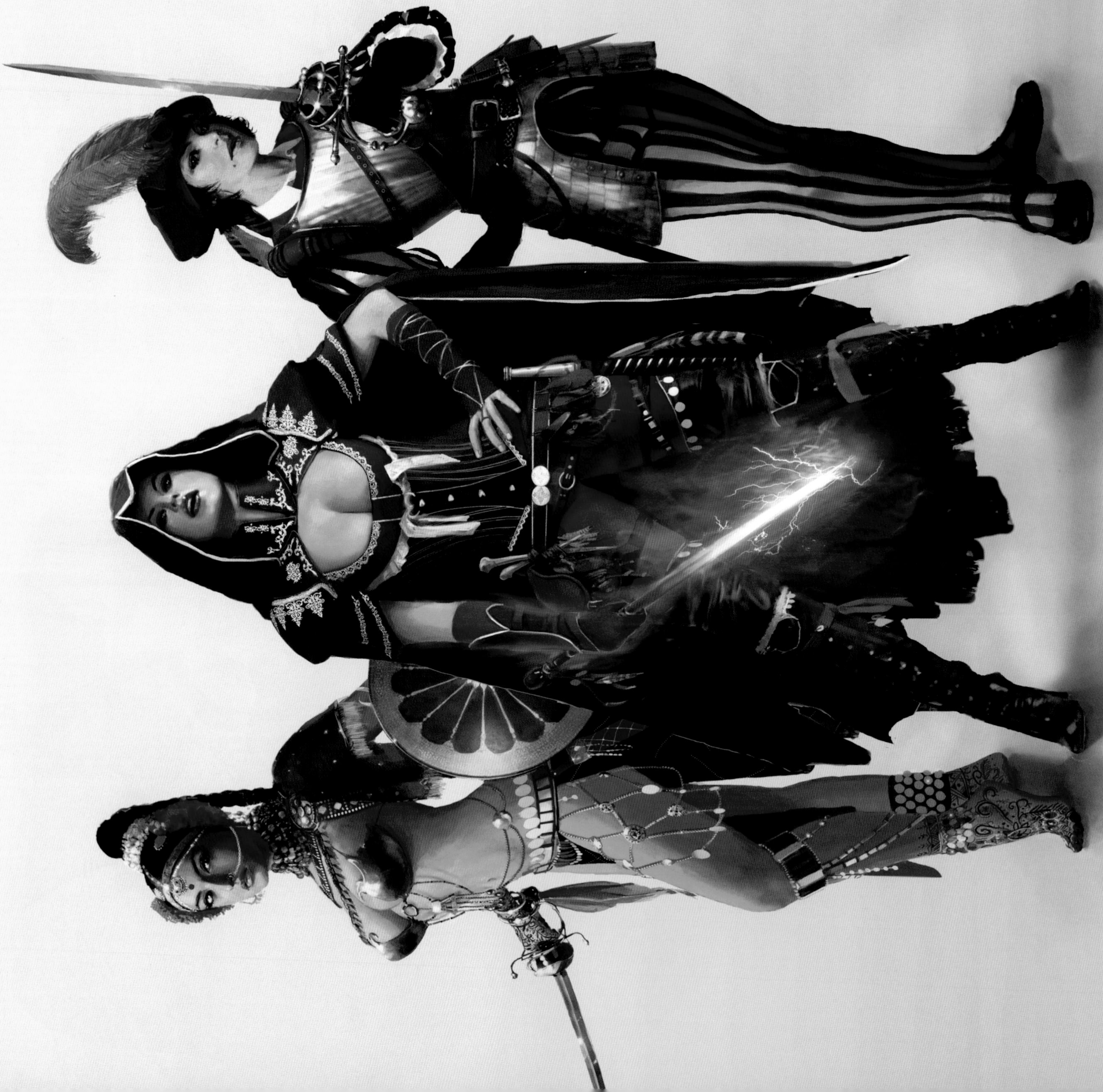

◀ **Dungeon of Doom Girls**
Nacho Molina
Adobe Photoshop
www.nachomolinablog.blogspot.com
www.nachomolina.deviantart.com

"These beauties are three of the seven main characters of the iOS game The Dungeon of Doom. *It is a project being lead by John Raymonds to reboot the classic '80s original that began on the Macintosh platform. My job was to design the 2-D concept art of the main characters before the guys at Luminous Arts built them in 3-D. You can see here The Jeweler, The Wizard, and The Fighter. It was interesting to imagine each character's personality and expression, as well as the different cultures, epochs, and traditions that could influence her style of dress. I had to put it all together based on just the short written description I was given."*

▶ **About Elves and Steel**
Uwe Jarling
Corel Painter
and Adobe Photoshop
www.jarling-arts.com

"I think the inspiration behind this piece is pretty obvious. Whenever I find some free time between my commissioned work, I try to create hot women in not-too-useful armor when it really comes to a fight. Seriously, I just love to paint things like that! As for the process, I mainly used Painter for this image with just a little color correction at the end in Photoshop. I used a lot of Painter's watercolor brushes to get the traditional media effect that I was looking for in this digital painting."

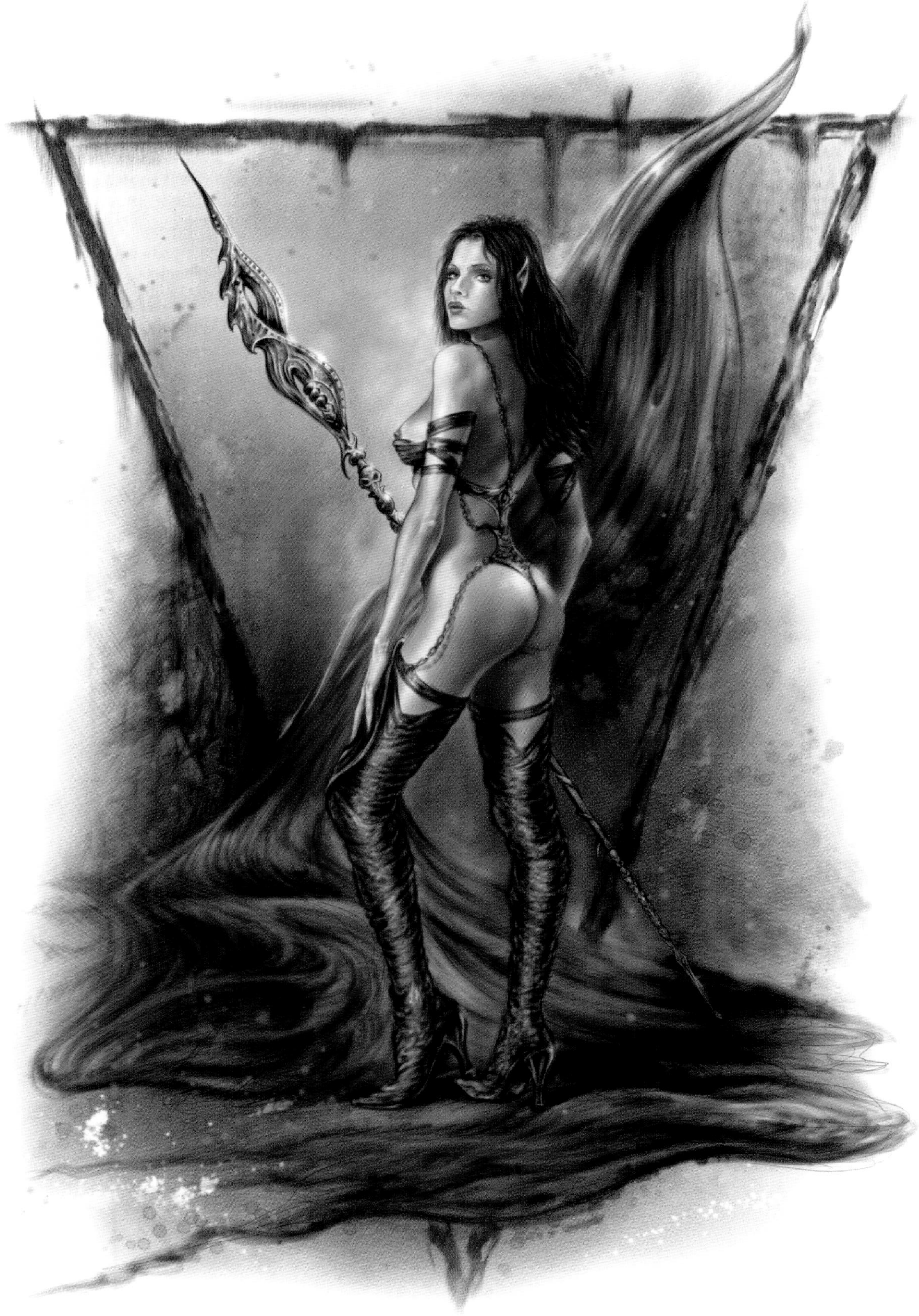

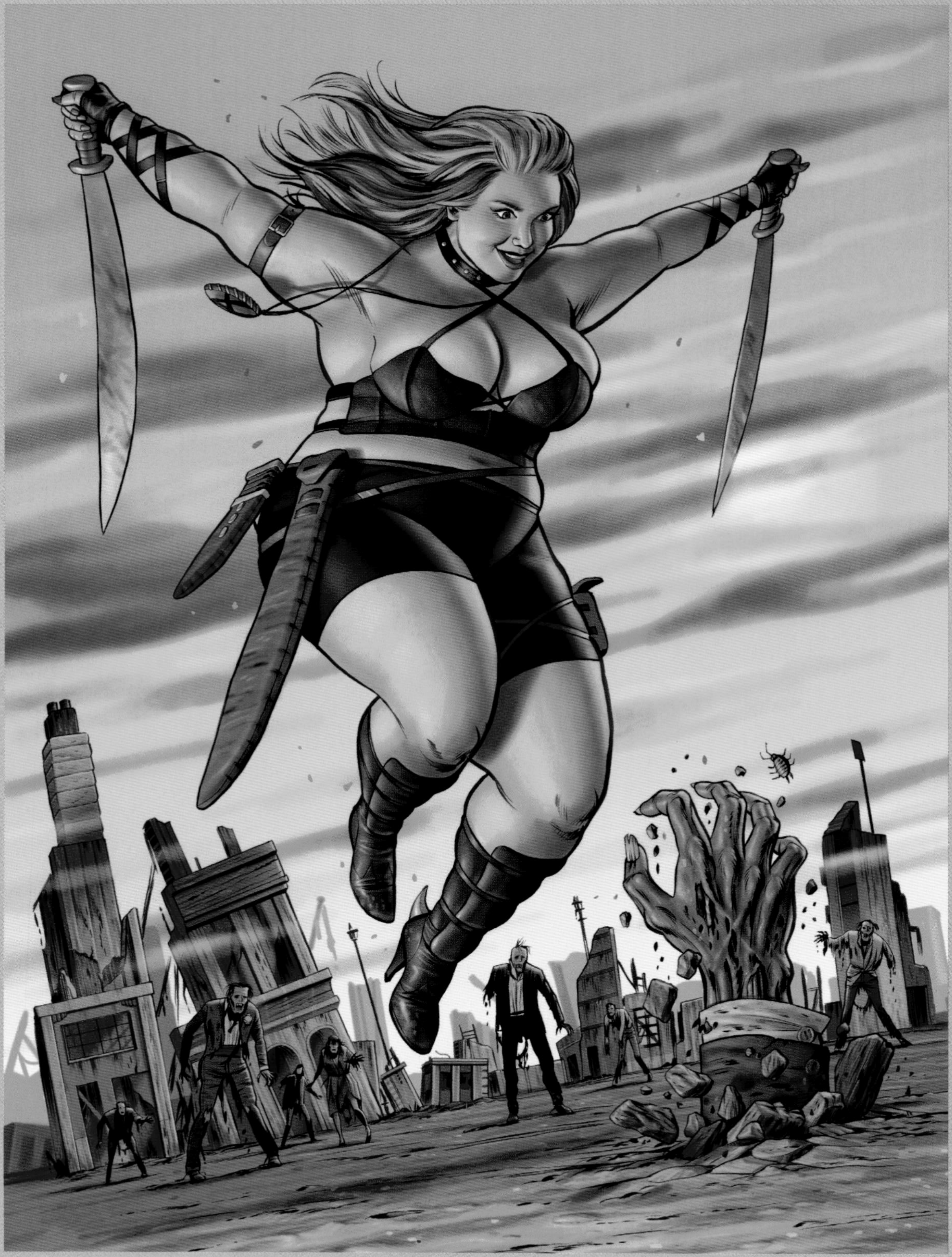

◀ **Carrie**
Les Toil
Pen, ink, and Adobe Photoshop
www.toilgirls.com

"I like confident zombie slayers and I like big, beautiful babes. At the crack of dawn, Carrie dresses herself in a provocative manner that implies the practice of turning the walking dead into moldy cold cuts is an act of eroticism to her. The expression on her face helps suggest that."

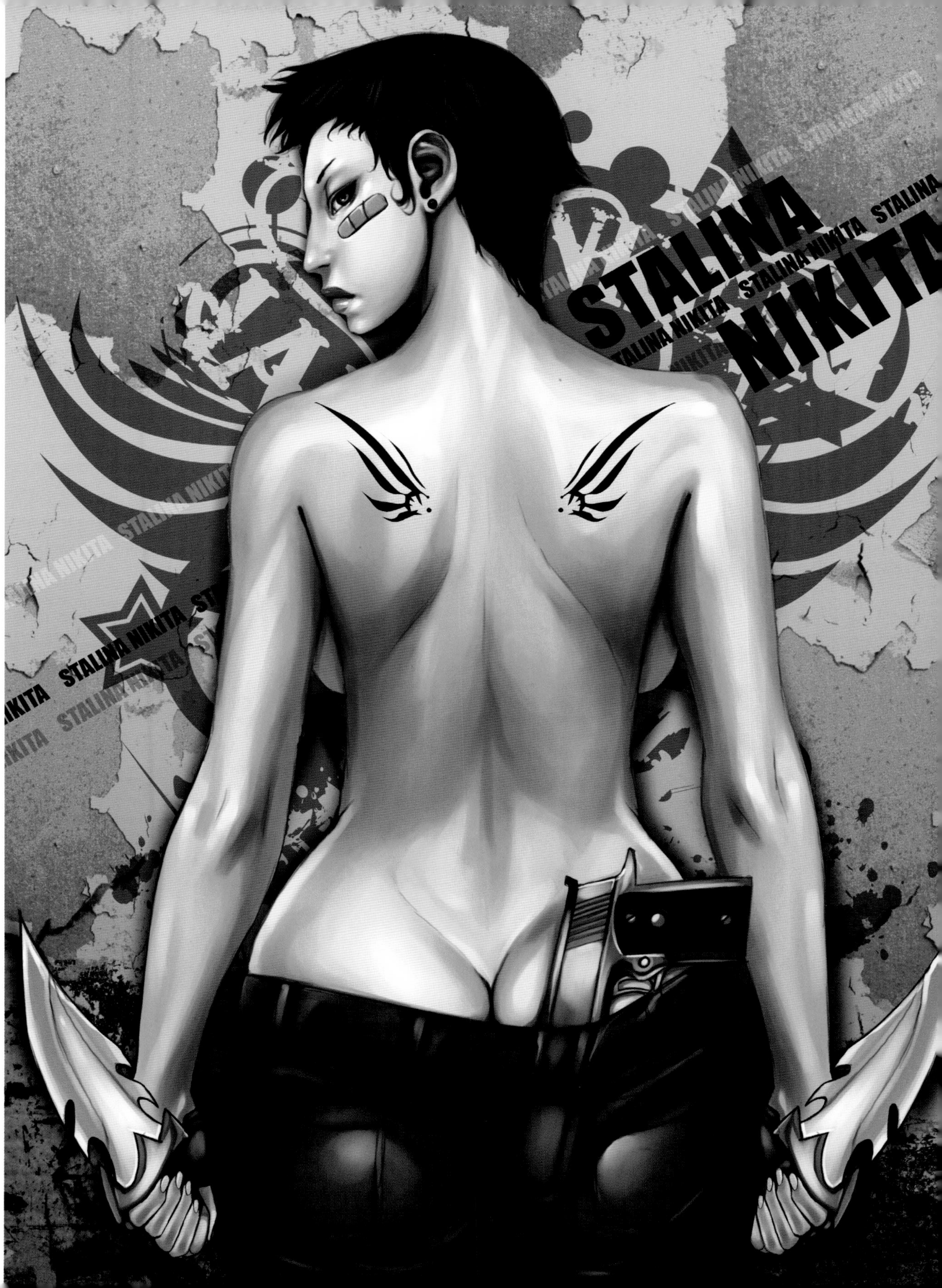
STALINA
NIKITA
STALINA NIKITA

Leaden Wings
Ricardo Landell
Adobe Photoshop
and Corel Painter
www.hardinkgirls.com

"Stalina Nikita is the protagonist of the upcoming HARDINKGIRLS.com comic, Plumbean Pinion. *Both are inspired by Revy from* Black Lagoon, *the* Hitman *video game franchise and movie, as well as movies and video games with distinct visual styles like* The Matrix, Equilibrium, *and* Max Payne. *The creation process begins with sketching in Photoshop using a Cintiq Wacom tablet. The sketch is then transferred to Painter, where it's retraced for clean ink lines. When inking is finished, the line work is transferred back to Photoshop for coloring."*

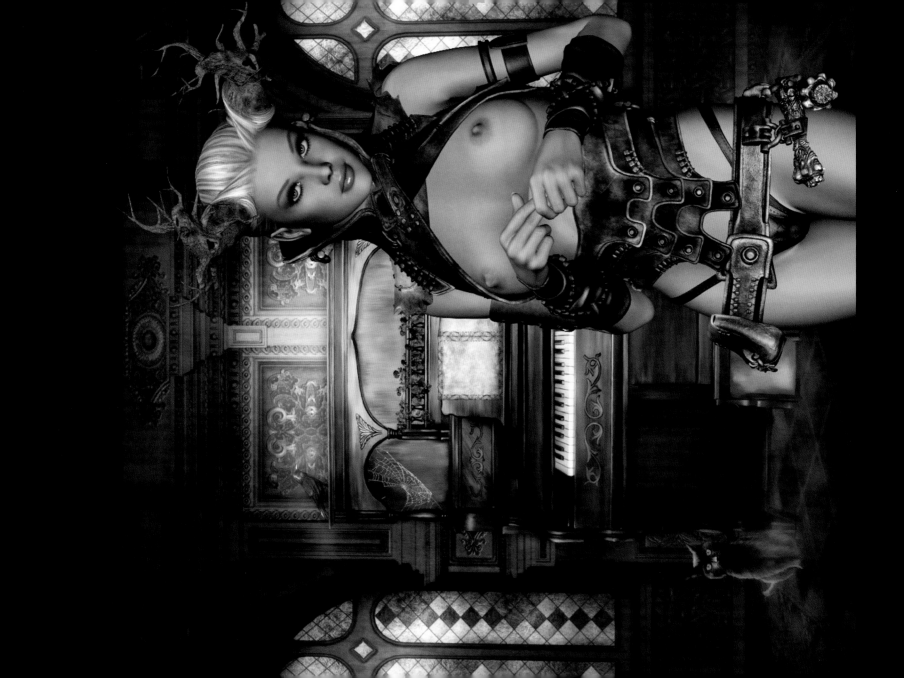

◄ **Woman or Beast**
Jane Dahl Jensen
Poser Pro and Adobe Photoshop
http://janedj.deviantart.com

This sexy wood nymph gestures suggestively, a slight smile playing on her lips. The world depicted in this quietly contemplative piece is rendered in meticulous detail right down to the plaintive look of the cat in the background. The coloring of this scene is expertly handled, its muted greens and browns creating an unearthly mood.

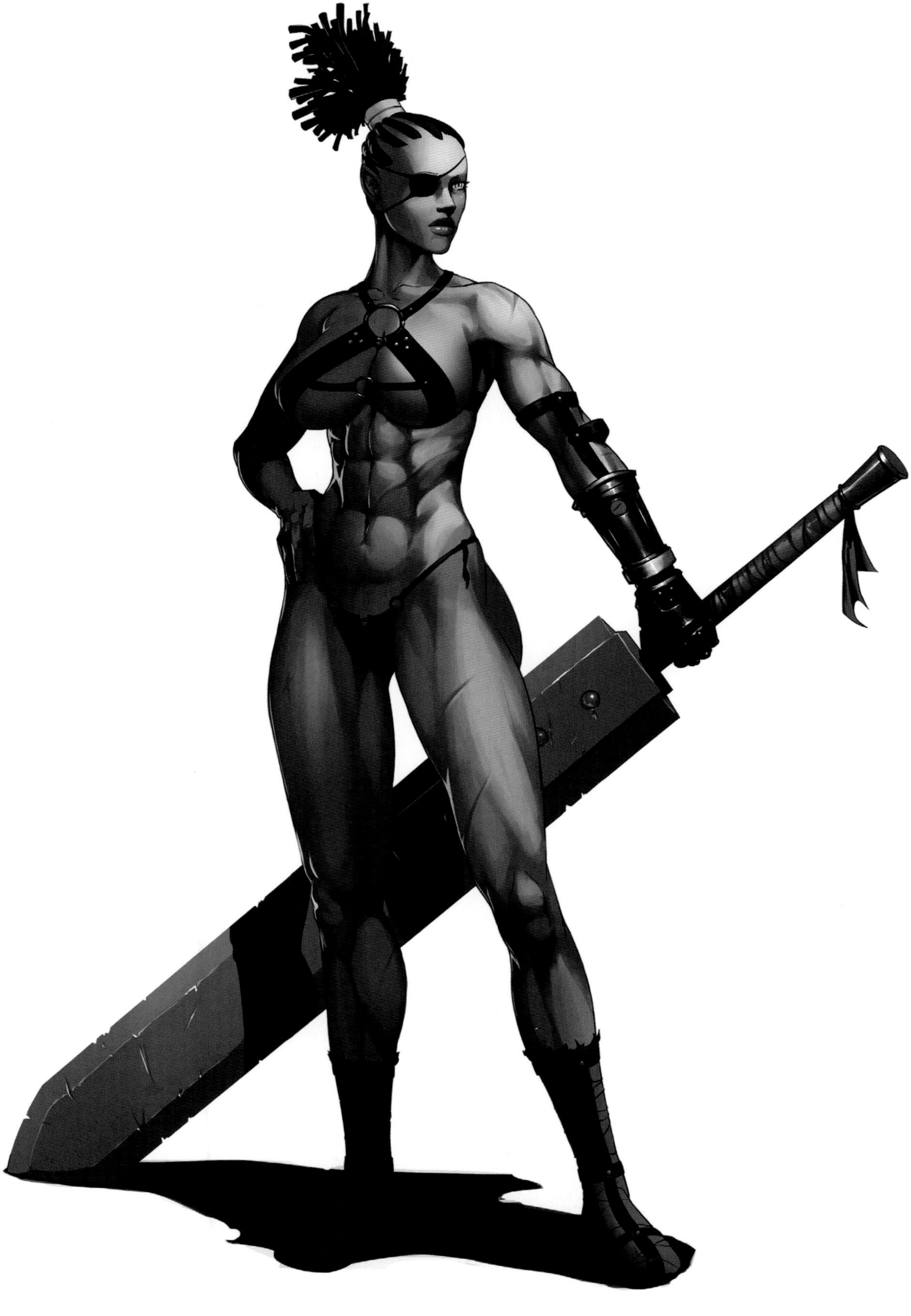

► **Ork Amazon**
Dmitry Sergeev
Adobe Photoshop
http://dmitrys.deviantart.com

Sergeev's scantily clad Amazonian warrior is incredibly toned. The artist took care to create accurate muscular details. "I'm a big fan of human anatomy, so I've tried to render this character to the best of my ability in this picture. Armor is overrated anyway."

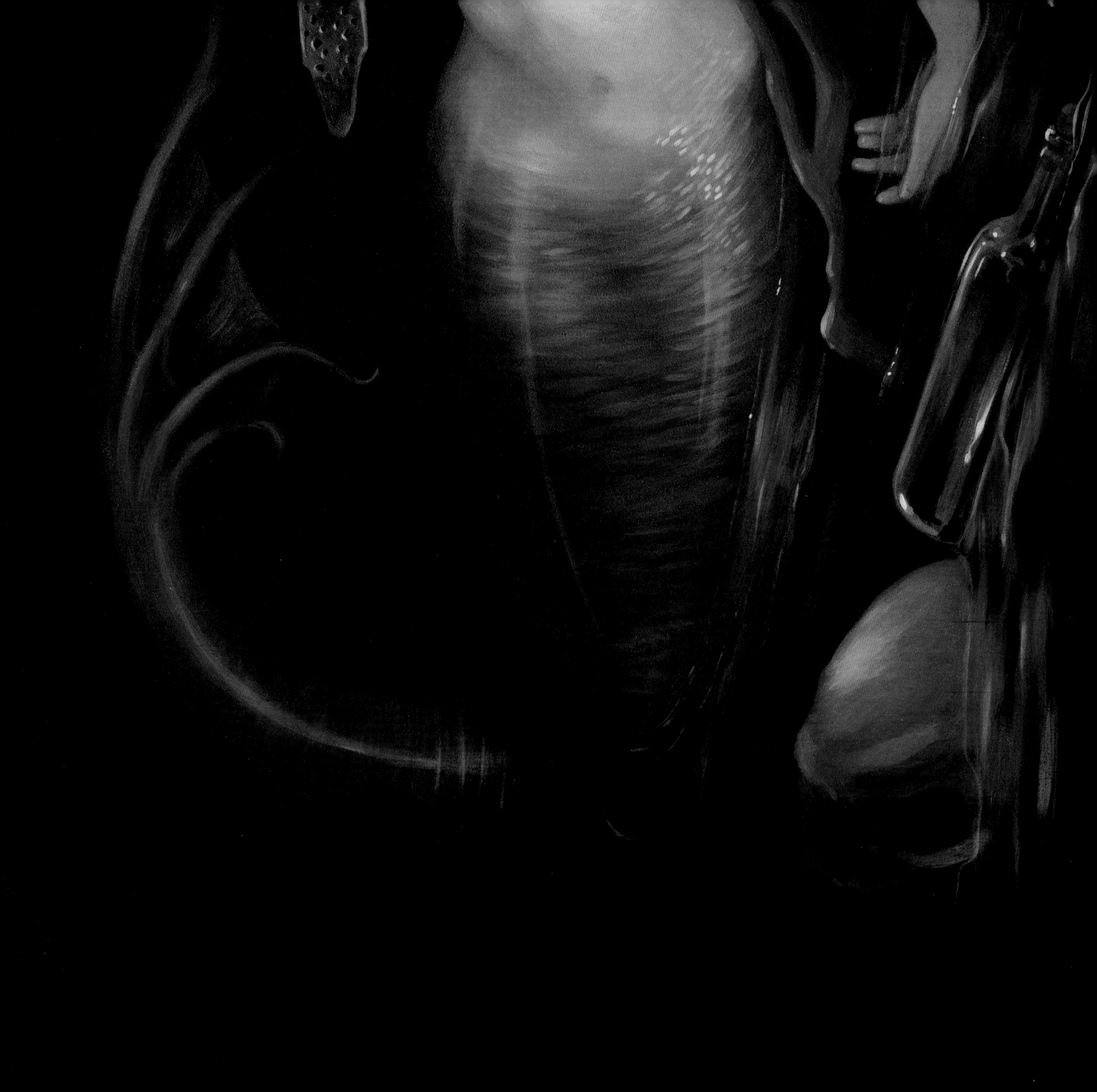

CHAPTER 2

PHANTASMAL BODIES

▸ **Absinthe Mermaid**
Jasmine Becket-Griffith
Acrylics
www.strangeling.com

"Oh, I love this painting! In the green colors of absinthe, this languorous mermaid seems to embody the indulgent spirit of the drink. Her eyes flash green, her luxuriant blonde hair streams over the roots and rocks (with sinister skull-like visages). You will see she holds a traditional absinthe spoon in one hand, and a green bottle floats away from her grasp on the absinthe-green waves. Her gaze has a seductive feel to it that gives this painting an air of eroticism."

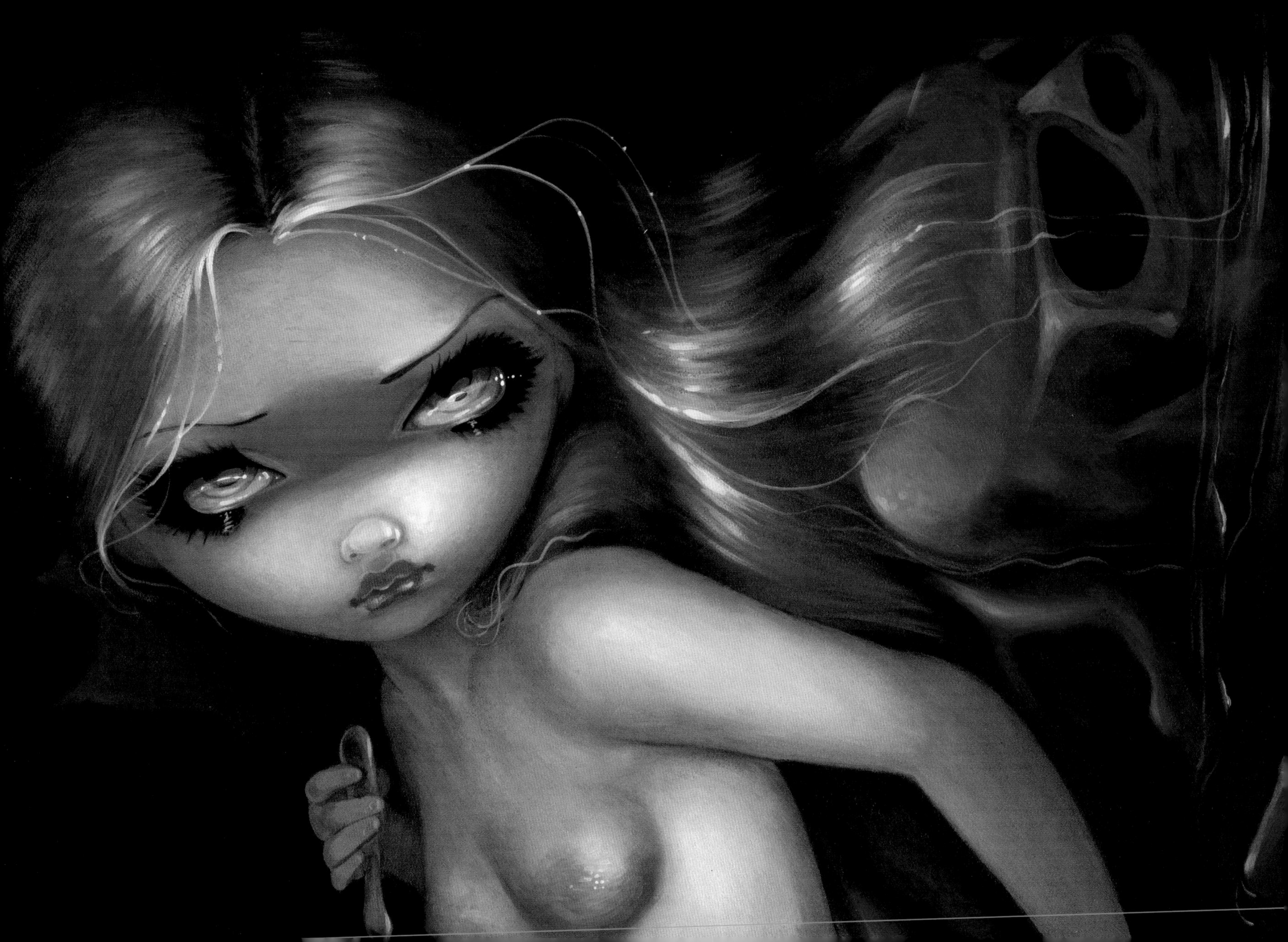

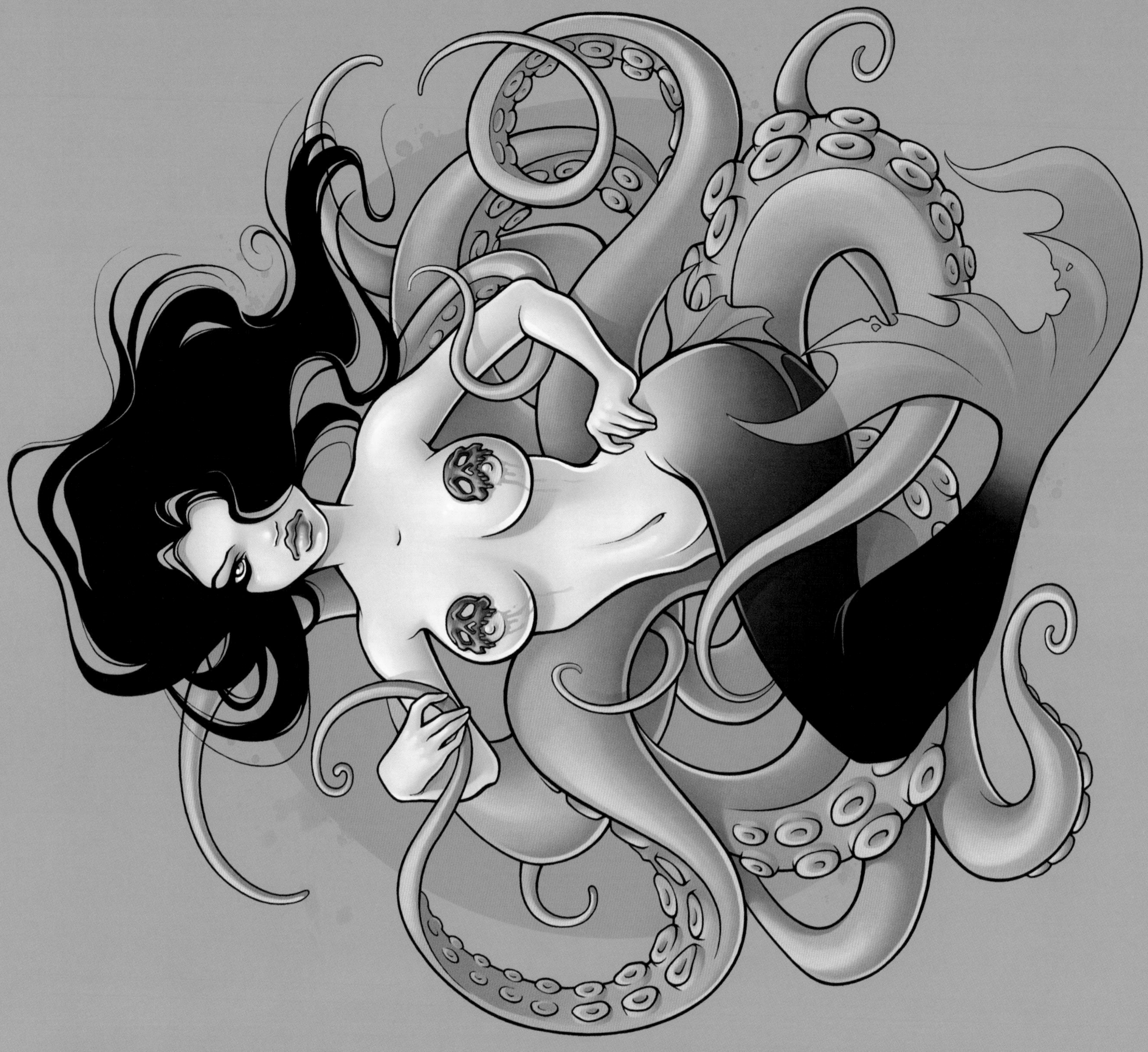

◀ **The Little Mermaid**
Aleksandra Marchocka
Adobe Photoshop
www.olamarchocka.com

"I love the dual nature of fairy tales because they provide strong and disturbing contrasts of cuteness and cruelty. This contrast inspired me to create a whole series of erotic pinup girls based on fairy tale heroines. I approached the Little Mermaid from Hans Christian Andersen's story with a much more sexy attitude, making her look more like a femme fatale than a Disney cutie. I also added a bit of a fetish undertone by drawing gothic skulls biting into her breasts. For the art style, I was strongly influenced by the organic and decorative art nouveau, which you can spot while looking at all those curvy and dynamic lines, the flowing hair, and tentacle ornaments."

▶ **Pink Tranquility**
Aleksandra Marchocka
Adobe Photoshop
www.olamarchocka.com

"Thanks to Japanese hentai, tentacles have become an erotic motif. I decided to combine them with a classic pinup girl from the 1940s and 50s, resulting in a modern approach to fetish fantasy. Originally the piece was designed as a tattoo concept, in which I tried to merge old-school themes with a more cartoon style. That explains not only the sexy pinup girl, but also the marine motif and little 'drooling' skull on the top. My main inspiration was again art nouveau style, with its characteristic sudden curves, dynamic whiplashes, and flowing lines."

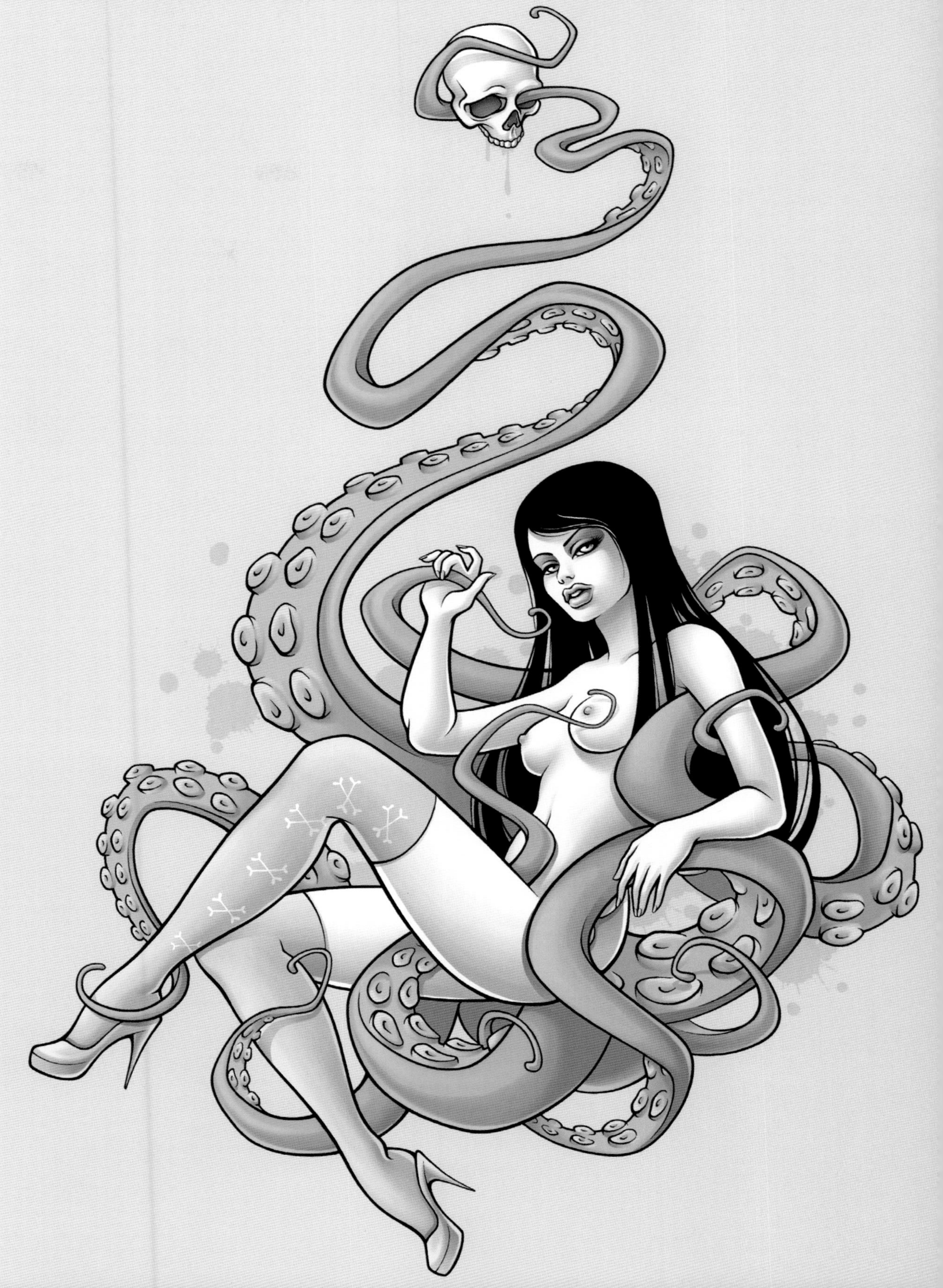

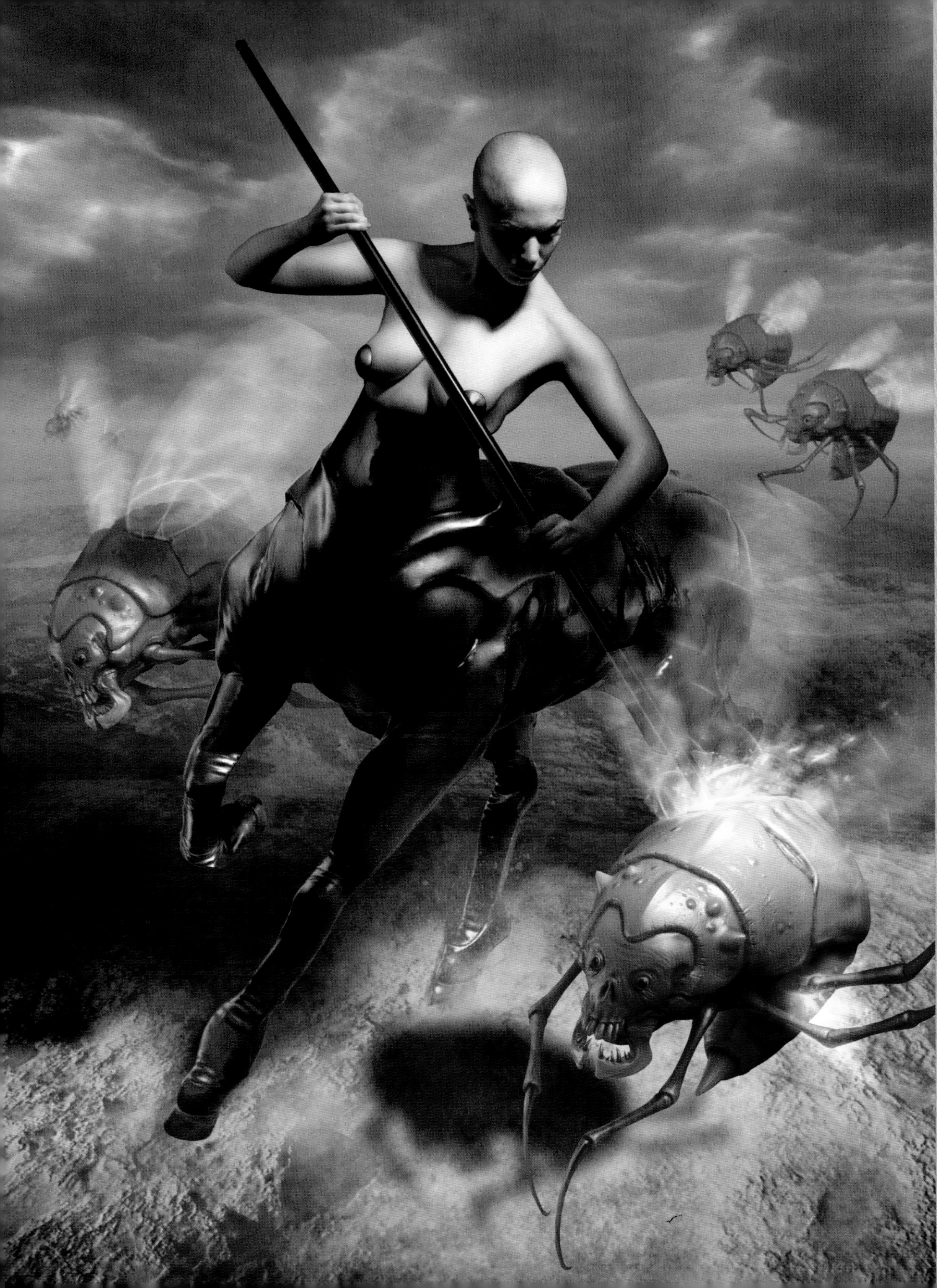

◀ **Centaur**
Jason Juta
Photography, Adobe Photoshop, Sculptris, and Modo
www.jasonjuta.com

"A discussion with the model resulted in choosing a centaur as one of the photo session concepts. My mythological creatures belong in a limbo where humanity has stopped believing in them. The body and hunted soul-insects resulted from an experiment integrating 3-D elements with painting and photography."

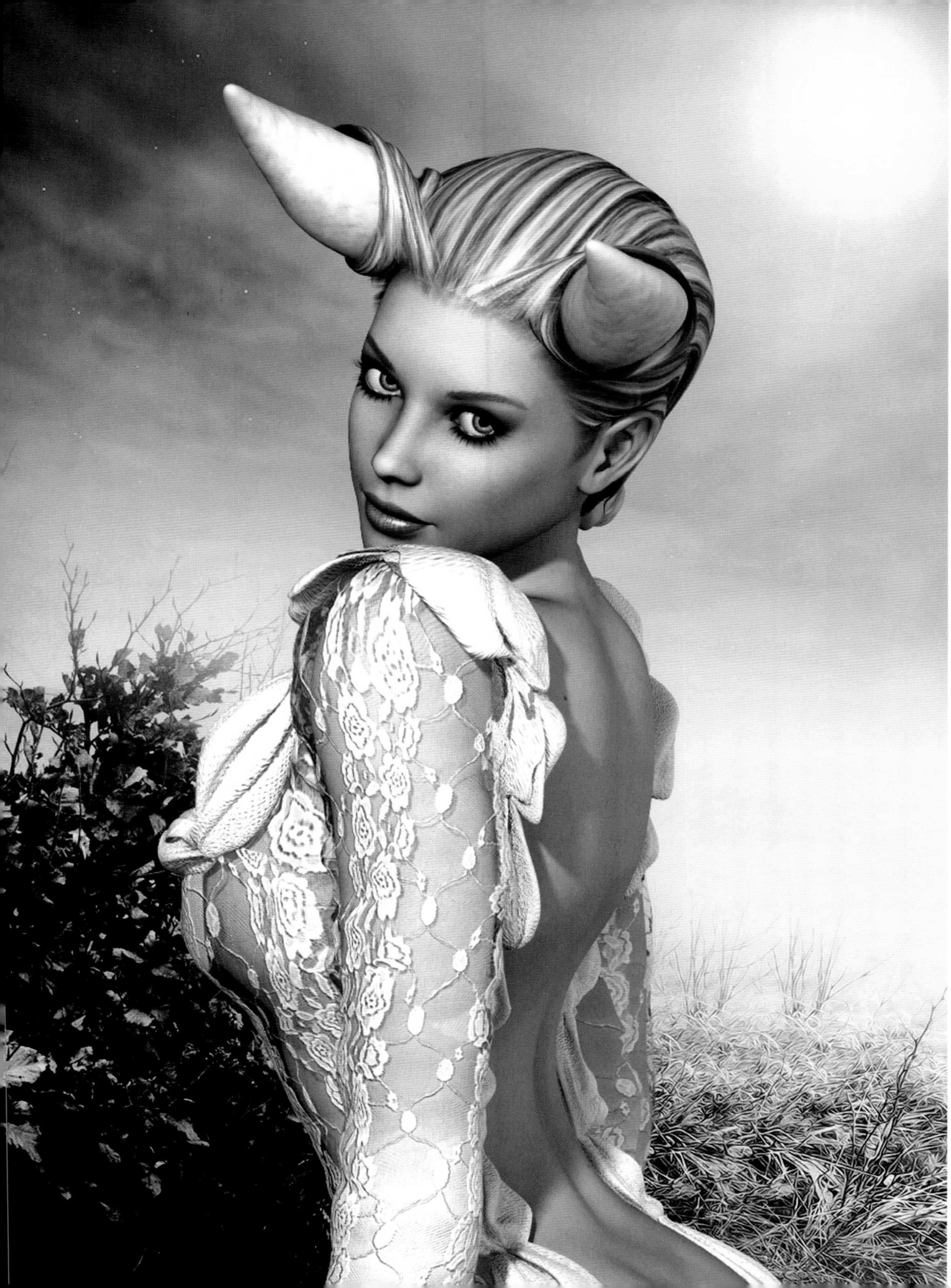

◀ **Shameless**
Jane Dahl Jensen
Poser Pro and Adobe Photoshop
http://janedj.deviantart.com

The detailed work in the leaves and lace displayed in this picture is something to behold. However the look in this lady's eyes is the real box-office draw. Jensen presents us with a conundrum: the subject is clearly a demon, although a thoroughly unconventional one, and despite her horns she promises heaven, not hell. We can only imagine the deeds for which she no longer feels ashamed.

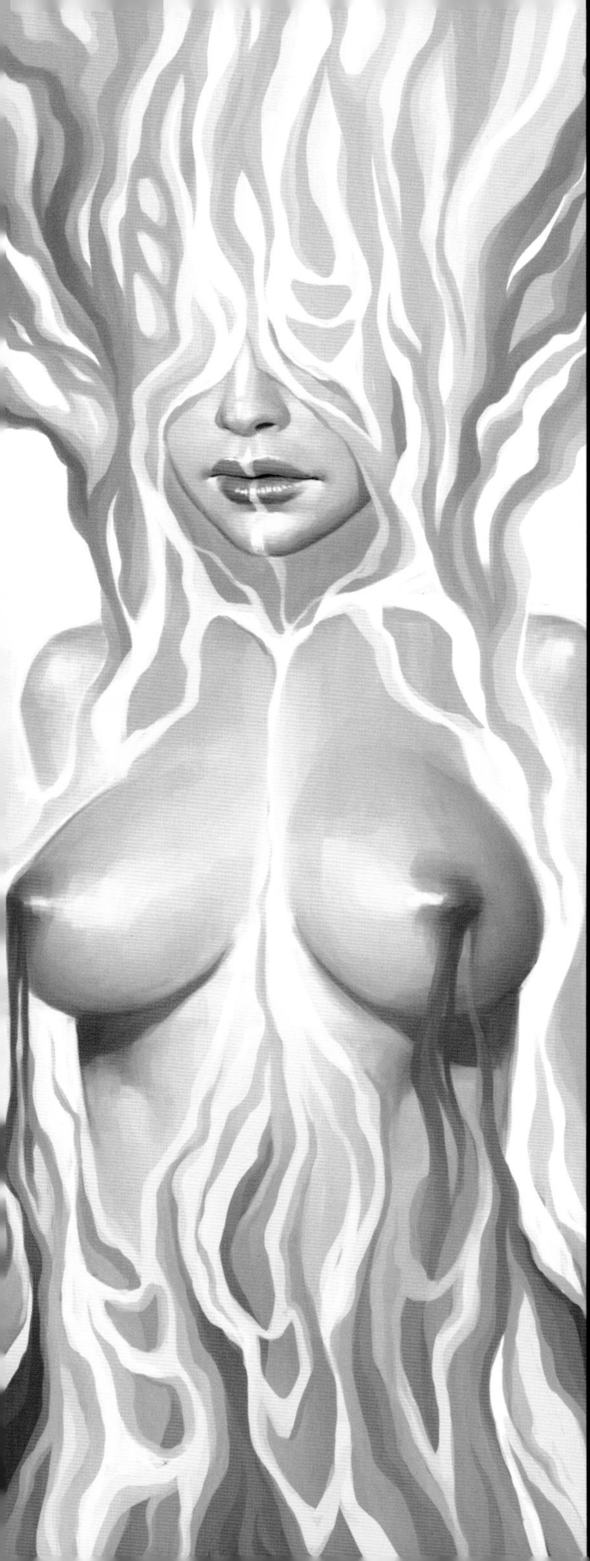

◄ **Melting**
Daniela Uhlig
Adobe Photoshop
www.du-artwork.de

"This painting is part of my Red Ink *series. There was no big inspiration or idea behind it; I started at the face with some sort of mask, and from this paint strokes began randomly flowing from my hand. To get a better composition in the end and to result in a high format like the others, I decided to continue with an upper body and through the melting nipples I got the idea for the title. For me, personally, it is one of the most erotic pictures I have ever done up till now."*

► **Red Ink II**
Daniela Uhlig
Adobe Photoshop
www.du-artwork.de

"Some time ago I painted a simple portrait of a red-haired woman (Red Ink), whose red hair merges into the red ink from a pen. This is its sequel. It's not really thematic of the content, but rather the style and the color scheme are the same. I really did not have great plans for the picture, so I just started to draw and paint. And because red is an erotic and sensual color, the sexy woman almost drew herself. Unlike the first portrait, this time there is a butt and a foot to look at. There was no need for a sketch, only a reference for the foot."

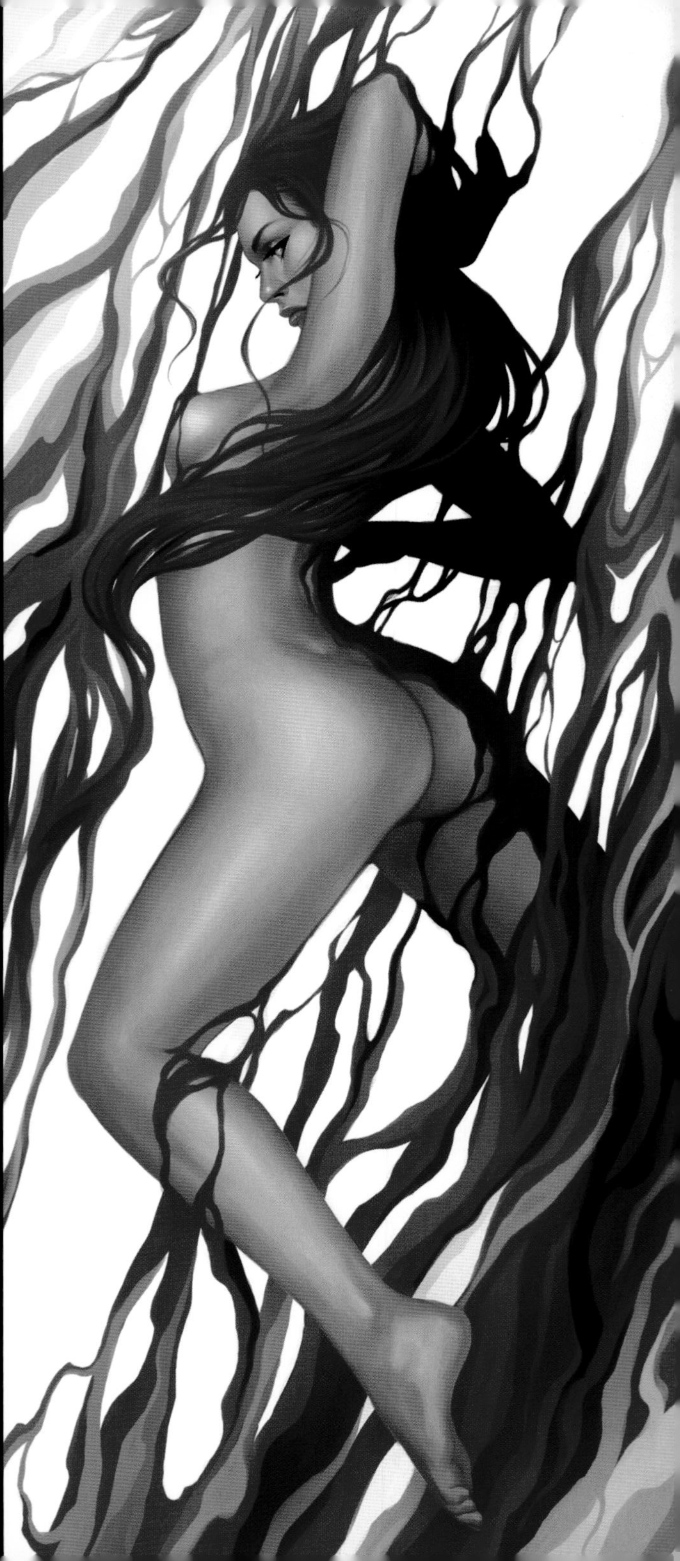

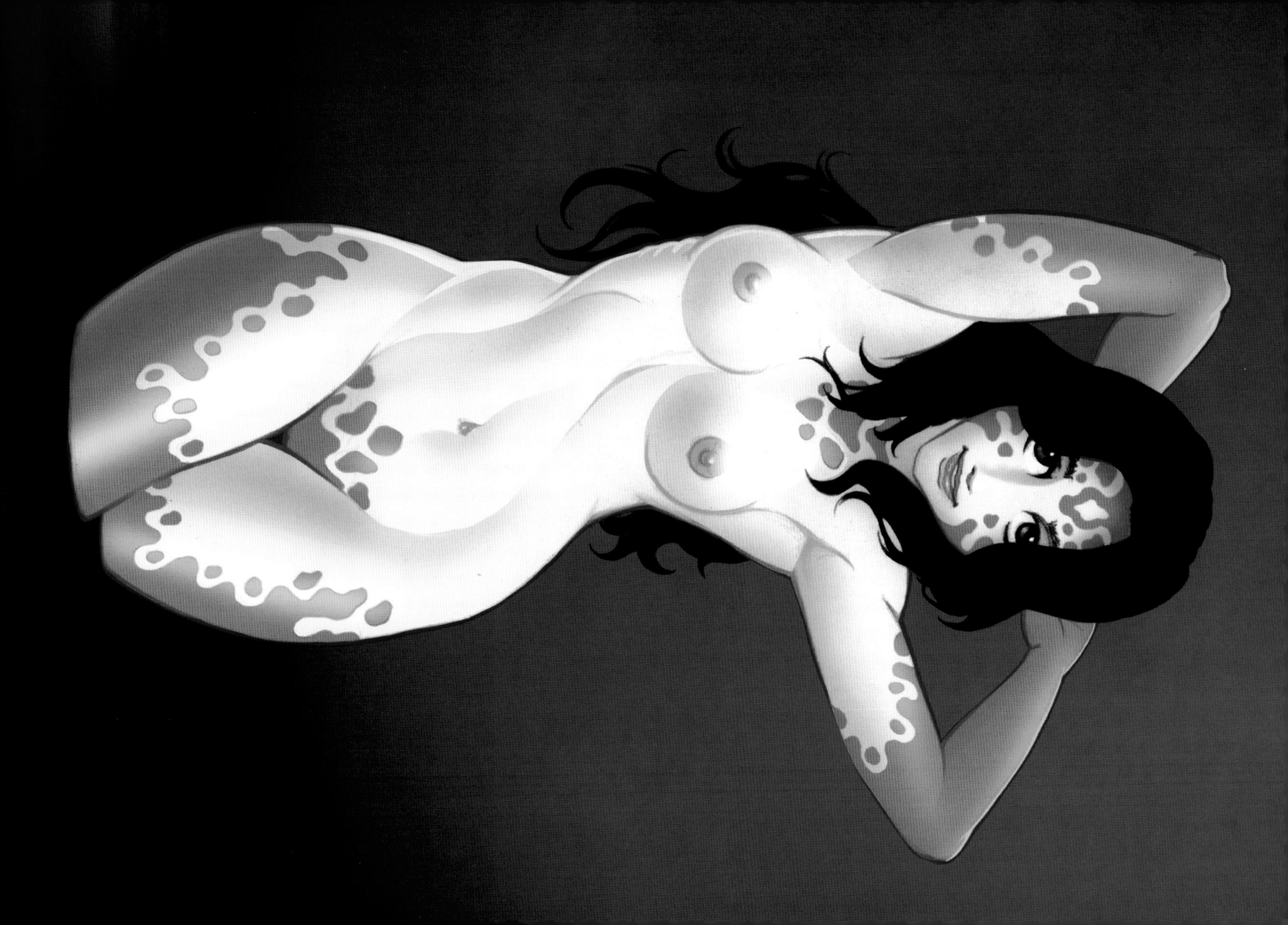

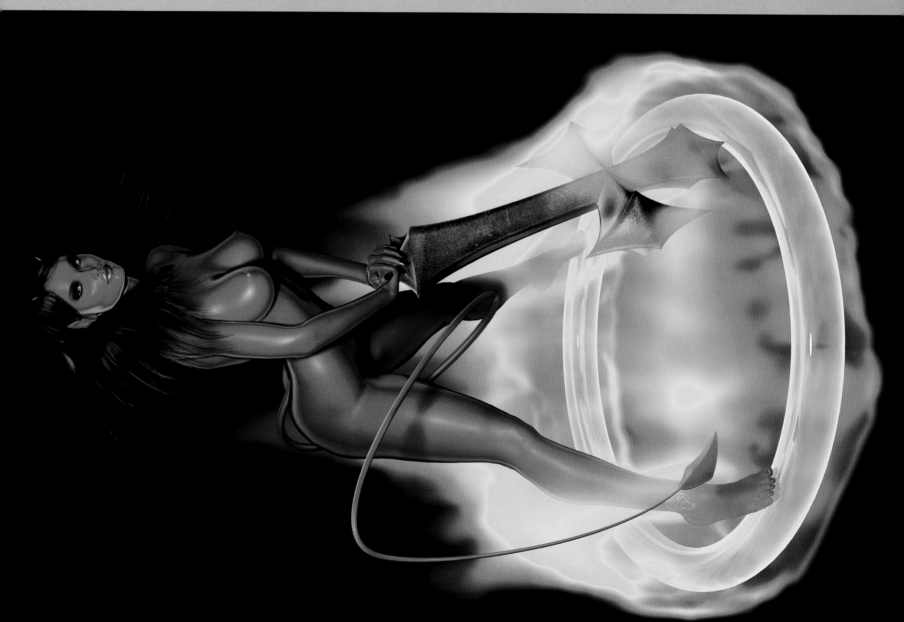

▼ **Burning Halo**
Darthhell
3ds Max
www.darthhell.deviantart.com

"I created this for an art jam some of my friends on deviantart.com were having. I was thinking something like an evil tooth-fairy-type demon who would hand out burning halos as rewards for especially evil deeds. Since the file had to be in PNG format with a transparent background, I didn't have a lot of options for postwork, so I didn't do any. This was a straight render out of 3ds Max."

▲ **The Naga Dancer**
Kassidi Keys
Poser and Adobe
Photoshop Elements
http://kassidikeys.deviantart.com

"Most of my images come about because I've become inspired by a small detail, such as a color someone's wearing. The Naga Dancer was that way for me. There was a girl in traffic who was wearing very long sleeves. Just the tips of her slightly curved fingers were visible below the cuffs of her sleeves. It was that elegant curve that inspired me to come home and paint something sleek and writhing. I have no idea what the actual girl looked like. I didn't see her face, but I do know that she had beautiful hands. With the image of delicate flowing hands in my mind, I could not resist adding more arms to magnify the effect. The snake body was the obvious conclusion to the image... all of those curves combined into one form."

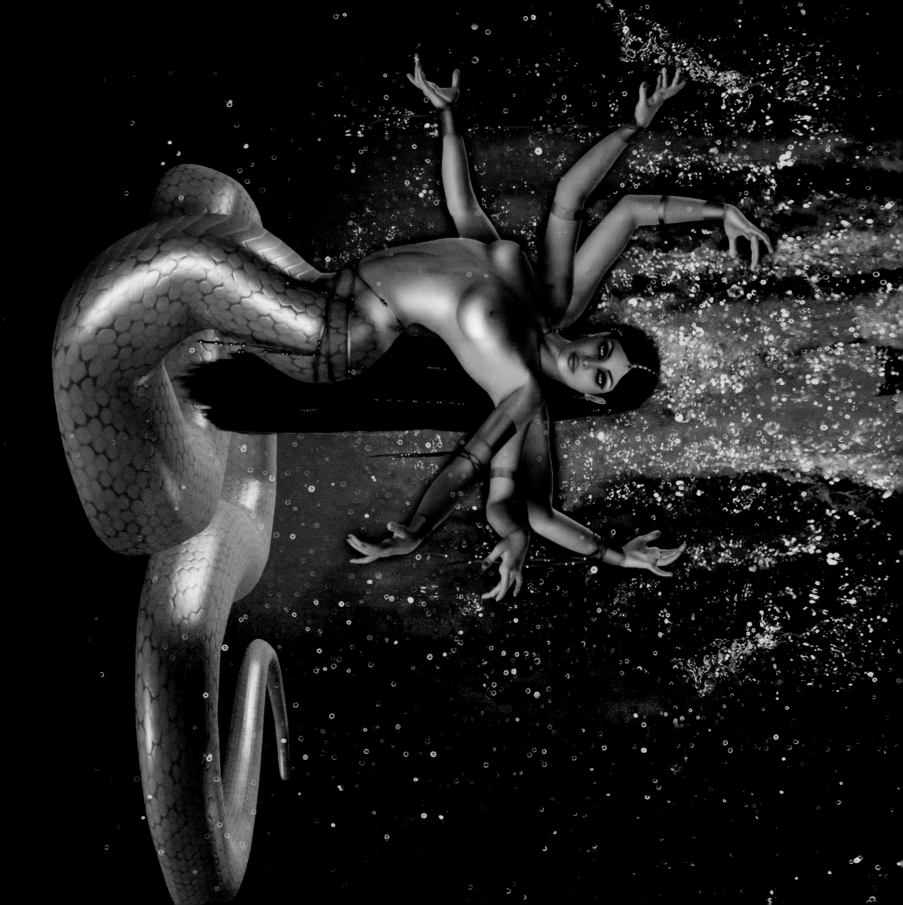

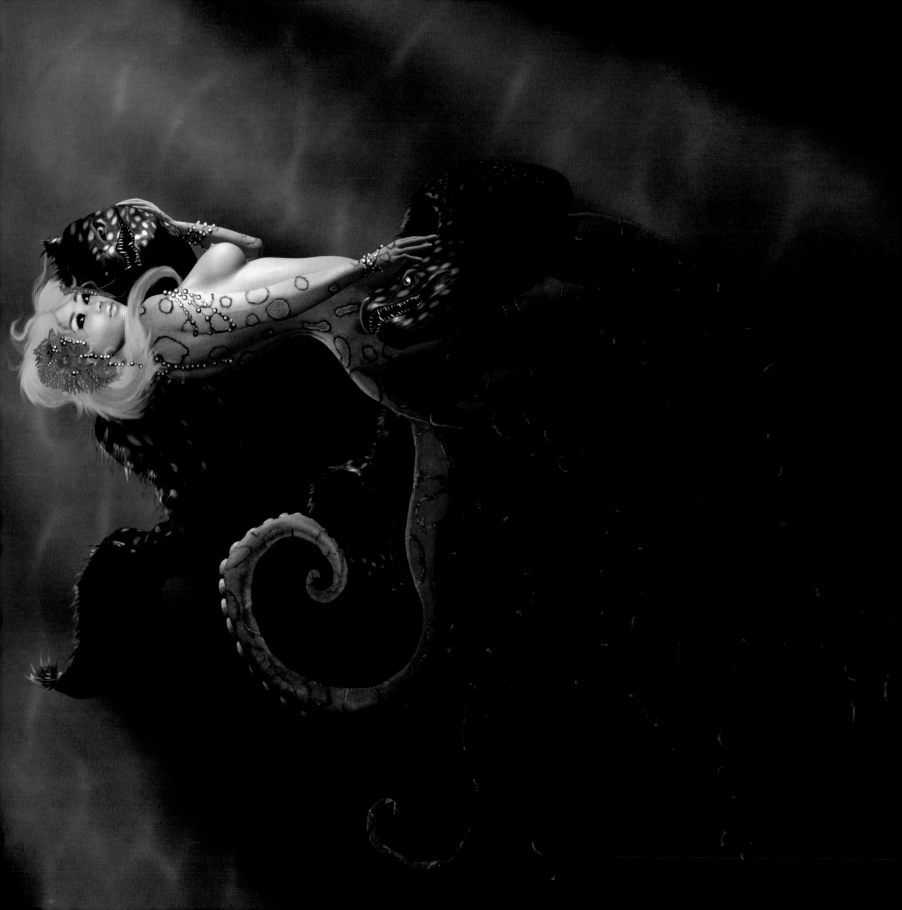

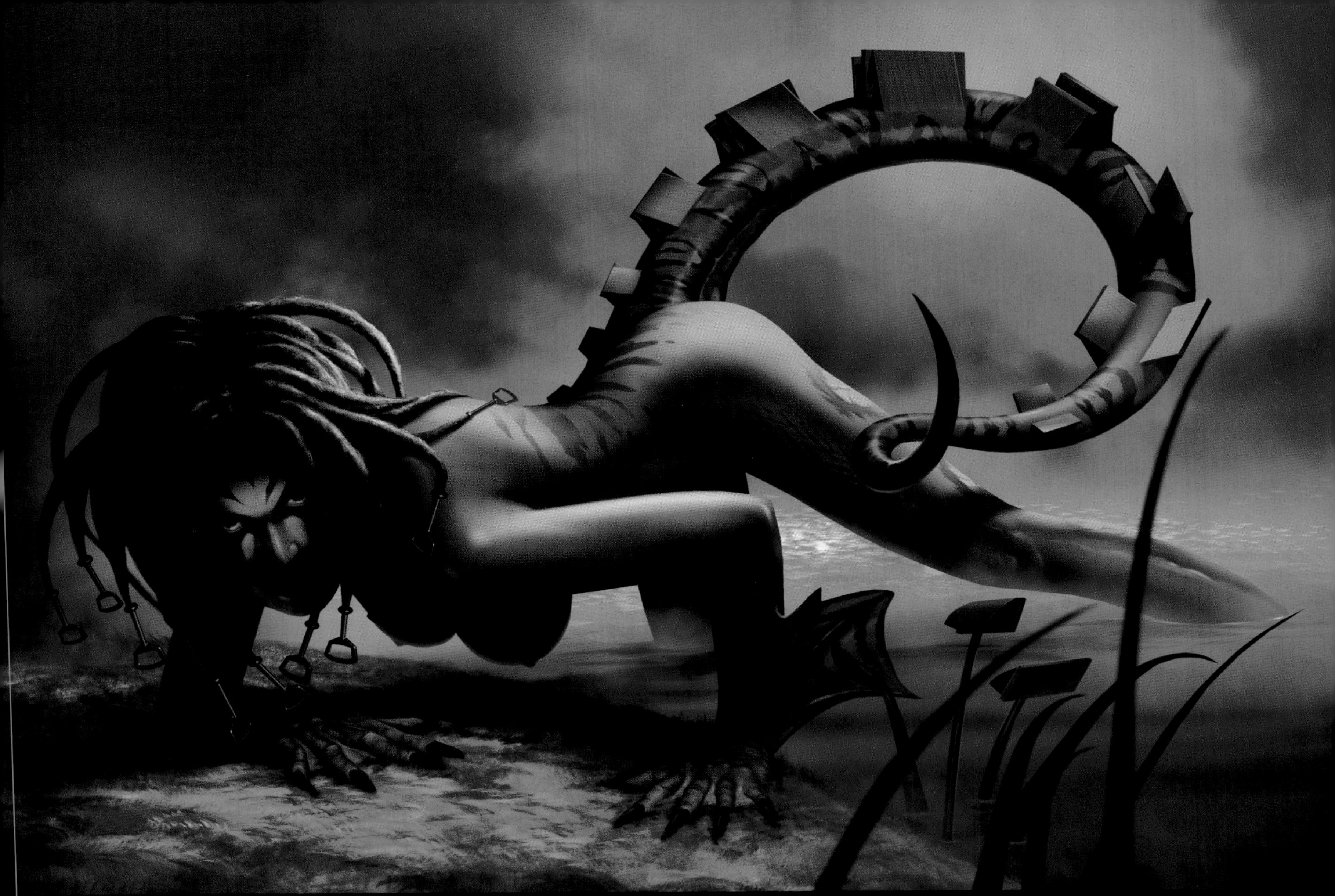

◀ **The Sea Witch**
Kassidi Keys
Photography, Poser, and Adobe Photoshop Elements
http://kassidikeys.deviantart.com

For this piece, Keys was inspired by the antagonist from Hans Christian Andersen's Little Mermaid. *She explains, "In all renditions I've come across she's always depicted as a hag, and I've always wondered, why would anyone trust an obviously deranged lunatic with what was ultimately their life? I couldn't see a princess trusting her soul to someone so obviously off their rocker, so I decided to paint the Sea Witch as someone much, much more vital, young, alluring, and obviously poisonous. She was definitely a challenge. I repainted several portions a number of times before settling on this incarnation, because, for me, the whole feel of the piece pivoted on two things: textures and her knowing glance that says, 'I know you're going to fail, but go ahead and try anyway.'"*

▲ **La Criatura Del Pantano**
Nestor Taylor
Adobe Photoshop
www.nestortaylor.blogspot.com

Taylor's atmospheric digital piece La Criatura Del Panto *(The Swamp Creature) depicts a curvaceous femme fatale. Bathed in green hues and a misty background, she is both sinister and seductive. There is more to the distinctive scales on her tail and hair adornments than first meets the eye. Taylor explains: "The creature is camouflaged with locks and keys. It was a commission for a client that made locks and keys, and this is the illustration for their almanac."*

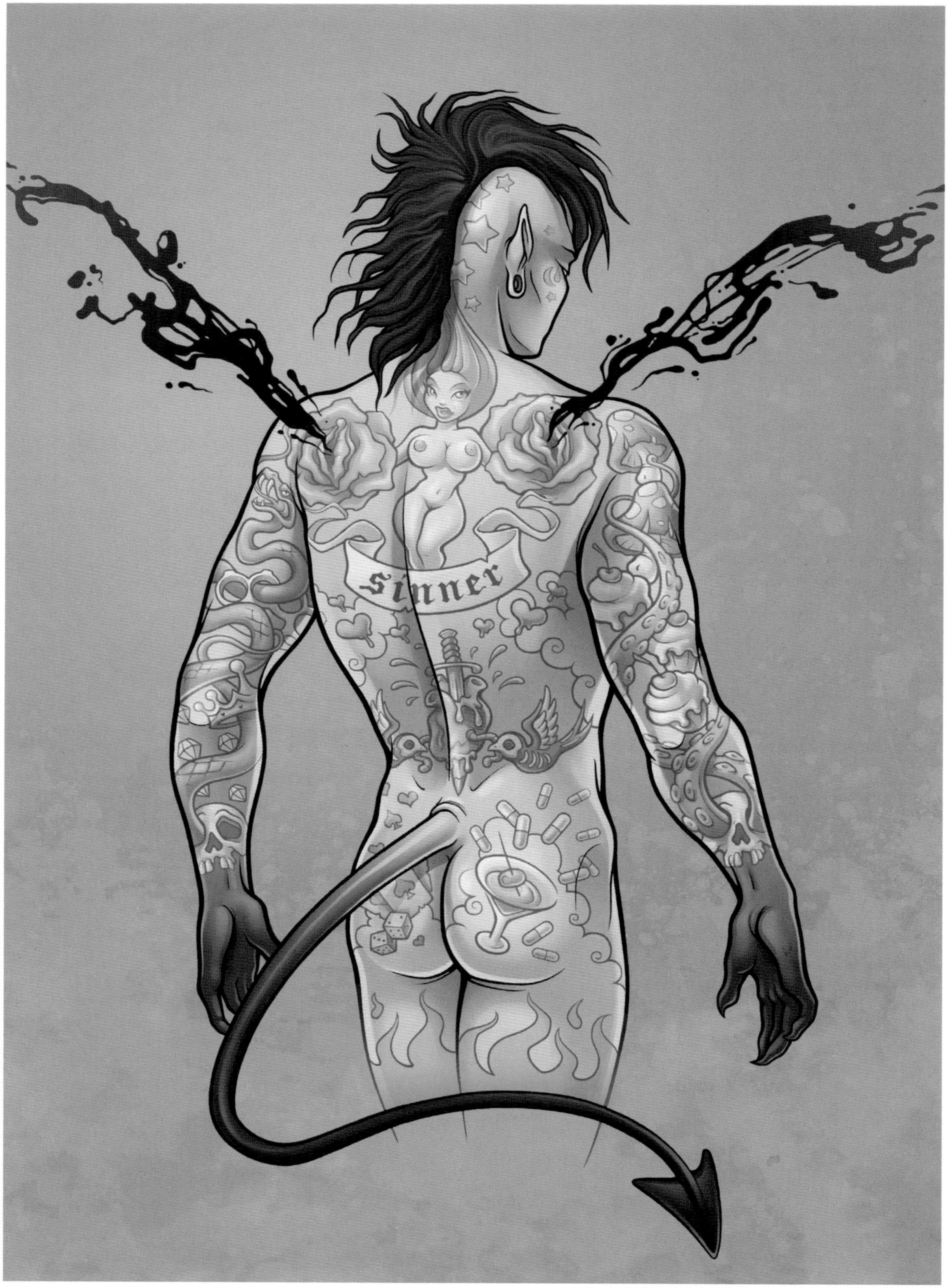
Sinner

◀ **Ink Devil**
Aleksandra Marchocka
Adobe Photoshop
www.olamarchocka.com

"I don't create male pin-ups too often, but I really enjoy drawing bad guys. This time I decided to add something modern and pop-cultural to the traditional character of the Devil. I have portrayed him as a punk rocker with a mohawk and tattoos covering his whole body. Each tattoo is related to a different sin and they all emphasize the evil, rebellious, and lustful nature of the fallen angel. My main inspiration for this piece was a mix of old school and yakuza tattoos, which created a decorative horror vacui composition on the devil's skin. I tried to highlight the tattoo theme by replacing traditional wings with ink squirting out of vagina-shaped roses."

▶ **Descendent**
Schin Loong
Pen, ink, Adobe Photoshop, and Corel Painter
http://lucioleloong.com

"I wanted to paint a piece with an East-meets-West theme. The idea of a beautiful Rococo-era beauty with a dragon half seemed very interesting to me. The painting began as a sketch on watercolor paper and eventually it turned into a Photoshop and Corel Painter affair. The dragon scales were reworked many different times in several sketchbooks until I had to force myself to stop editing them."

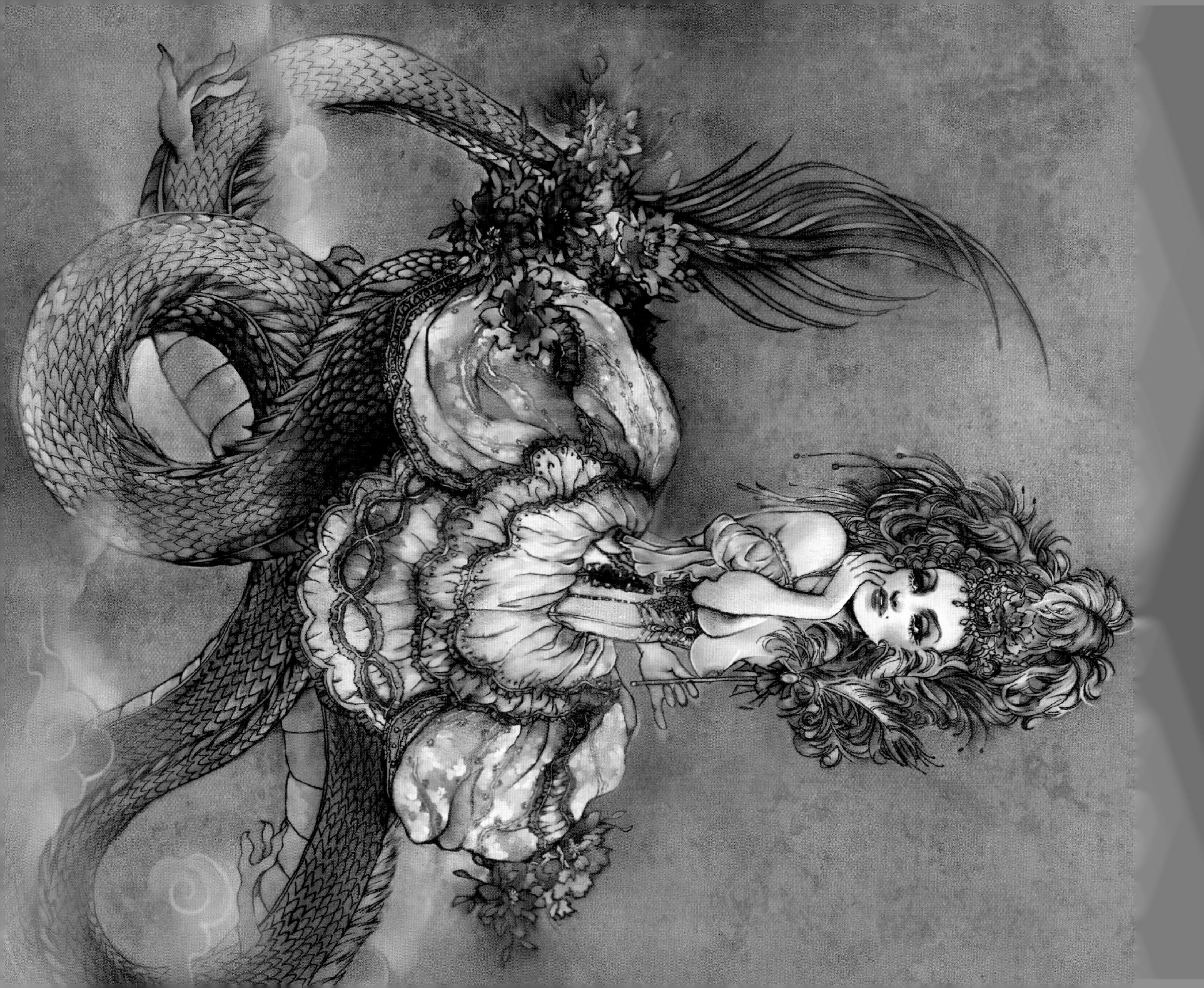

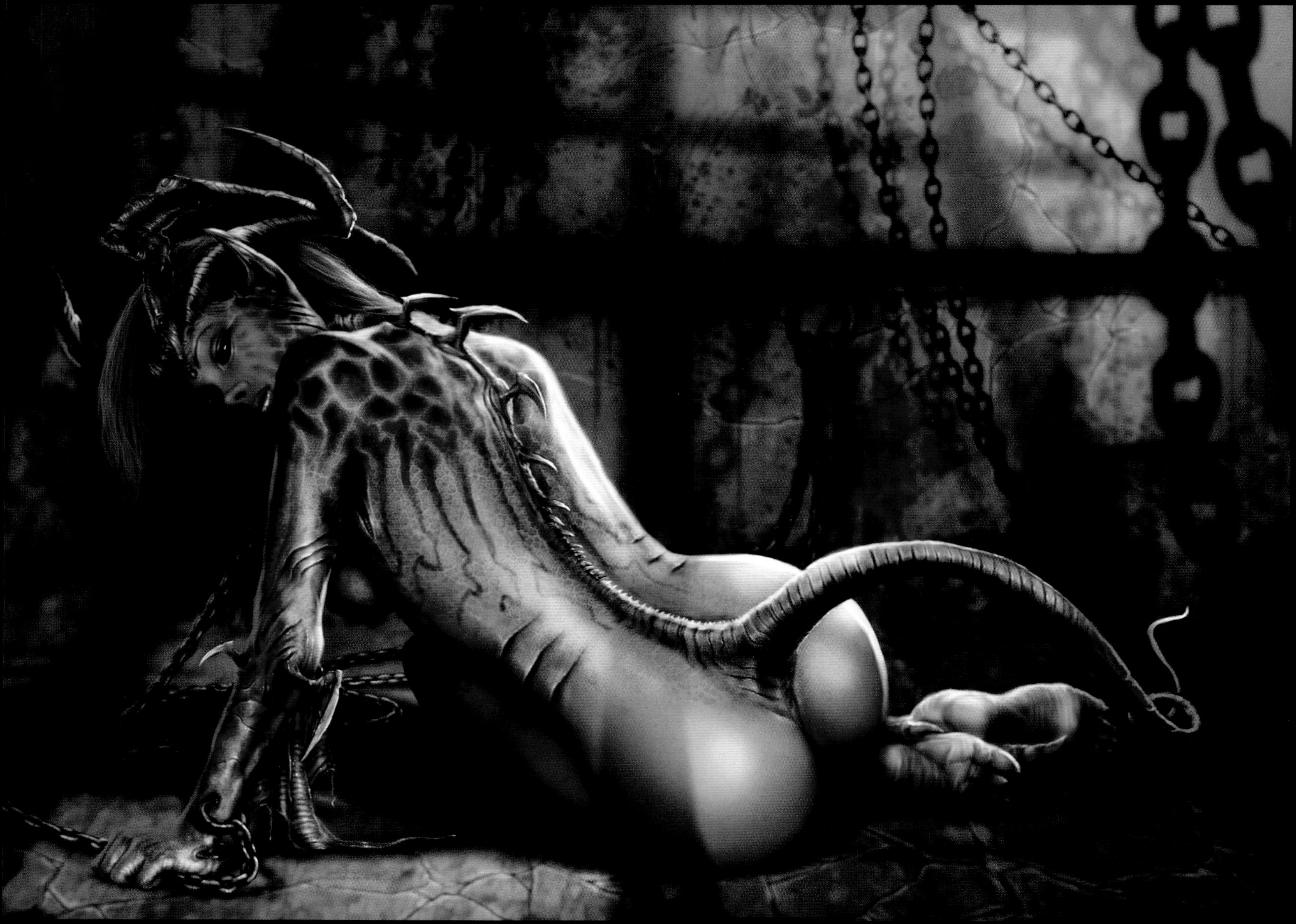

▲ **Creatura**
Tariq Raheem
Adobe Photoshop and Corel Painter
www.tariqart.net

"Held in a human prison, she awaits her fate. Born of a woman who loved a dragon—the last of its kind. She was distraught and overwhelmed by the numbers of attackers when captured. She has the ability to generate armored scales and breathe fire. Her father was the last of the water dragons . . . she is his legacy. I have an affinity to this piece as it closely resembles the style of one of my favorite artists, Dorian Cleavenger. It is in fact a homage to his beautiful creature paintings."

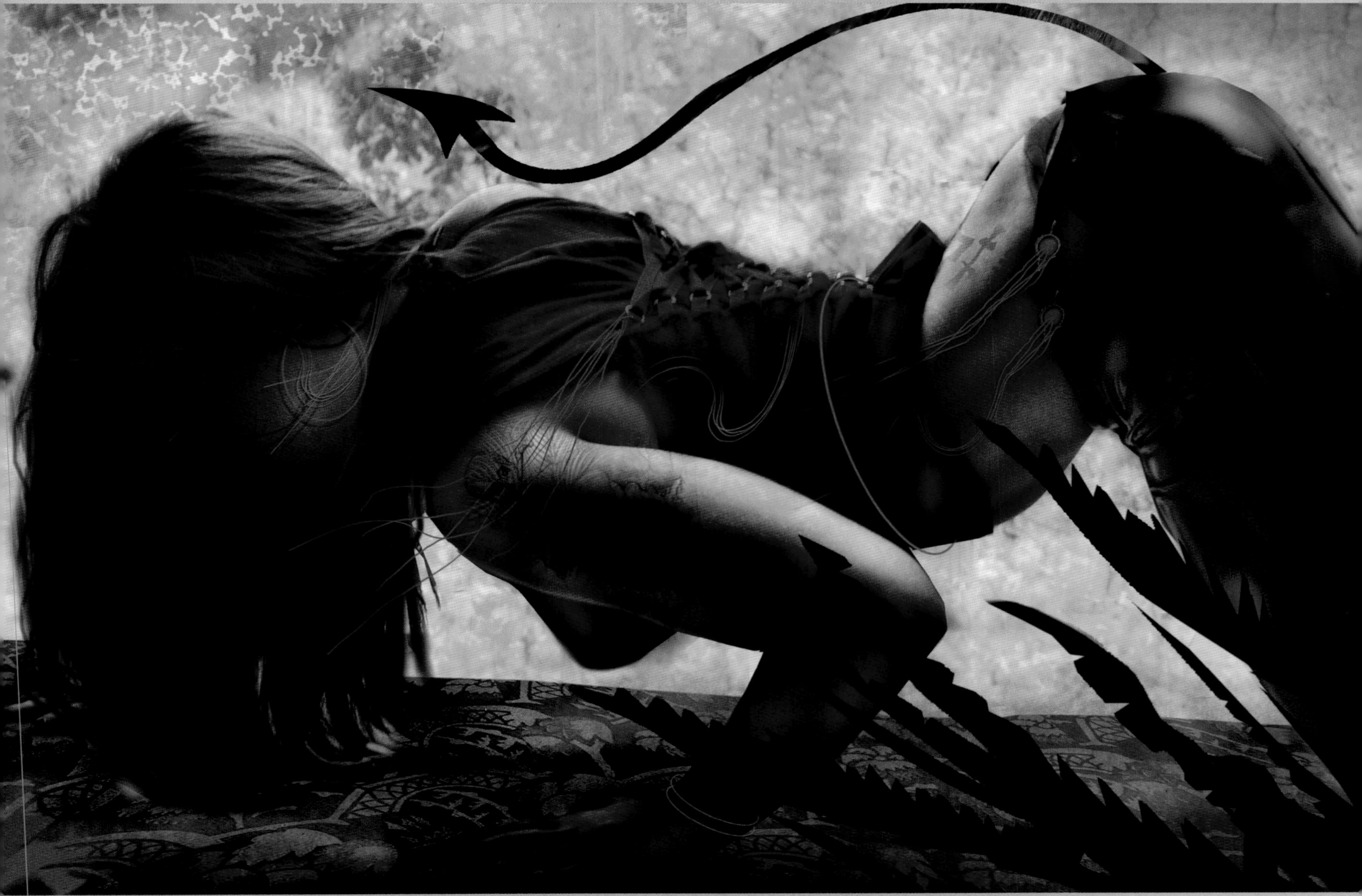

▲ **Lake Girl**
Chris Spollen
Adobe Photoshop
www.illoz.com/spollen

"The inspiration for this was the sort of spirits that reside in the depths of unknown spaces or sirens that draw men to the sea, rocky shorelines, and their deaths. The process for me starts when a mental image forms. I make thumbnails to get the idea on paper. Quick compositional sketches are made in a free flow of thought, which I do not edit until the flow stops. Then I locate a model for a photoshoot. I work in grays then add color slowly. I draw on proof printouts then go back to the Photoshop document."

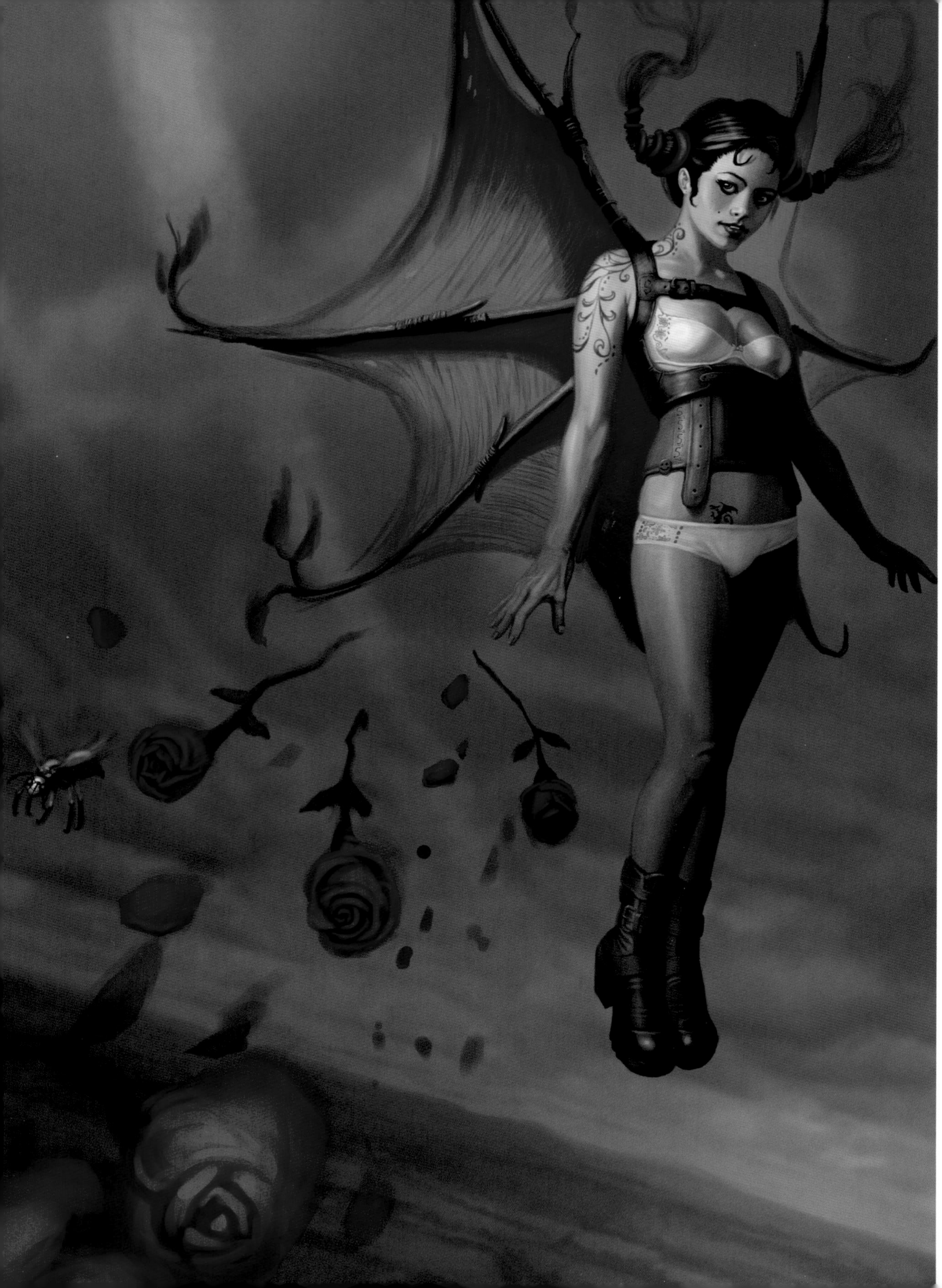

◀ **Flight and Roses**
Jhoneil Centeno
Adobe Photoshop
www.jhoneil.com

"I saw a friend of mine standing on her toes and it seemed to me like she was floating. I like painting someone flying or floating as I don't have to follow the laws of gravity as much. Originally, the painting only had the floating woman above a landscape, but composition-wise it was not working. The roses were added after chatting with a friend about love, relationships, and freedom. Not only were they a perfect solution to a bland composition, but they also added depth and meaning to the image."

▶ **If I Had a Heart**
Kassidi Keys
Poser and
Adobe Photoshop Elements
http://kassidikeys.deviantart.com

"There are various folktales of mermaids and sirens across the world. They almost all universally center around partially female creatures designed to lure men to their death. When I began painting If I Had a Heart, *that murderous intent was my inspiration. I didn't set out to paint a character so beautiful that she could lure anyone to their death (although she is). Mostly, I just wanted to paint her expression: one that was cold and apathetic. I wanted her to openly display her contempt for human life. I left the background very simple so as not to distract from her icy glance as she sinks back into the depths of the ocean to wait for the sound of another ship passing nearby."*

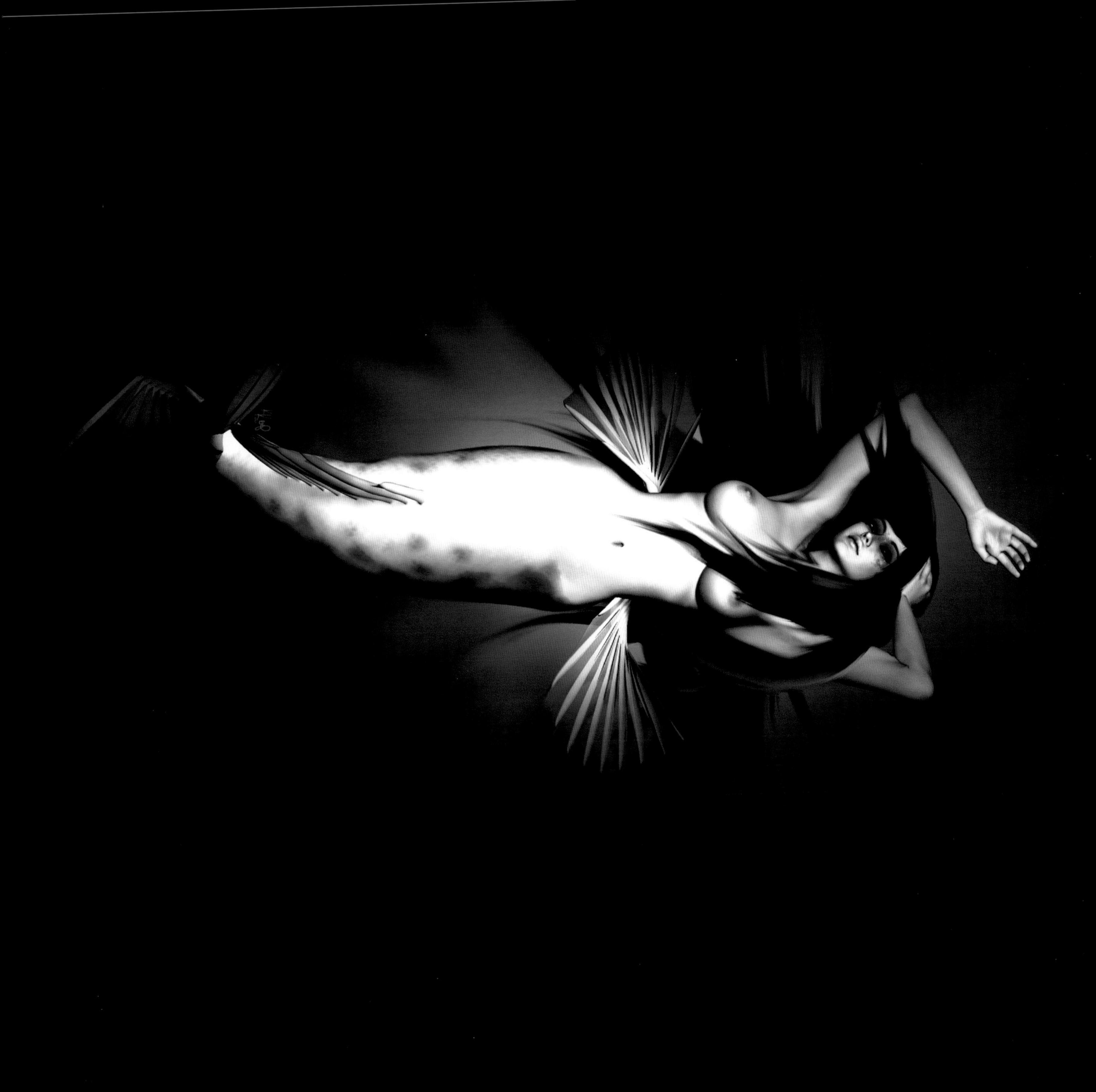

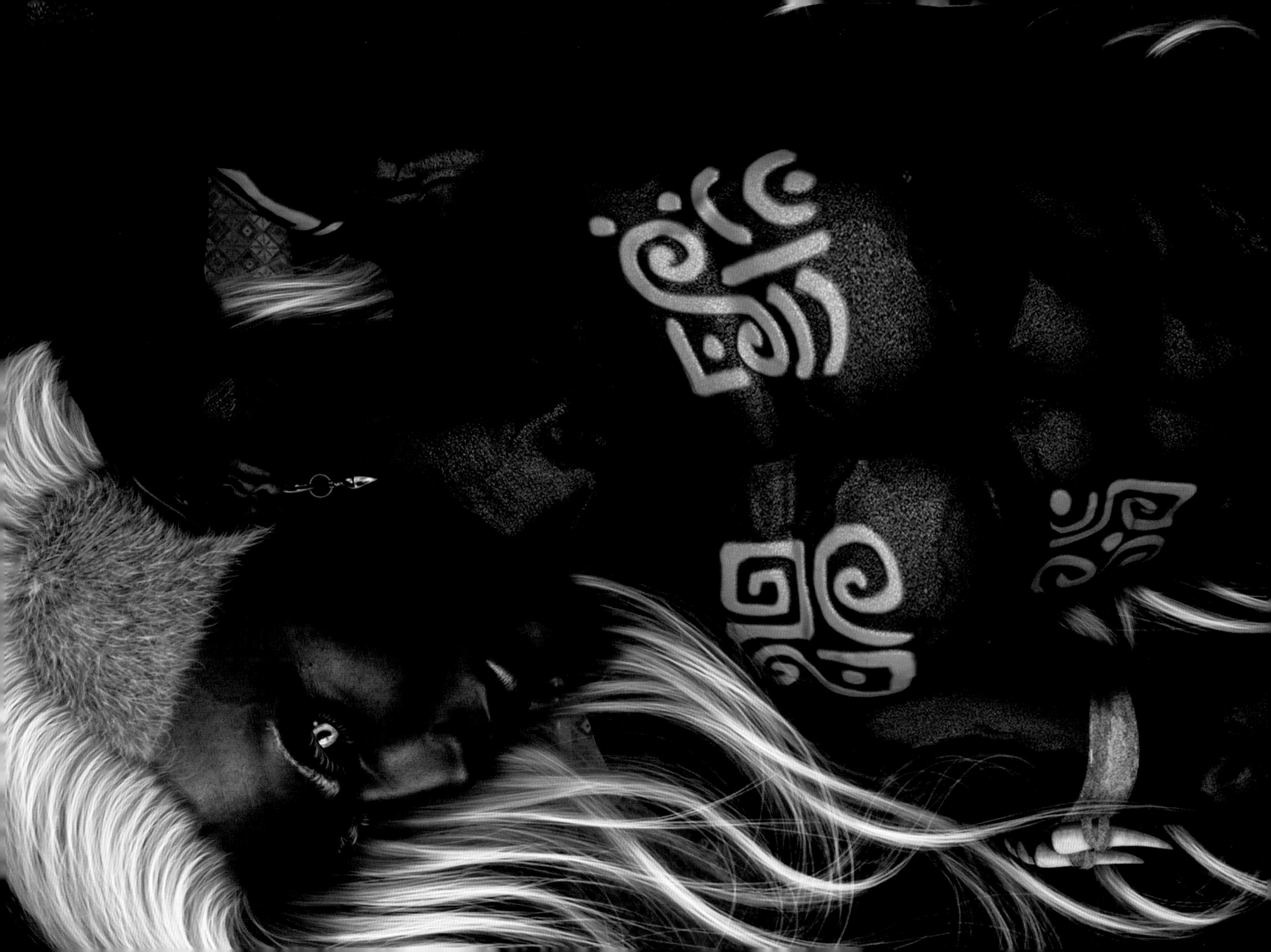

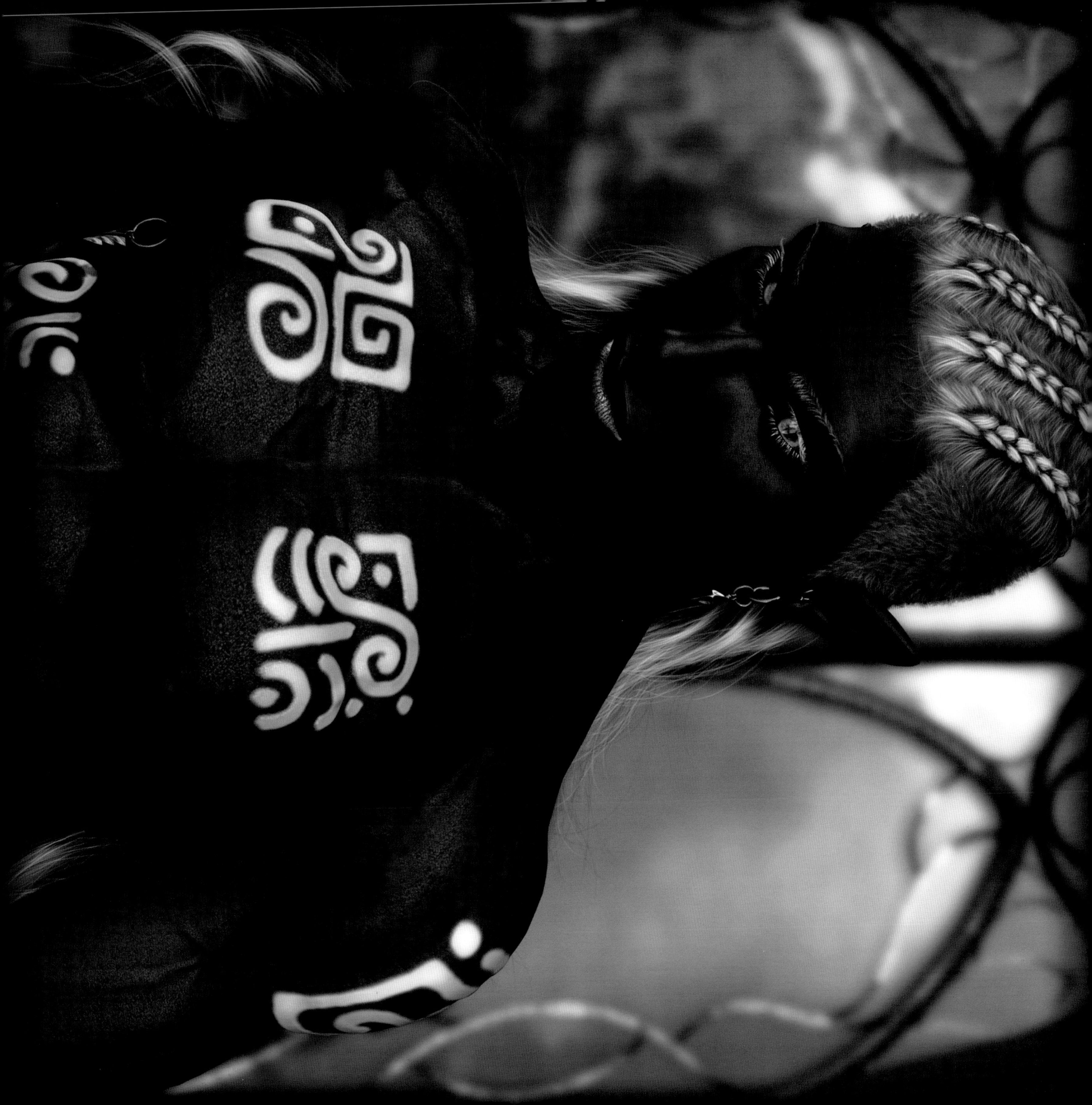

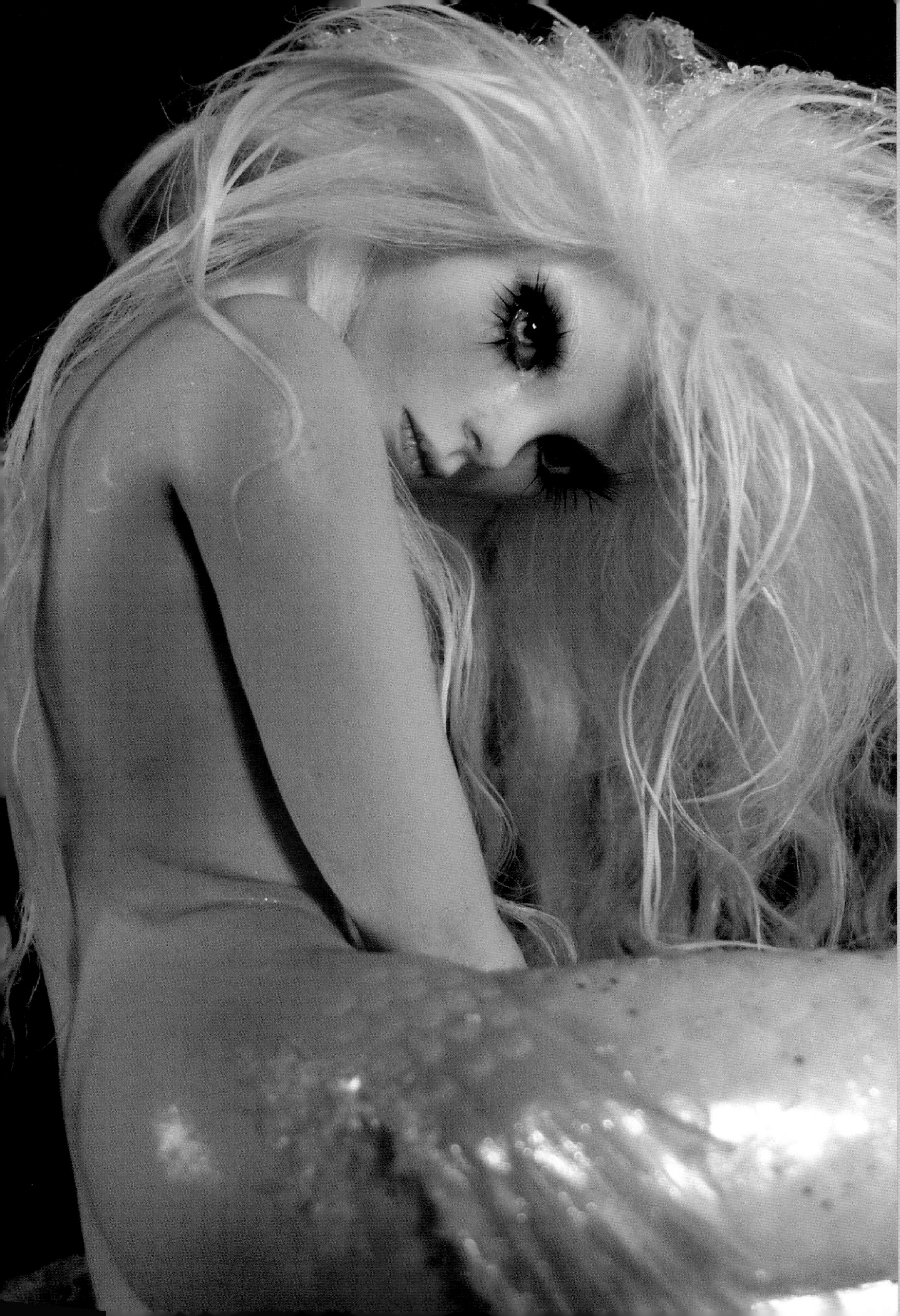

◄ **Ice Crystal Mermaid**
Nicole West
Polymer clay and various fibers
www.pbase.com/nicolewest

"To this day this is still my favorite piece I've created. I wondered how someone would go about making something simultaneously cold and hot. It took some very subtle paint work to pull it off. Layering fleshy pink over frozen blues gave me this effect. For me, eyes are really the most important element in my sculptures. I want them to draw the viewer into another world. I want them to feel as though a true living, breathing entity resides within that clay."

► **Angelblues**
Pascal Blanche
Adobe Photoshop, 3ds Max, and ZBrush
www.3dluvr.com/pascalb

"I started this illustration as a test for the new brushes in ZBrush and the new shaders in V-Ray in 3ds Max. I wanted to get a sculptural feel and it progressed into this beautiful fallen angel. The bloody tattoo mark on the back of the neck is a recent addition and it gives more of a story to the overall picture."

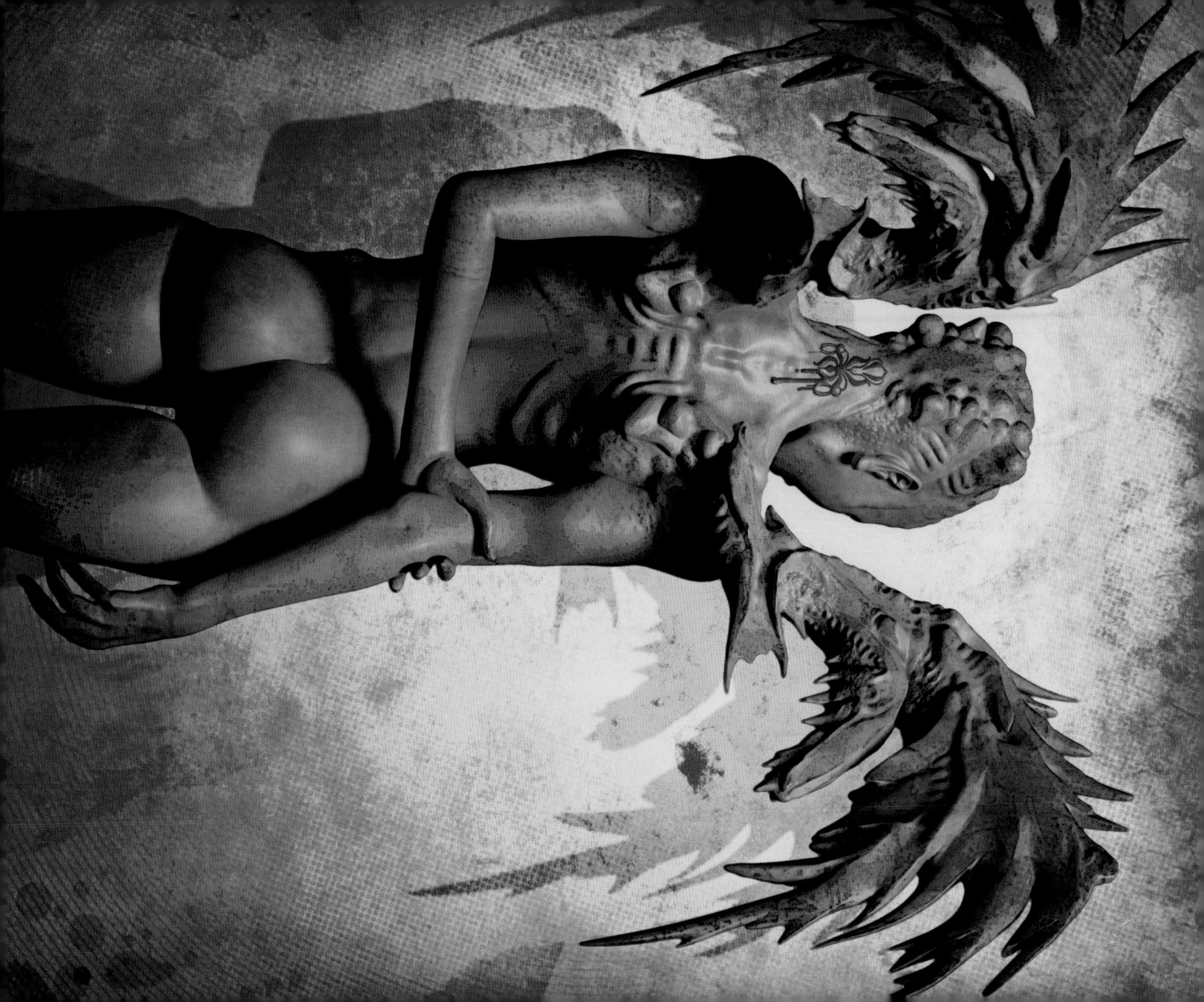

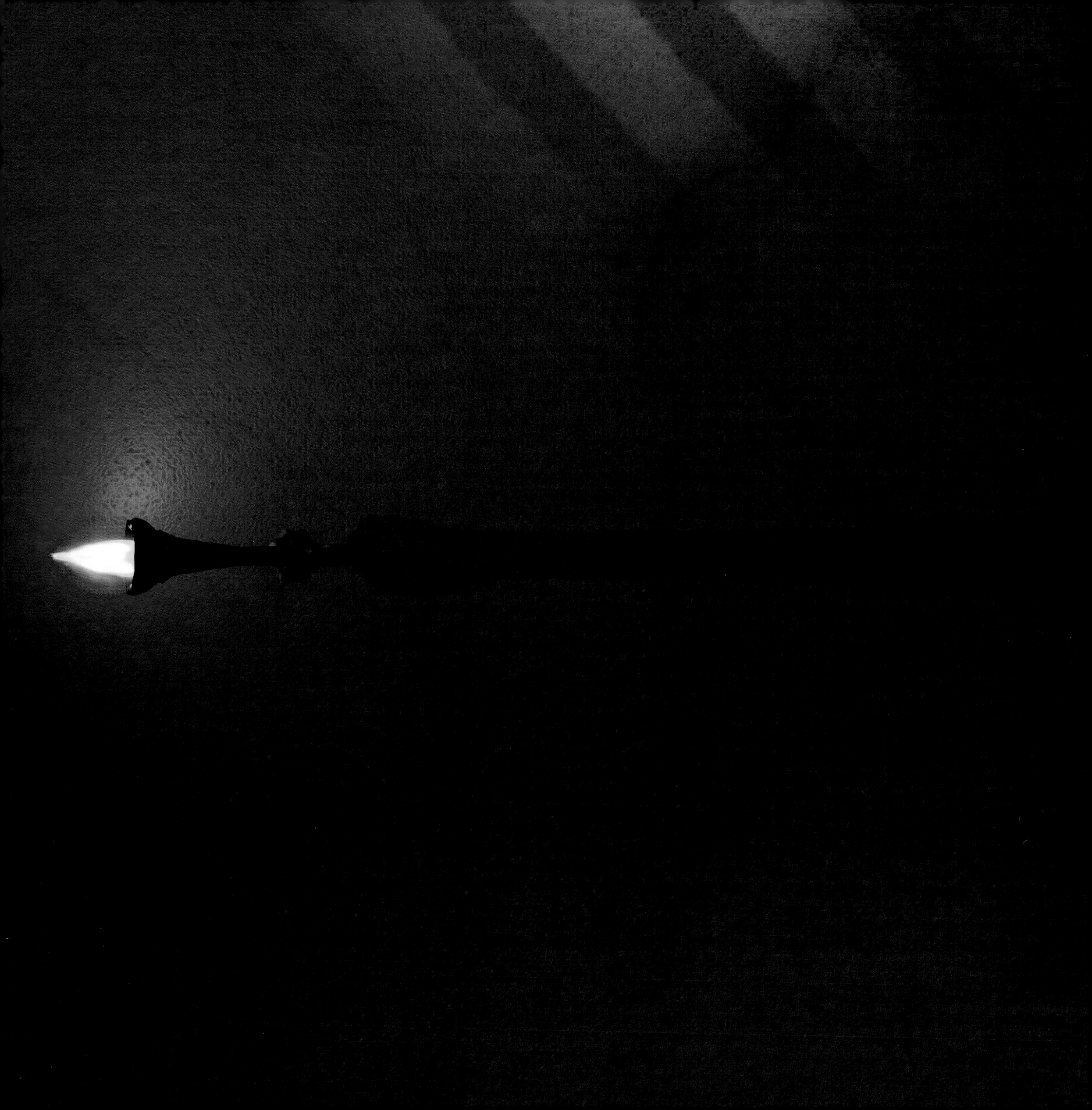

CHAPTER 3

ILLUMINATING URGES

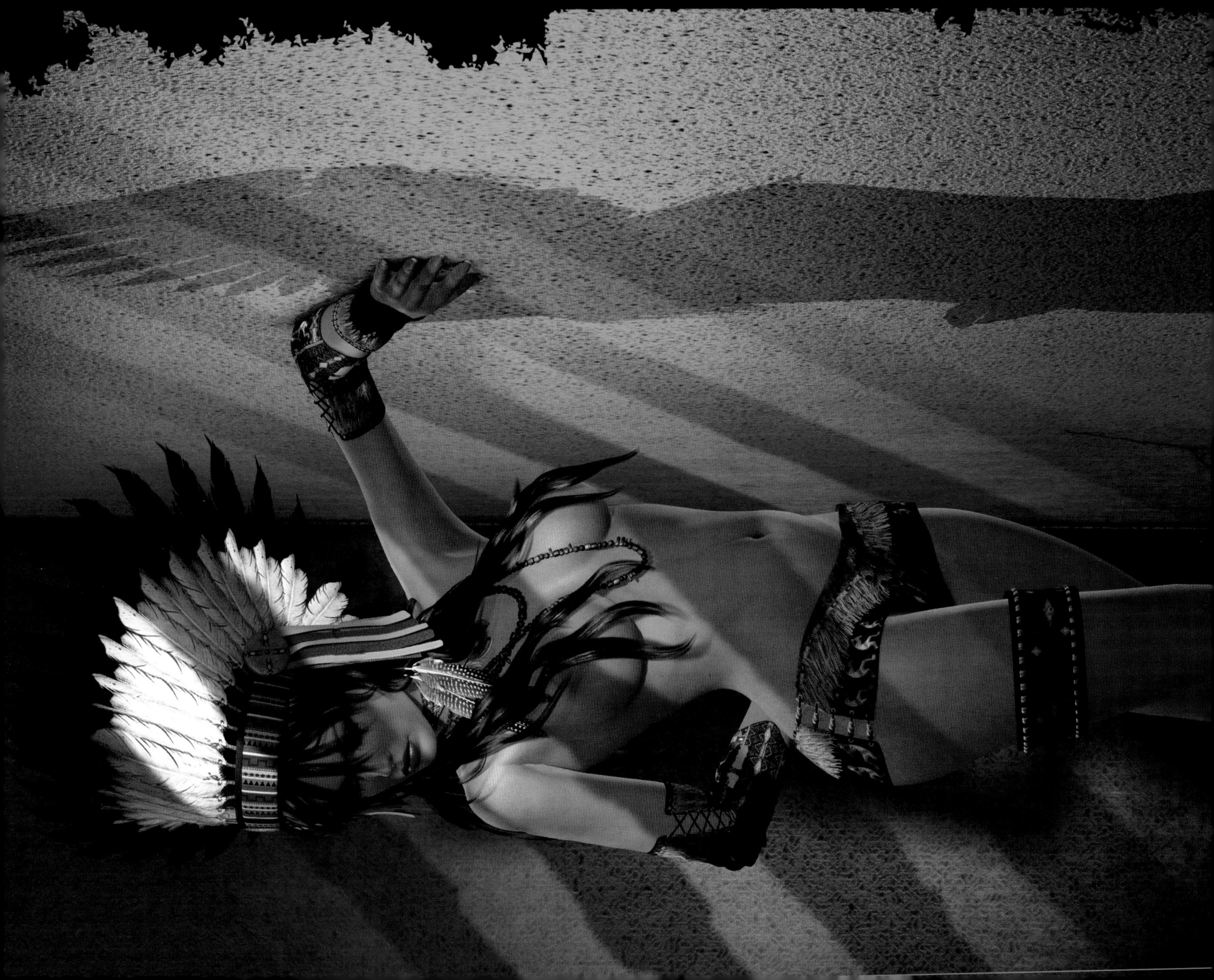

▼ **Taming the Wild**
Artemis aka Sharyn Yee
Poser Pro and Adobe Photoshop
http://dragonfly3d.deviantart.com

"For taming the wild, who better than a beautiful Native American maiden? I wanted her to be strong and fierce, yet not above using her feminine wiles if needed. While she is someone's prisoner, I didn't feel the need to use shackles to show this, as the lighting was more appropriate to convey the feeling of being imprisoned in a cell or a cage. My inspiration was the desire to do something very simple and sexy, carrying the message that a free spirit cannot be tamed by chains, real or imaginary. I built this scene in Poser Pro, exporting the image to Photoshop to lay the finishing touches of color and lighting."

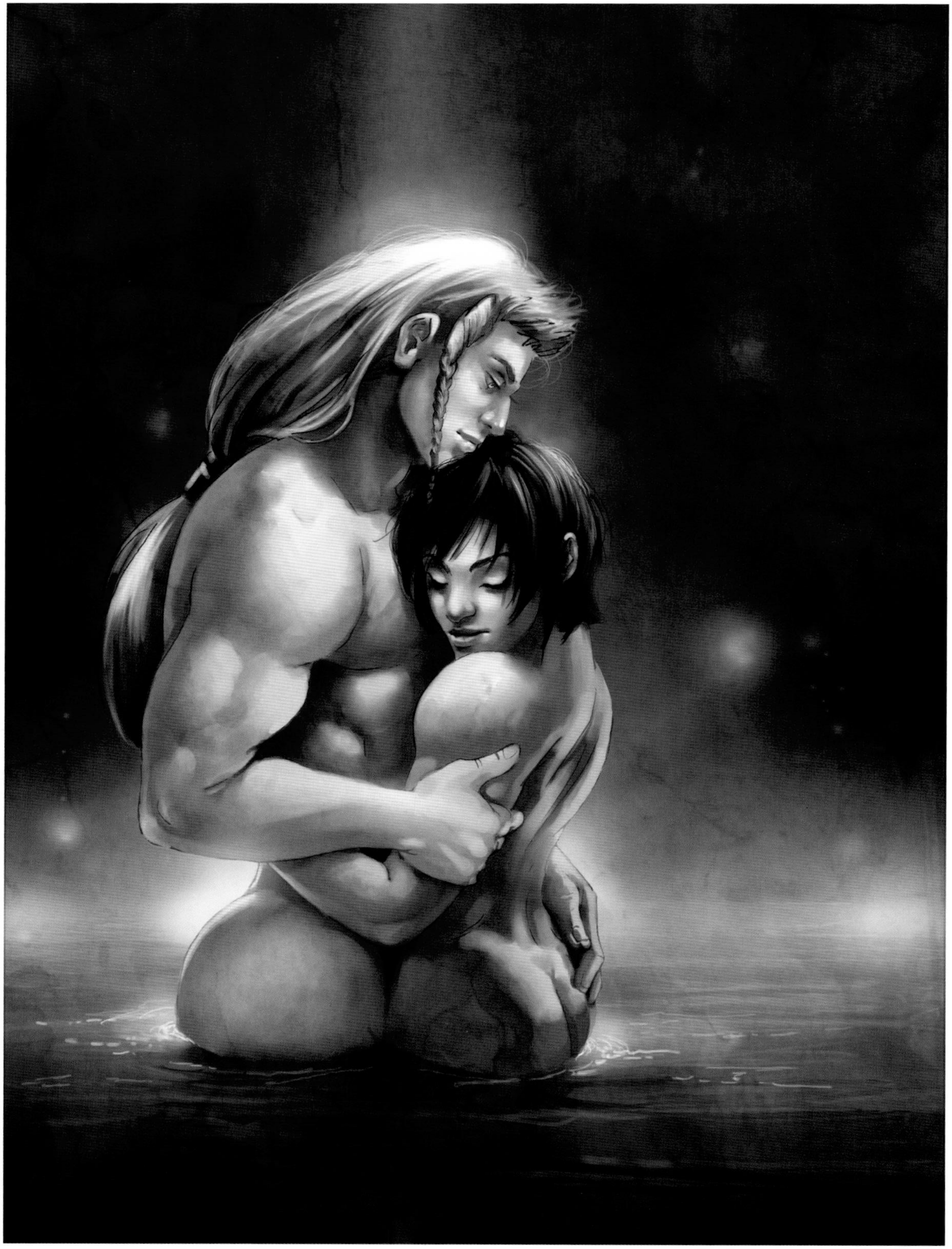

◀ **Lotus in the Wild**
Anne Cain
For Dreamspinner Press,
LLC Graphite and Adobe Photoshop
www.annecain-art.com

"This was commissioned for use on the cover of Fae Sutherland and Marguerite Labbe's Lotus in the Wild, *a fantasy-romance novel. Color and light are powerful tools in adding to the sense of intimacy between characters. However, I did not want the tenderness of the lovers to overpower the subtle allusions to magic and fantasy. My color palette plays with warm and cool tones to create an otherworldly air. They are beings of magic and sexuality, yet with an innocence, or rather, a purity to their love that I wanted to convey by making the pose more romantic than graphic. This enhances the eroticism, while at the same time downplaying it."*

▶ **A Knowing Touch**
Artemis aka Sharyn Yee
Poser Pro and Adobe Photoshop
http://dragonfly3d.deviantart.com

"For this piece, I wanted to simply convey the feeling that for love or comfort there are no boundaries. All human beings crave to be wanted and loved, or just to be comforted in hard times. I put the scene together in Poser Pro, adjusting the lighting to build the mood. The characters are dressed in sensual and sexy attire, yet maintain an innocent air. The woman comforting the distressed female is a woman of power, revealed by her clothes, and the distressed female is a lady in waiting or a slave. I leave it up to the viewer's imagination as to what happens next. Finally, I used Photoshop to do the final touches of lighting and color."

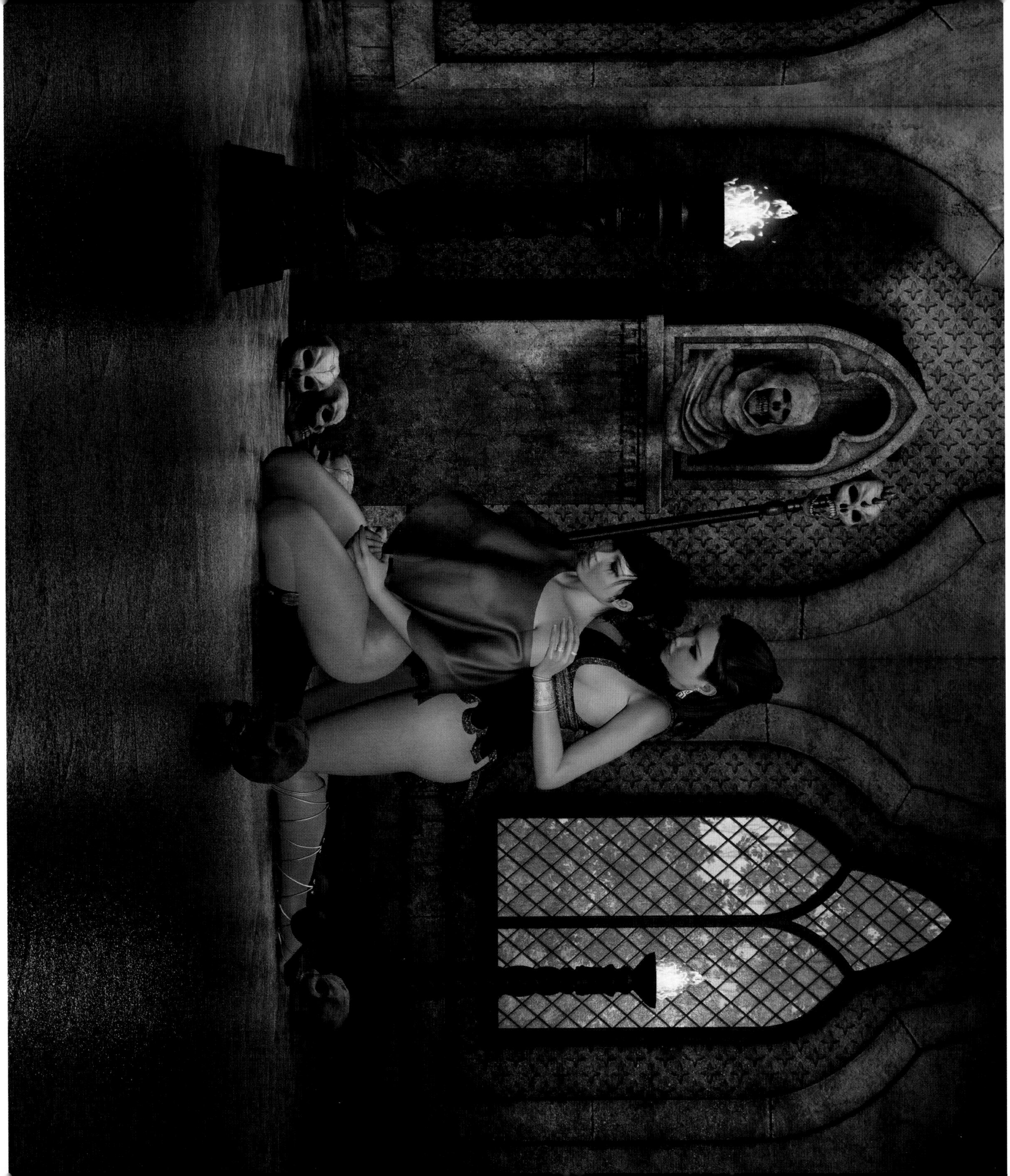

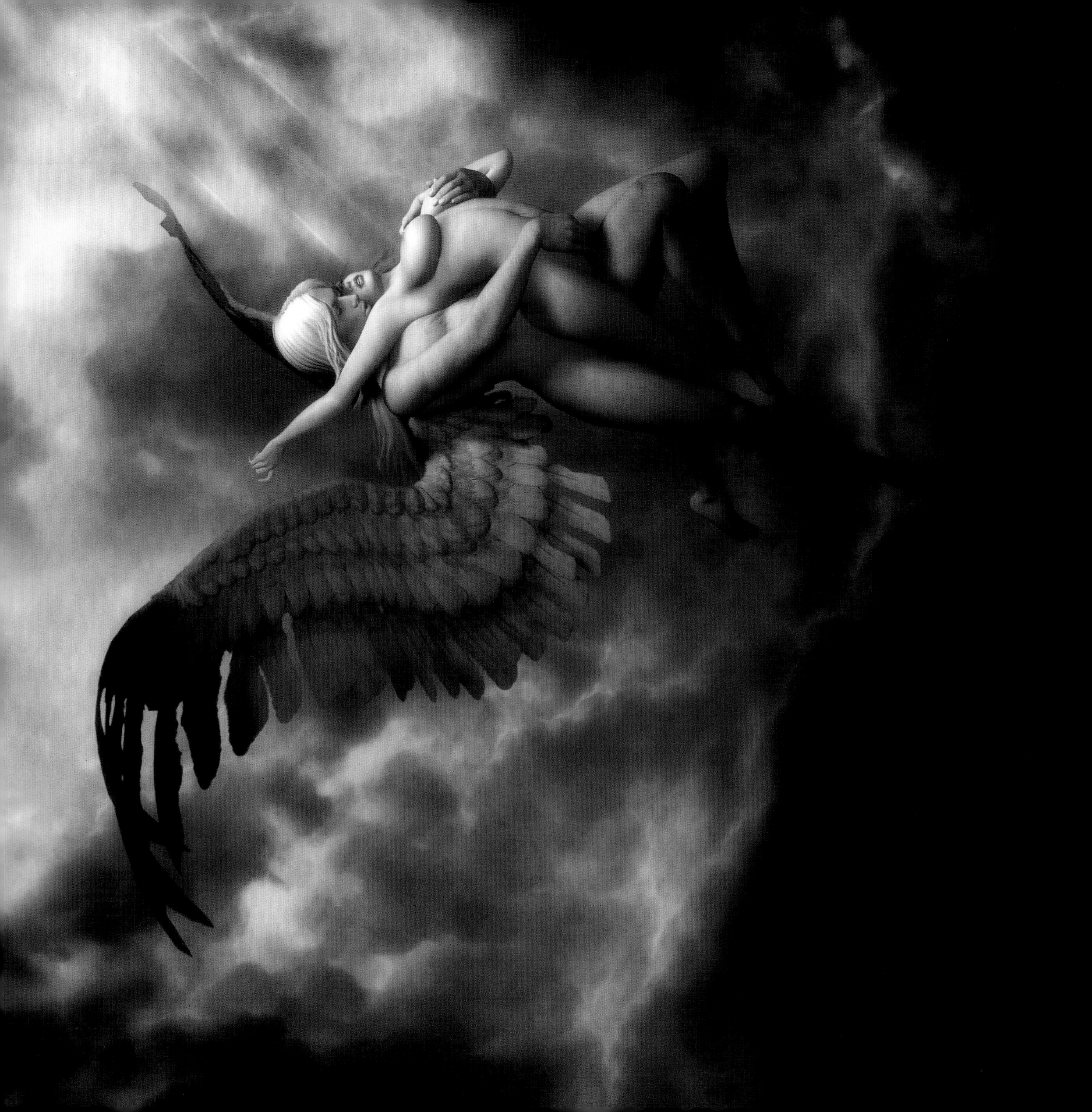

◀ **Heaven Sent**
E. Crellin aka DarkElegance
Poser and Adobe Photoshop
http://art-of-darkelegance.daportfolio.com

"From the birth of heaven, lust bounds us in mortal coils. Angels dare to taste such temptations. This was inspired by the Nephilim. I tried to capture the ethereal flight of such unbound passion and lust. The arch of the back, the sweeping line of the bodies as they fly to the very heights of heaven, drawn almost by the shine of light from above. This picture was created from a 3-D render (the figures) and from stock images (the clouds in this case). Using Photoshop, the colors of the clouds were changed, lighting and effects were added, and there was correction to a joint or two."

▶ **Where Heaven and Hell Meet**
Deedee Davies
Poser, Vue 6 Esprit, and Adobe Photoshop
www.seedydeedee.co.uk

"A friend challenged me to make this picture, giving me the outline idea of 'a female demon and a male angel enjoying an intimate moment where heaven and hell meet.' I wanted to make the female demon as capricious-looking as possible, and hopefully her sense of mischief comes through in the picture. I wanted the male angel to look a little nervous, as he's probably a bit out of his depth here, but still keen! I went for a blend of golds, reds, and greens to keep the picture vibrant and lighthearted, and added a few comedic gargoyles to emphasize the humor of the piece."

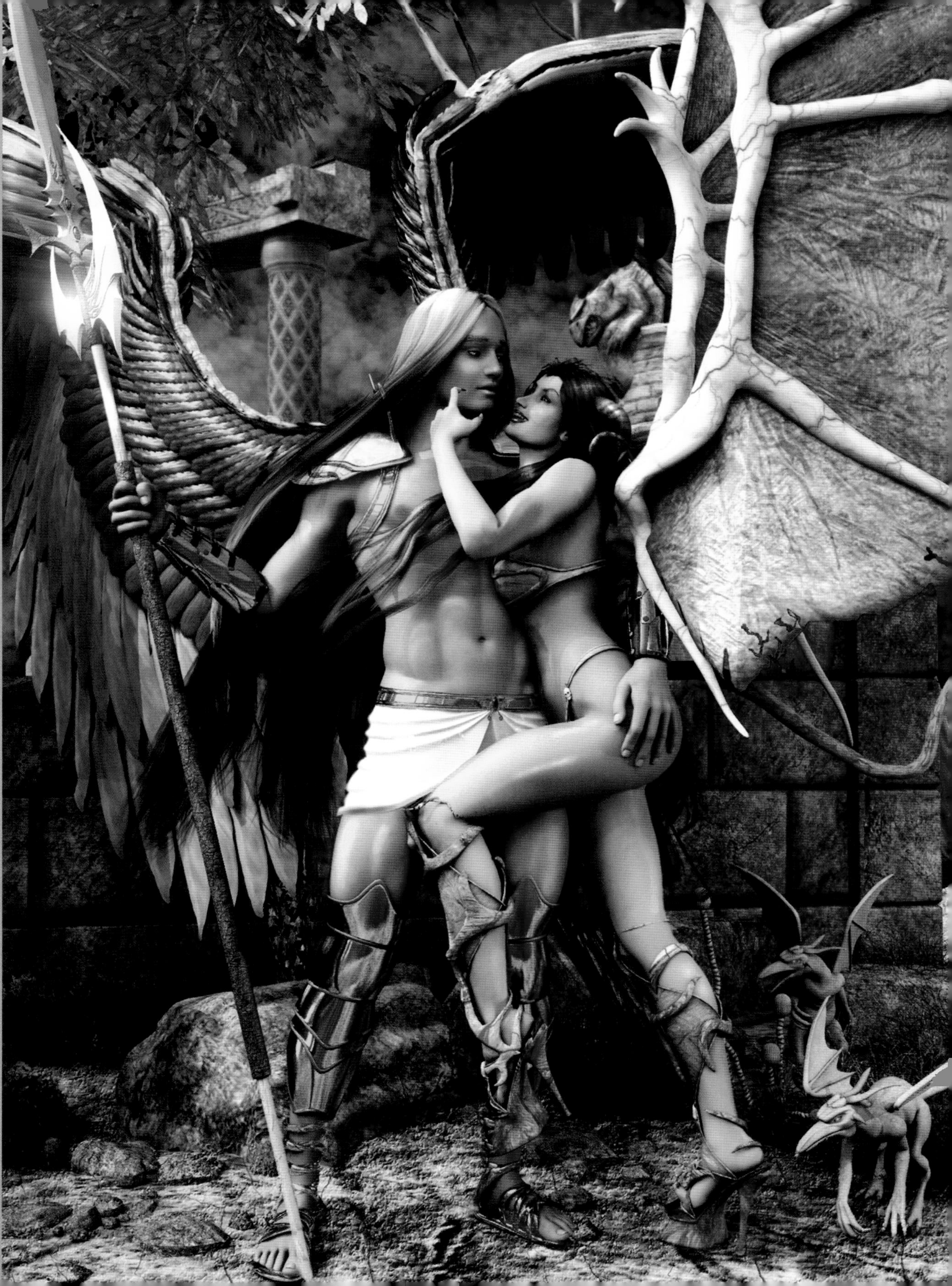

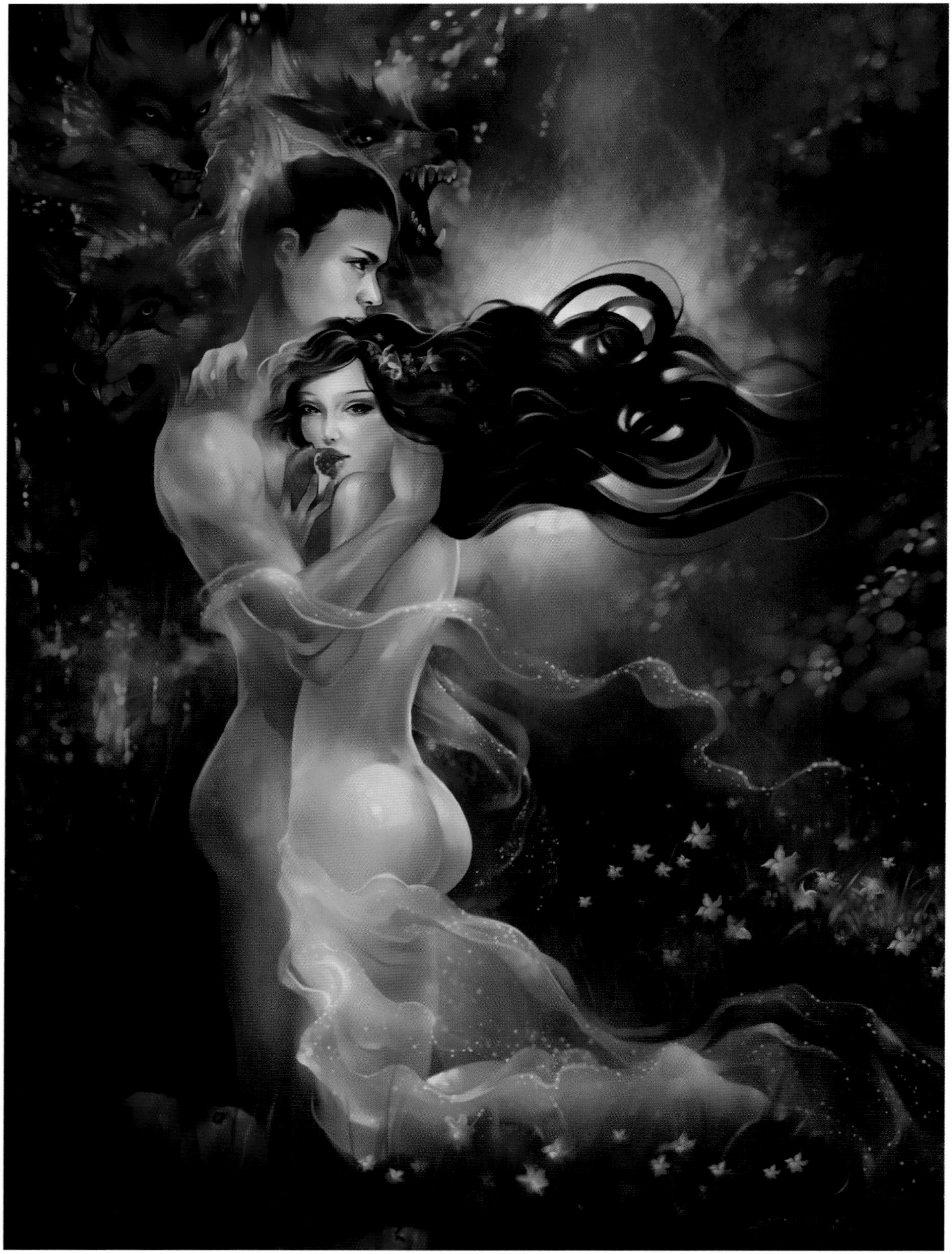

◀ **Persephone Destroys the Light**
Schin Loong
Adobe Photoshop
and Corel Painter
http://lucioleloong.com

"This is my depiction of Persephone and Hades. According to legend, Hades, the God of the Underworld kidnapped Persephone to be his bride. Whilst in captivity, Persephone ate some pomegranate seeds, which resulted in winter every year. Personally, I always thought that Persephone secretly loved Hades and ran away with him. I painted her seductively and willingly taking a bite out of the cursed pomegranate while he holds her tightly and looks on behind her protectively. Behind him, the three-headed dogs of hell, Cerberus, signifies the dark future in store for them both. This painting is their misunderstood love story."

▶ **The Unicorn Kiss**
Kassidi Keys
Poser and Adobe
Photoshop Elements
http://kassidikeys.deviantart.com

"Some days I just feel like fooling around with my tools with no particular direction in mind. Always challenge yourself! Without experimentation, we don't learn new things. The Unicorn Kiss *was born because I wanted to test out new brushes and models. While posing the horse, I realized I could easily make it a unicorn and obviously it needed a rider . . . no! Why not two riders? It wasn't intended as a serious piece, but it took on a life of its own, and before I knew it I had spent three days painting an elf and a fairy making out on the back of a unicorn."*

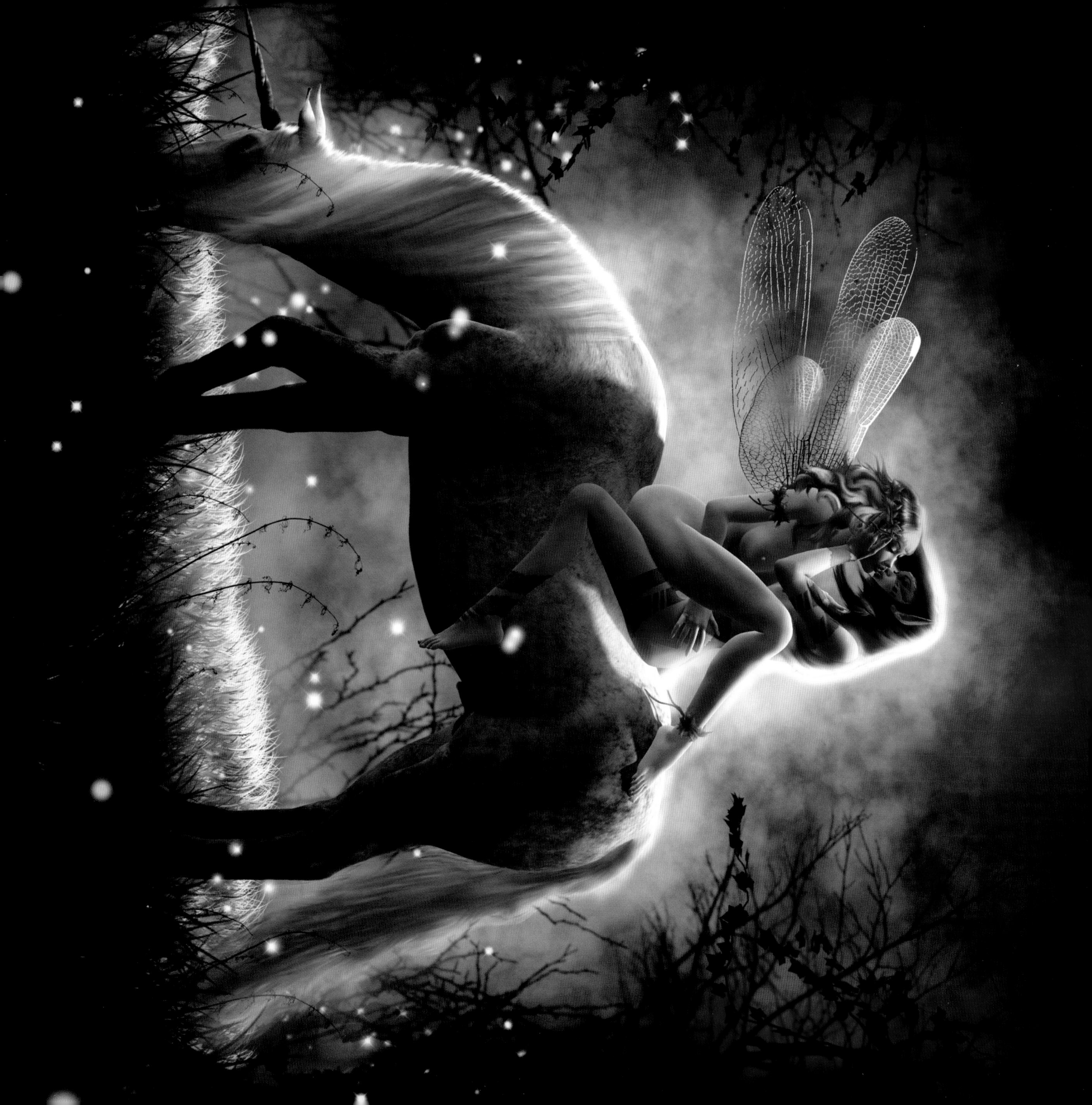

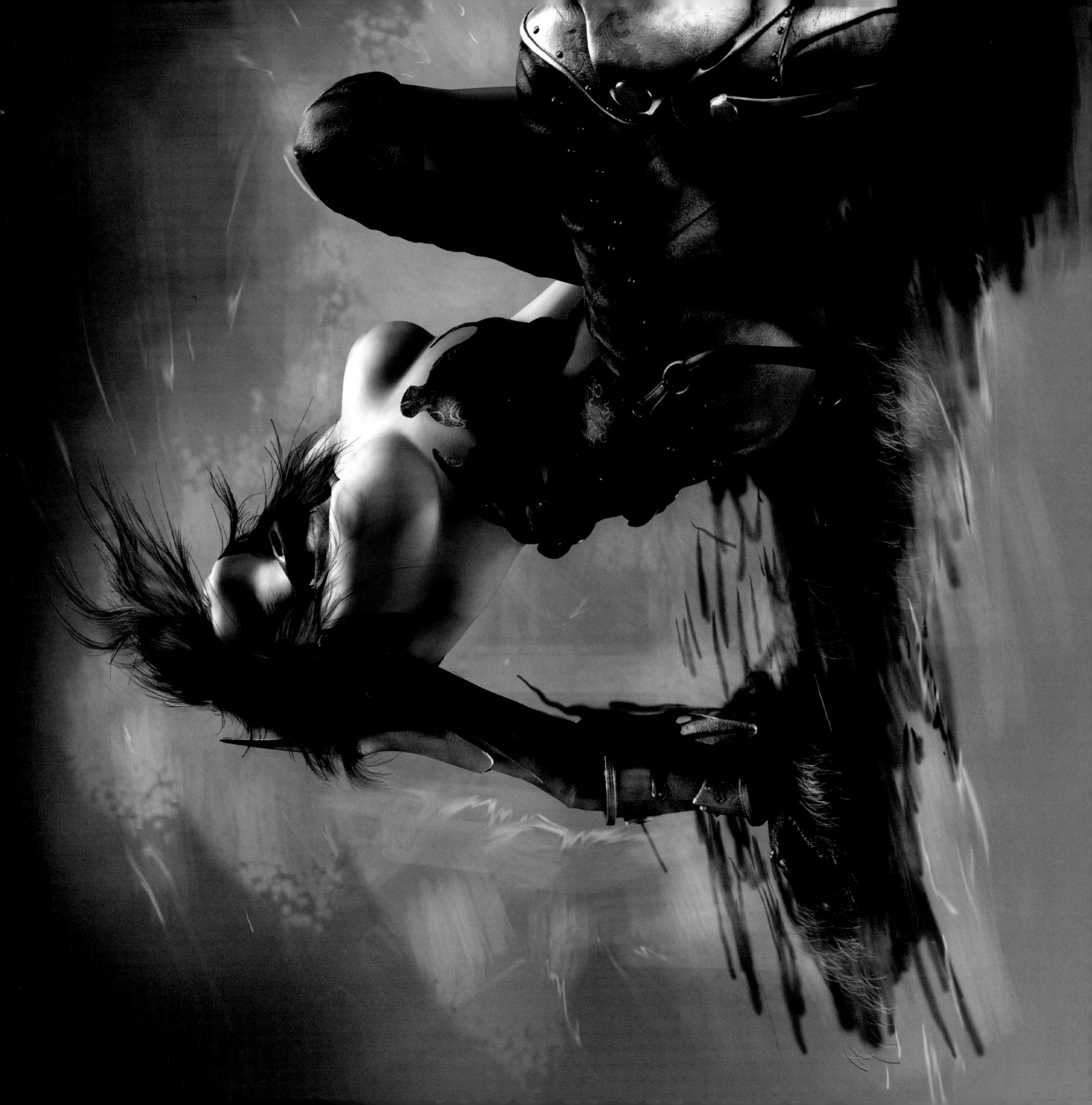

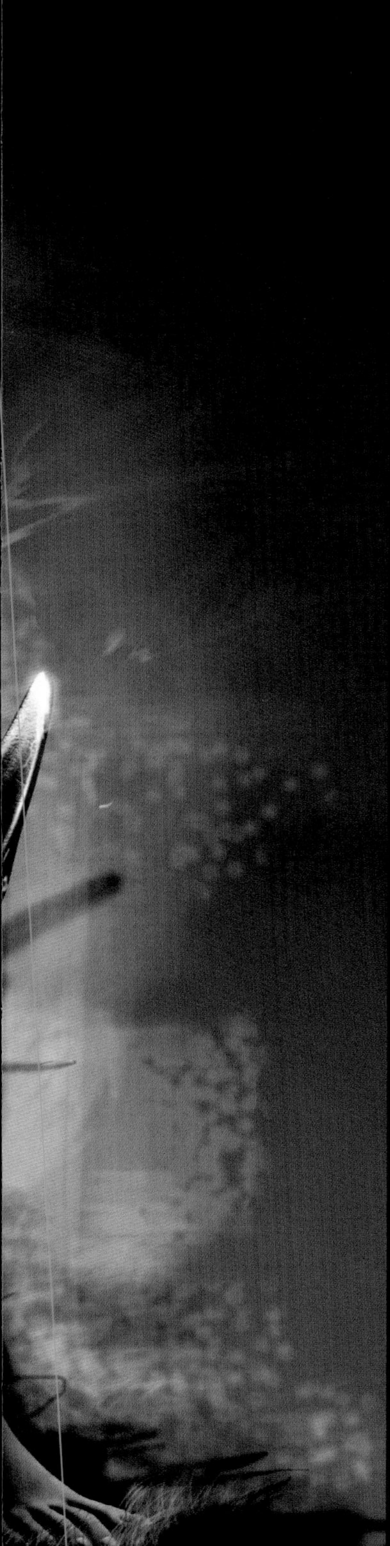

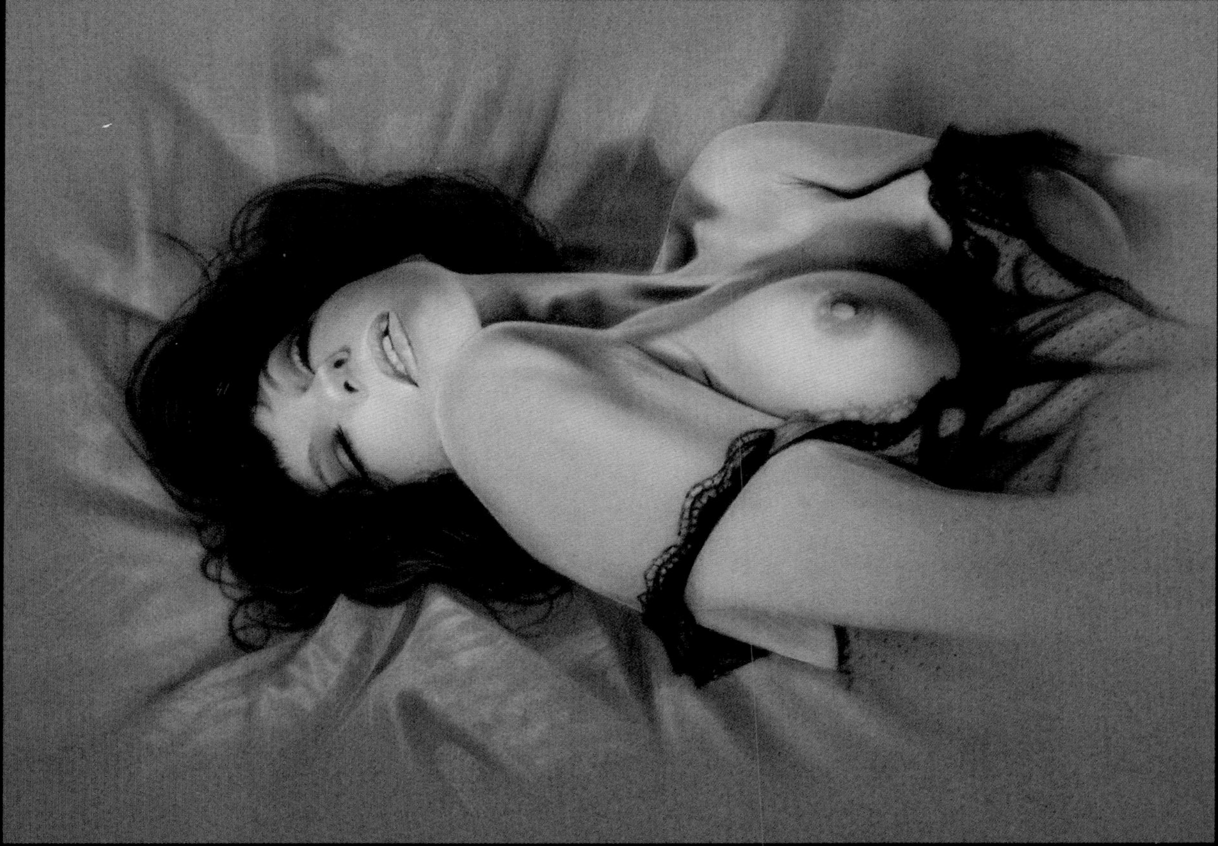

◀ **Blow**
Guido Leber
Poser and Adobe Photoshop
www.goor.deviantart.com

"A warrior after a successful battle. The body is heated. The wind sweeps through the wet hair, it cools, and plays with the heated skin. The figure was created with the 3-D rendering program Poser and the post-processing was done in Photoshop."

▲ **Awakening**
Michael Calandra
Acrylics and colored pencil
www.calandrastudio.com

"When creating the image Awakening, *I wanted to invoke the feelings and colors of a dreamlike state — that brief moment in time between consciousness and unconsciousness. I used a soft airbrush technique and colored pencil to give my model, Seffana, a soft quality and a sense of movement that would express this theme."*

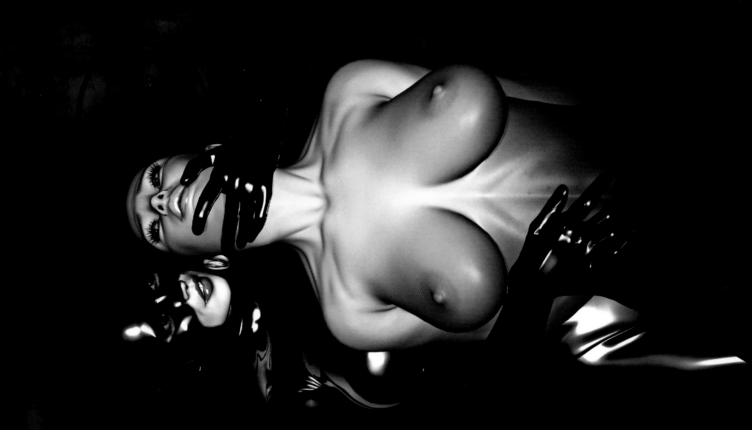

▼ **Latex Bound and Love**
E. Crellin aka DarkElegance
Poser and Adobe Photoshop
http://art-of-darkelegance.
daportfolio.com

"These two visit my imagination often. There is the twinning of hard and soft: the synthetic shine of latex and the soft glow of supple flesh; the domination and the submission. Something about seeing that shine against bare flesh is enticing. You can get a particularly striking contrast of the two using digital techniques, either to render or to enhance it in photos. You can render textures with an almost alien intensity or you can go for something a bit more supple and less reflective. Either way, fetish work is moving at light speed via digital art. The latex here is created with Shader Nodes, which allow for the sheen. It's the same for the flesh or fabric, Shader Nodes allow you unimaginable options."

▲ **White Snake**
Carmen Indorato
Poser and Adobe Photoshop
http://shantetoo.deviantart.com

"I love tentacle hentai and the fascination with the snake is, in part, a carry over from that. There is also an obvious fascination with the phallic representation of the snake and its correlation with the embodiment of the Devil from the Old Testament as the seducer of women's purity. However, here, it seems the woman is just as beguiling as the snake and possibly a more dangerous seducer."

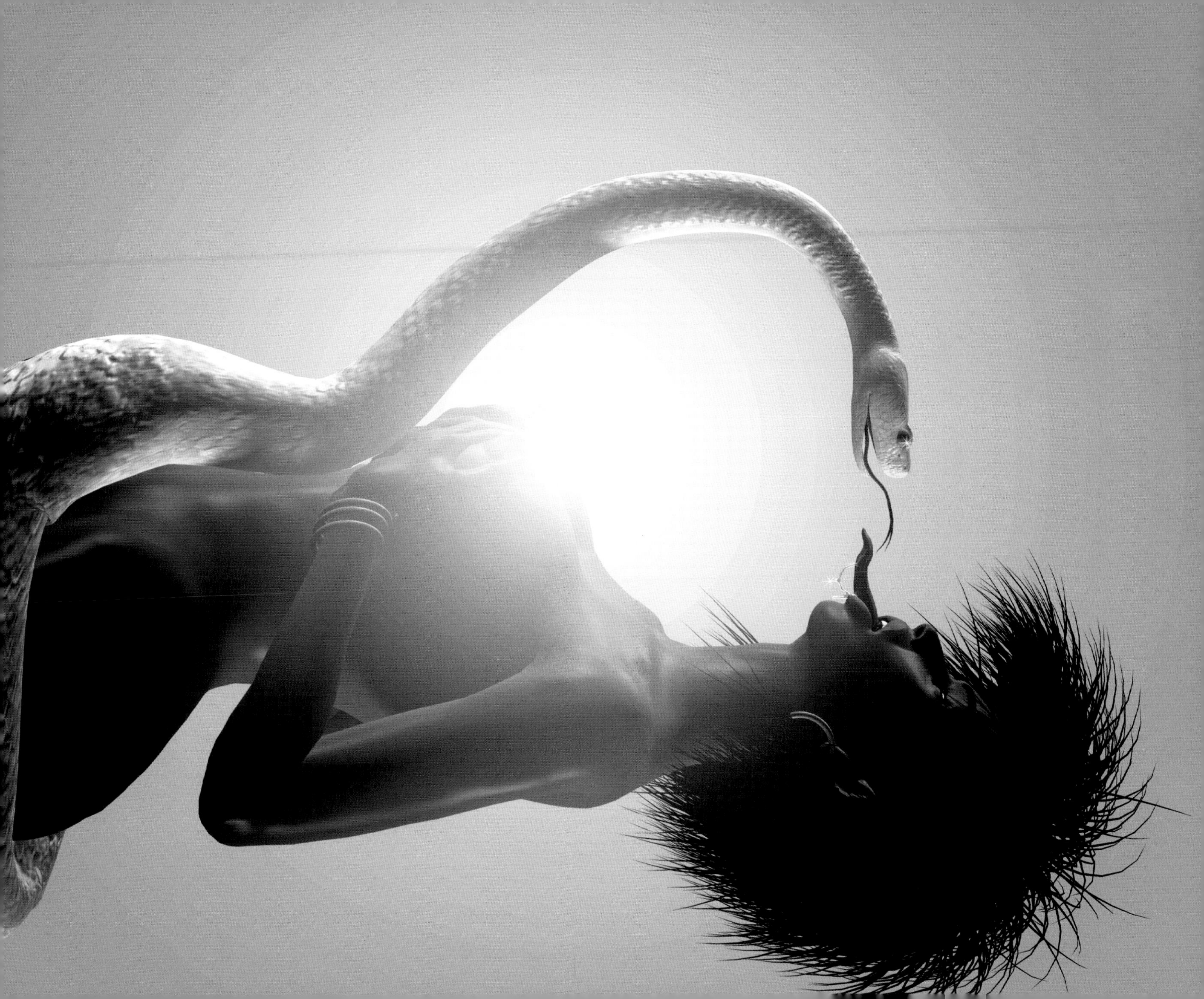

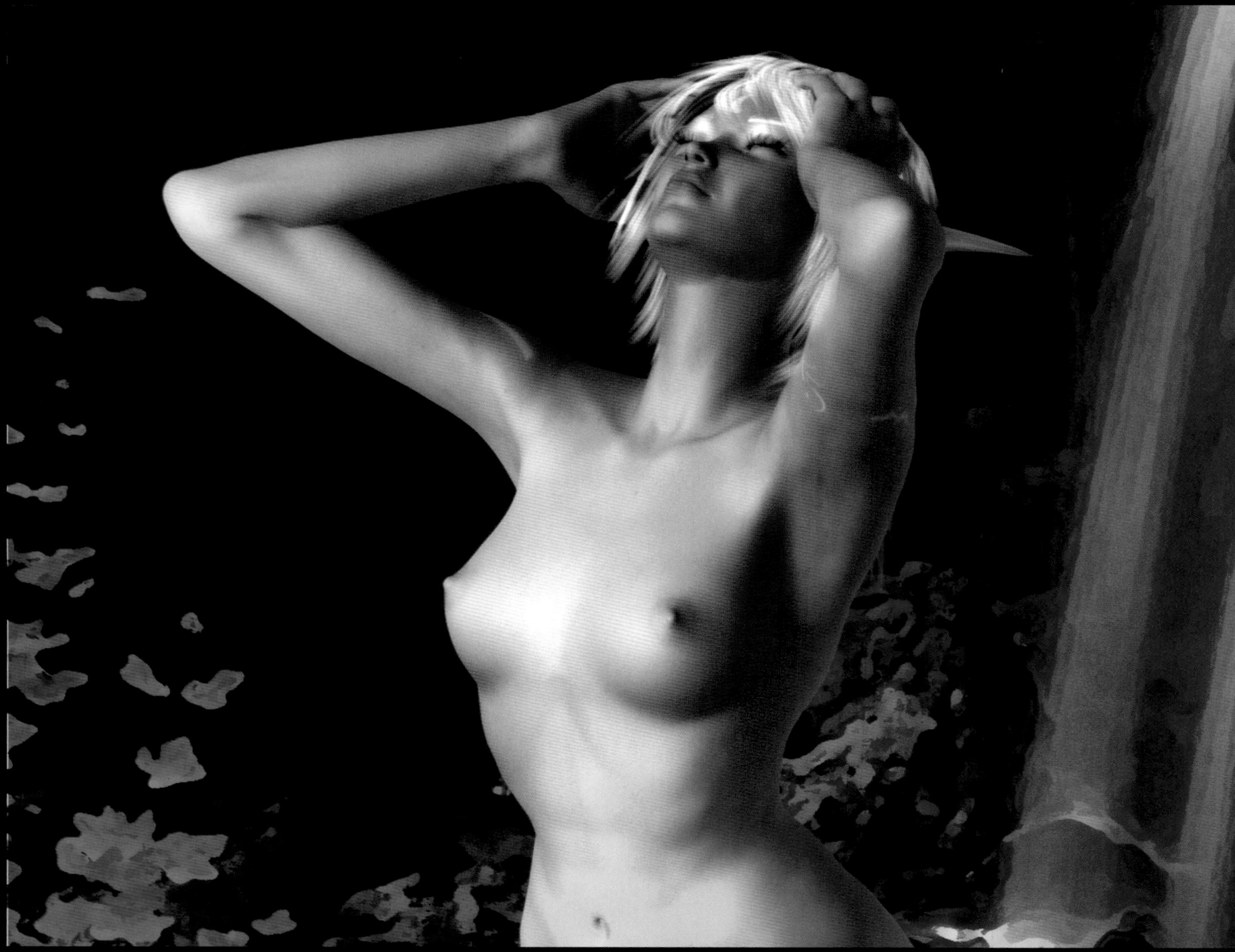

▲ **Lunarix—Moonwell**
Aaron Birch "Lunariis"
Poser Pro and Adobe Photoshop
http://lunariis.deviantart.com
www.treeworx.org

"Lunarix was my main character when I used to play World of Warcraft*. I have Blizzard Entertainment to thank for a great jump into the fan-art genre. I was always captivated by the graphics of the game and their simplicity, inspiring me to paint a more imaginative picture. I wanted to convey how I saw that world, and this is an example. The model was based on the generic 'Victoria 4' model from DAZ 3D. I designed the pose in Poser Pro, and then added hair, textures, and lightning effects. After, I rendered her, which takes anywhere from half an hour to 12 hours based on an image's complexity, and exported the render into Photoshop. Then I added the final effects, softened the look, and added vibrant colors."*

▶ Hunger
Deedee Davis
Poser, Vue 6 Esprit,
and Adobe Photoshop
www.seedydeedee.co.uk

"I have a long-standing interest in vampires and their innate sensuality has always fascinated me. I wanted to create a picture that would express raw, primal hunger and sexuality, as well as a sense of danger. After a lot of prevaricating and blushing, I created this piece. I used strong blue tones for the vampire's skin and much warmer pink ones for the girl's to emphasize the difference between them. I also added some gothic spires in the background, along with a bat, just to set the scene a little. I tend to think, when I look at this, that the vampire's snarl is just fading."

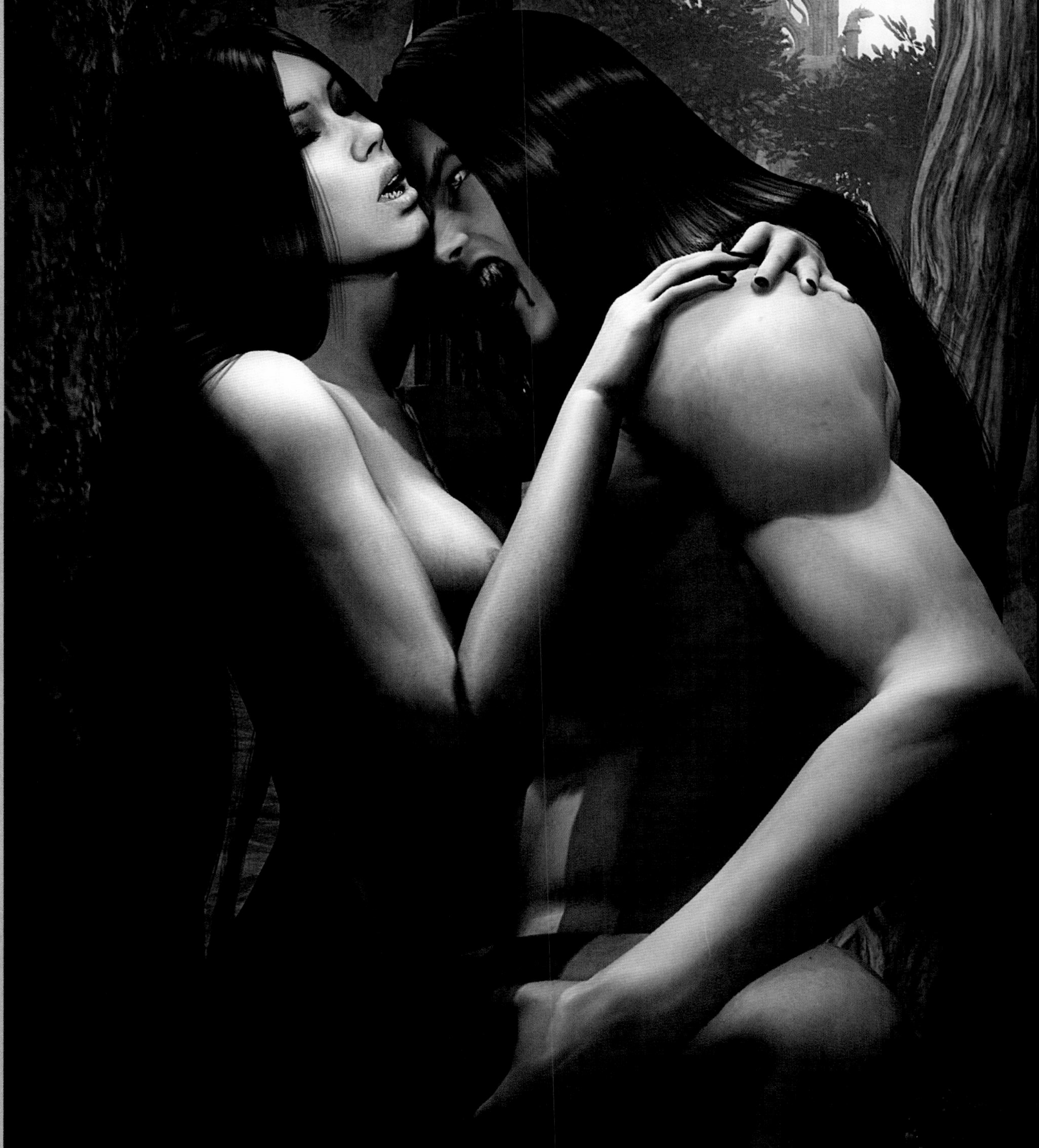

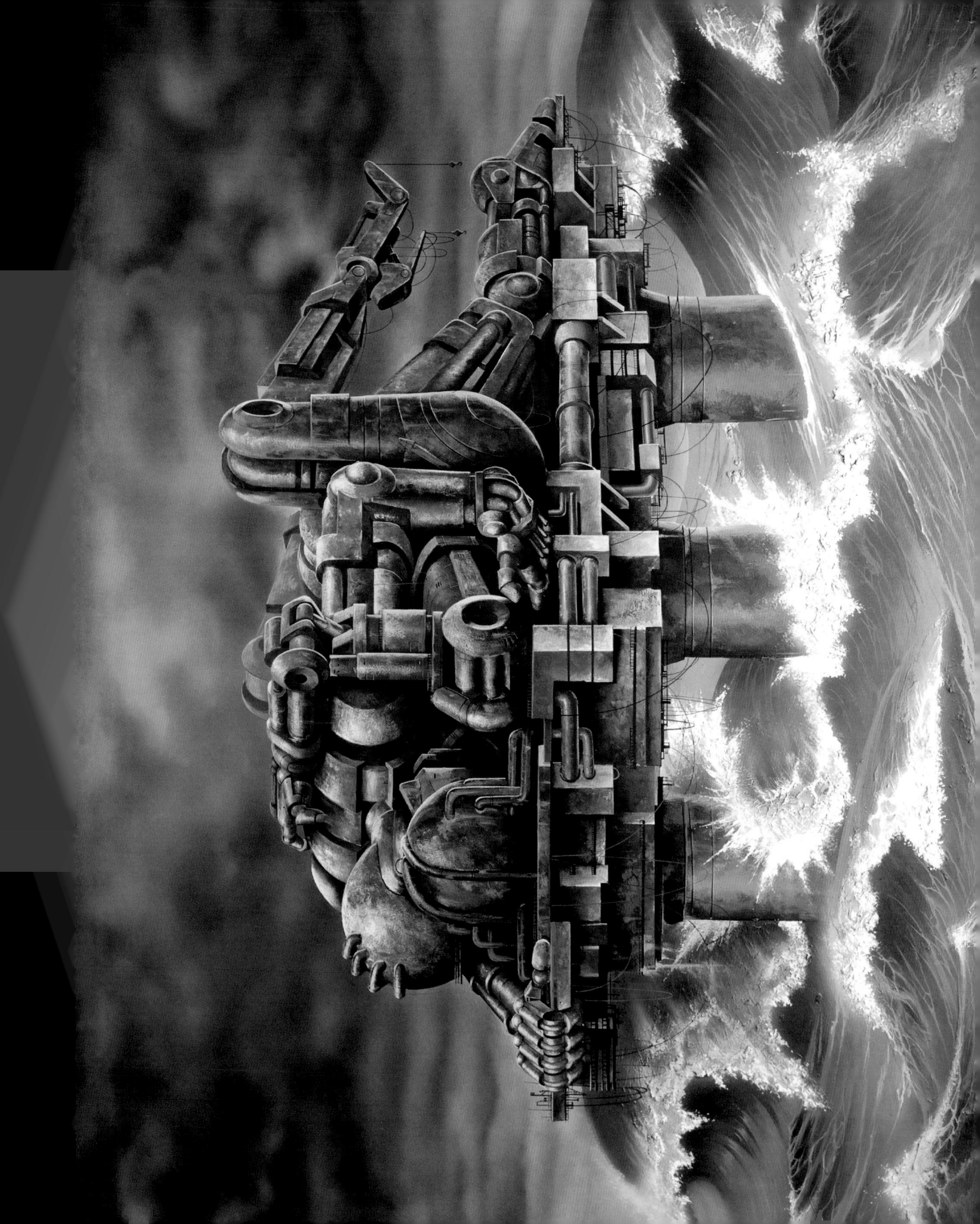

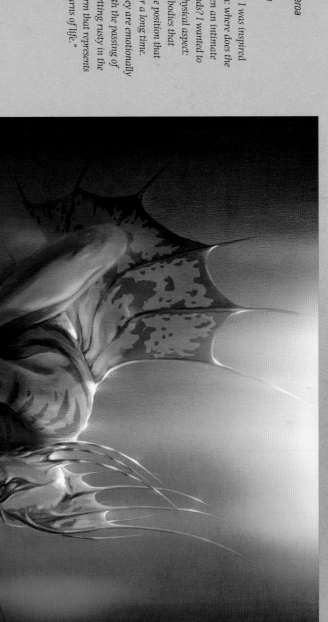

Storm
Raúl Cruz Figueroa
Acrylics
www.racrufi.com

"For this piece, I was inspired by the question: where does the passion go when an intimate relationship ends? I wanted to represent the physical aspect: I depicted two bodies that remained in the position that they were in for a long time. Now empty, they are emotionally empty, and with the passing of time they're getting rusty in the middle of a storm that represents the different turns of life."

▼
Amantes Marinas
Nestor Taylor
Acrylics
www.nestortaylor.blogspot.com

Taylor's skillful use of acrylics to create highlights and shadows captures the luminous effect of sunlight underwater. "Blue-green hues give the ideal atmosphere for two marine lovers. The illustration creates a vision of the fantastic world of mermaids and tritons."

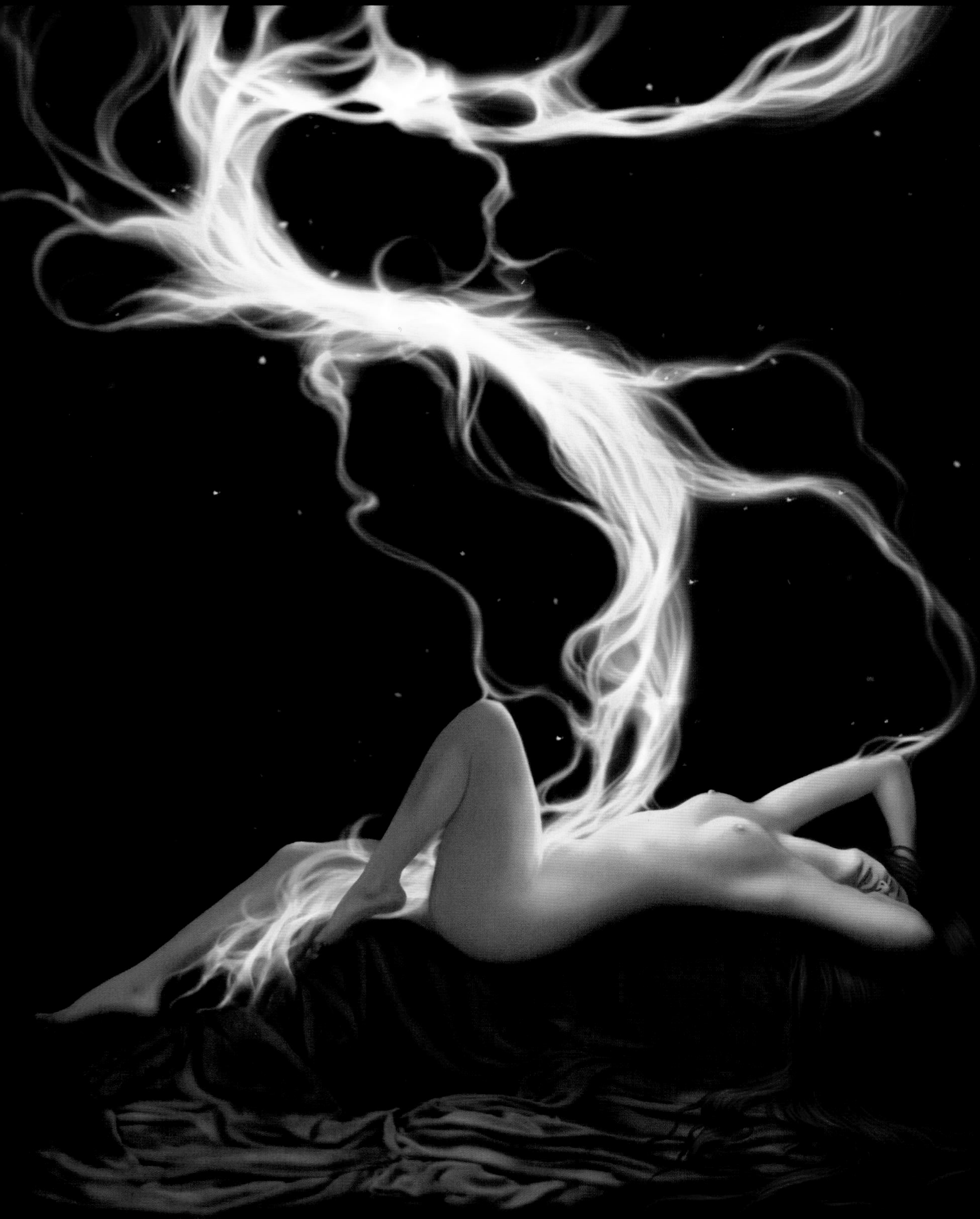

◀ **Danae**
Manon
Adobe Photoshop
www.artbymanon.com

"Ancient myths are a huge inspiration for me — endless juicy stories to be plundered! I painted Danae *in Photoshop using oodles of photo references for the figure and fall of the fabric. I use mainly hard-edged brushes and the Smudge brush to paint, and also plenty of layers.* Danae *was being held captive by her father Acrisius in a bronze tower, and Zeus, being a God and feeling a bit frisky, thought the only way to get to her was in the form of a shower of gold — an image which was beautifully represented by Klimt in one of my all time favorite paintings. For the gold shower, I used a lot of soft airbrushing in various opacities and many layers with the Overlay and Multiply settings. The shape and form of the gold was inspired by the shapes made by plasma balls — I wanted the shower to be electric and powerful, rather than a falling rain of gold."*

▶ **Deadly Seduction**
E. Crellin aka DarkElegance
Poser and Adobe Photoshop
http://art-of-darkelegance.daportfolio.com

"Using digital media anything is possible, such as tentacle-like growths sprouting from a hazy alien world to cradle a feline creature that is coaxing the viewer to her. The idea is a deadly beauty, like the exotic flowers that devour insects in the jungle. Exotic, enticing, and ultimately deadly. This is actually three renders in one. There is the foreground (main figure) and two background scenes (additional growths). Using Photoshop, I marry them into a scene that is a bit more lush."

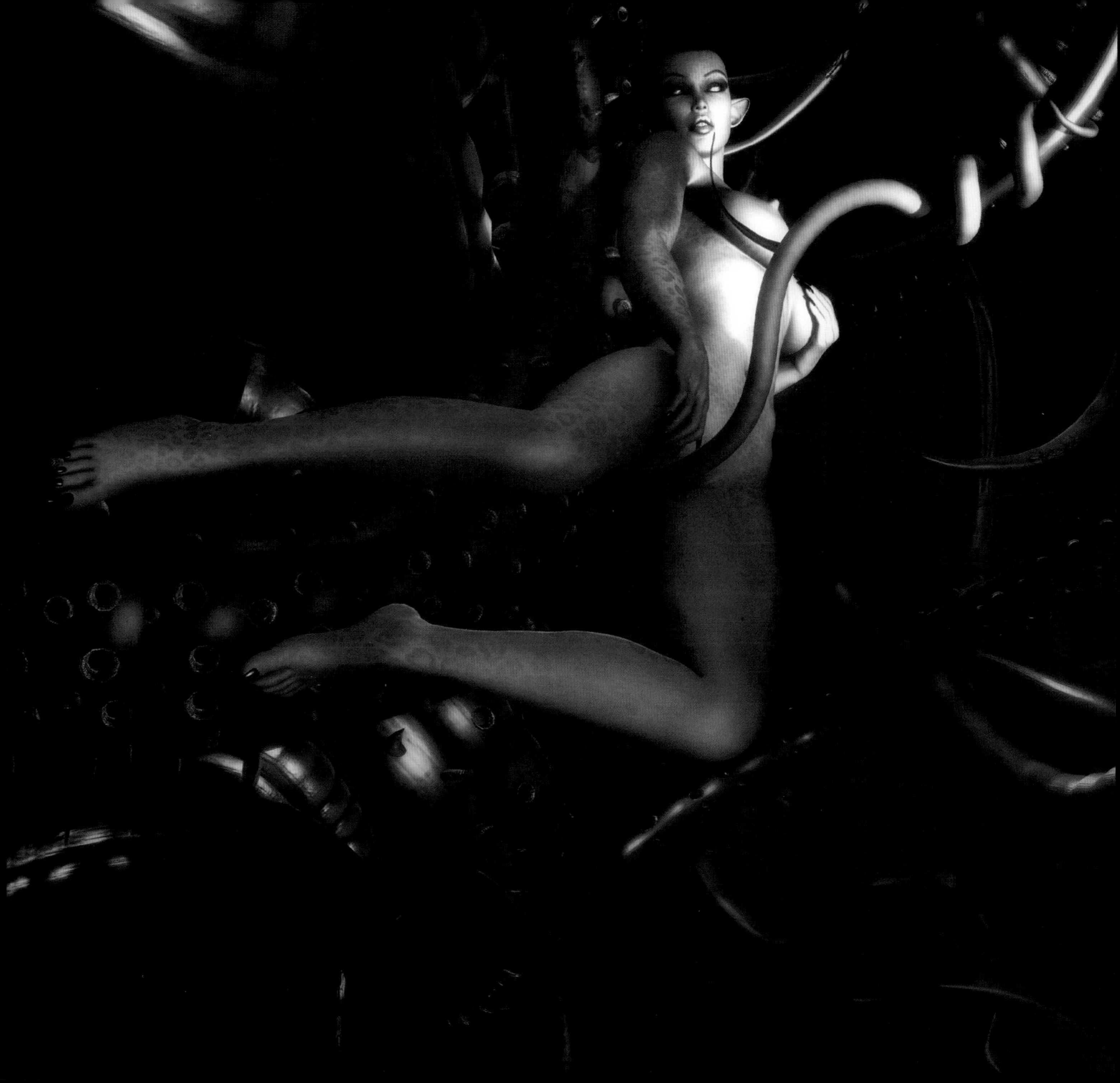

▶ **Blue Butterflies**
Jasmine Becket-Griffith
Acrylics
www.strangeling.com

"A red-haired nymph lying in a green field gazes up at the sky as blue butterflies fly above her. Though not overtly seductive, the nymph's hand and the flying butterflies give the impression of fleeting modesty—adding only a bit of coverage, but hinting at the beautiful body below. I love the color combination of her red hair as it snakes through the green grass. This is an acrylic painting on a long narrow canvas."

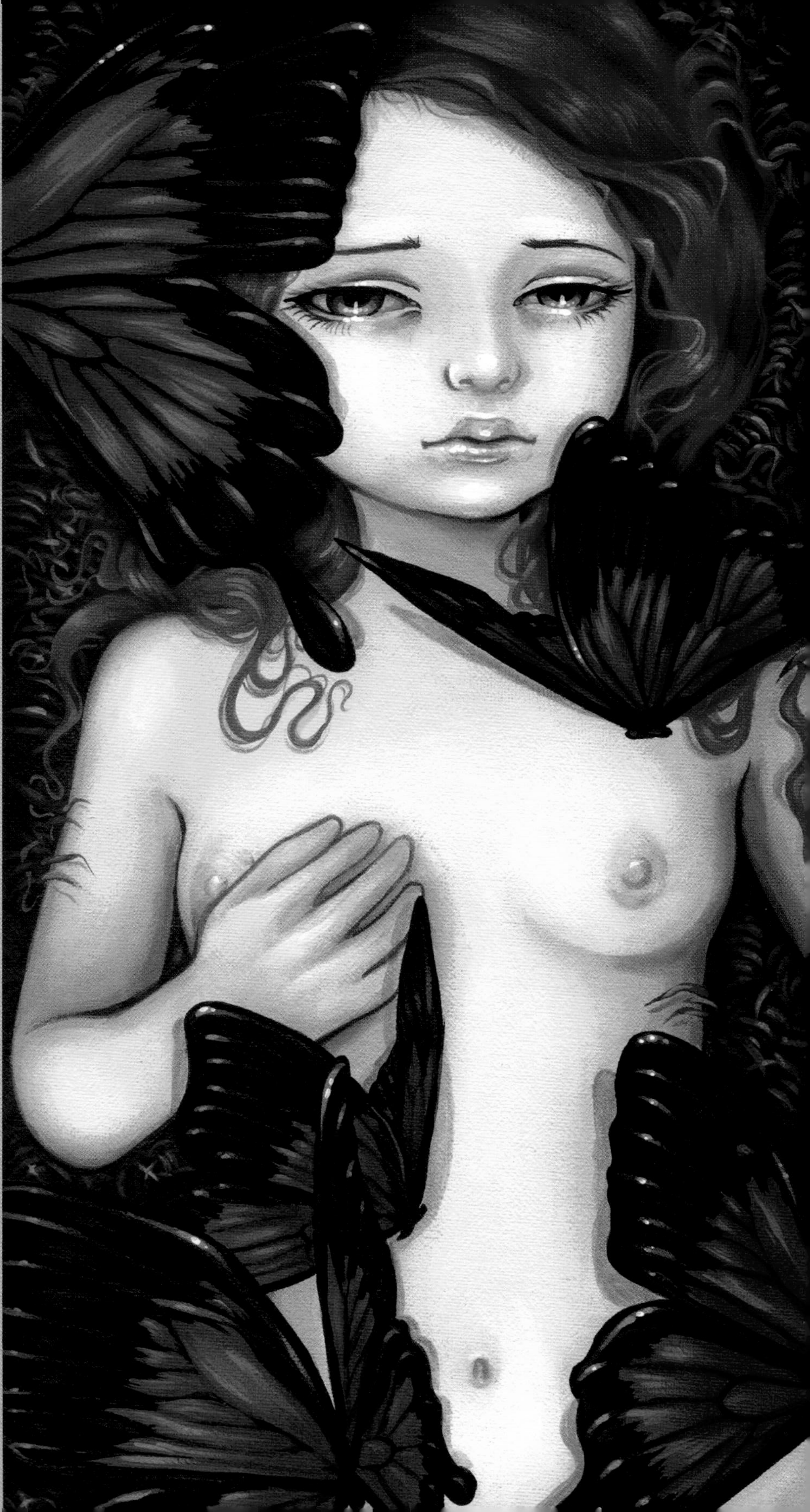

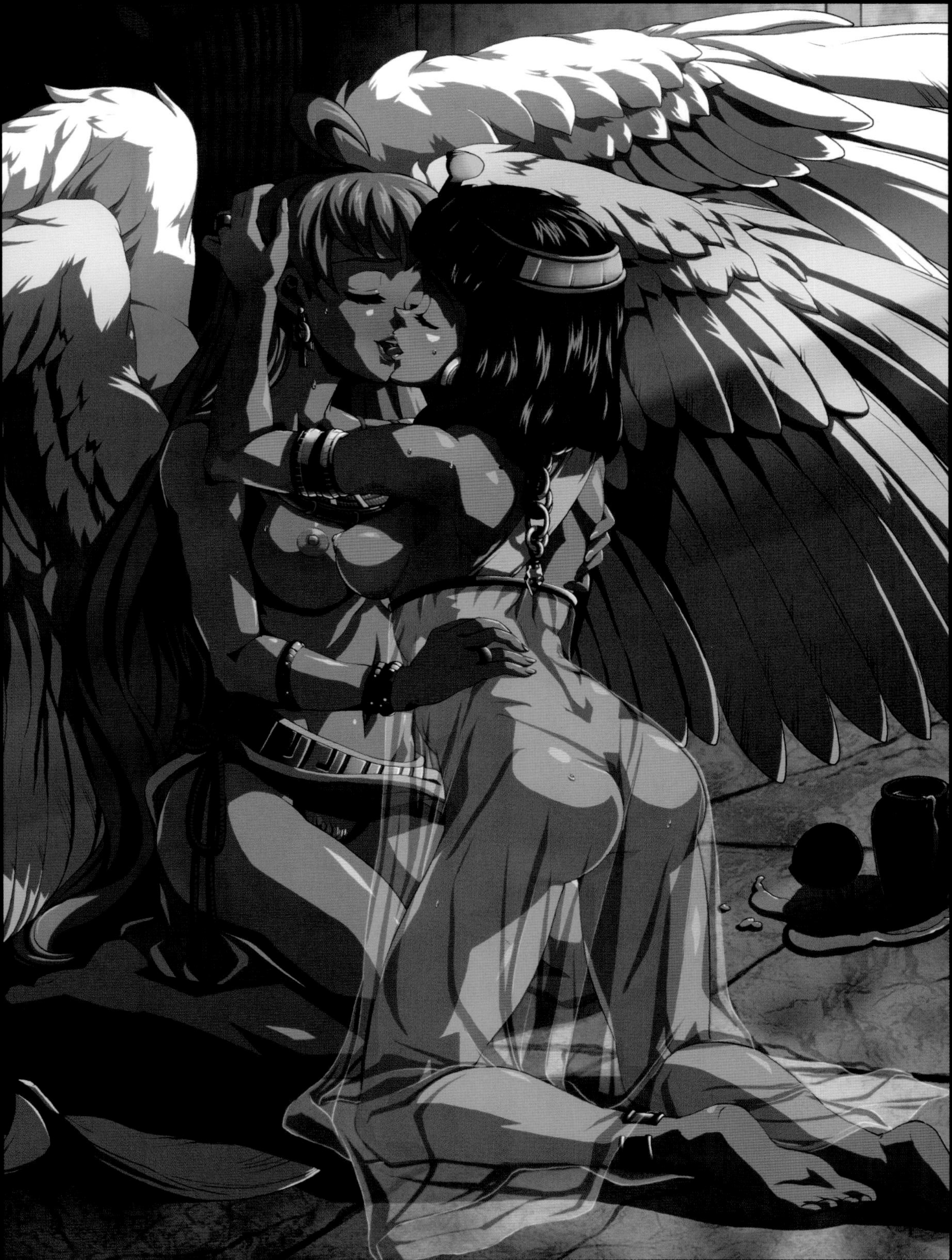

▶ **Angel in Egypt**
Mr. Ecchi
Pencil, Corel Painter, and Adobe Photoshop
www.cutepet.org

"I work in a style reminiscent of detailed cel animation. My work starts on paper as a pencil drawing encompassing the character and background art. When the drawing is complete, I scan it into Photoshop and proceed to paint the background elements. At this stage, I largely ignore the character-filled portions of the image. Unlike background art in animation, I can save time by only rendering the areas of my paintings left unoccupied by the characters. Next, I ink the character portion for my sketch using Painter. When I'm done replacing the rough graphite drawing with perfectly smooth black lines, I export the character art into Photoshop for coloring and recombining with the completed background plate. To achieve the look of an animation cel, the character is colored without tonal blending, using the harshly aliased Pencil tool."

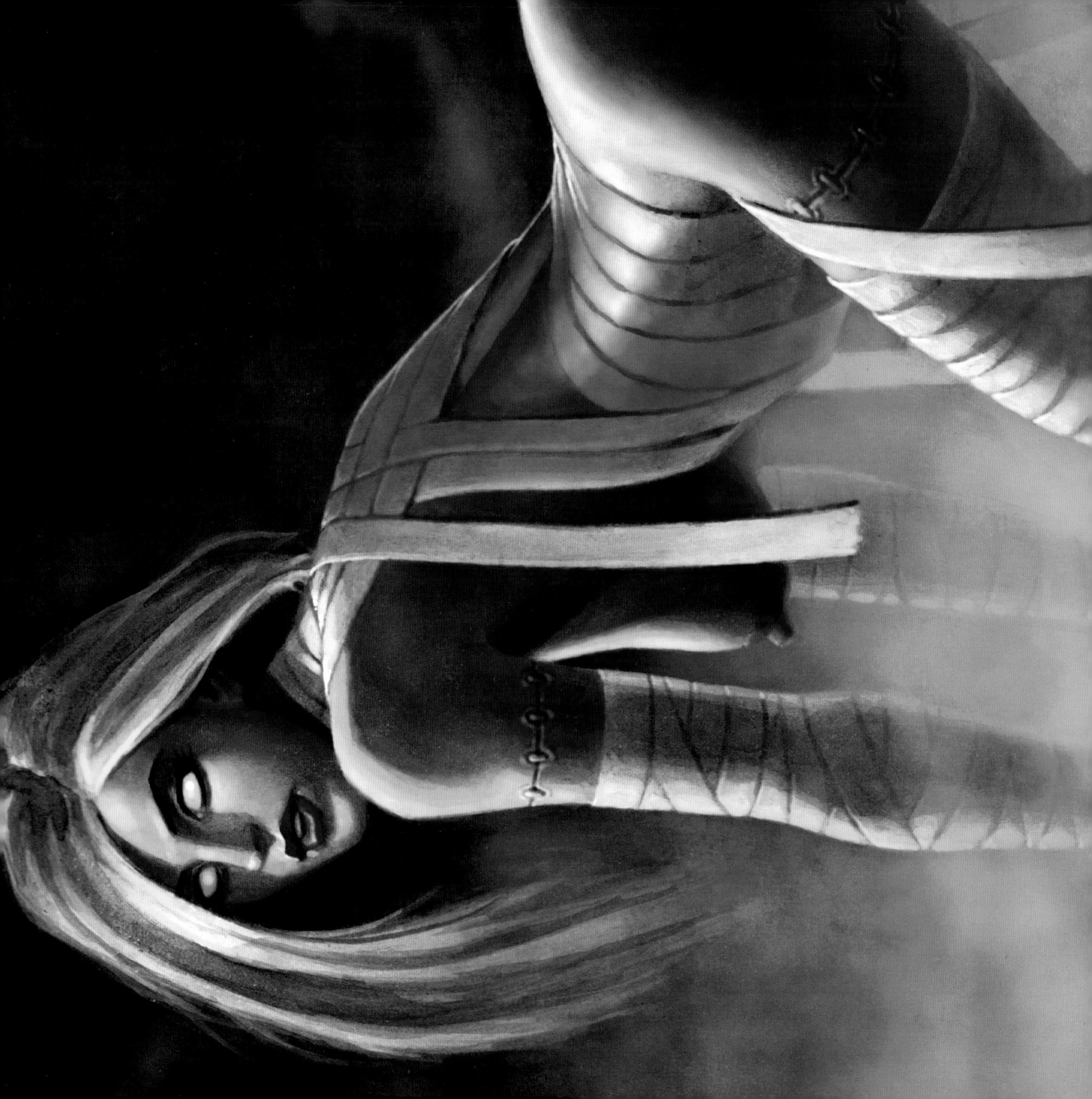

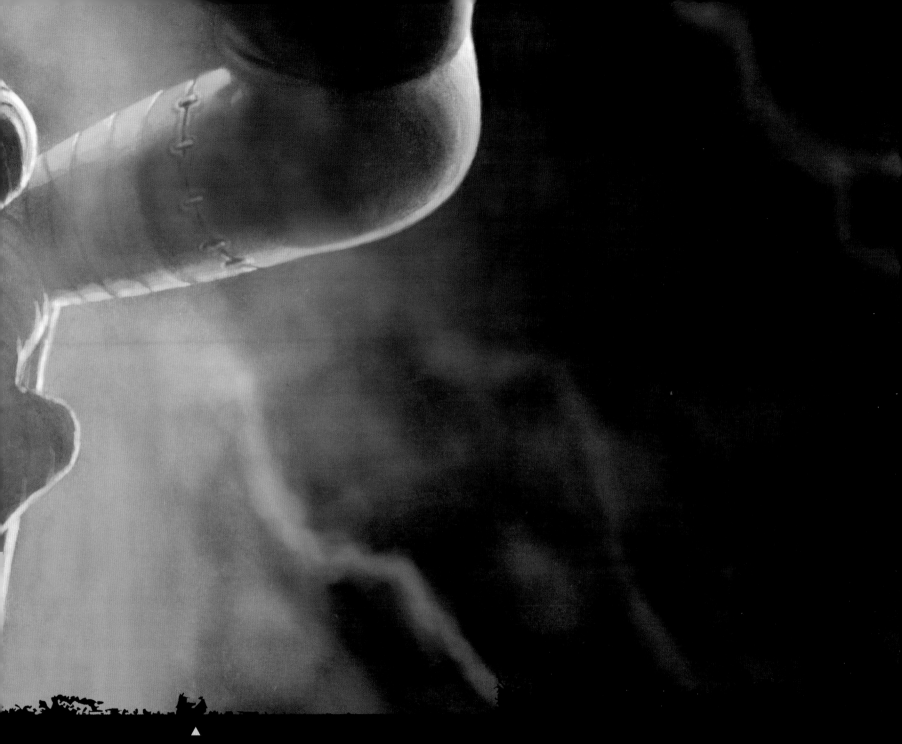

She's Alive!
Paul McCaffrey
Acrylics and Adobe Photoshop
www.coroflot.com/paul_mccaffrey

"This is my take on the Bride of Frankenstein, which I'd watched—yet again!—shortly before I began this piece. I suspect James Whale would not have approved . . ."

CHAPTER 4

SINISTER SENSUALITY

▶ **Dark Elves: Awakening**
Anne Cain
For Loose Id, LLC
Graphite and Adobe Photoshop
www.annecain-art.com

"This illustration was created for use on the cover of Jet Mykles' Dark Elves: Awakenings, *a fantasy romance novel published through Loose Id, LLC. I was thrilled to be a part of the project given my fascination with elves and the fantasy genre, and Jet's stories are themselves fantastic. Sensuality is at the core of this image, with the characters having forsaken clothing in favor of having nothing conceal their romanticized physical beauty. They are beings of magic and sexuality, with a complex history between the characters that's only hinted at in the image. Much of my work as an illustrator and graphic artist is in publishing as a cover artist, and* Dark Elves: Awakening *remains one of my favorite projects."*

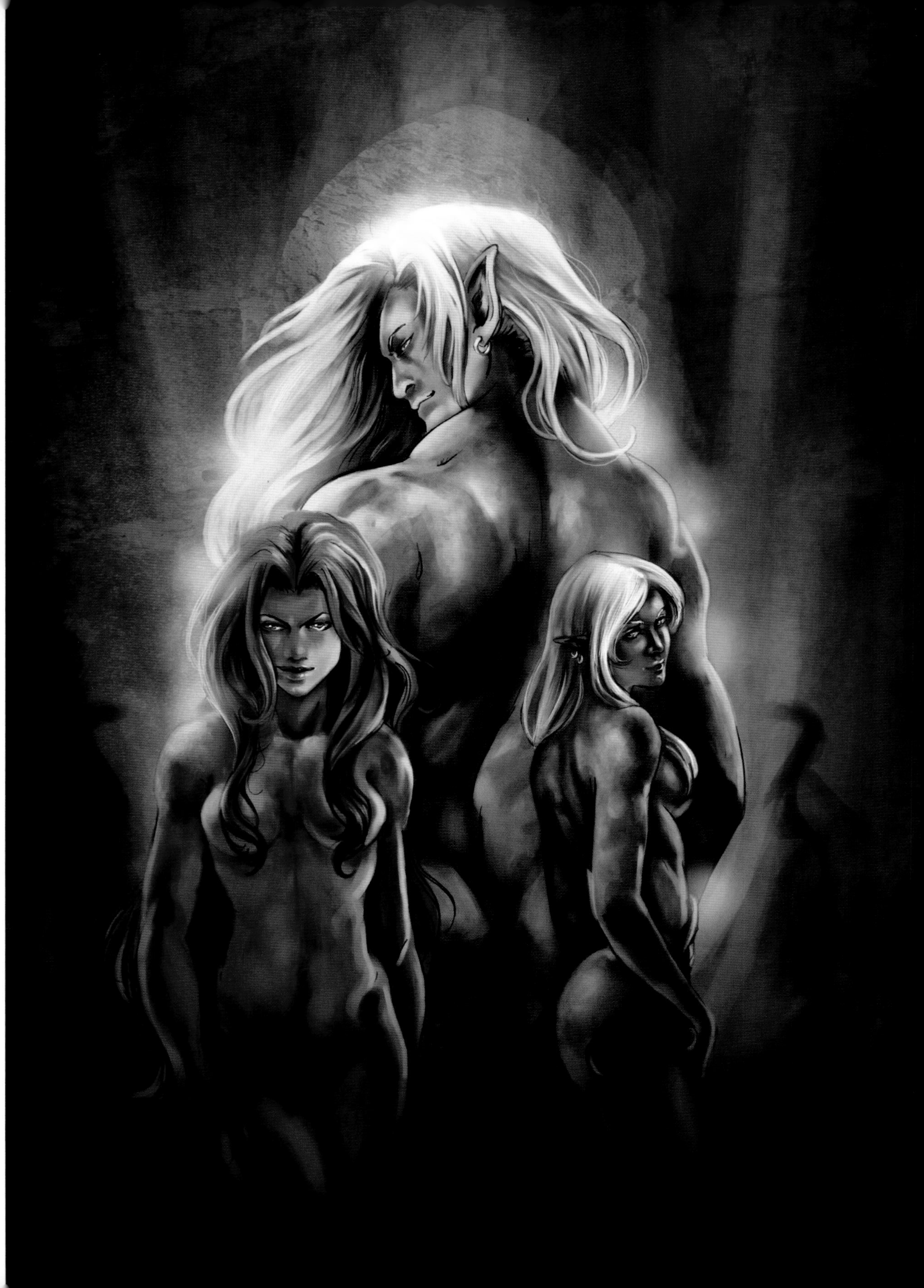

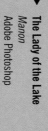

The Lady of the Lake
Manon
Adobe Photoshop
www.artbymanon.com

"How can one resist the Arthurian legend? The Lady of the Lake has many names and there are various versions of her story. The best known is her keeping of the Sword Excalibur. She is often depicted as clothed, but I thought this would be highly impractical if you are living underwater, so I decided to go for yet more naked skin with the magical light that comes through water. I used lots of layers for this one, painted in Photoshop, and studied photo references for the downlighting on the face."

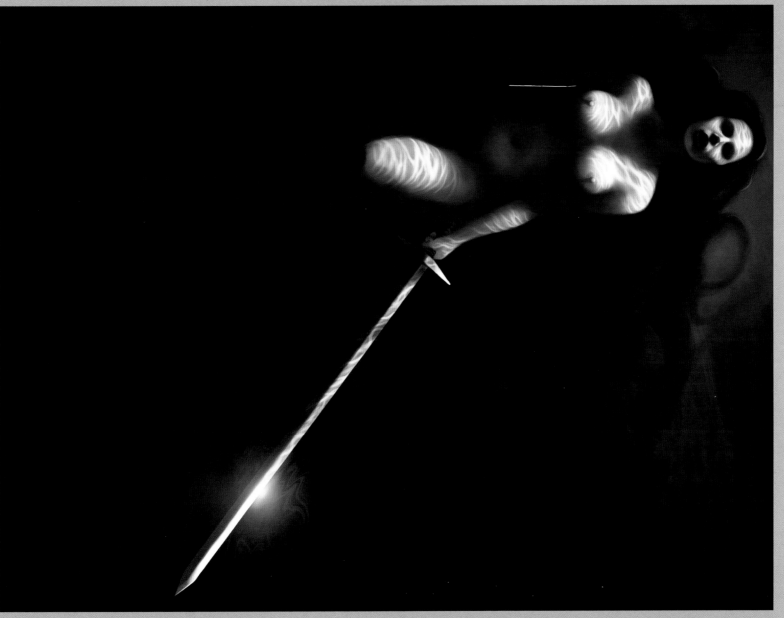

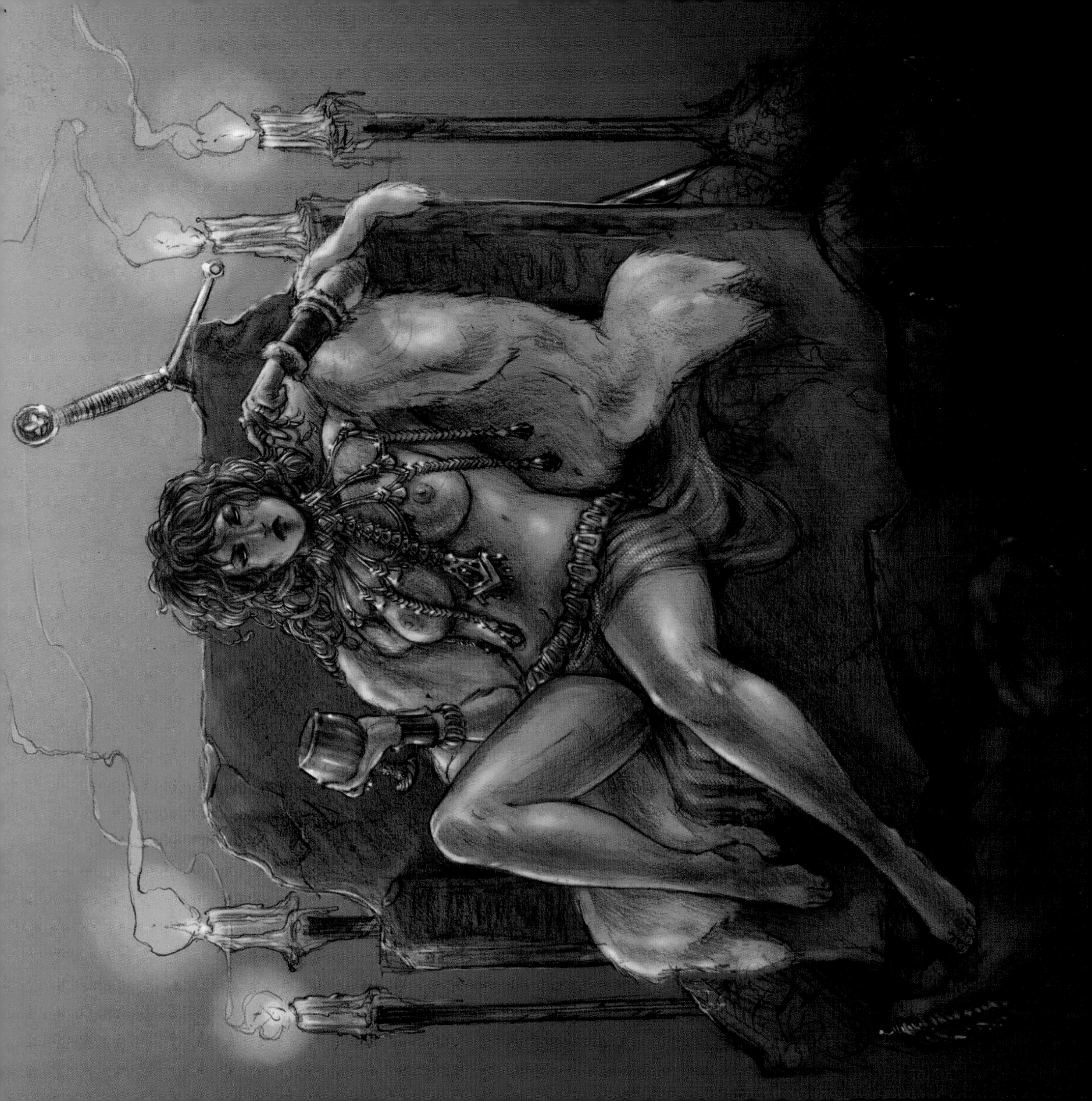

◀ **Mars In Furs**
K. Wainwright
Pencil and OpenCanvas
http://yilamstation.com

"I owe my inspiration for this piece and others like it to the sources that gave me my earliest grasp of beauty. When I was little, other girls would read gossip magazines or watch rom-coms. I would read X-Men *or* Slaine*. As I've grown up I've come to love the art of Vallejo, Brom, and Frazetta, to name a few, with their captivating mixtures of beauty and danger. My idea of gorgeous has always been dependent on some kind of strength; Venus tempered with a dash of Mars resplendent, this time lounging among the cloud-soft folds of a mantle smelling of smoke and plundered spices. Perhaps those furs are a tribute, perhaps a prize claimed from the corpse of an enemy. My idea was to leave a little bit of mystery in this piece: who is the figure? Did she gain that barbarous throne by cunning, force, or perhaps seduction?"*

▶ **Cold Marble Floor**
K. Wainwright
Pen, Corel Painter, and OpenCanvas
http://yilamstation.com

"I used Painter for this piece because I like the way the brushes look a bit more organic, and I wanted this to look like the sort of portrait you might find hanging on the walls of some strange manse. The Duchess of Snard is quite the attention-seeker, best known for her worst behavior and reputation as a libertine incapable of keeping her priceless silk knickers on. Being sentenced to appear publicly exposed was a punishment meant to humiliate and chasten. Instead, she only found it entertaining."

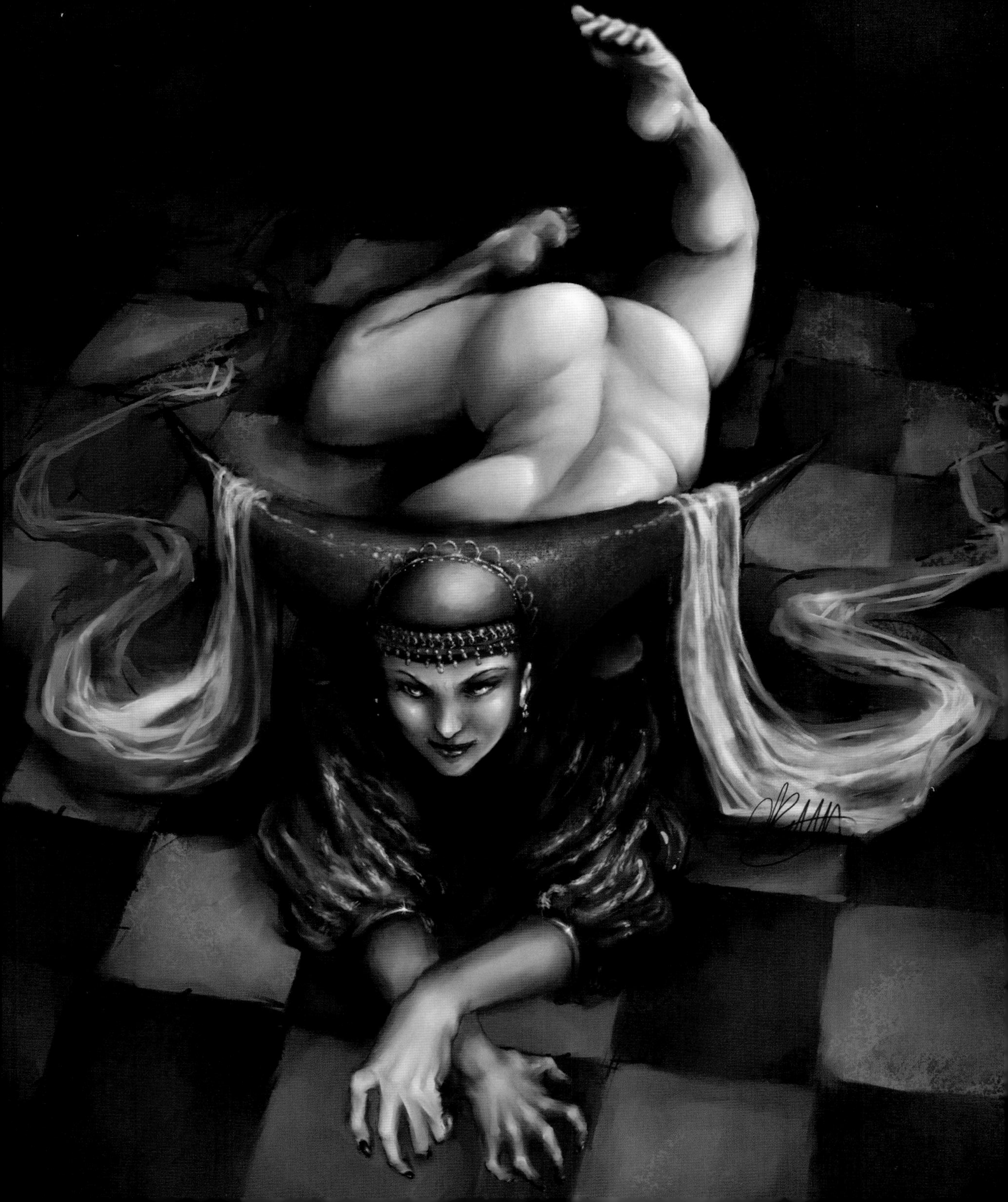

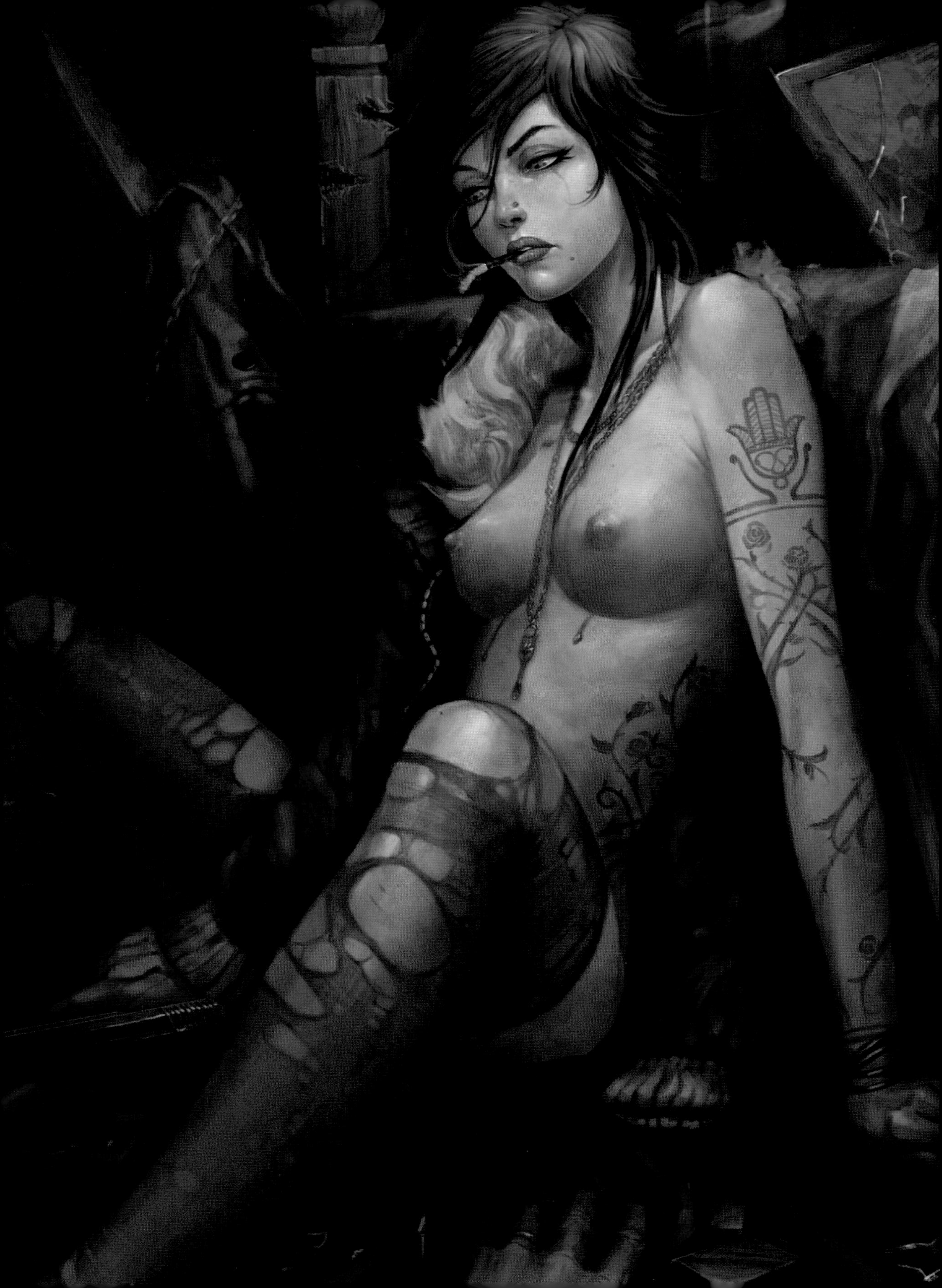

◀ **Close Call**
Devon Cady-Lee
Adobe Photoshop
www.gorrem.cghub.com

"I wanted to capture a film noir feeling in a modern setting, to be different from my usual choice of science fiction or fantasy. I was also trying to narrate a story without being too explicit, keeping the motivations of the character(s) ambiguous and scattering clues throughout the composition. I tried to use colors that were outside of my familiarity."

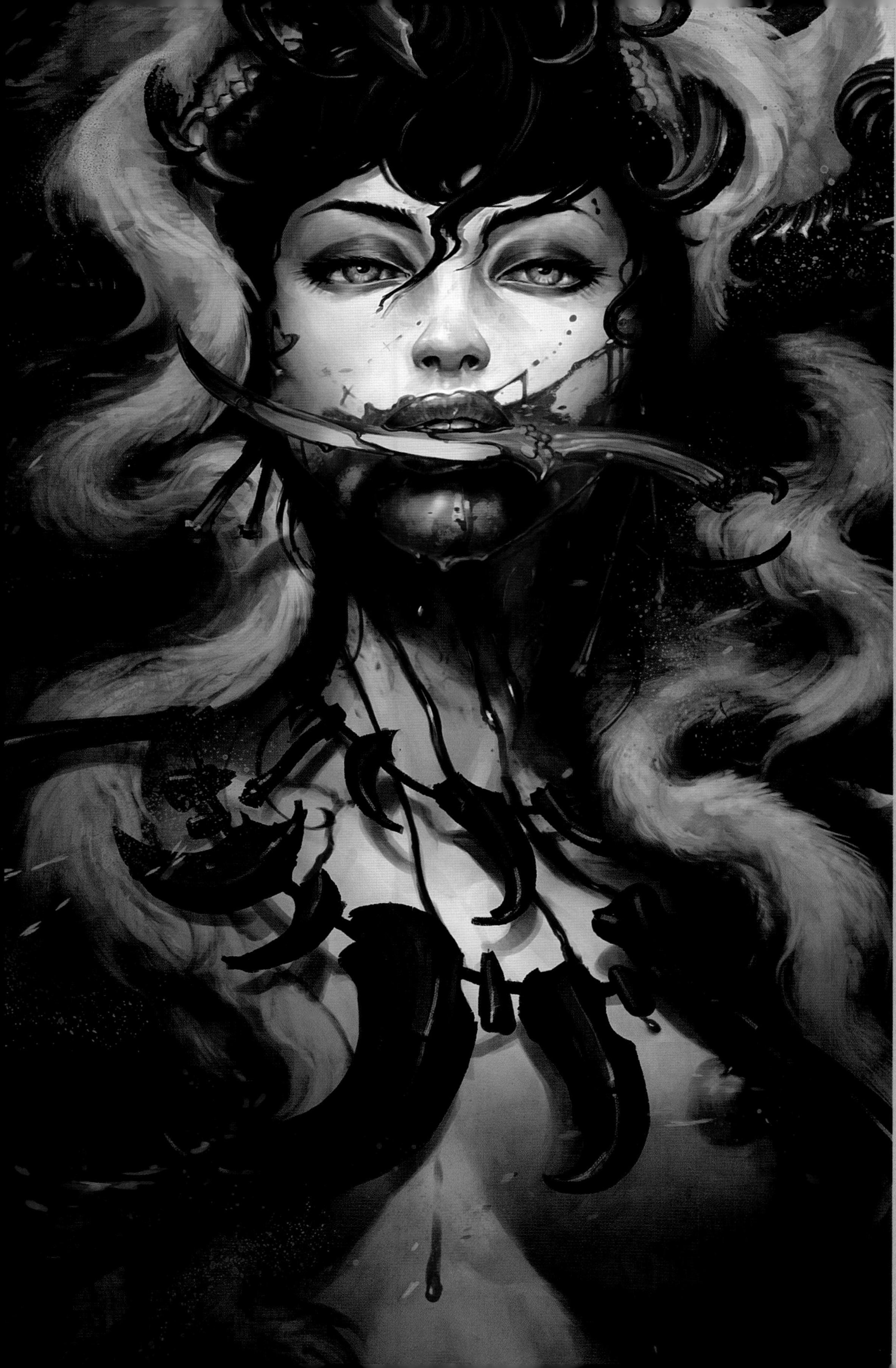

◀ **Sacred**
Devon Cady-Lee
Adobe Photoshop
www.gorrem.cghub.com

"This was inspired shortly after the death of Frank Frazetta; I was motivated to paint a fierce cavewoman, like he often did. I wanted to include warm elements of blood and fire, versus the cold colors of her skin and furs. I started in shades of gray-blue and built up the rest from there."

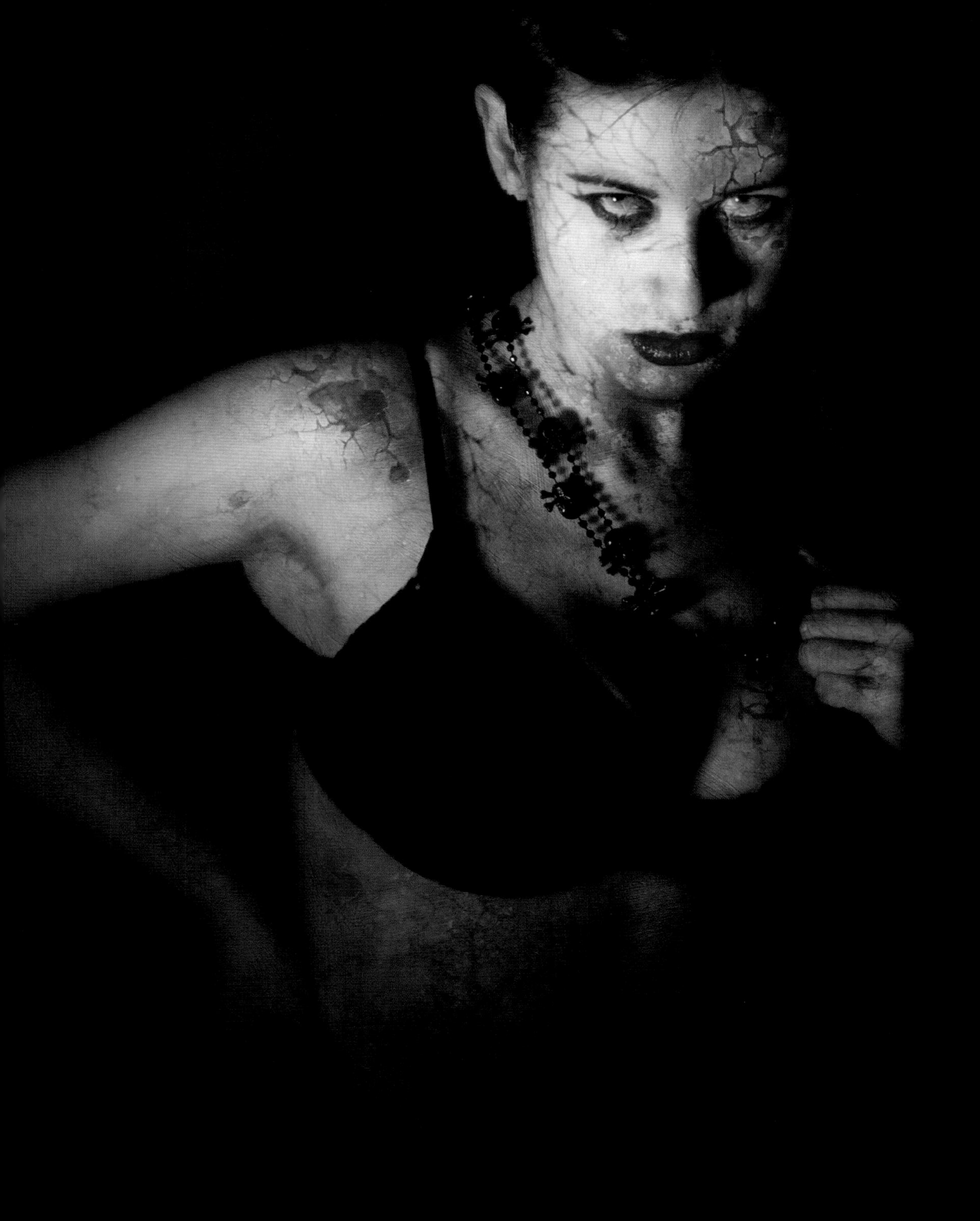

◄ **Zombie**
Jason Juta
Photography
and Adobe Photoshop
www.jasonjuta.com

"At the end of a photographic session I thought it would be fun to try a simple zombie pinup idea. I employed my typical strong spot lighting and used overlaid textures, color manipulations, and hand-painting to get the end effect in Photoshop."

► **Spellbound II / Lady Blue**
Oliver Wetter & Anita Collins
Adobe Photoshop
http://fantasio.info

"This collaboration piece is a result of being inspired by a sculpture by Anita Collins that screamed to me to be painted in a realistic manner. Her sculpture had a very haunting expression that inspired me to imagine this fragile creature within a jail-like, captive environment, without making it obvious where she was, leaving enough room for the viewer's imagination."

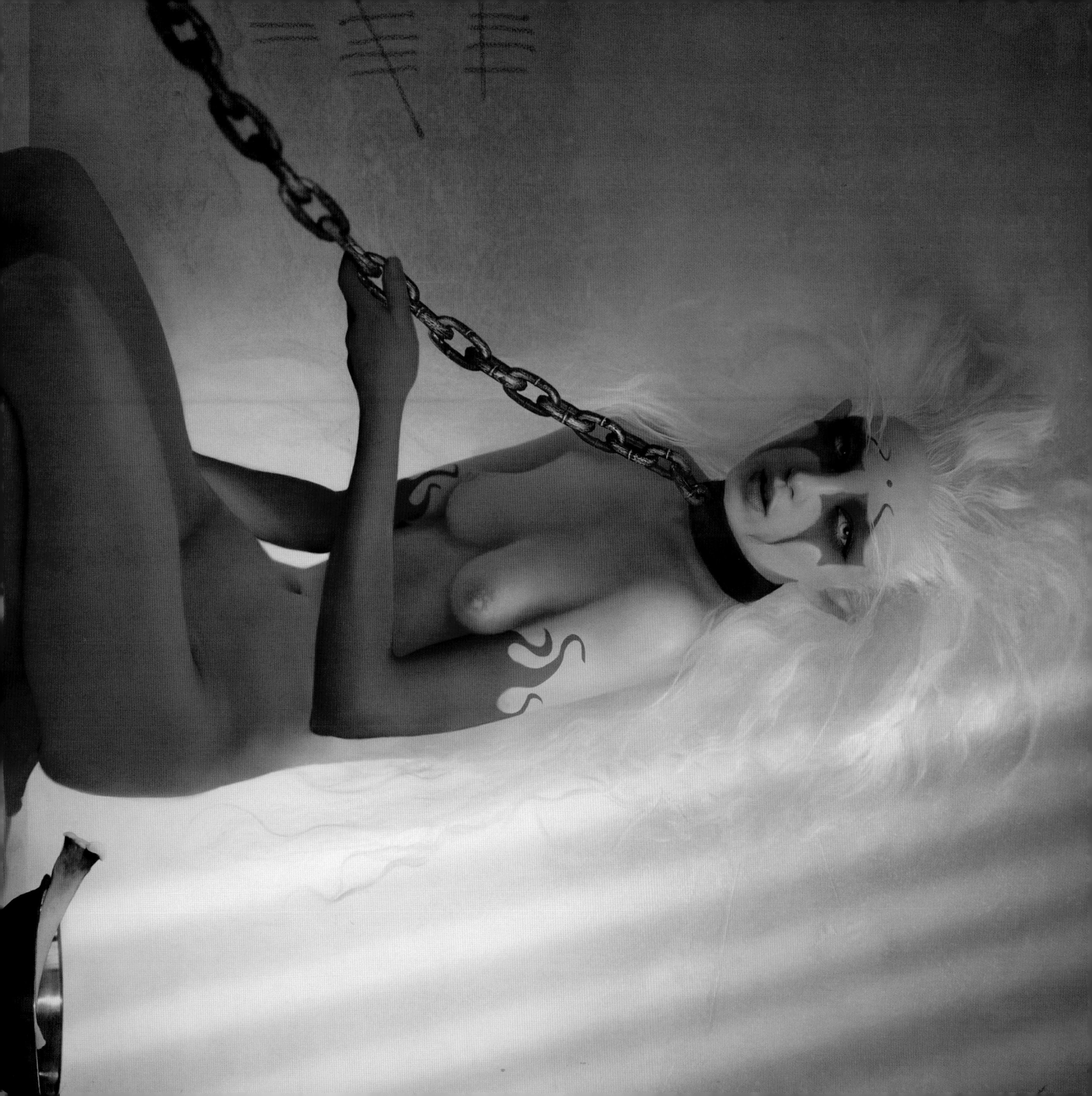

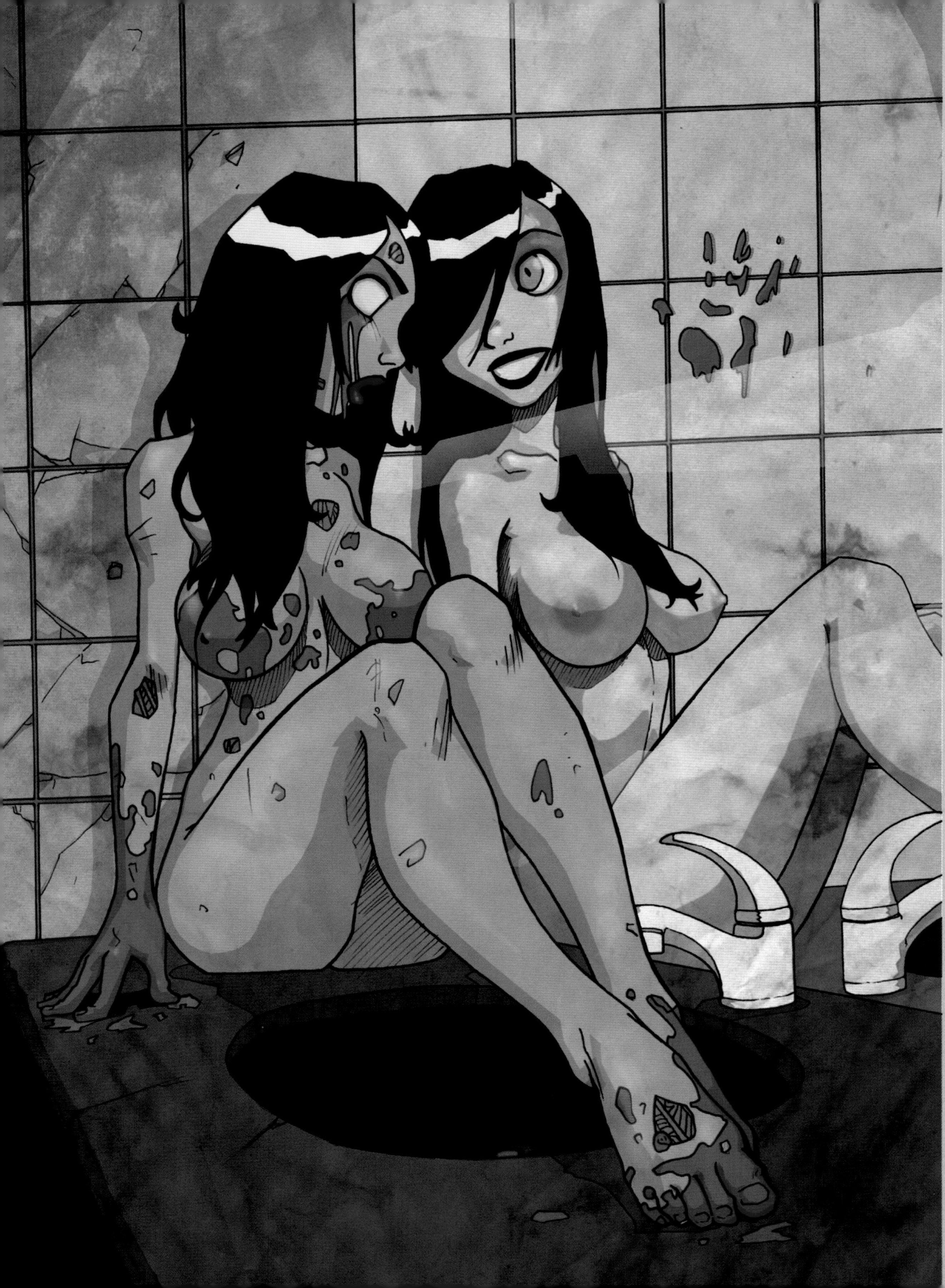

◀ **What Was Lost**
Dan Mendoza
Pencil, Micron and Prisma Pens, and Adobe Photoshop
www.toxiccandie.com

"This is a poster I designed to promote my comic book ZOMBIE TRAMP. It's a promo piece that I sell at conventions I attend. I also ended up using it for the main page of my website. In this drawing I wanted to portray Janey as missing the life she once had when she was human and lived a life of sex and luxury as a call girl. All my drawings start off as pencil on paper. This one was on smooth Bristol board. Afterward I add ink using Micron or Prisma pens. When that's all done, I erase the pencils underneath and scan it with my A3-size scanner from Mustek into Photoshop. From there I darken the lines and color with my Wacom tablet."

Vampyr
Charlene Chua
Adobe Illustrator
and Adobe Photoshop
www.charlenechua.com

"My version of the vampire is a creature of dark romance, a symbol that's as much about love and lust as it is about death and eternal suffering. It is a very beautiful if somewhat twisted thing, both cursed and blessed. My depiction of her is simple in concept—a female vampire about to kiss a small, devilish thing in her hands. The figure is slightly distorted in order to retain the original sketch, which I thought had more raw emotion than a tidied up one. The color scheme was chosen for its feminine quality; I wanted to contrast the dark nature of the creature with its association with that which we all long for—love."

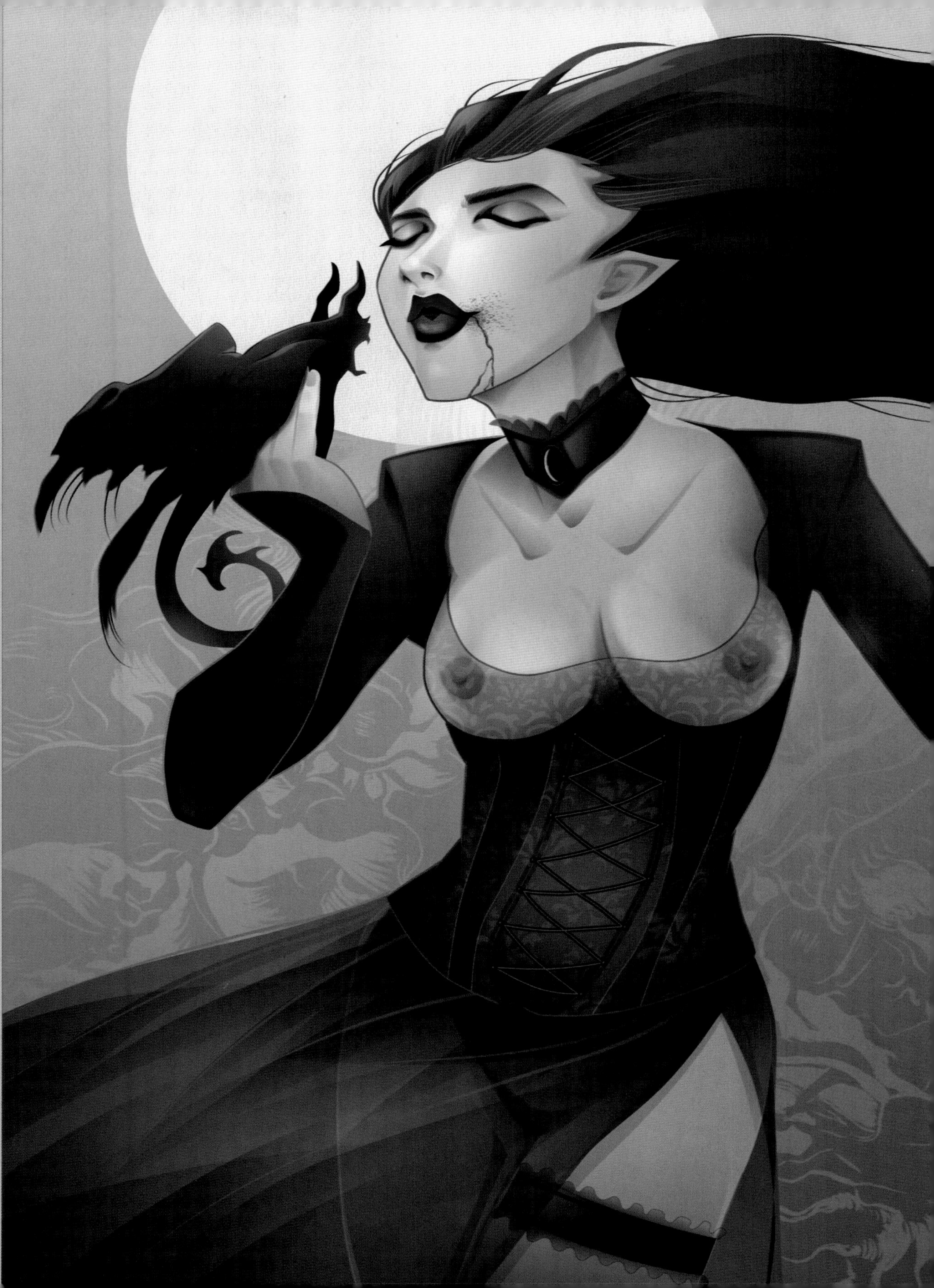

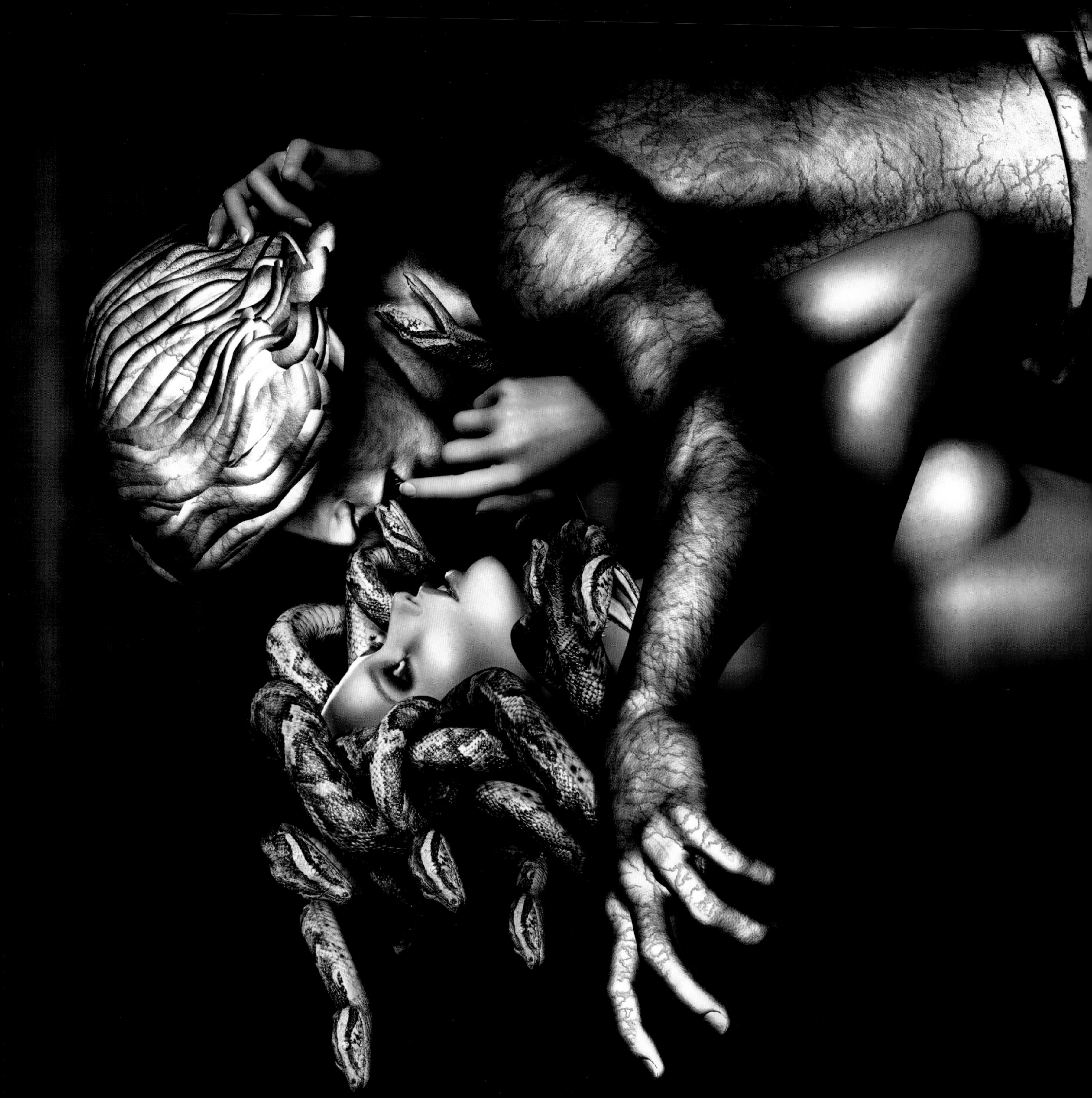

◀ **Medusa's Lover**
E.Crellin aka DarkElegance
Poser and Adobe Photoshop
http://art-of-darkelegance.daportfolio.com

"I have a very big fetish for Medusa, I think she has been dealt a bad blow by most modern myths. How frustrating it must have been always to turn the men to stone. How lonely it must have been for her. It was easy for me to see her wandering her caverns, touching the now stone men, wondering what it would've been like to feel them in the flesh. That was the inspiration for this work; her curiosity at the touch of his lips. Her snake hair was a bit of a headache for me. I used multiple snakes parented to a ball in Poser that was then hidden within her head. Then the snakes had to be posed individually to get them to 'perform.'"

▶ **Lilly**
John Blumen
Adobe Photoshop
www.johnblumenillustration.com

"Vampires never get old—nor does illustrating them. In this work, I speculated that even in their relationships, there comes a time when it just isn't working any longer and the rift between lovers grows wider than a gift of flowers can bridge. In the end, someone always gets hurt."

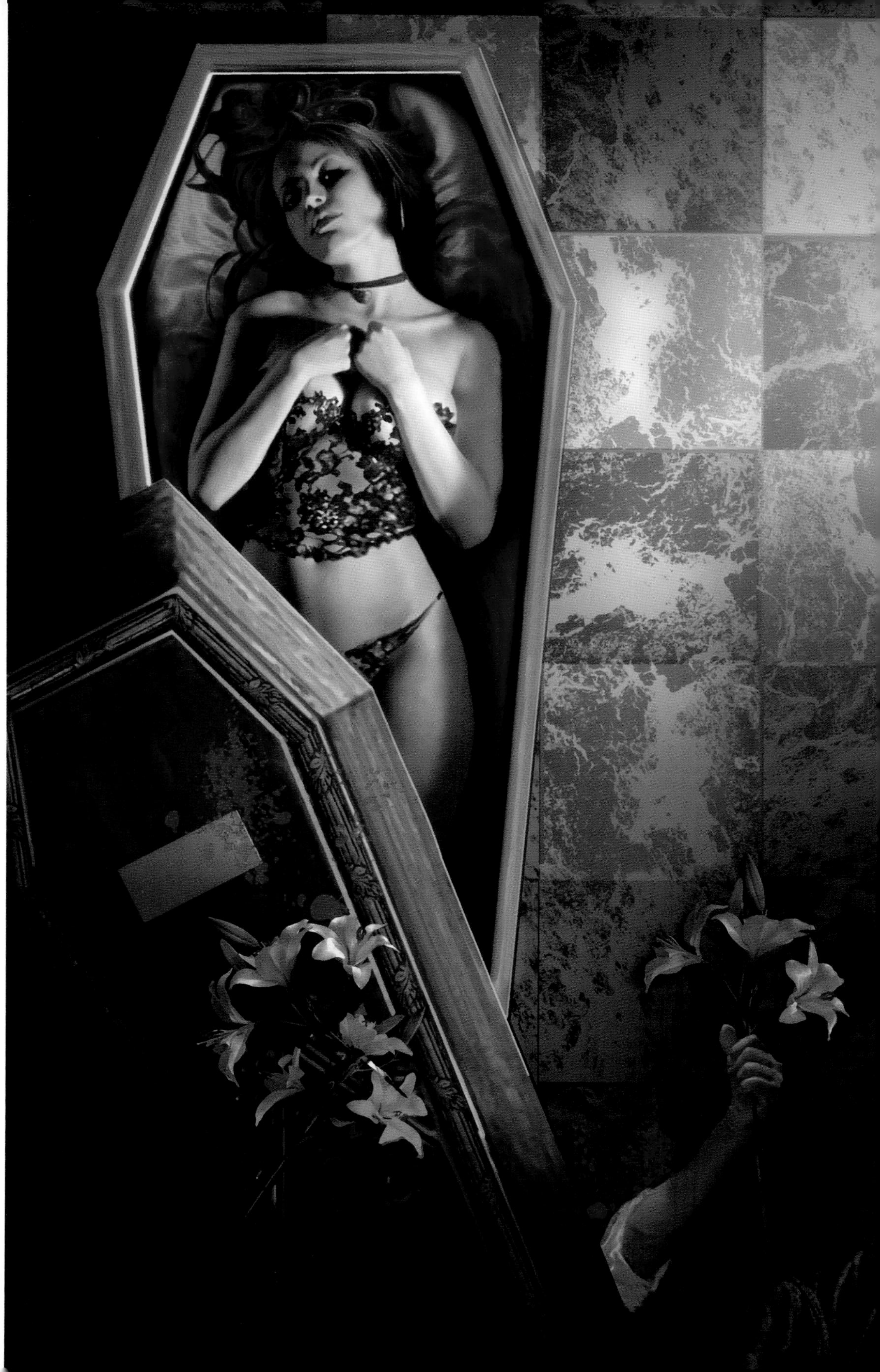

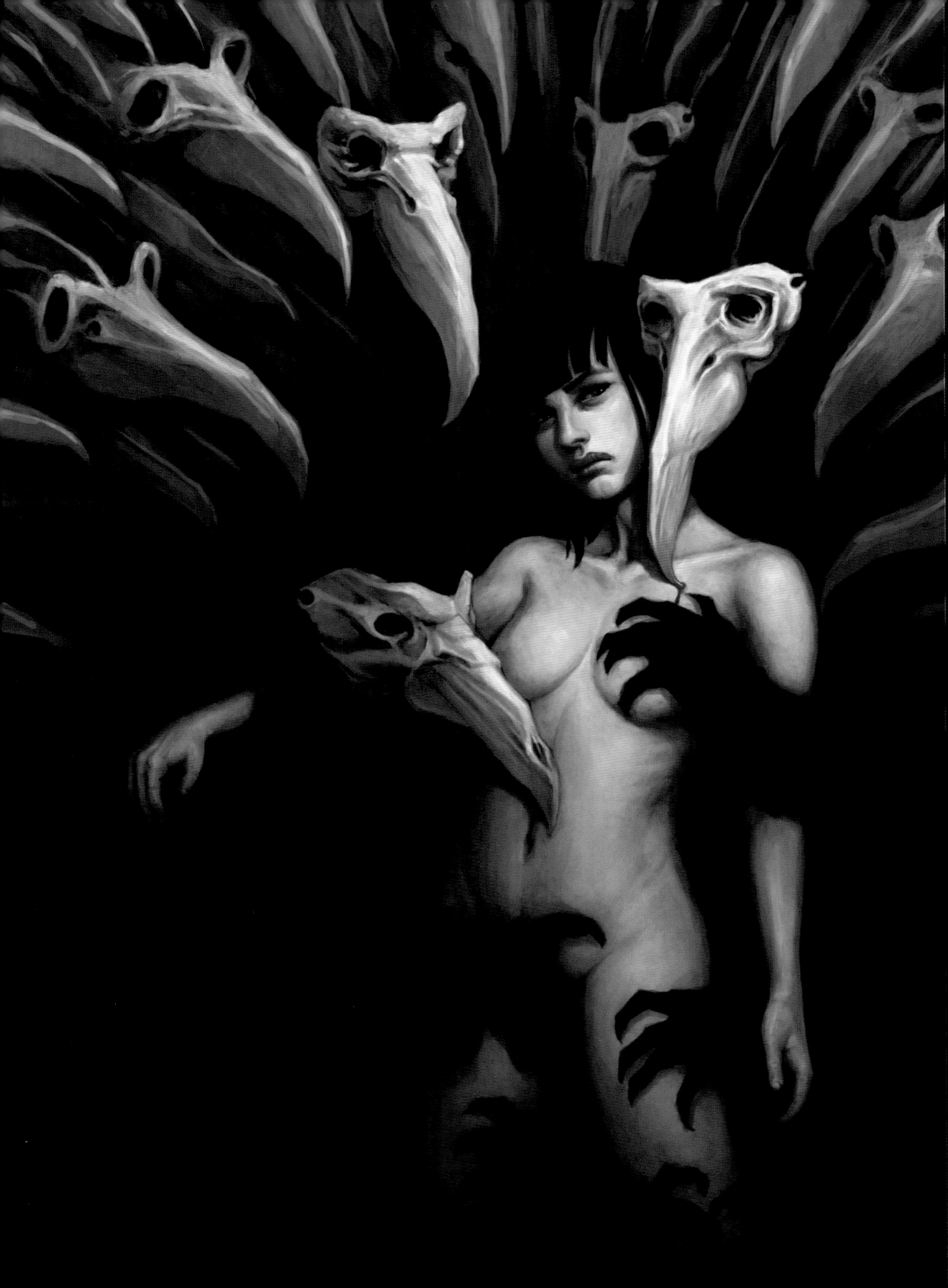

Promises
Ben Newman
Adobe Photoshop
www.bennewmanart.blogspot.com

"I drew this for an exhibition themed around various types of masks. I've always been fascinated by the eeriness of the long-nosed plague doctor masks and their Venetian counterparts, and this image is an exploration of that. Originally the bodies of the doctors were a lot more visible in the picture, but I felt the more fantastical approach of having them blacked out with the masks starting to blend together in the distance worked better for the feel I was trying to achieve."

anys Defiant
Andrew Hunter
adobe Photoshop
www.zarathul.deviantart.com

"This is a book cover for a dark antasy novel. I hoped to capture he vibrant, fiery character of anys — the warrior girl of a barbarian tribe — shining against he backdrop of a shadowy and dangerous world that threatens o consume her at every turn. used photo reference for her pose and painted everything in Photoshop. My familiarity with he program gives me a much greater sense of control and ease of workflow, even though sometimes I may feel as though 'm fighting with the brushes. Experimentating in Photoshop s quite simple and allows for many happy accidents, not to mention a quick cleanup after he unhappy ones."

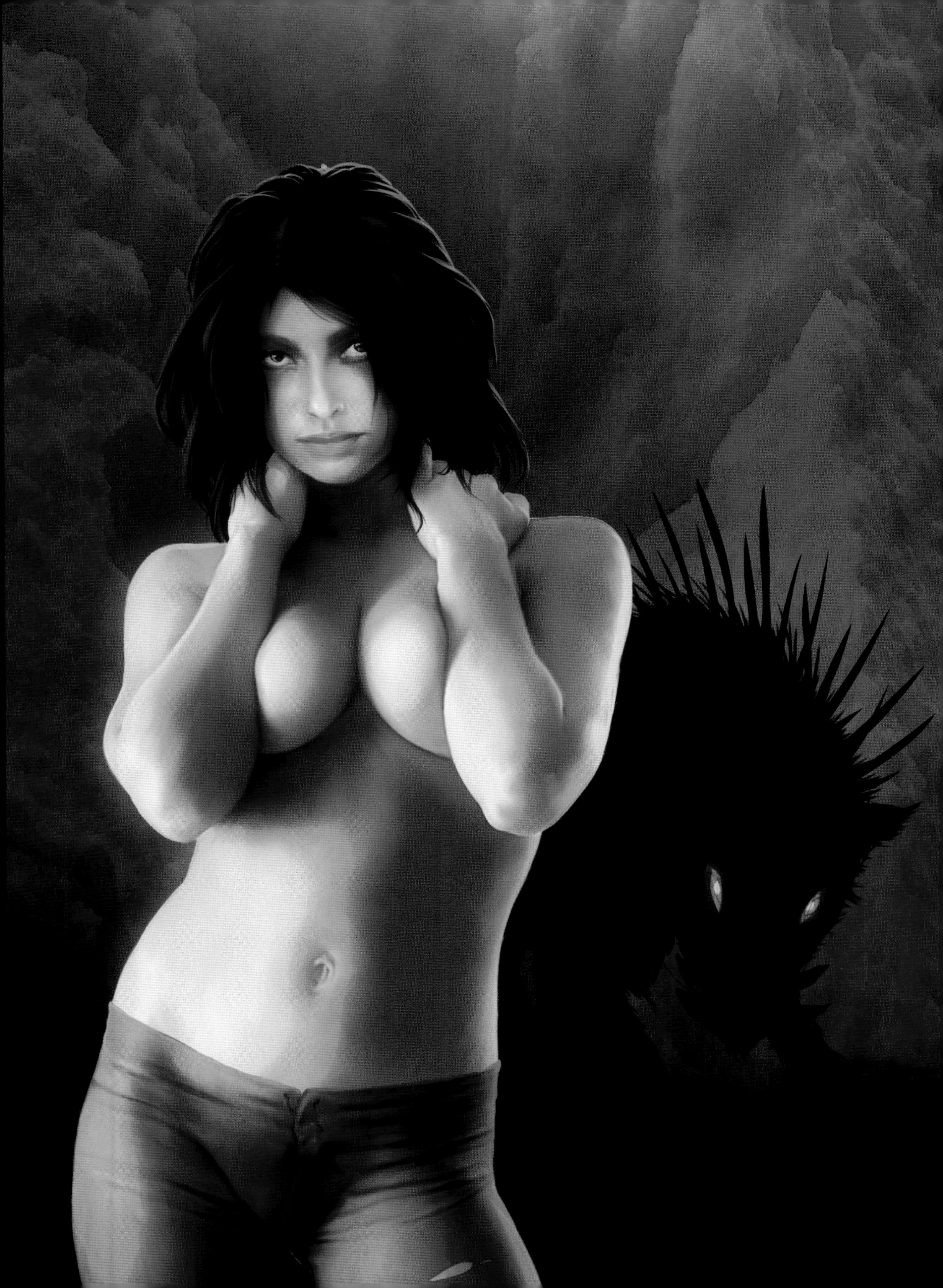

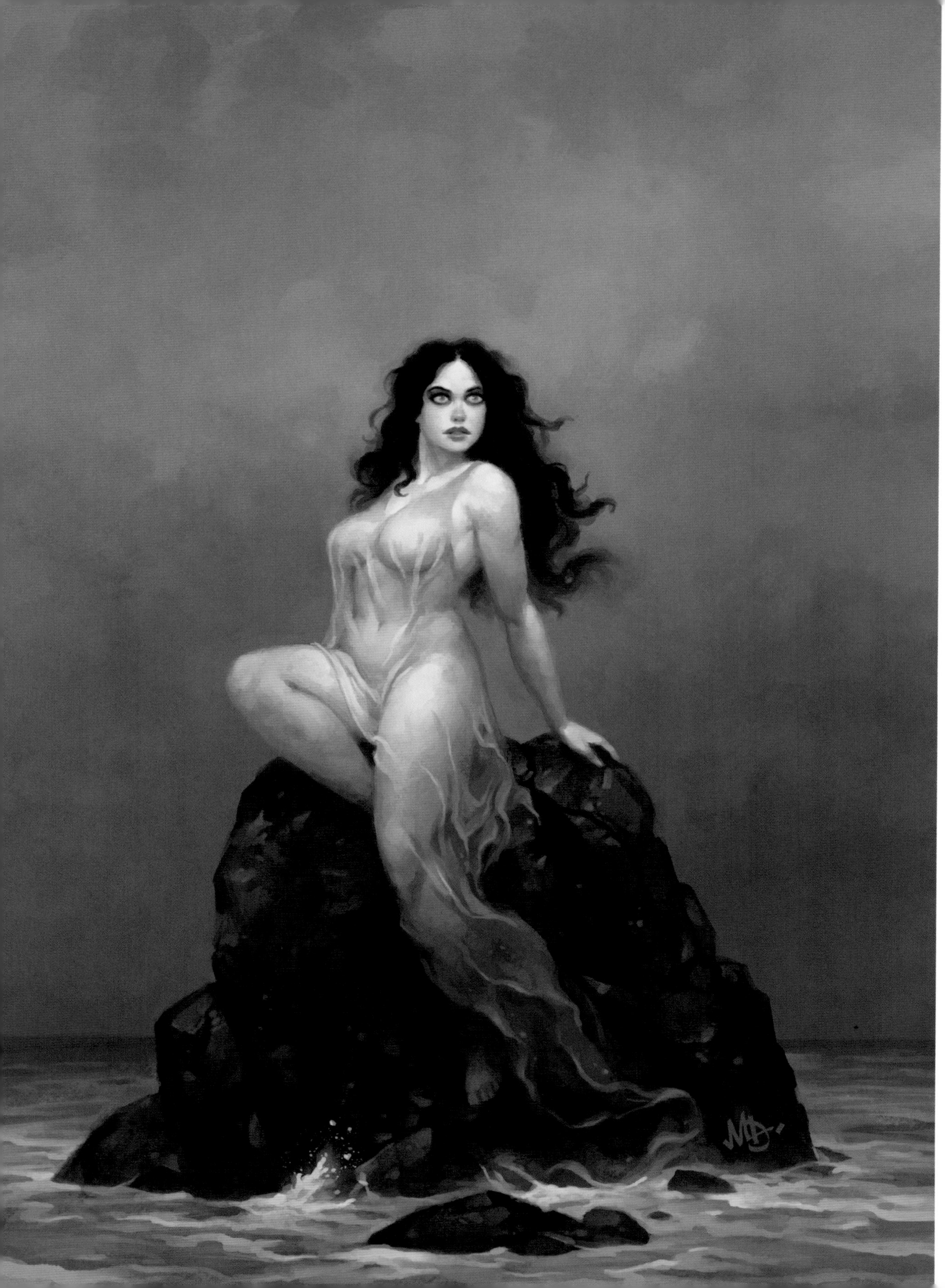

◀ **Selkie**
Matt Dixon
Adobe Photoshop
www.mattdixon.co.uk

"This piece was inspired by a cold winter walk along a rock-strewn Cornish beach. The heavy sky, wind, and colors of the sea were incredibly evocative and set me thinking about the legend of the Selkie, a creature that appears as a seal but can shed its skin to become human. Folk tales often tell of humans falling in love with Selkies in their human form with tragic consequences. I felt those melancholic stories perfectly suited the weather that day and this image was the result. The woman's gown is a metaphor for the Selkie's skin, but whether she's rising from the sea to find her lover or taking a final look at her human life before retiring back beneath the waves forever is up to the viewer."

▶ **Prey**
Steve Sampson
Pencil, Adobe Photoshop, and Adobe Illustrator
www.thedarkinker.com

"I've always had a fascination with vampires and Prey *is my first real attempt at creating a vampire character of my own. I wanted to try and capture a moment in time where she is just about to feed and something has disturbed her. I also wanted her to have a kind of old world feel and at the same time be modern. Her hairstyle is inspired by African tribeswomen and the color tones were chosen because purple has cultural associations as the color of death."*

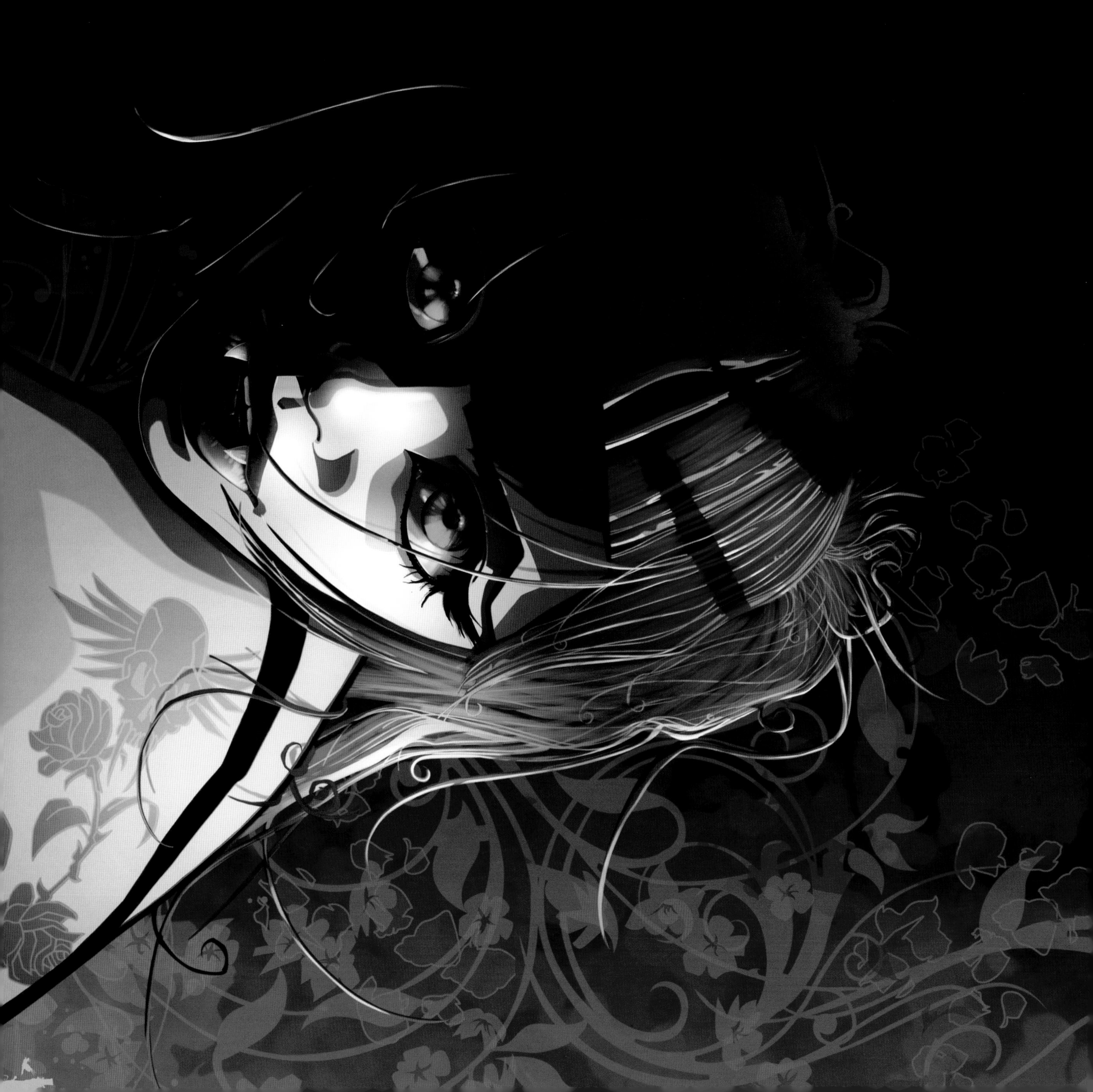

▼ **Siren**
Manon
Adobe Photoshop
www.artbymanon.com

"This is one of my favorite paintings – again inspired by ancient myth. The siren's song was said to lure sailors to their deaths. The ultimate femme fatale, I wanted her to be slightly sinister-looking, but magnetically alluring at the same time. I love the light that plays on naked skin underwater, an effect very easy to do with a semi-opaque brush on a separate layer using a light color with low opacity on an Overlay setting. I used photo references for the body and some textures for the scales on her shoulder and hip. I always paint dark to light; I find this a faster technique than starting on a blank white canvas."

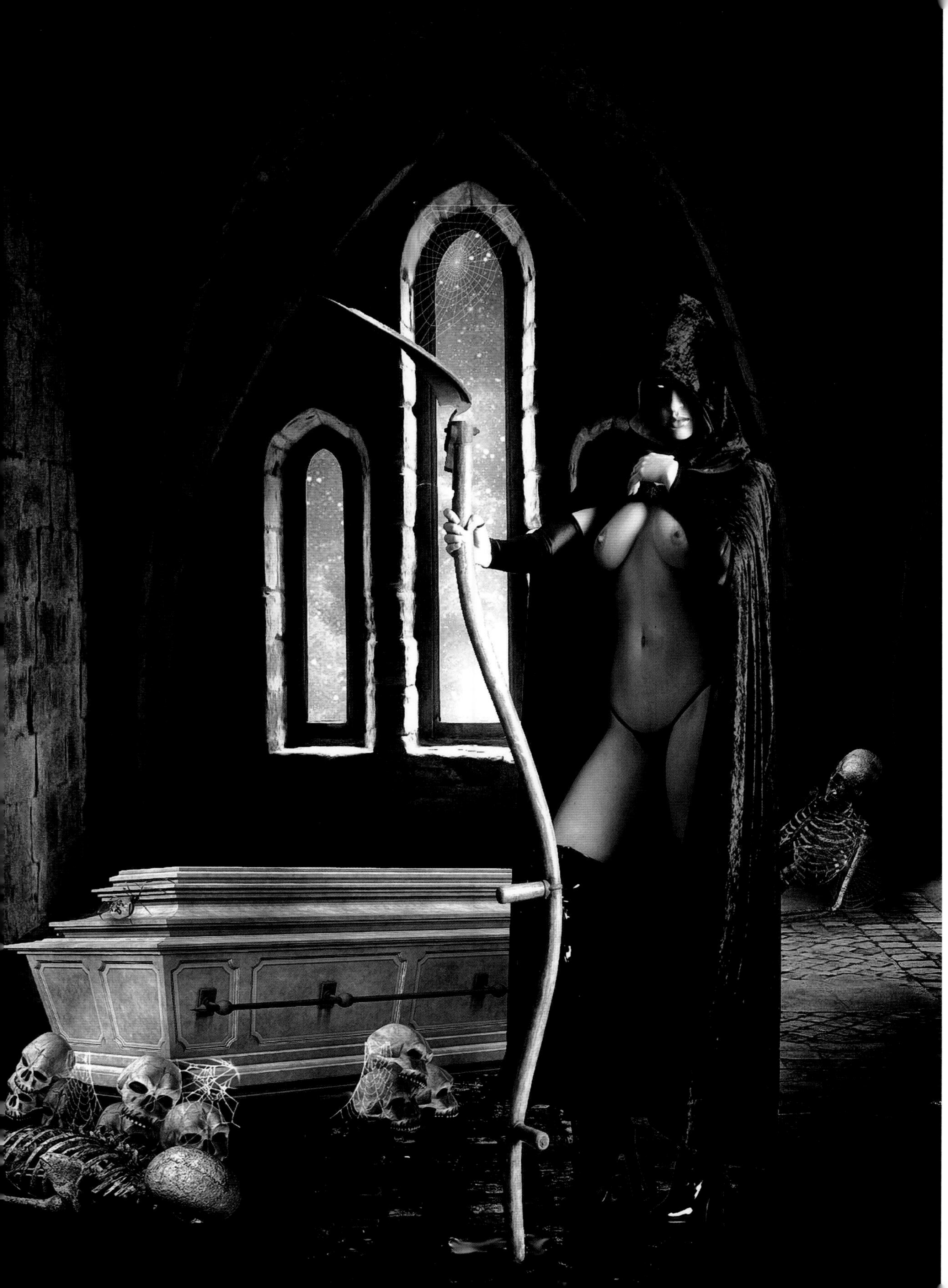

◀ **Ever After**
Logan Knight
Adobe Photoshop
www.knightmanproductions.com

"This was created using Photoshop and would be categorized as photo manipulation. Using stock images and 3-D-generated stock models, I layered each piece onto the background image, which was pre-made. After placing all the layers where I wanted them, I then saved everything as one layer and began the main coloring and effects additions, blending everything just right to get the look I wanted. For this piece, I wanted to create a playful, yet dark emotion, inspired by the idea of Death being a sexy woman instead of the standard skeleton we all know, and place her in a scene that perhaps is a crypt of collected souls, past lovers, or those she feels especially connected to."

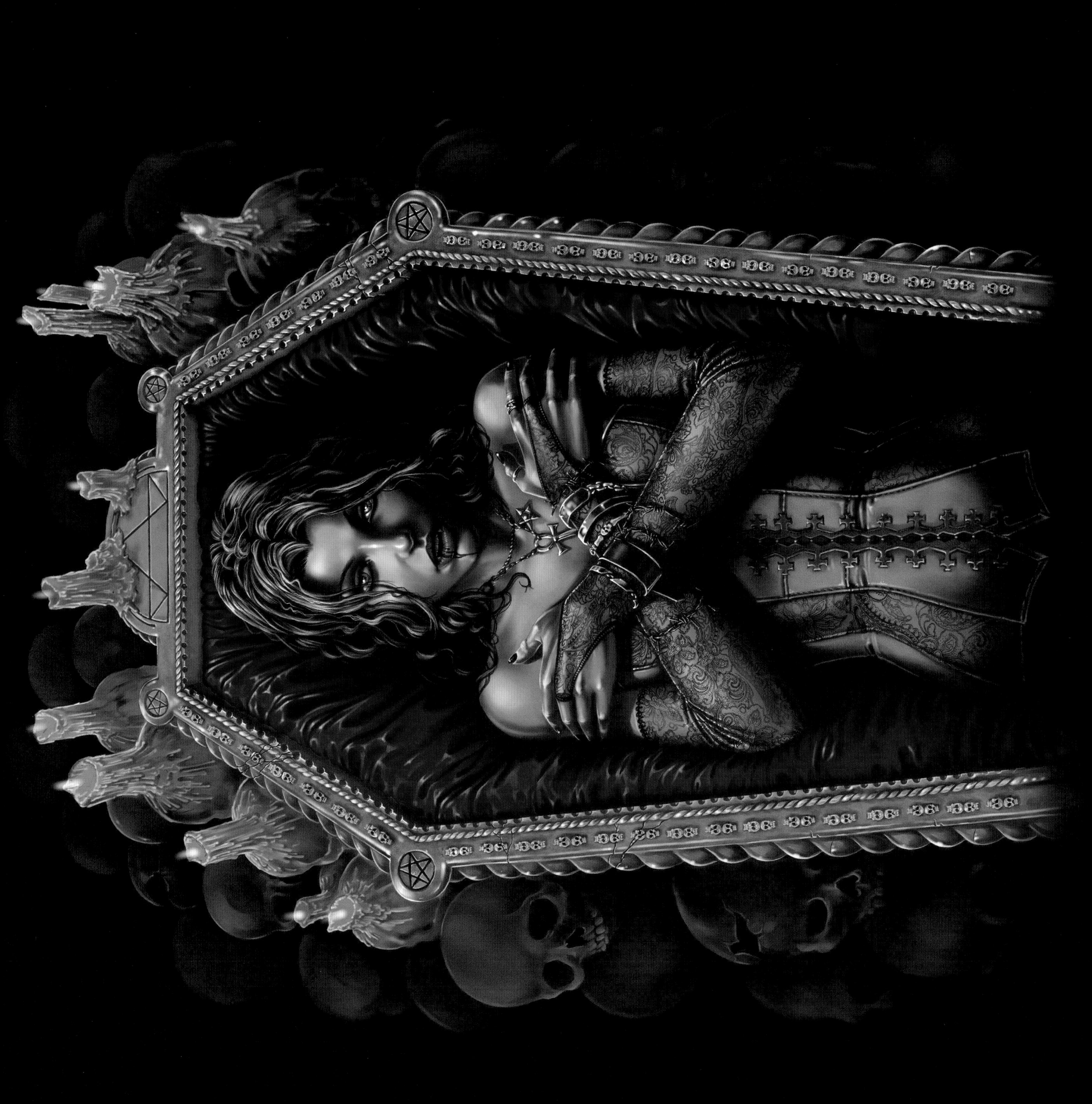

▲ Velvet Dreams
Andy Hepworth
Corel Painter
and Adobe Photoshop
http://andyhepworth.blogspot.com

*"This was the first T-shirt design
that I produced for Spiral Direct.
In many ways—for someone
who does a lot of monochrome
work—it was a gentle step to
only have to account for an extra
color, and it allowed me to
explore the advantages and
limitations of Gel, Overlay, and
Colorize layers in digital media
as a method of adding hue to a
grayscale underpainting."*

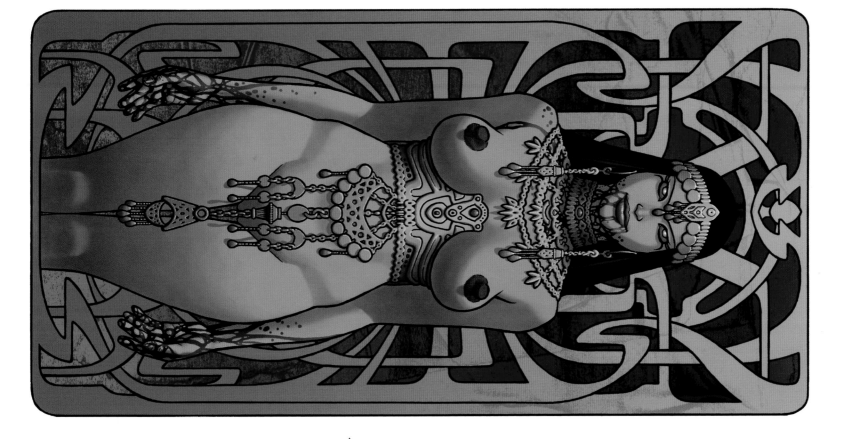

▲ Vampire Nouveau
Paul McCaffrey
Pen and Adobe Photoshop
www.coroflot.com/paul_mccaffrey

*"Being a life-long fan of horror
fiction in all its manifestations,
choosing the vampire as subject
matter was a no-brainer. As I
worked through my ideas, other
influences such as art nouveau,
Alphonse Mucha, psychedelic
posters, and the Tarot began
to surface. These directed me
towards a more static or formal
composition. I wanted the
vampire to look relaxed and
satisfied after feeding, but still
predatory and confrontational,
almost mocking. The jewelry
and body adornments were an
attempt to suggest something
Eastern European/Middle Eastern."*

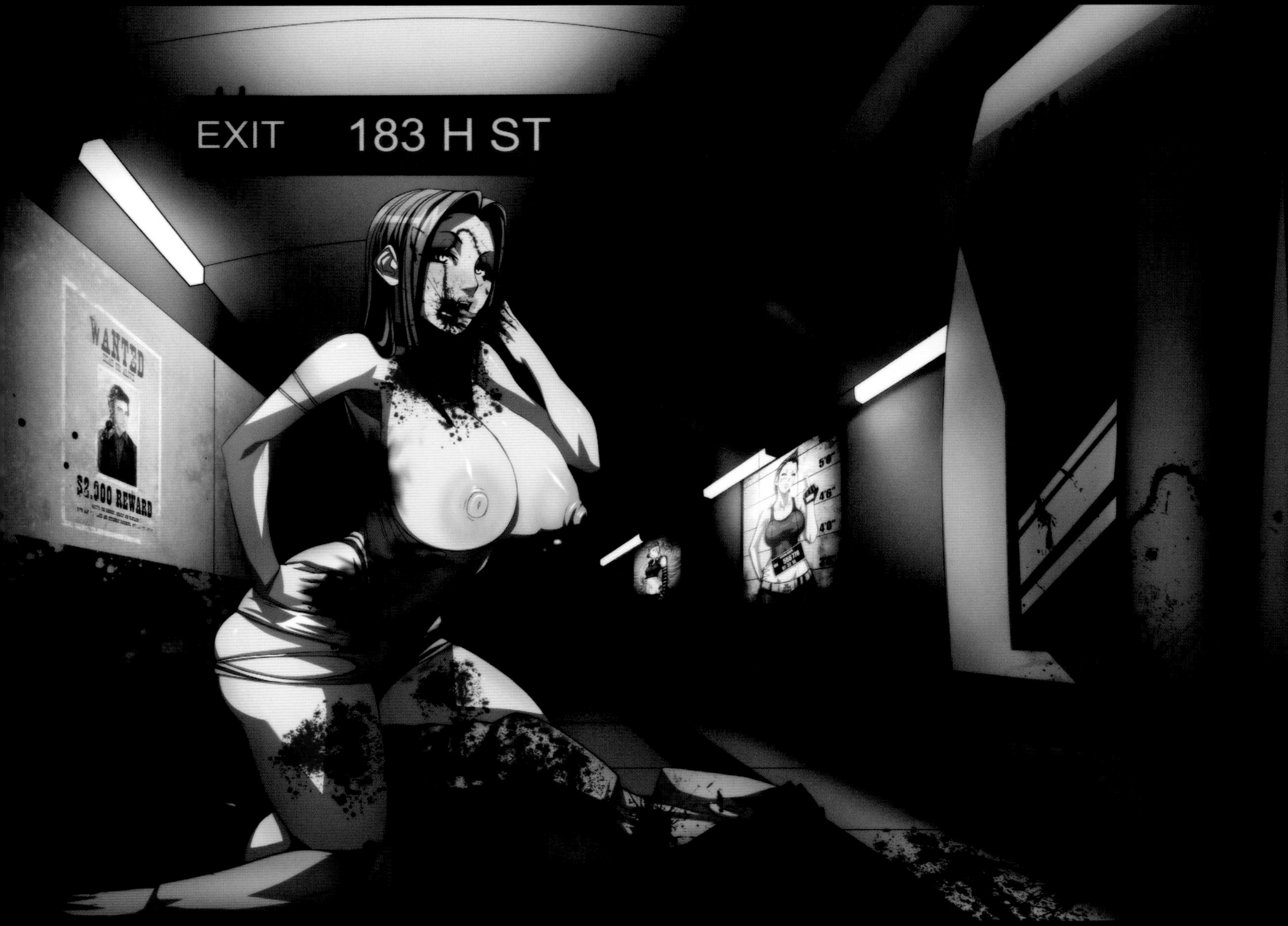
EXIT 183 H ST
WANTED
$2,000 REWARD
5'0"
4'6"
4'0"

▲ **Vampire Bloodlust**
Ricardo Landell
Adobe Photoshop and Corel Painter
www.hardinkgirls.com

"An original HARDINKGIRLS model inspired both by Halloween and bloody vampire movies like Let the Right One In*. This vampire girl hunts at night for blood to satisfy her thirst. The methodology used to create the picture starts with 'ideations,' followed by sketching in Photoshop, then transferring the image to Corel Painter for the cleaning and line-inking processes before exporting the image back to Photoshop for coloring."*

▶ **Succubus Aflight**
Ricardo Landell
Adobe Photoshop and Corel Painter
www.hardinkgirls.com

"This succubus, backlit by a full moon, was inspired by Halloween, the classic femme fatale archetype, and the long-standing fantasy art tradition of the erotic demonesses. As before, the methodology used to create the picture starts with 'ideations,' followed by sketching in Photoshop, cleaning and line-inking in Corel Painter, then exporting back to Photoshop for coloring."

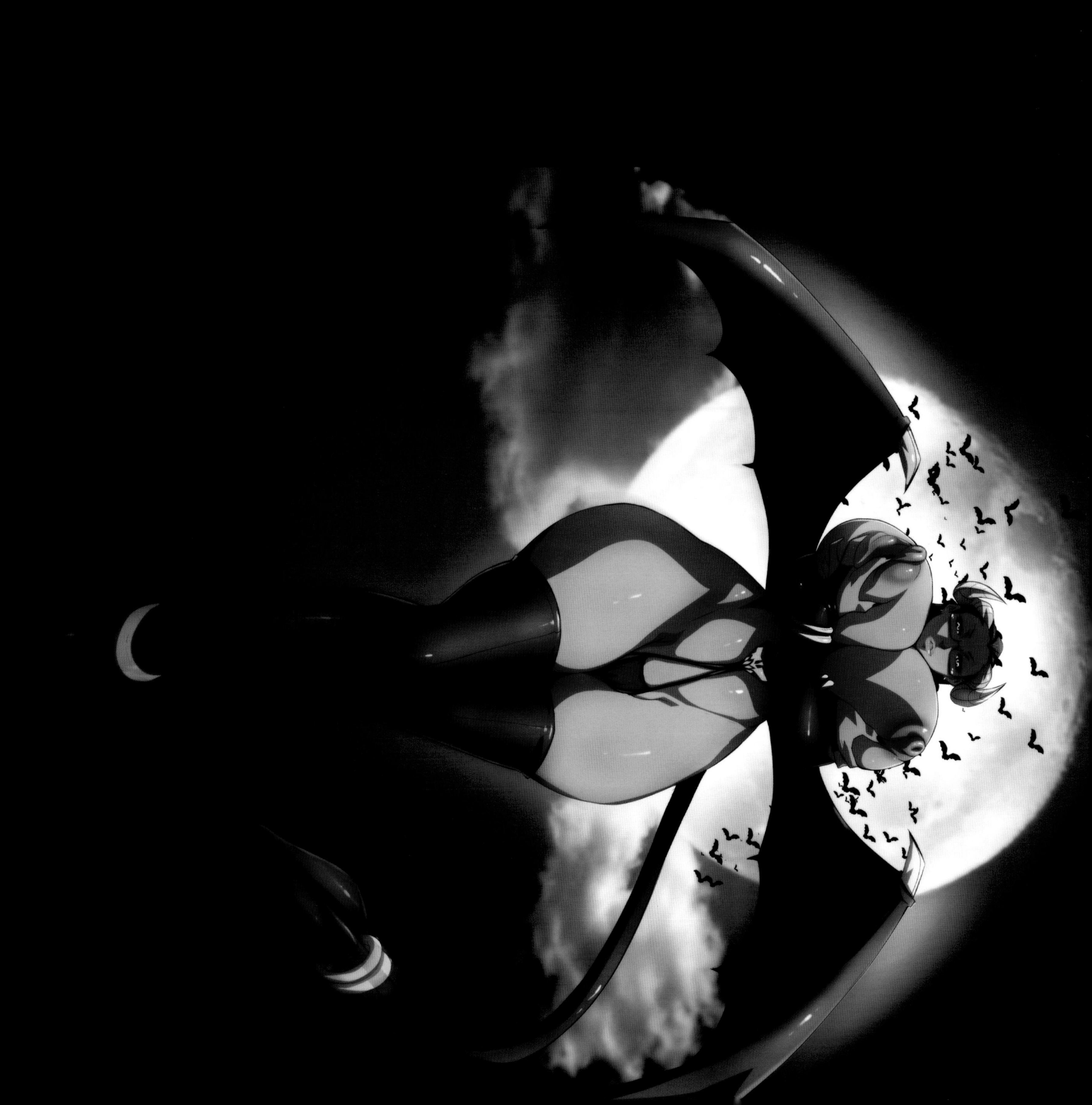

▶ **May Flower**
Chris Spollen
Adobe Photoshop
and Adobe Illustrator
www.illoz.com/spollen

"I am not ashamed to admit that this one is simply about beauty, no more, no less. I am a great admirer of all things beautiful: woman, flowers, and airplanes. What can I say? The art says it all for me. I love when the earth comes alive in early May; the birds, the flowers, the sweet smell of spring. I also enjoy the allure of a beautiful woman, so for all the above, I am truly guilty. The process is thumbnail sketches are made and then I have a photo shoot with a model. The small red accents in this piece were done in Illustrator, and I finished the image in Photoshop."

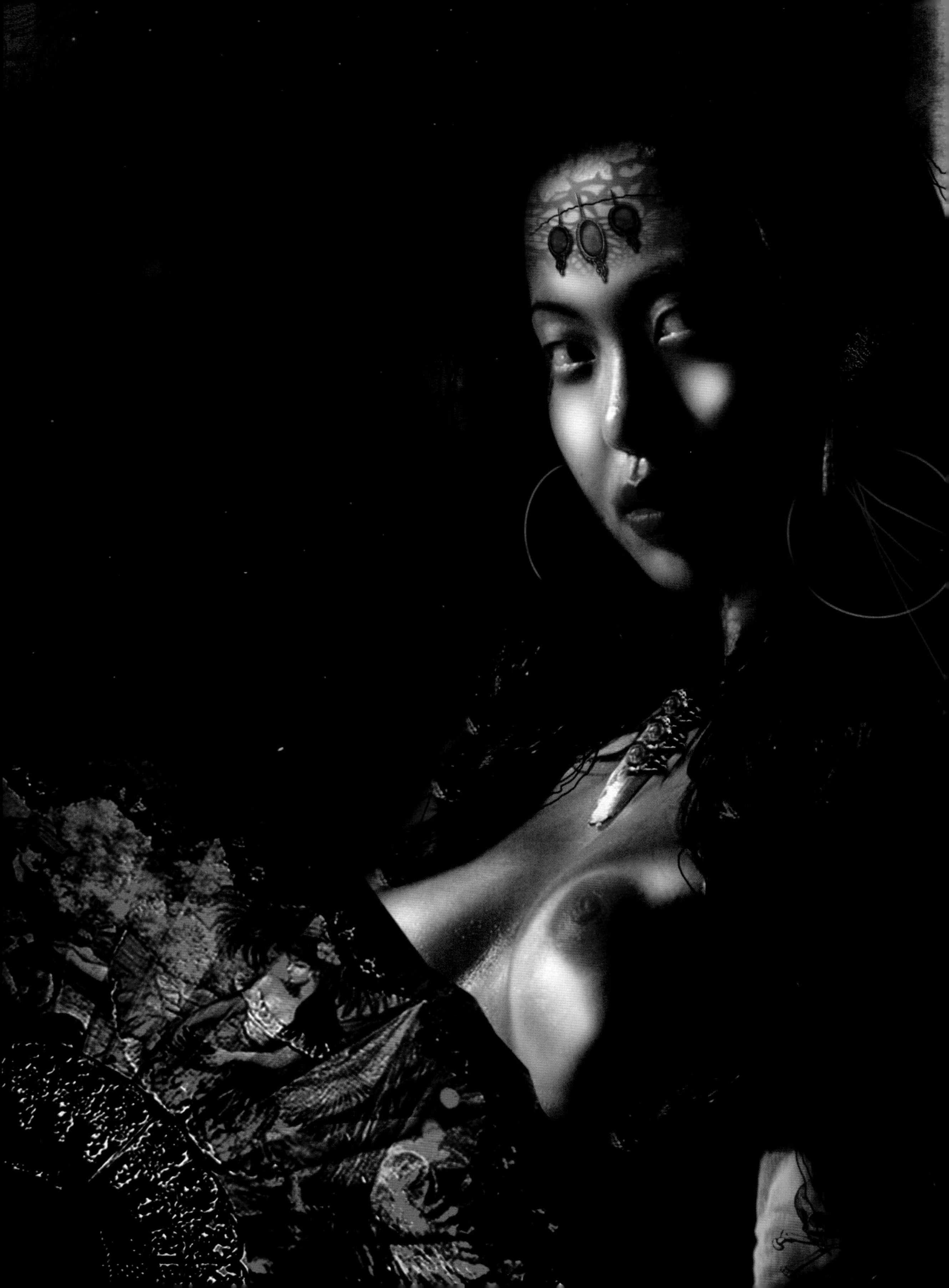

Night Watch
Chris Spollen
Adobe Photoshop
www.illoz.com/spollen

"Ideas and inspiration for me come from the sea. I have always lived near the water so it's a part of my work and me. My studio is only a twenty-minute walk to the water, and the sea has always been a source of awe, wonder, and most importantly, a feeling of great calm. This piece evokes the idea of the lost seaman and the angels or sea spirits that guide and watch over him. As a boy, I was told red lanterns were lit at night and placed in fishermen's wives' windows to guide the lost fishermen home. The process is the same here as with my other artworks—thumbnail sketches are made and then I have a photo shoot with a model. For this piece, I also shot a lantern that I have in the studio, as well as the fence, and added it to the finished art."

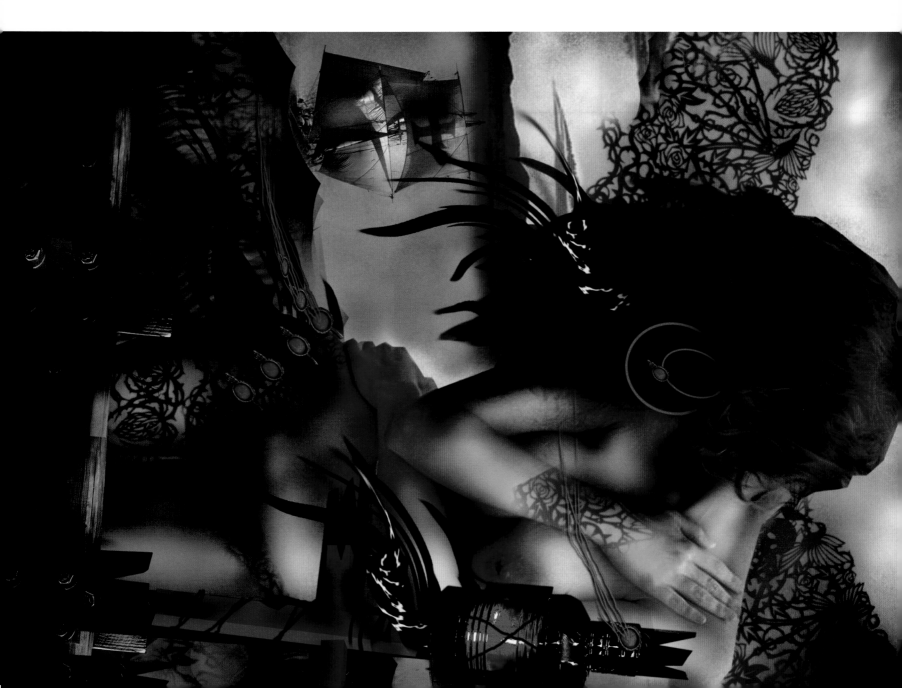

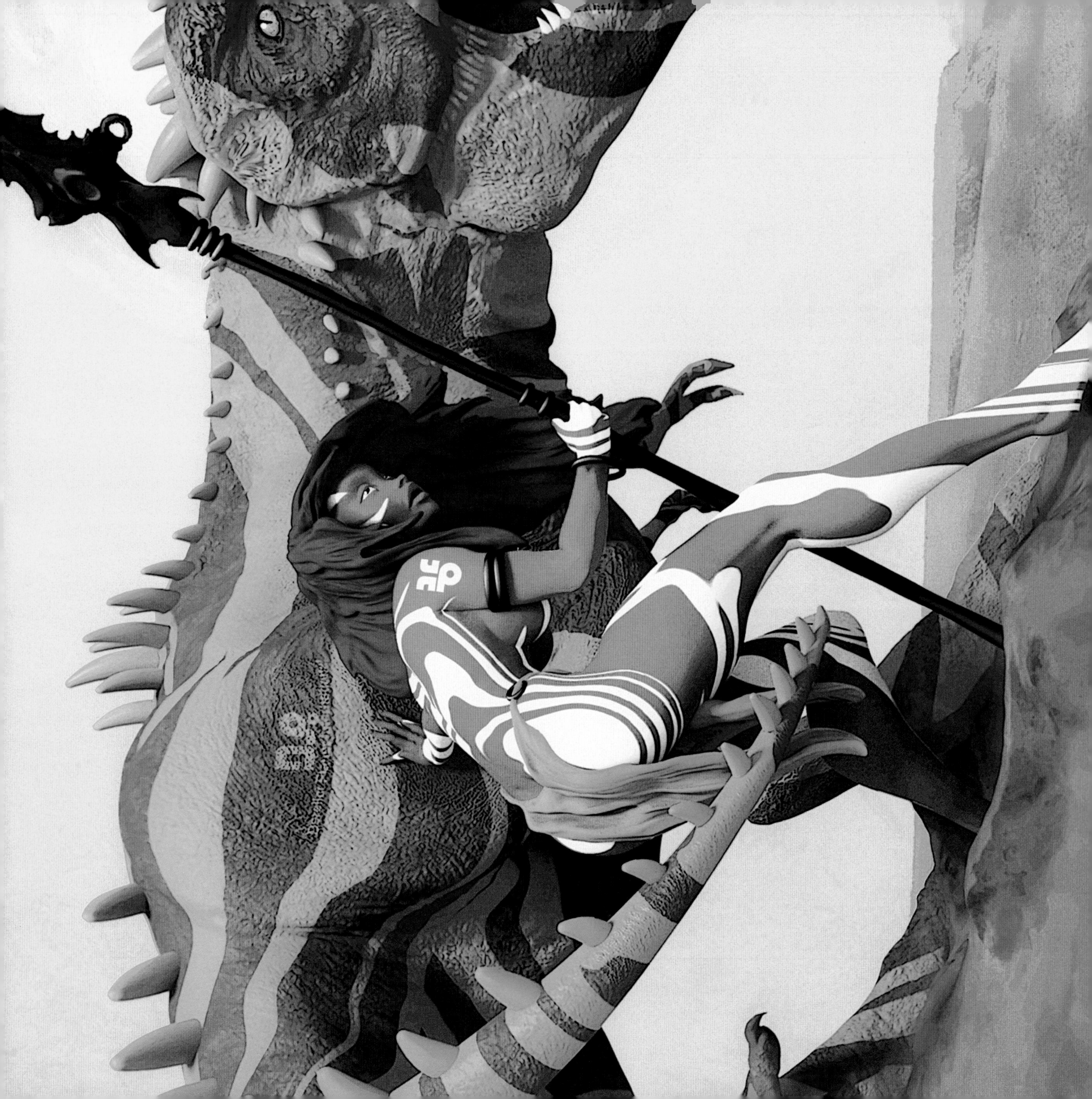

CHAPTER 5

GODS AND MONSTERS

Dinoblues
Pascal Blanche
Adobe Photoshop,
3ds Max, and ZBrush
www.3dluvr.com/pascalb

"This is a tribute to one of Frank Frazetta's fantastic works." Inspired by the great painter and illustrator, Blanche pairs his warrior girl with a Tyrannosaurus who presumably fills the role of her hunting dog. The composition of the piece is dynamic, allowing the figures to appear to be in motion despite the fact that they are still, poised to deal with some unknown threat off-screen. Blanche's designs for the characters suggest a distant, imagined past and a very bleak future.

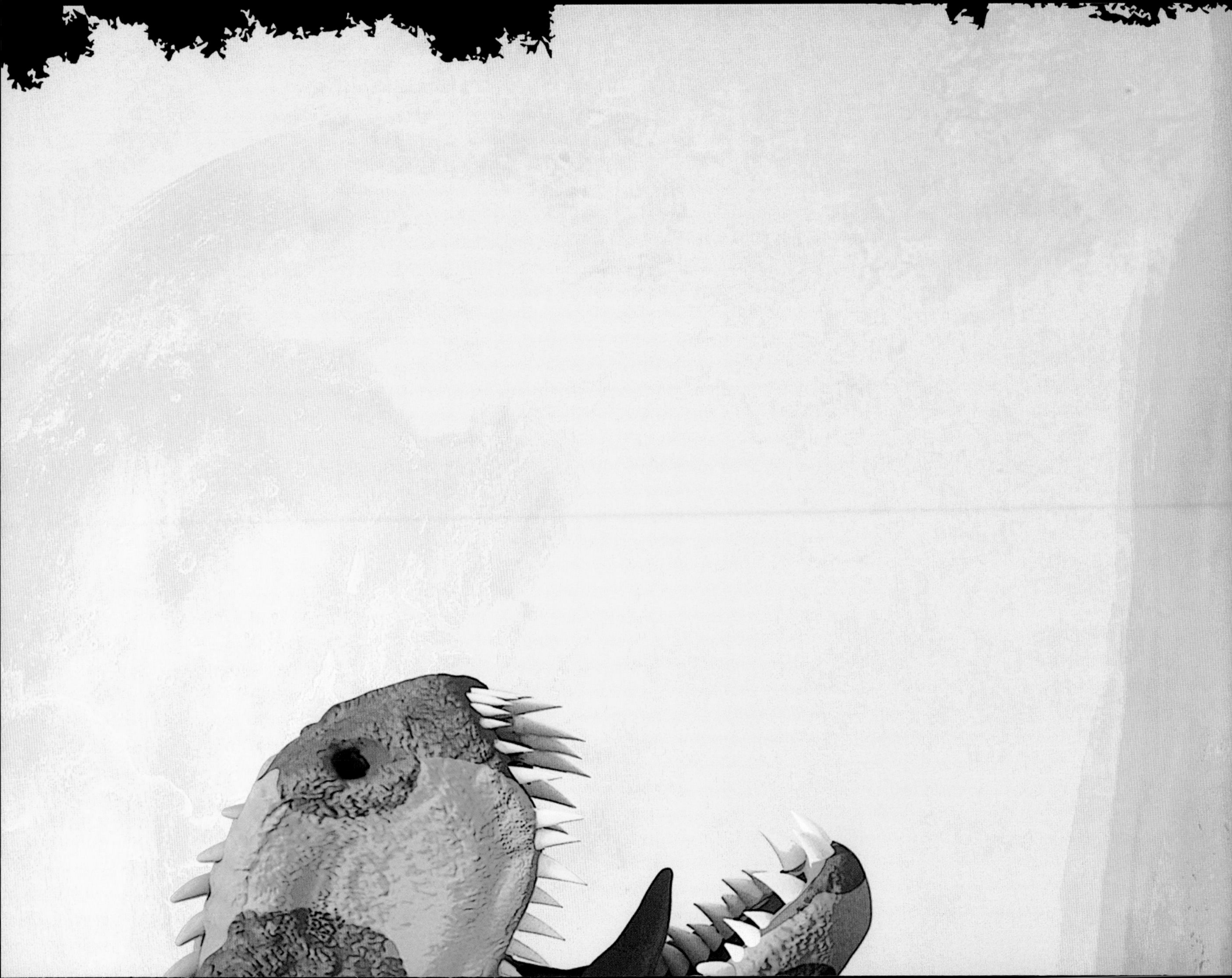

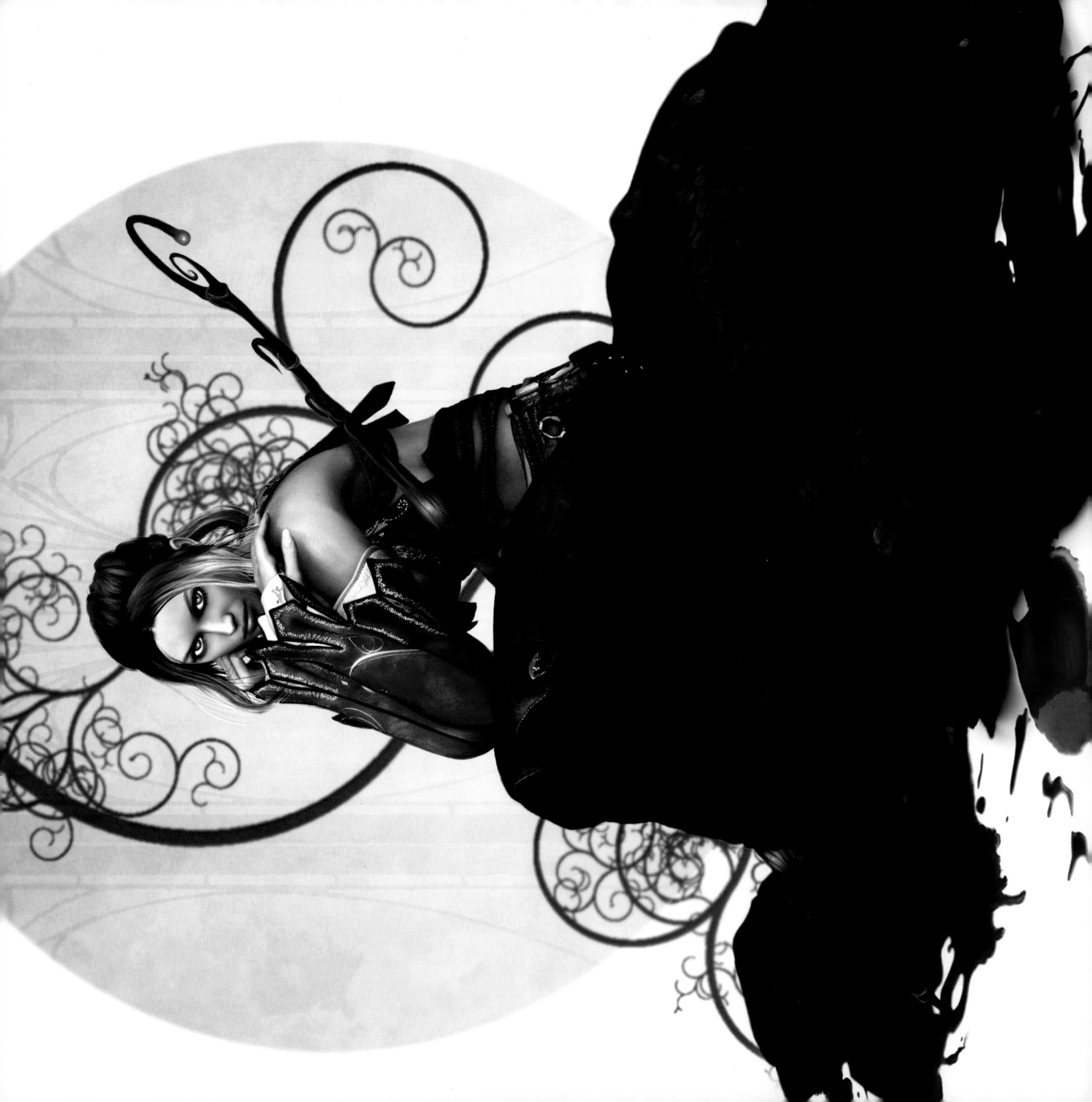

◄ **The Mage**
Susanne Korff-Knoblauch
Poser and Adobe Photoshop
www.kaanamoonshadow.deviantart.com

"The mage is one of the classics when it comes to fantasy character portraits, and I think every artist tries his or her hand at creating one sooner or later. For my first attempt, I chose to go with a female wizard. I imagined her to be quite the tease, both adventurous and very skilled at casting her spells in battle. I decided to show all these aspects of her nature by adding a little twist to the image, the slain foe that now serves as a stool while my mage poses for her observer. I wanted her to truly catch the eye, so I gave her clothes in bright colors and underlined her silhouette further by surrounding her with swirls and a different background."

► **The Duel**
DCWJ
Adobe Photoshop
www.dcwj.deviantart.com

"This piece is about a face-off between a giant and a female warrior. I wanted to do a series of artworks depicting a one-on-one battle. For this piece I wanted the monster to be towering over the female warrior to show that it's very powerful and menacing. As for the girl, I wanted to portray her confident and strong as if she fights monsters like this on an everyday basis."

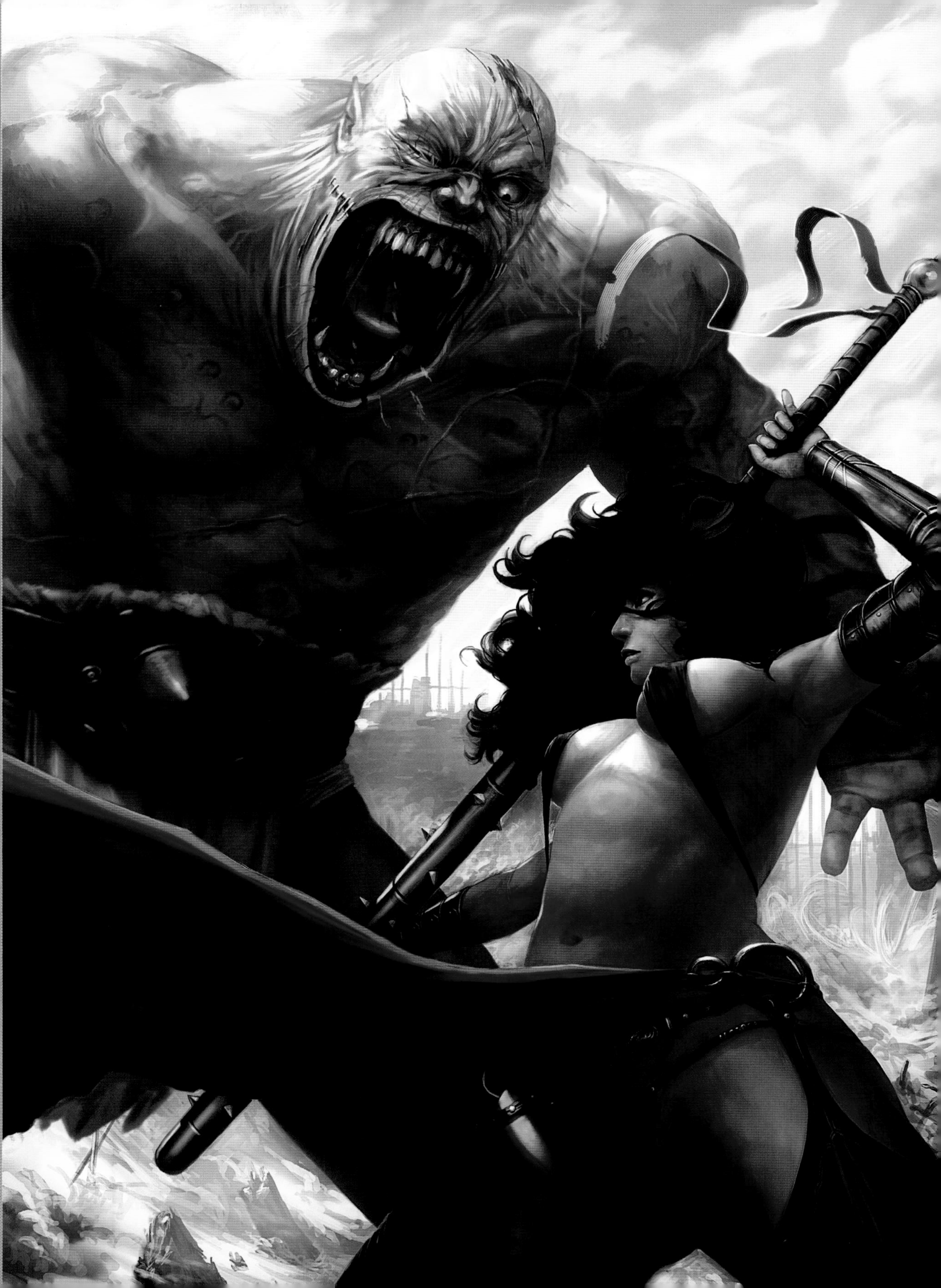

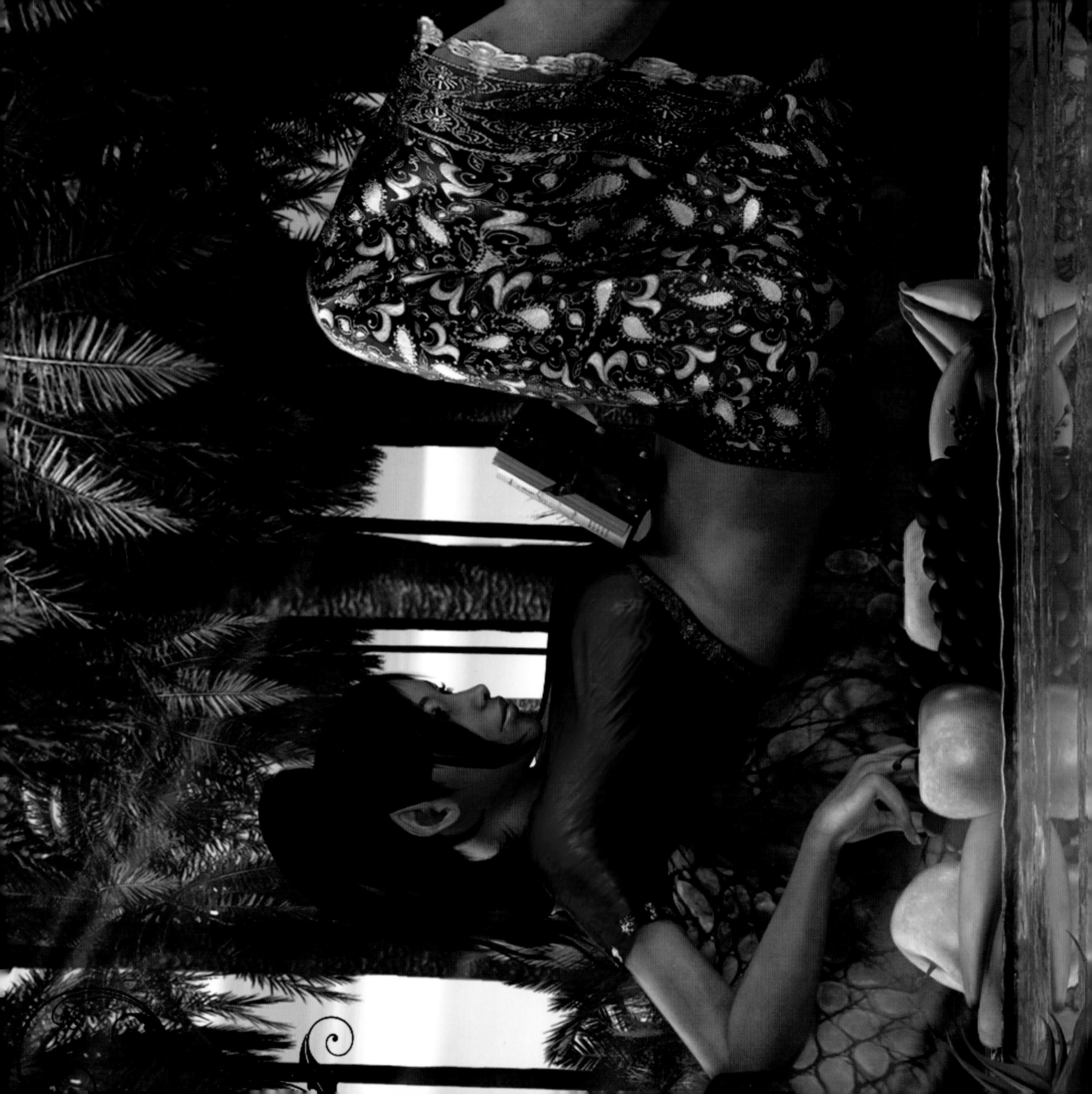

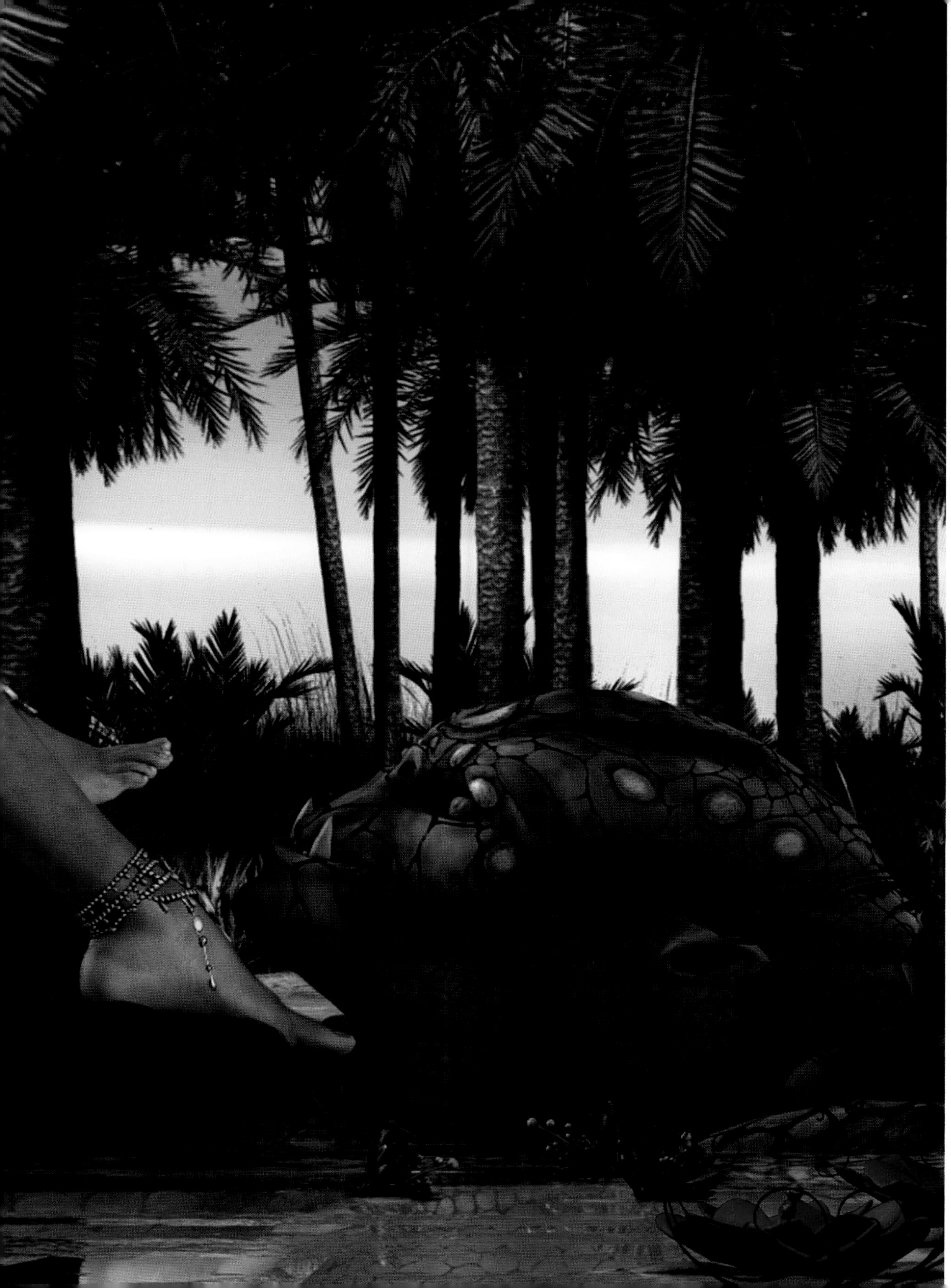

◀ **Quality Time**
Susanne Korff-Knoblauch
Poser and Adobe Photoshop
www.kaanamoonshadow.deviantart.com

"A playful fantasy image showing an elf maiden and her troll companion, relaxing on a bright, sunny day from their work as adventurers and soldiers of fortune. I wanted to create a summery feel and used bright, shiny colors to enhance that theme and make the girl stand out from the background, while giving her all the things that, in my opinion, are part of every successful vacation: a pool, a good book, something to eat, and sunshine. I imagine Troll to be quite the gentleman, inviting his friend to this luxurious fantasy resort, gallantly offering his services as a living float so that the lady can enjoy her vacation to the utmost . . . not minding the fact at all that he is getting a good look under her skirt while he is at it."

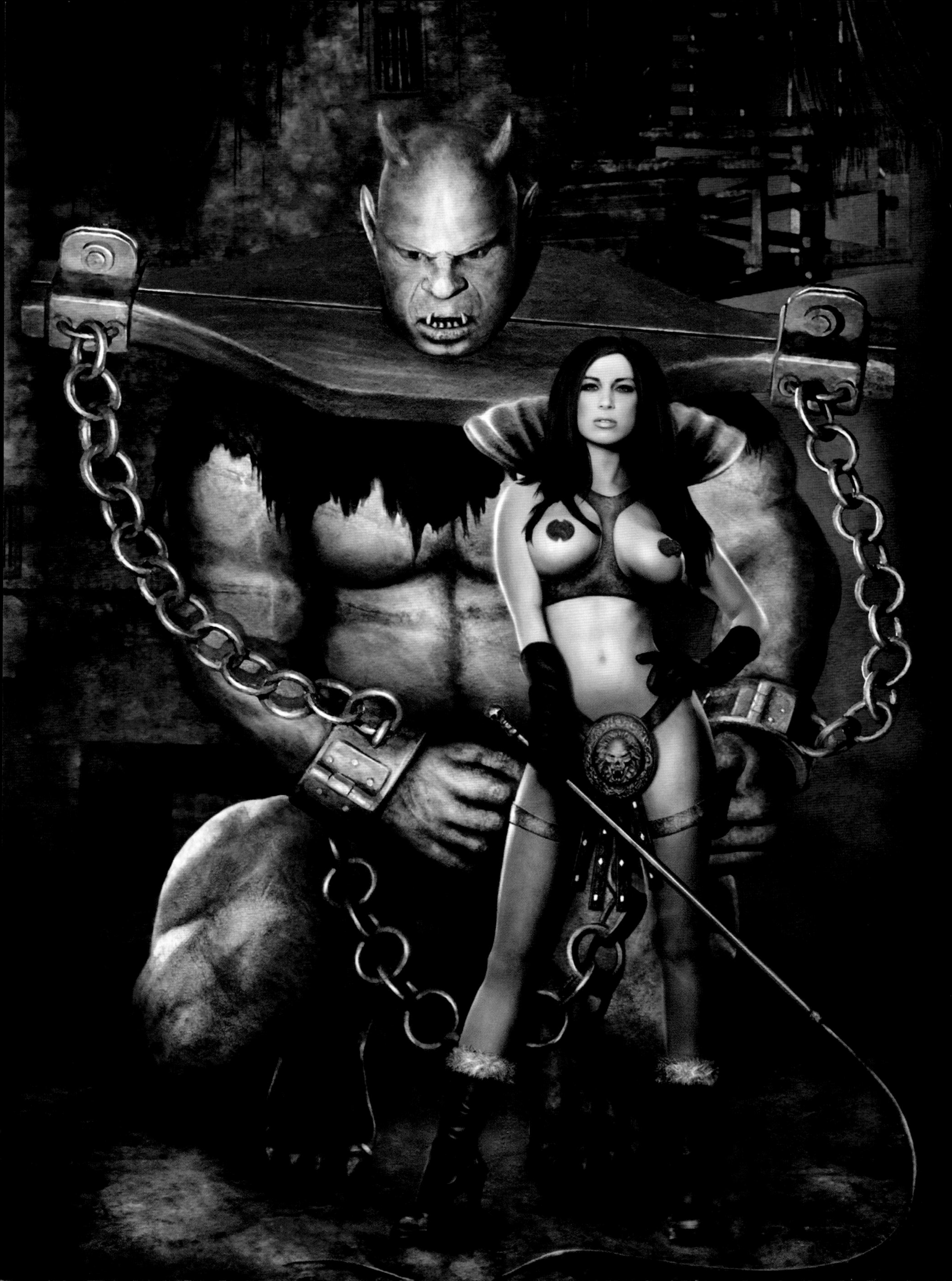

◀ **The Mines of Barrad-Mishar**
Al Serov
Cinema 4D and Adobe Photoshop
www.alserov.com

"This is a little fantasy about a land of ferocious beasts and exotic women. The beasts might be enslaved and turned into obedient miners, the shining beauties might become overseers. This work was done primarily in Photoshop, though I used Cinema 4D software at the beginning of the process. It helped me to establish the basic shapes and the lighting. I used textured brushes a lot and also some photo textures. No monster was harmed during the creation of this picture."

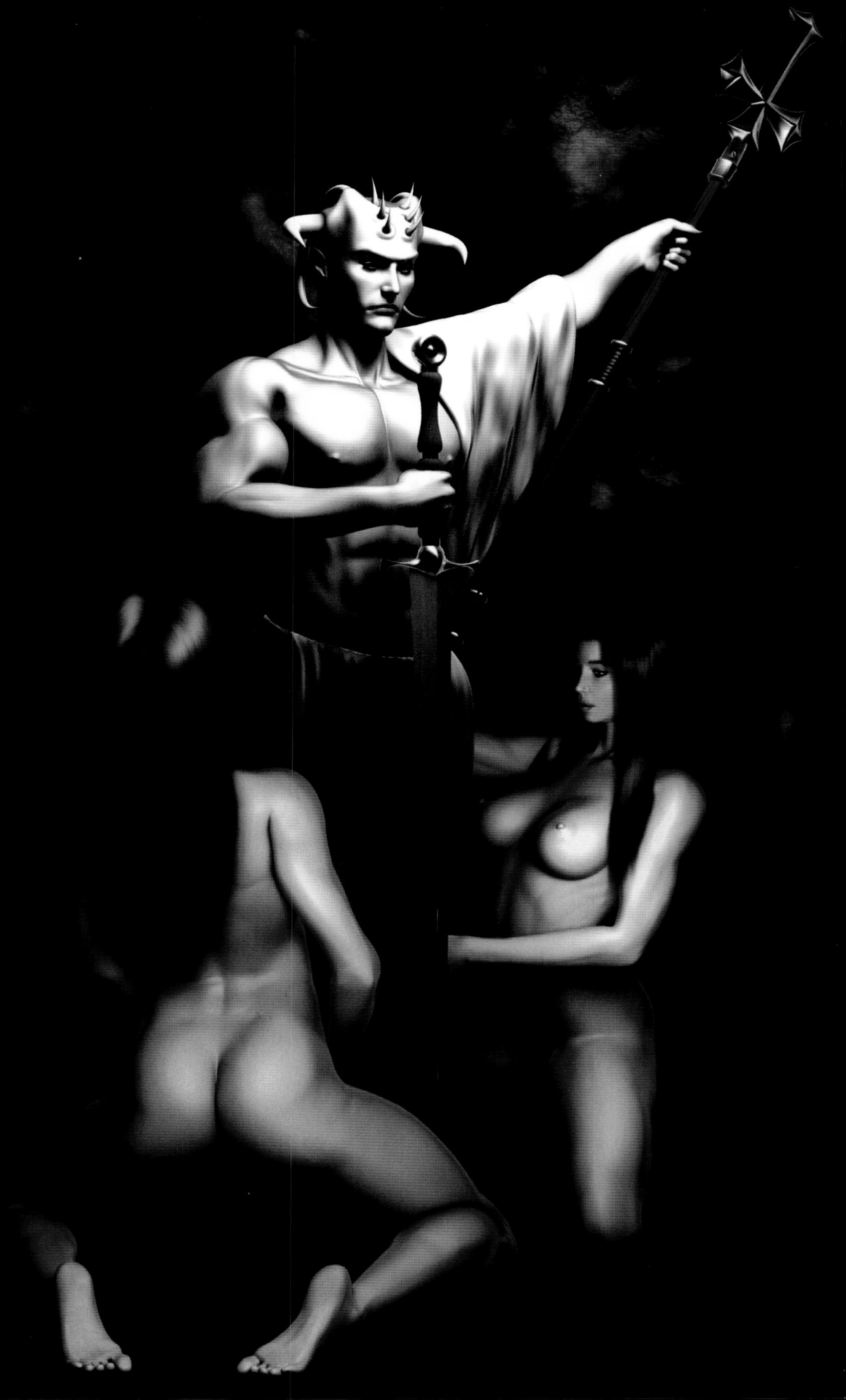

Belial
Darthhell
3ds Max and Adobe Photoshop
www.darthhell.deviantart.com

"This piece was requested by an acquaintance of mine. After seeing my other work, he knew the demon stuff was my kind of thing. I came up with a new kind of look for a demon who is top in the hierarchy, and I wanted him to have ten horns—sort of a biblical reference. I figured a white, shining, noble-looking demon would look best, since evil and dark is so overused, even by me. Belial is the champion of mankind and represents the carnal and base urges of humans. I rendered the scene in 3ds Max and did all my postwork like filtering, smoothing, and hair-painting in Photoshop with my Wacom tablet."

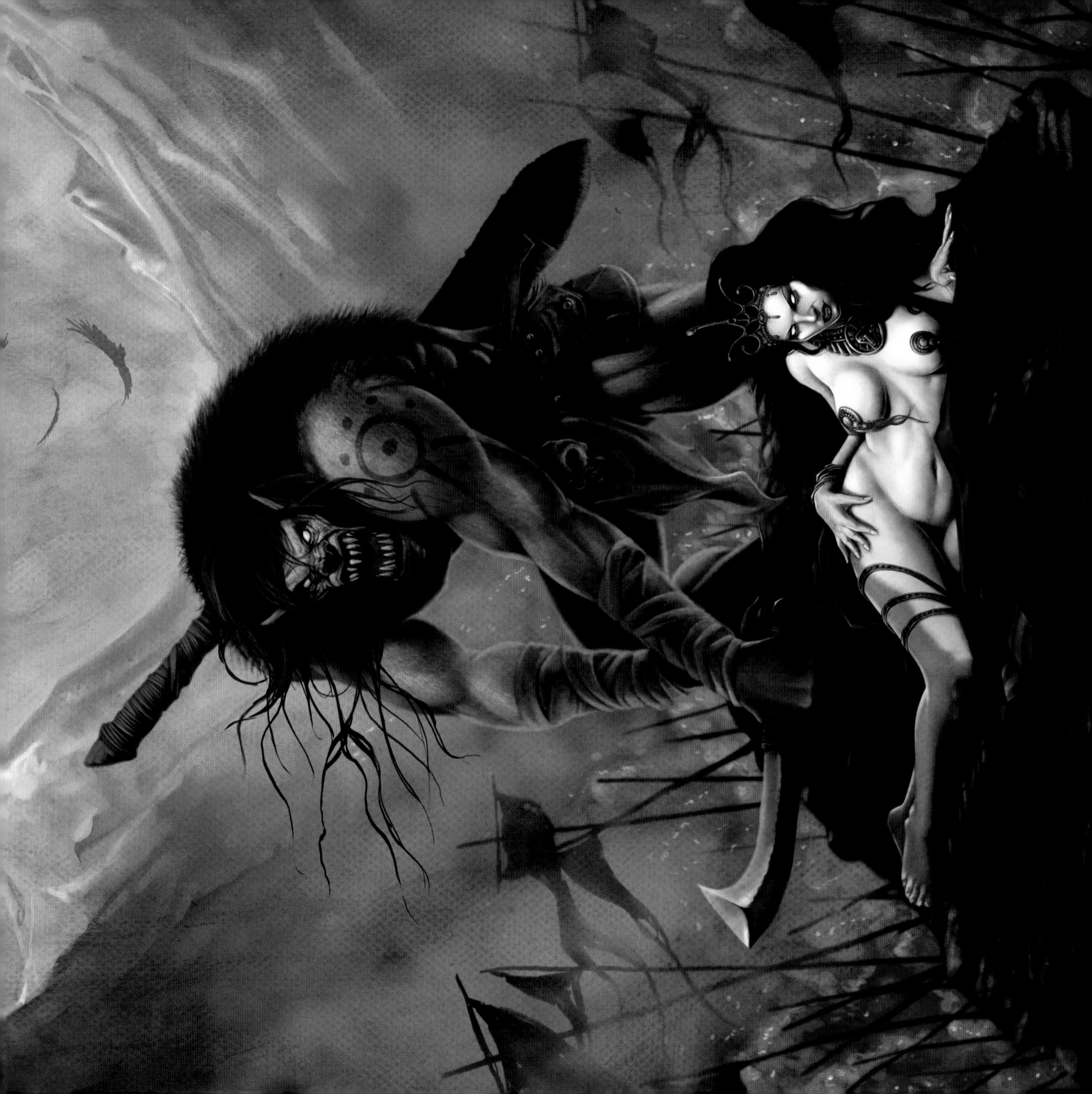

◀ **The Beauty of the Beast**
Daniel Bernal
Pen and Adobe Photoshop
www.imaginante.deviantart.com
www.danielbernalportfolio.blogspot.com

"I wanted to make an illustration of a wolfman and evil maidens that allowed me to play with the duality of beauty and bestiality. My illustration process is to start with a drawing in my sketchbook. I then generate a color base to help me imagine the atmosphere and the action that I want to represent. Afterwards, I find the first planes and details. I generally use a few layers in Photoshop. I like to work as if I'm painting in an oil technique on a real canvas."

▶ **The Head Collector**
Daniel Bernal
Pencil and Adobe Photoshop
www.imaginante.deviantart.com
www.danielbernalportfolio.blogspot.com

"I believe there are two recurring features in my illustrations. The first is beautiful women protagonists. The second is an enviroment that generates enough tension for the spectator to construct his or her own history for the piece. In The Head Collector, *maybe this is the end of all hope, where a king's daughter is taking revenge, or is she a work-in-progress assassin . . . the root of all evil perhaps? The illumination was crucial in this illustration, and it is the first part that I worked on. I was inspired by Rembrandt to reveal, little by little, what the light is letting us see."*

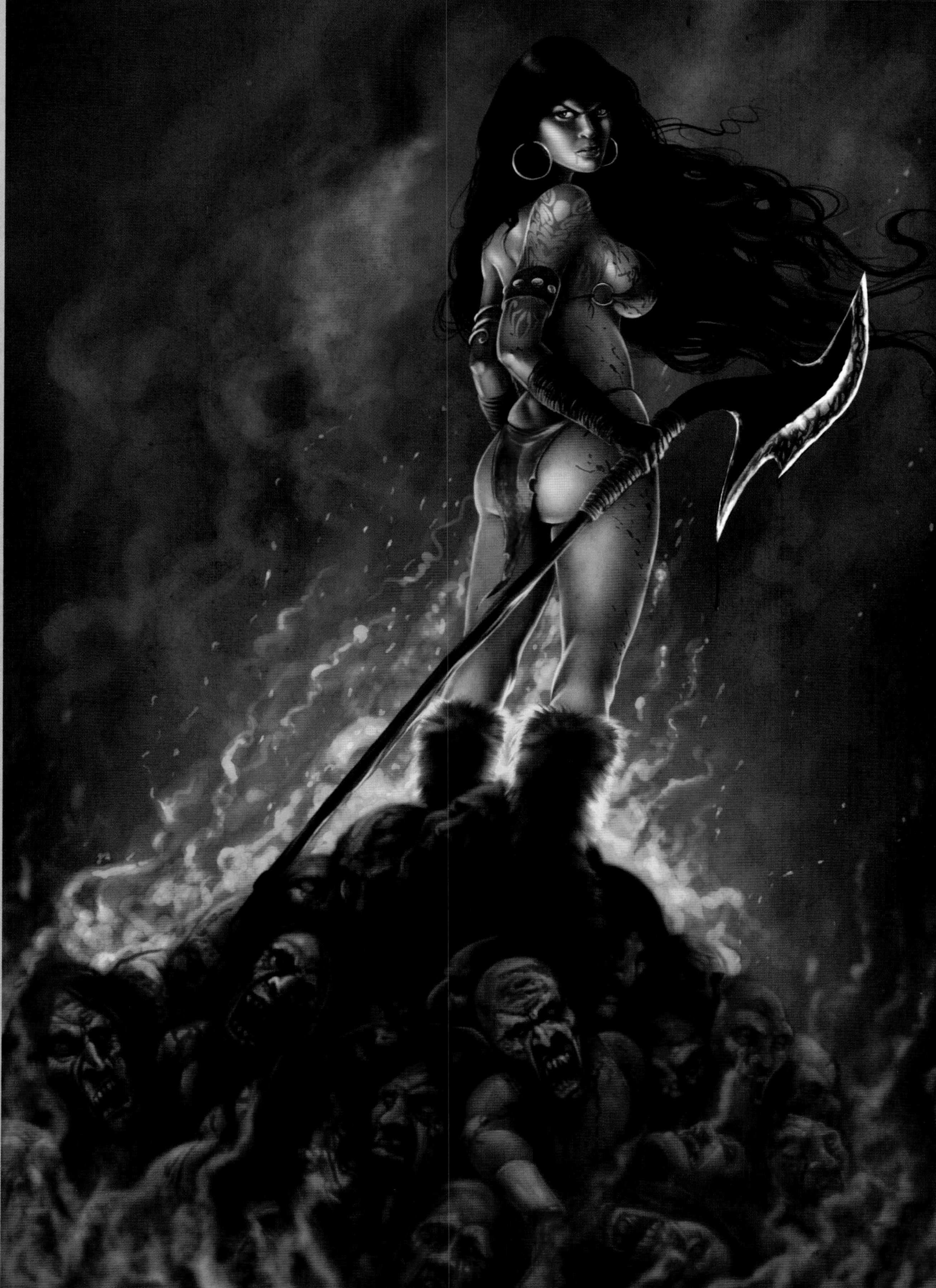

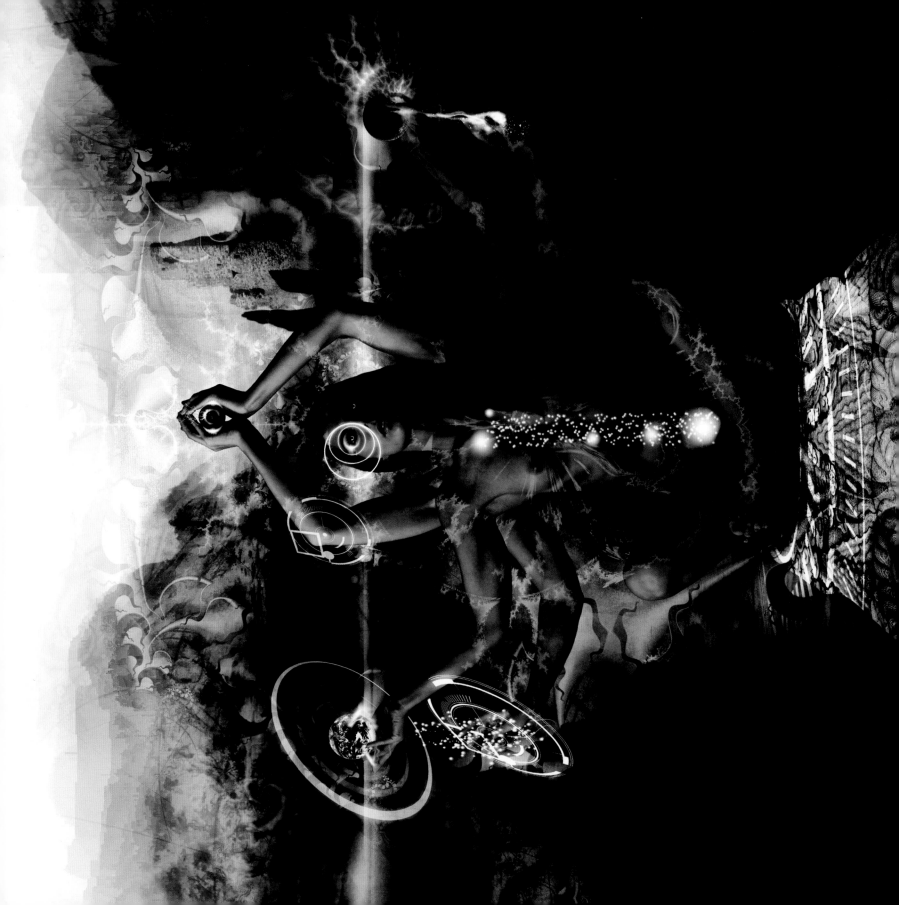

◀ **MultiVerse**
Logan Knight
Adobe Photoshop
www.knightmanproductions.com

"I used a combination of stock photography, fractal art, and 3-D renders to create this piece of photo manipulation. Inspired by the subject of quantum physics, this piece takes us deep into my imagination. The idea of multiple universes or realities existing at the same time all around us. It is kind of hard to wrap your head around, but for me this subject and all its possibilities really open the floodgates to my creative process. The piece here shows what my idea of a controller (if you will) of these multiverse realities might look like and what a moment in her life might be like."

▶ **Bad, Barbarian, Marian**
Jhoneil Centeno
Adobe Photoshop
www.jhoneil.com

This piece is a study in the controlled use of color. The figure is surrounded by shades of gray, which draw the eye to the "warmest" spot—the four red diagonal stripes across her belly. Jhoneil has a strong sense for design and the reality of a scene. His design for the belt, tattoos, and weaponry is delicate and original. But the most impressive attention to detail is in the actual shape of her body. Rather than a wafer-thin supermodel, the artist displays an athletic, strong woman with realistic proportions. He also gave her uneven breasts, a deft touch. Jhoneil says, "I love the idea of a female warrior who seems vulnerable at first, but is surprisingly deadly."

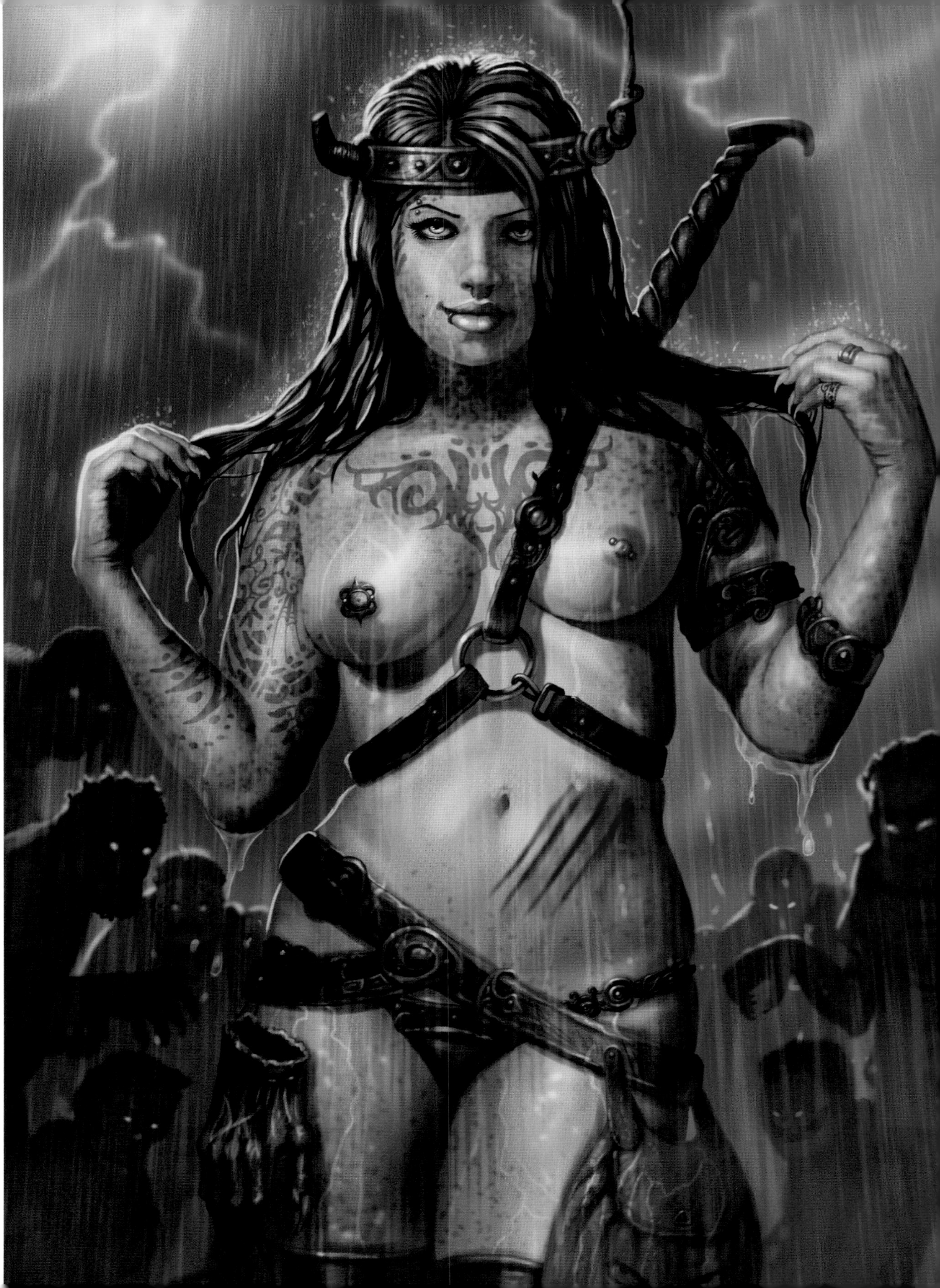

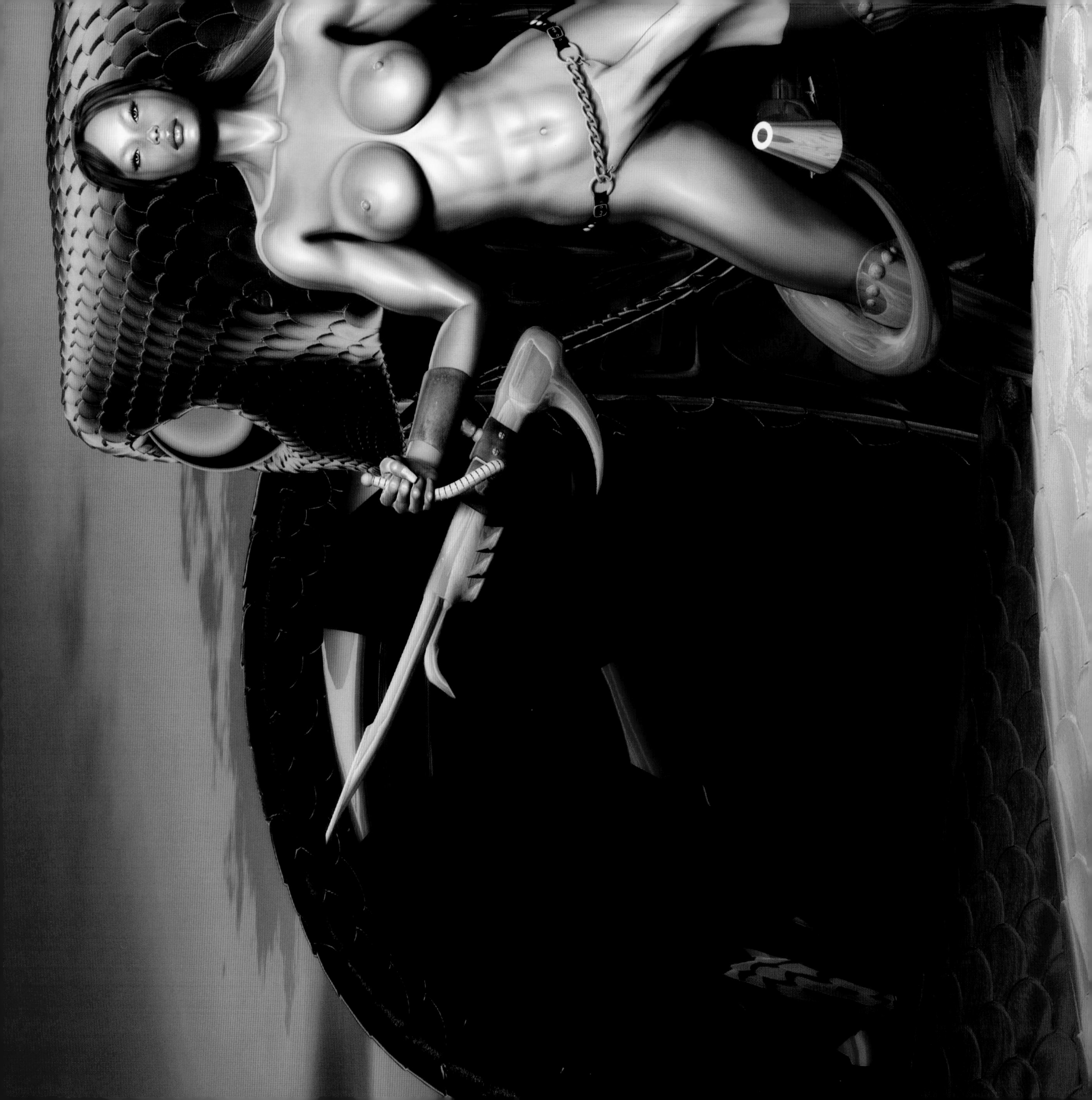

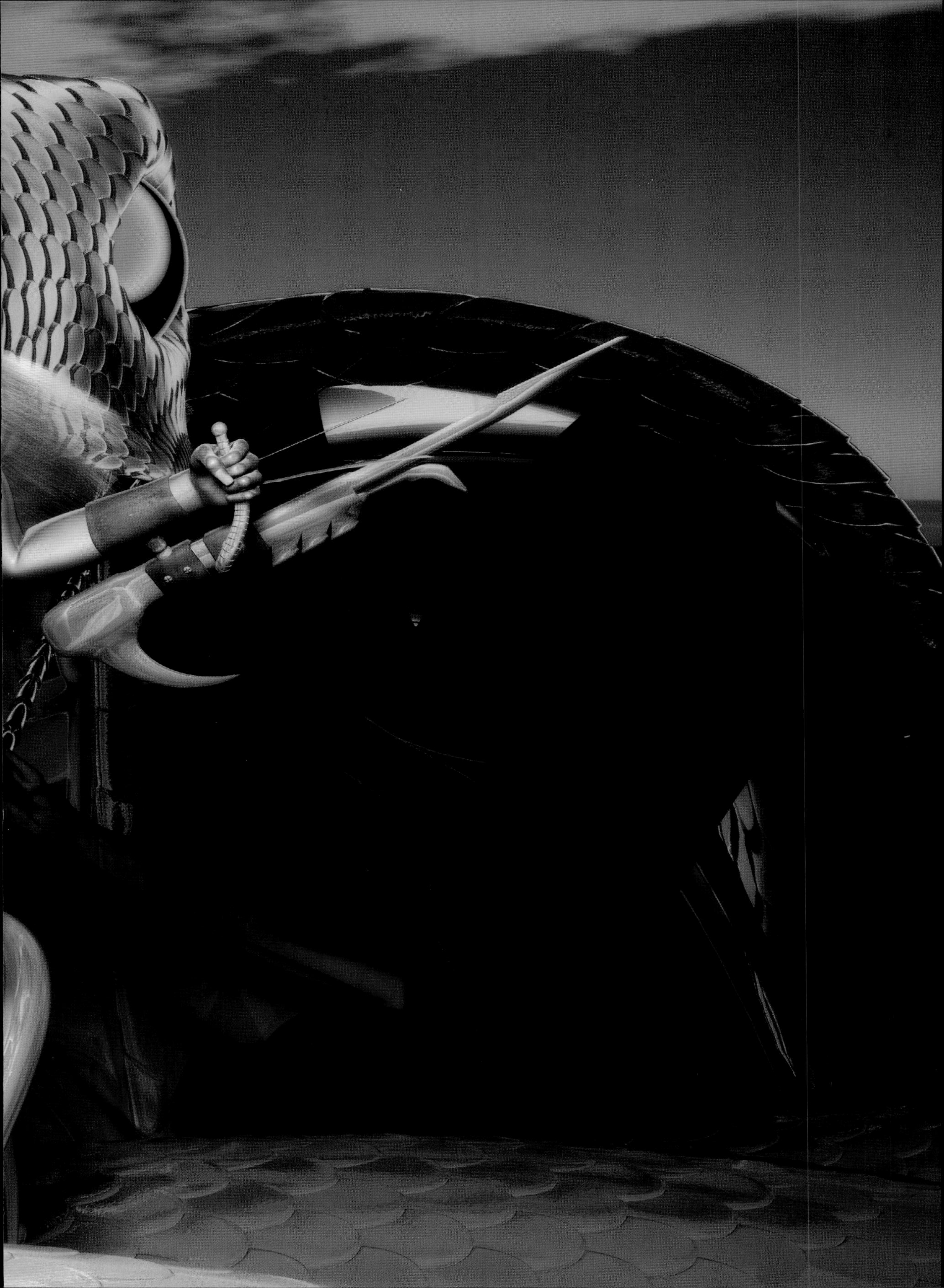

◀ **Pay Homage**
Darthhell
3ds Max and Adobe Photoshop
www.darthhell.deviantart.com

"Frank Frazetta had just died and being a long-time fan of his (I mean, what teenage boy wasn't back in the day?), I wanted to do a sort of tribute to his genre, but in my own style. So, a scantily clad, topless warrior girl with a metal snake seemed good. I tried to match the feel and color tones of his work without copying him outright. I rendered in 3ds Max and did postwork in Photoshop. The hair was rendered, which is not something I normally like to do, so mainly I did some layering and hard-light blurring in Photoshop for this effect, and smoothed out some mesh flaws from the model."

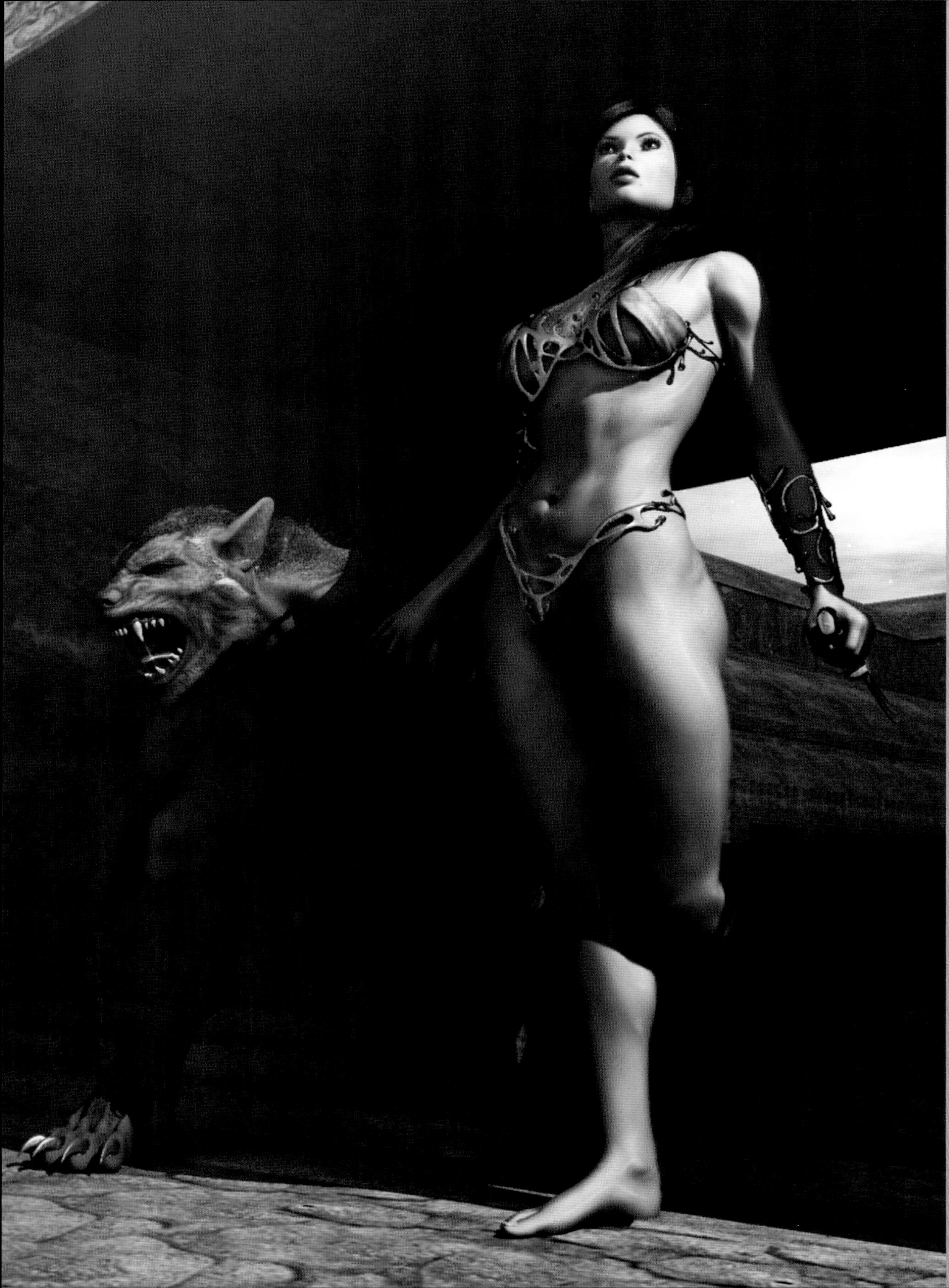

◀ **Tread Softly**
Deedee Davies
Poser, Vue 6 Esprit,
and Adobe Photoshop
www.seedydeedee.co.uk

"This was created for a competition where you had to try to do something that emulated the work of classic fantasy artists like Frazetta and Vallejo. I went for a fairly voluptuous female figure in the requisite impractical metal bikini, along with a werewolf to depict a 'beauty and the beast' type of scene. I've gone for quite a low point of view to give the impression they're being watched. The story behind the picture is that the werewolf is actually the girl's enchanted lover, and they've come to solicit the aid of a dangerous sorcerer to try to get him to lift the curse."

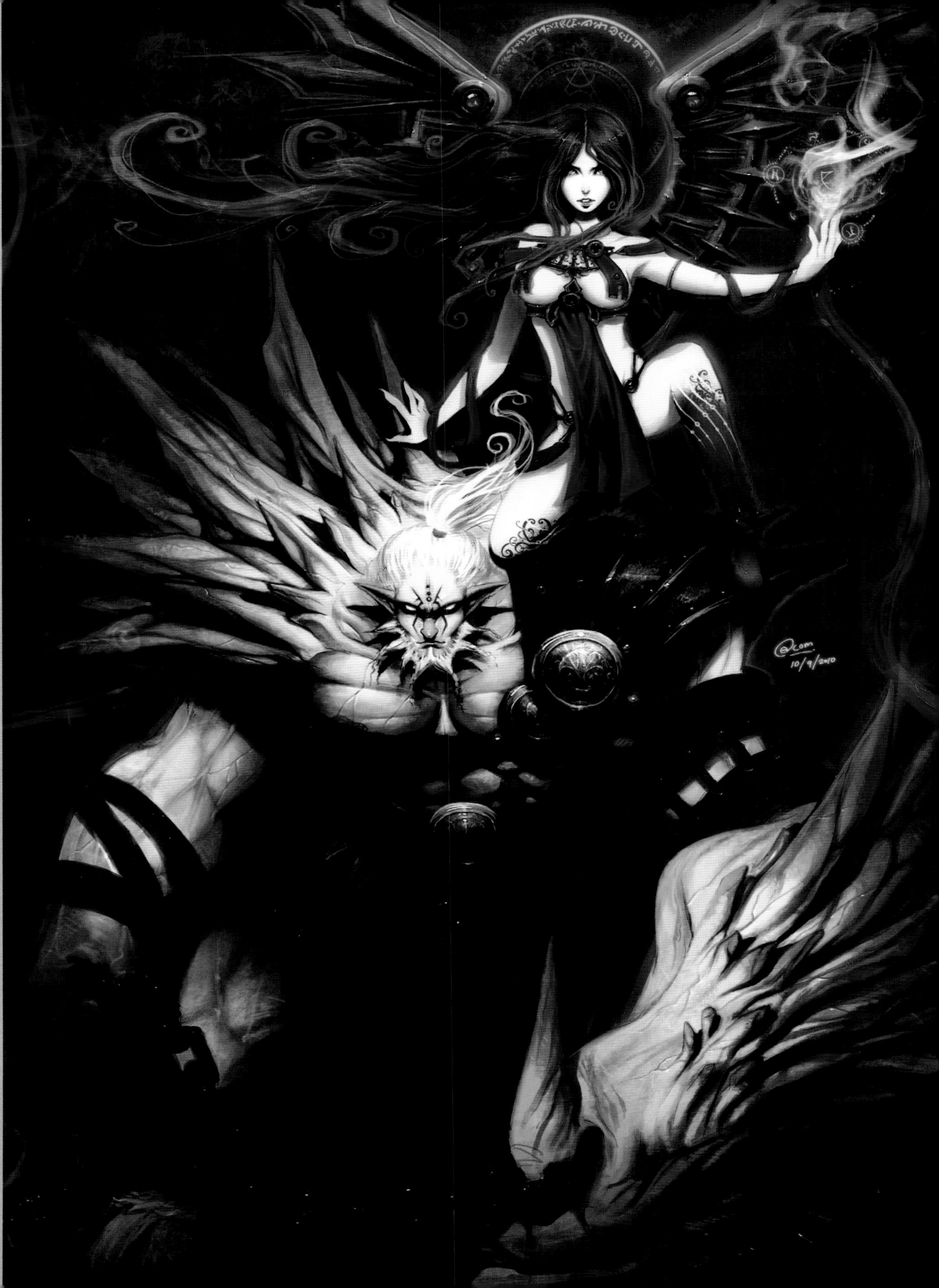

@com
10/9/2010

Earth and Fire
Chung Yee-Ling
Adobe Photoshop
http://syncmax.deviantart.com

"Earth and Fire *was one of my random character designs. It was also an attempt to paint an illustration that has more than one character. I tried to create a good overall composition using the characters' positionings, poses, and size contrast. One of the most time-consuming parts to paint was the monster's stone-like spikes."*

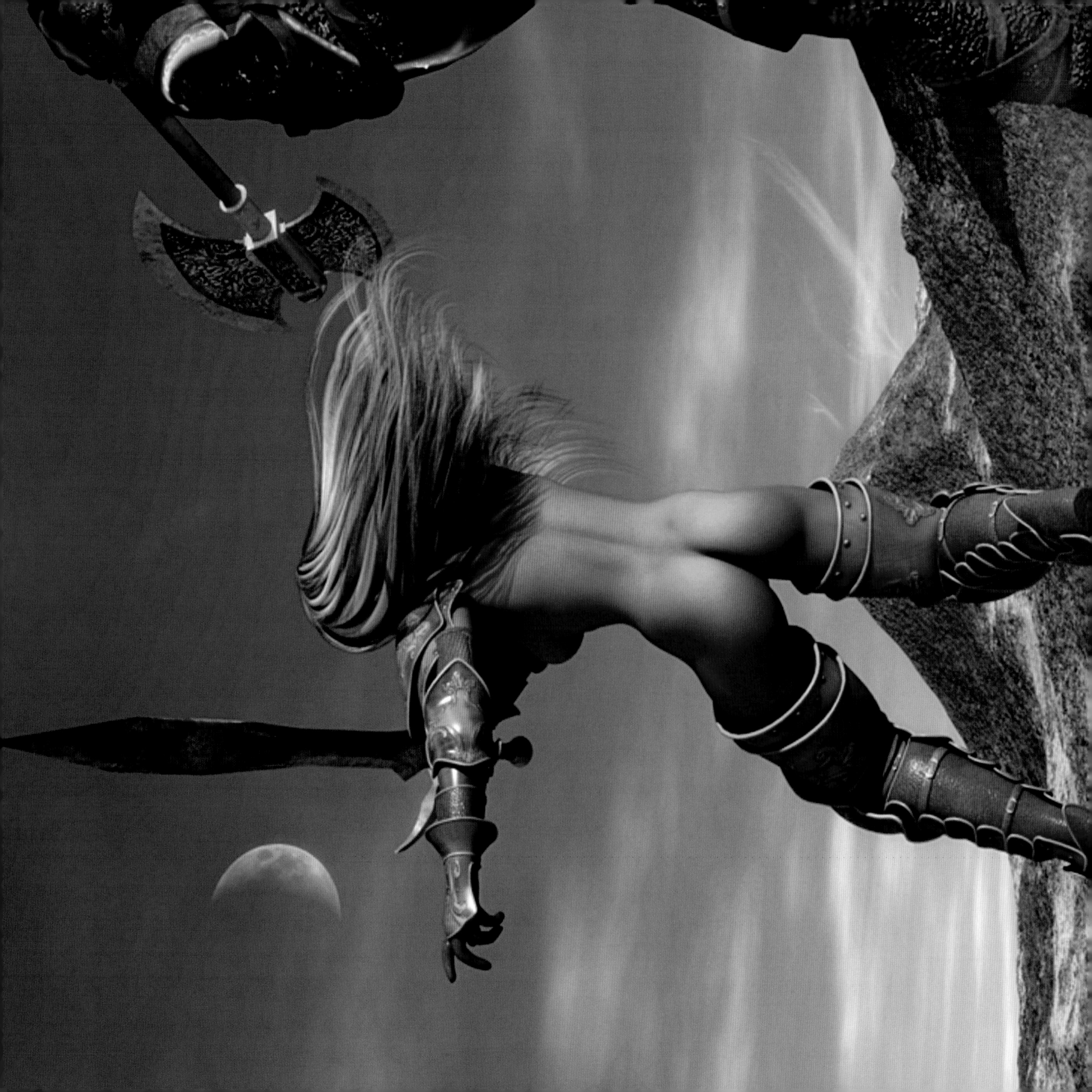

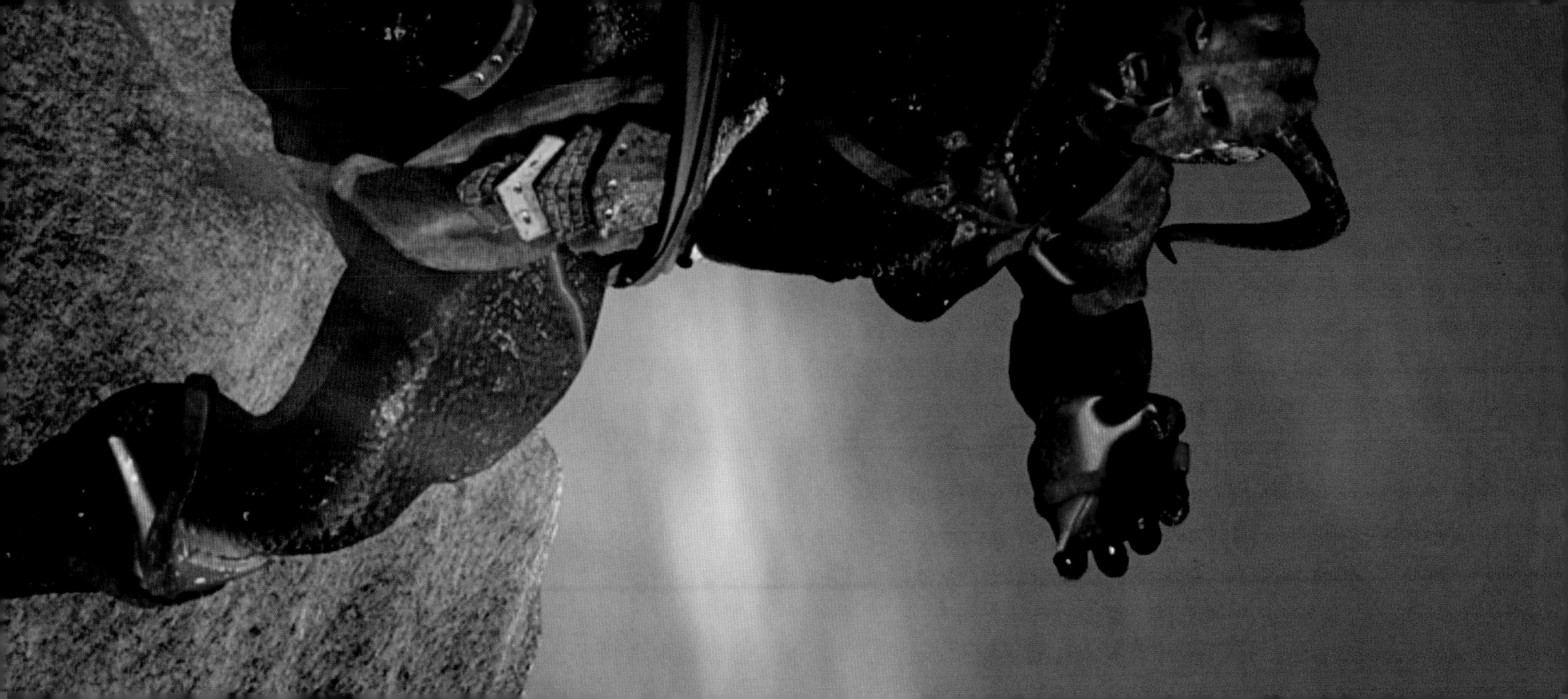

▶ **Dragon Pet**
Uwe Jarling
Corel Painter
and Adobe Photoshop
www.jarling-arts.com

"What could be more fun for a fantasy artist than to paint a dragon or a well-formed amazon? The answer: paint them both in one picture! This was a really fun piece done mostly for my own enjoyment and hopefully for yours too. As for the technique, I used Painter for painting and Photoshop for color corrections. I mostly used Painter's watercolor brushes to get the desired effect, and for the opaque colors I used Painter's oils and its wet grainy blender."

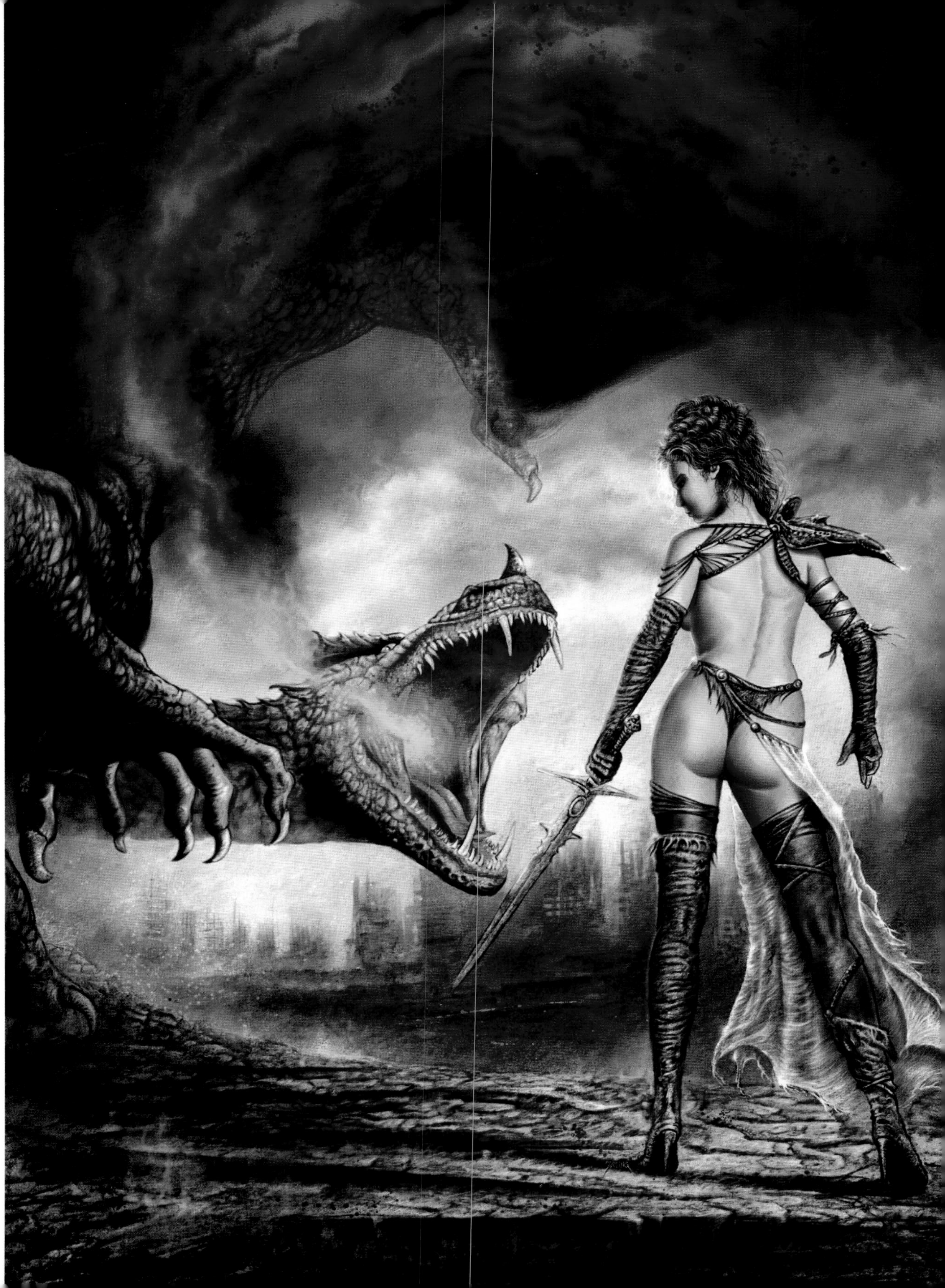

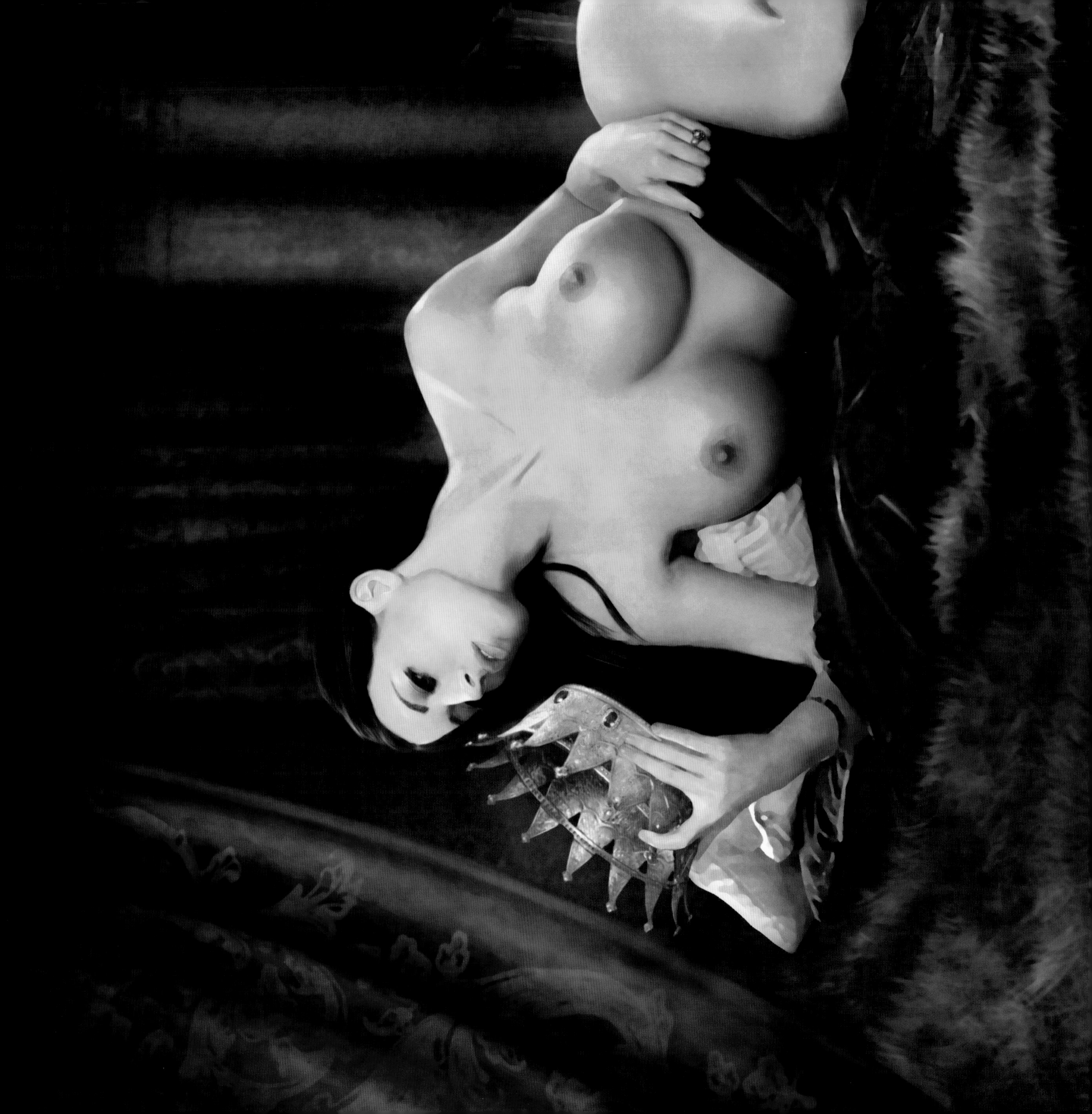

CHAPTER 6
VIVACIOUS VIXENS

▲ King's Favorite
AJ Serov
Cinema 4D and Adobe Photoshop
www.ajserov.com

"This is a scene from the long forgotten past. A quick look at the royal chamber. In the absence of the king, a serving wench is playing with his crown. The king believes that it is he who possesses the highest power in the land. But is this really so? I wanted to create a sensual portrait in a medieval environment. Some elements were created and rendered in Cinema 4D first. Then they were brought into Photoshop for painting. The more I work in Photoshop, the more this program amazes me. The textured brushes, the alpha adjustment layers, the alpha masks — they were invaluable in making this picture. I was striving to create the illusion of tons of details without actually detailing everything."

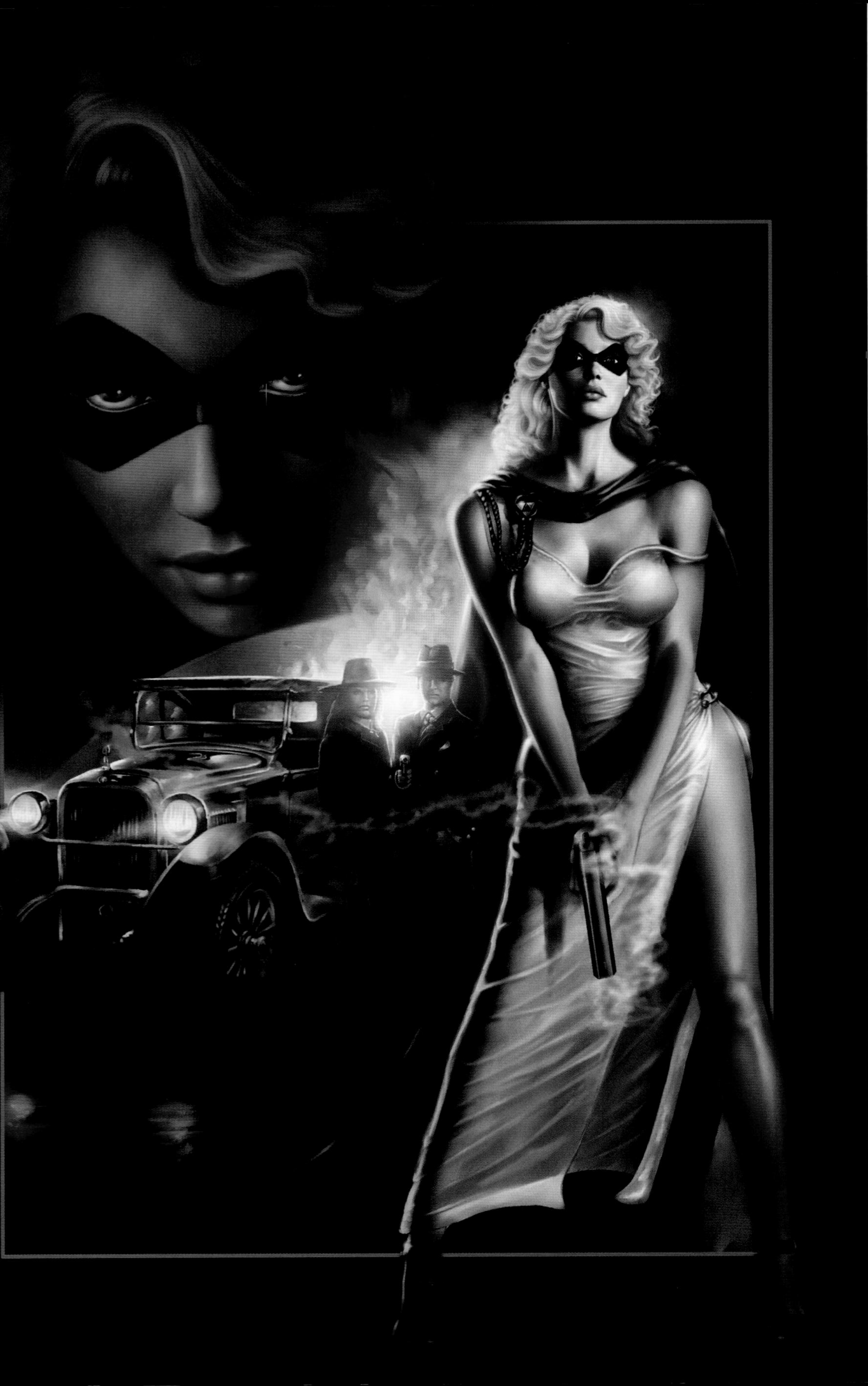

◀ **Domino Lady**
Uwe Jarling
For Moonstone Books
Corel Painter
and Adobe Photoshop
www.jarling-arts.com

"This piece was a commission from Moonstone Books for a Domino Lady *graphic novella. This piece was extremely fun to paint as I really enjoy doing some pulp covers every once in a while. As for the process, as usual I used Painter and Photoshop, Painter for painting and Photoshop at the end for minor color corrections. I'm really glad I used digital media for this illustration as there were so many changes before we got the look we wanted that it would have been extremely frustrating had I done it with traditional media. The painting process is almost the same for digital and traditional media, but when it comes to changes, digital is much, much easier!"*

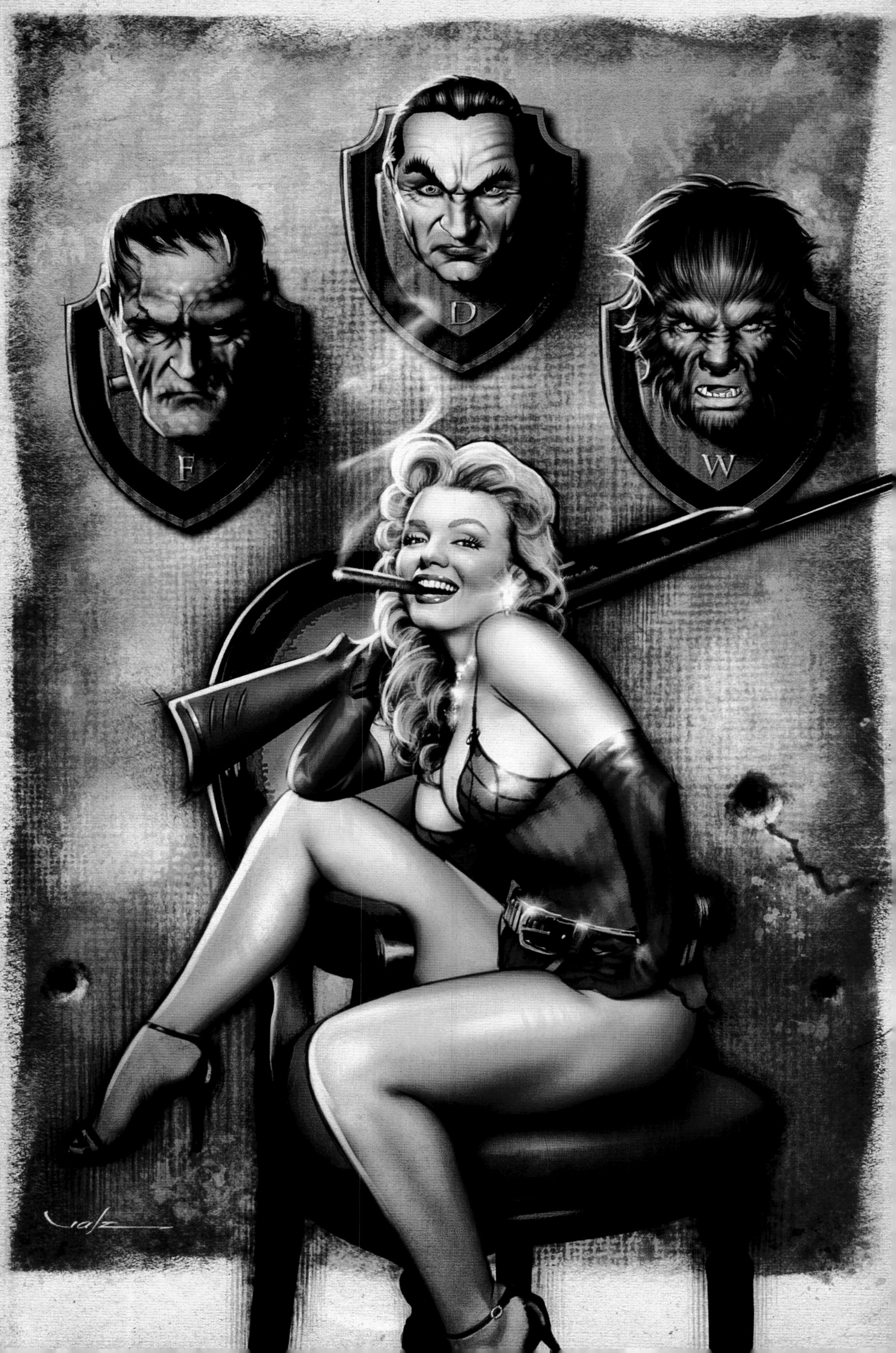
D
F
W

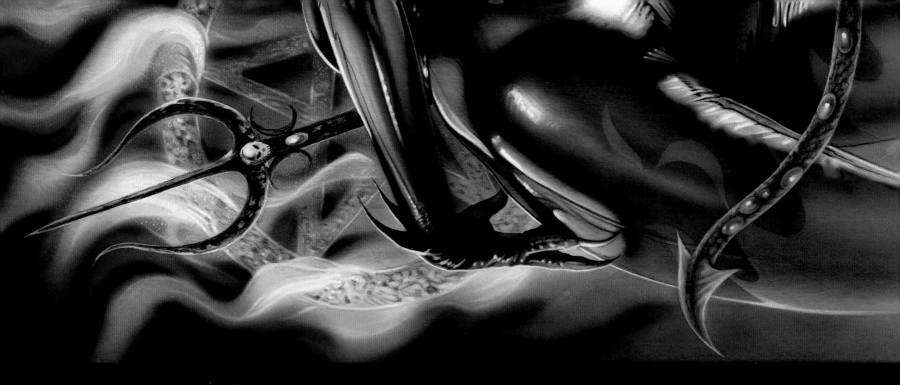

▲ **Devil Girl**
Michael Calandra
Acrylics and colored pencil
www.calandrastudio.com

"I was intrigued with the idea of doing a devil girl, but I didn't want to do a 'cute', pinup-style painting. I wanted to paint a 'real' devil girl, so I chose model Bianca Beauchamp to collaborate on a sexy latex devil girl, complete with pitchfork and flames. The idea was to create a seductive image and give it some motion with the flames."

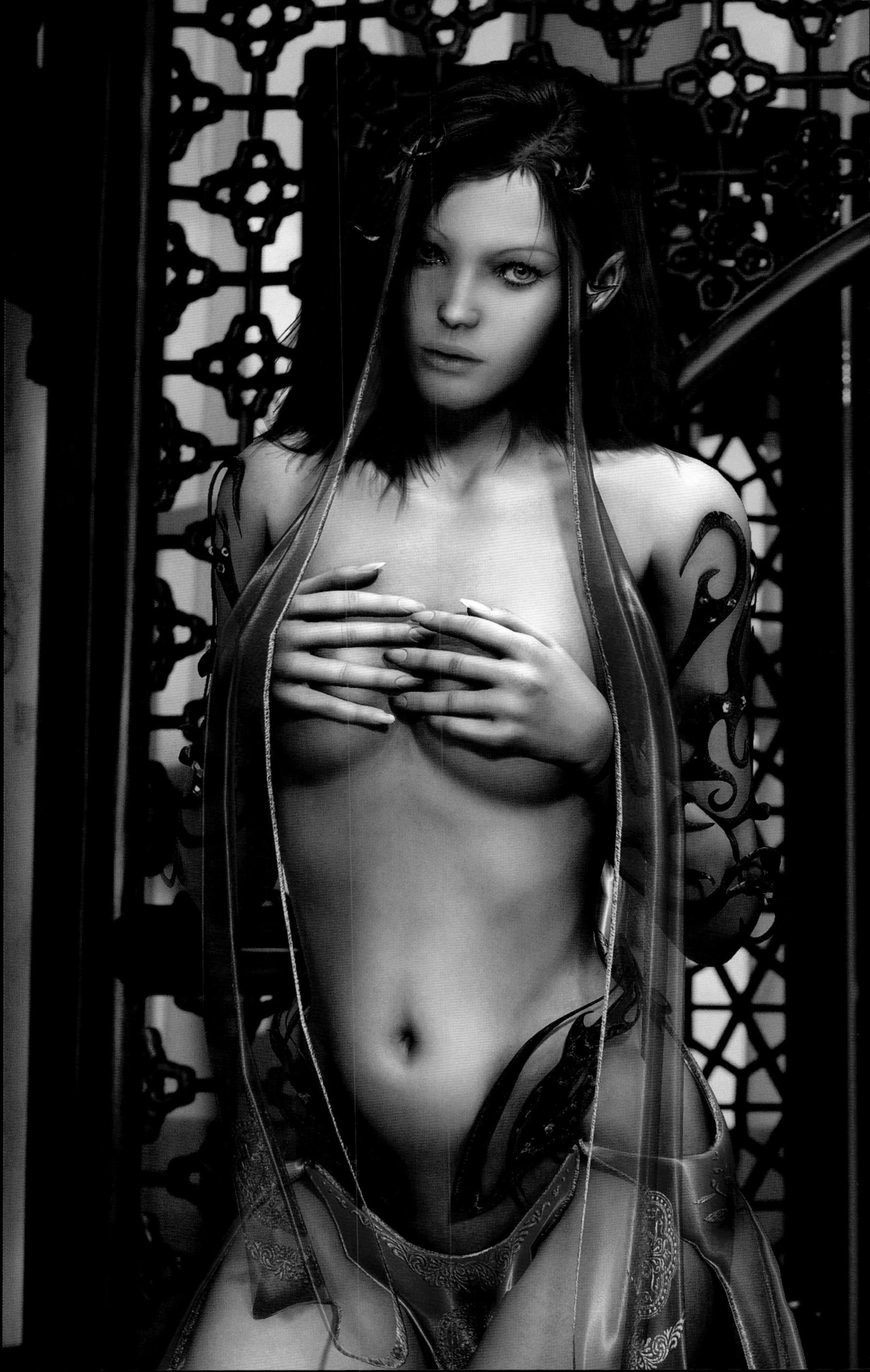

▶ **Shy**
Guido Leber
Poser and Adobe Photoshop
www.goor.deviantart.com

With this piece Leber confronts the viewer with the sexuality of the character facing us. There is something innocent about her, as if she challenges you to be worthy of her trust and the bounty that would bring. She forces us to look at our desire for her, to test our motives. The image started with a rudimentary 3-D model created in Poser in order to get the anatomy entirely correct, then rendered in Photoshop for details. The quality of the finish is extraordinary, we really feel her skin, and we don't doubt the reality of her presence.

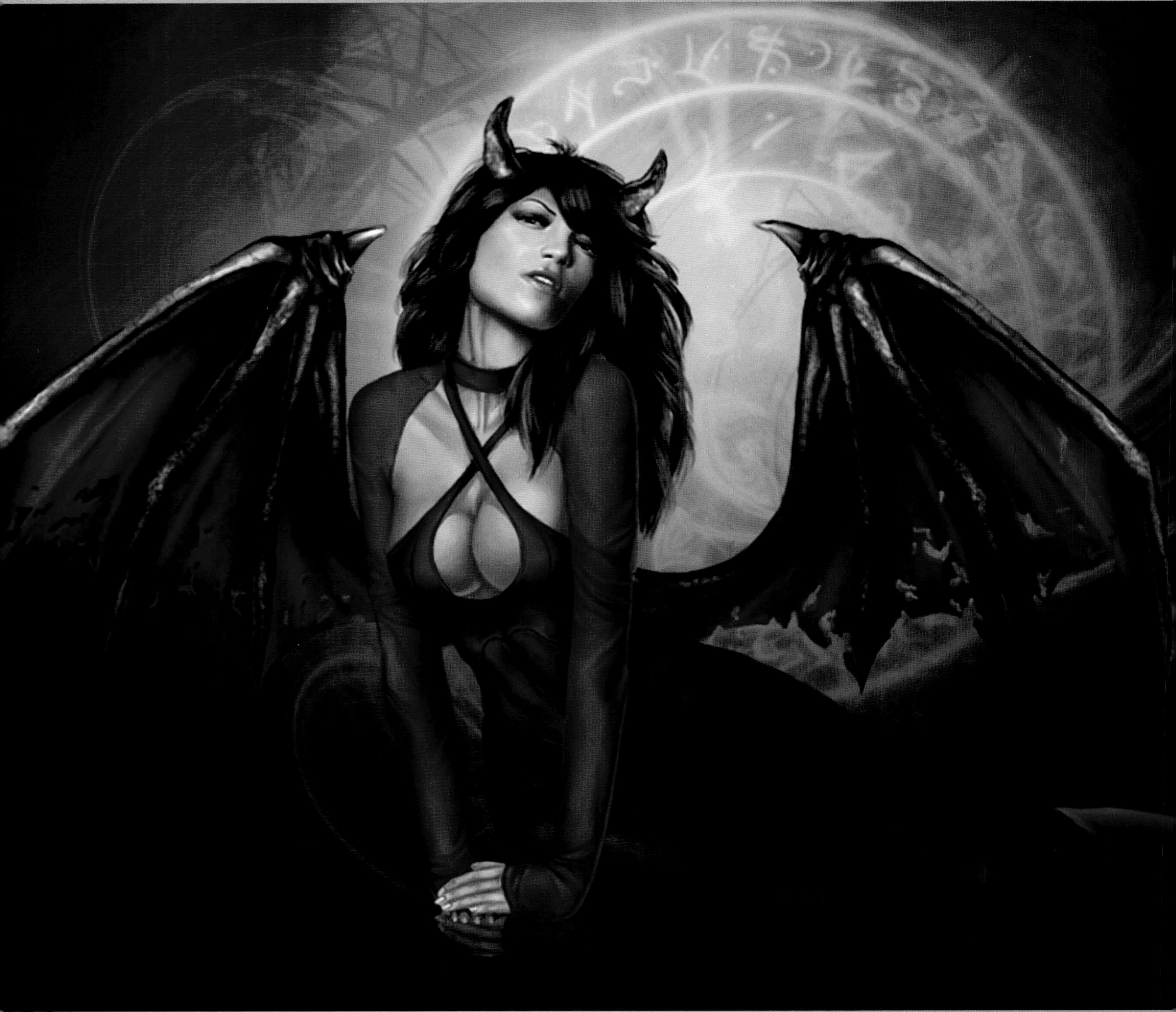

◀ **Demonic Obsession**
Vanette Kosman
Adobe Photoshop
www.vanettekosman.artworkfolio.com

"This character is a very sensual and voluptuous succubus who attracts men to devour them. I decided to create this character in a hyper-realistic style to bring her fully to life. I did not use a detailed background because I wanted to keep it simple to enhance her beauty. Her pose is erotic, showing her attributes, with her head tilted back and her hair in the wind. Red is the principal color, because I associate it with demons and blood, and it is very powerful tone, which captures perfectly the essence of the succubus."

▶ **Succubus by the Sea**
Vanette Kosman
Adobe Photoshop
www.vanettekosman.artworkfolio.com

"This drawing was inspired by the art of Gonzalo Ordoñez Arias. I tried to apply his technique and combine it with my style, and the result was a sassy and sensual succubus. Backgrounds are always an issue for me, but I managed to break this barrier of my previous drawings (where I work with simple patterns and very few colors) and give this character a physical area with an extensive sky and a vast ocean. I chose hard and shiny fabrics for the clothing to symbolize domain, and I tried to express in her face a mix of playfulness, sensuality, and wickedness."

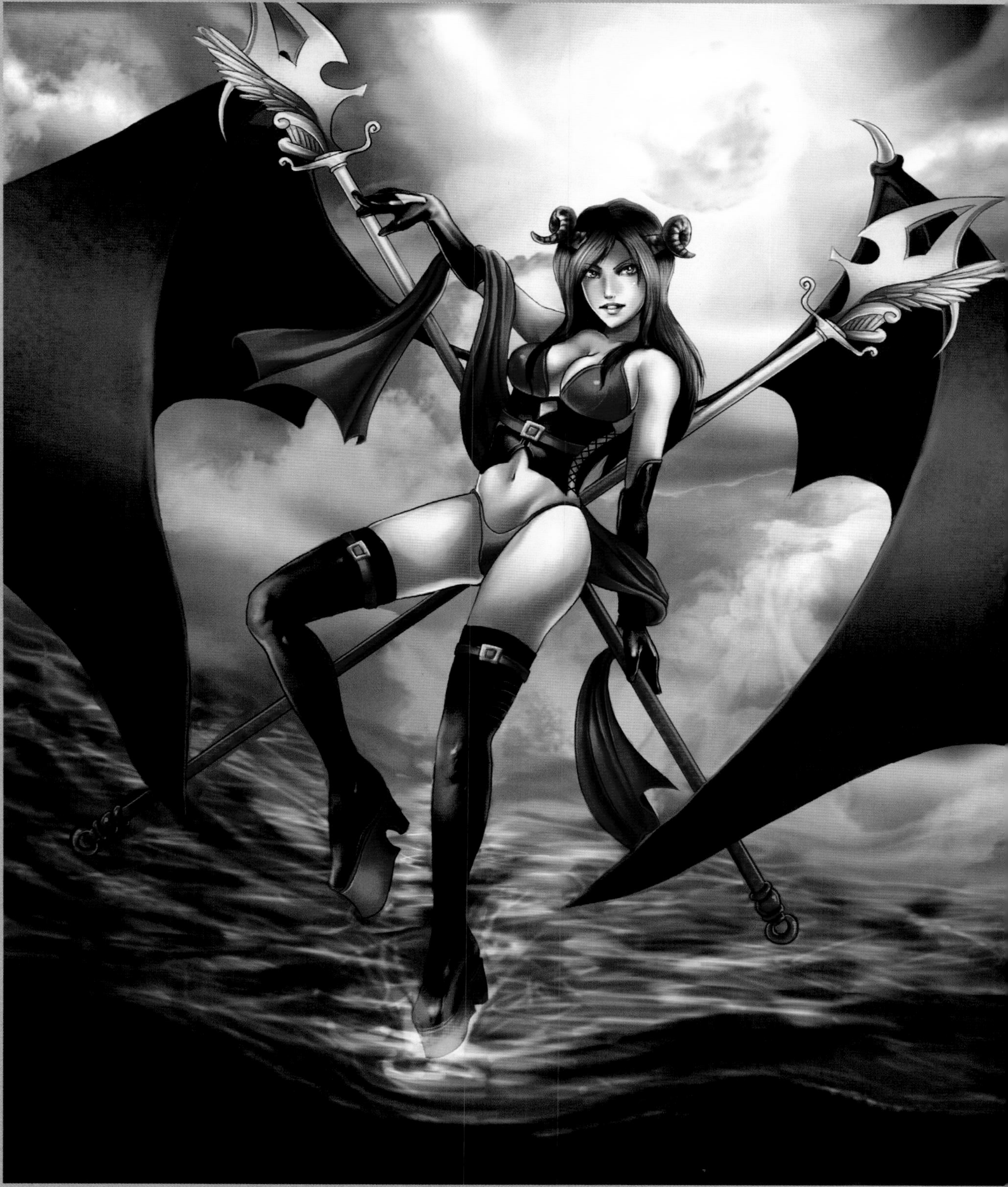

▶ **In the Throne Room**
Al Serov
Cinema 4D and Adobe Photoshop
www.alserov.com

"I wanted to create something dark and yet beautiful, something strange and sexy at the same time. I wanted to depict an exotic queen surrounded by her guards. At first it was difficult to decide how the guards were supposed to look. Should they be humans? Should they be beasts? They had to look spooky and weird but I did not want them to steal all the attention from the girl. After some consideration, I decided to choose the look of the Grim Reaper for the guards. I think it worked in the end. Some elements of this picture were at first created using 3-D modeling software. I like to work with Cinema 4D, as it is very intuitive and logical. After some fast modeling and quick rendering, I brought everything into Photoshop and started to paint."

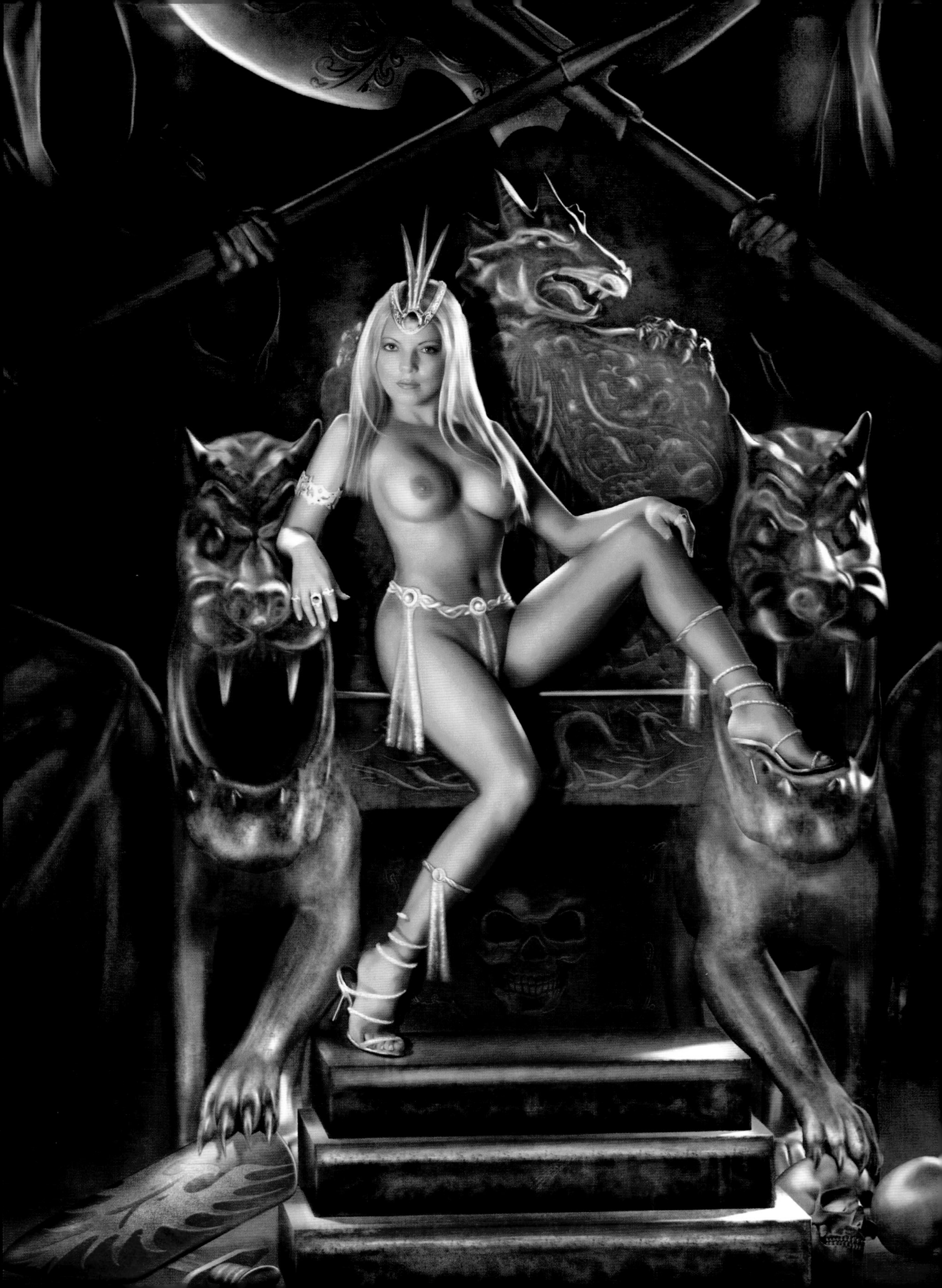

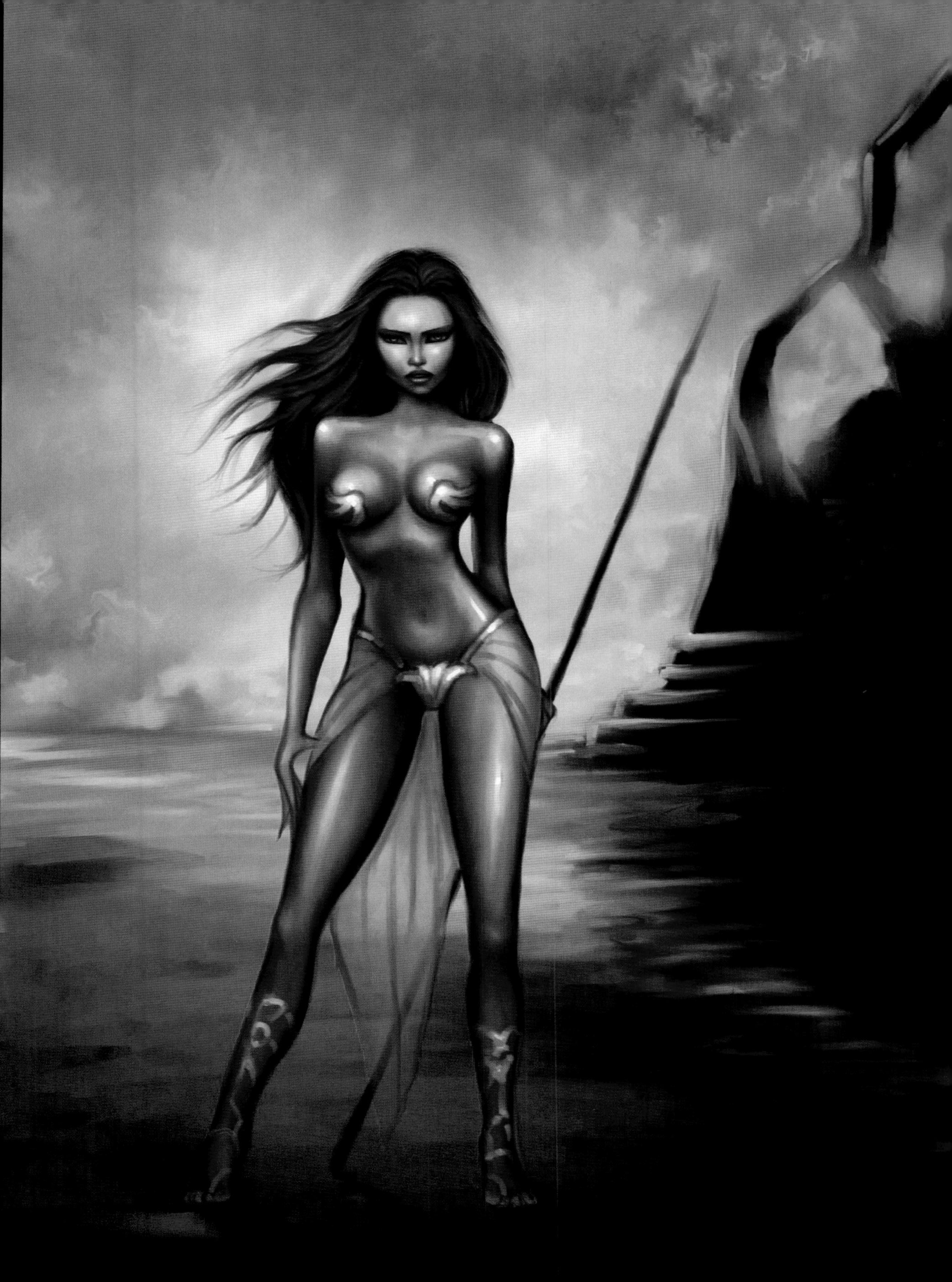

▶ **Vixen of Venus**
Frank Granados
Corel Painter X
www.granados602.deviantart.com

Granados describes this lady as "one of the seven guards of the temple of Venus." The atmosphere of this piece is desolate. "I have always loved drawing and painting the female form. I love the way the female body captures the light and shadows, and I have always tried to depict that in my artwork. I tend to put as little clothing as I can on the figures, so that the beauty of the female form can be seen and expressed through the play of light and shadow on the body. The attitude of the character is bold and defiant. I use the female face as the focal point in all my work, concentrating on the eyes. I don't go for that accurate photo-realistic look."

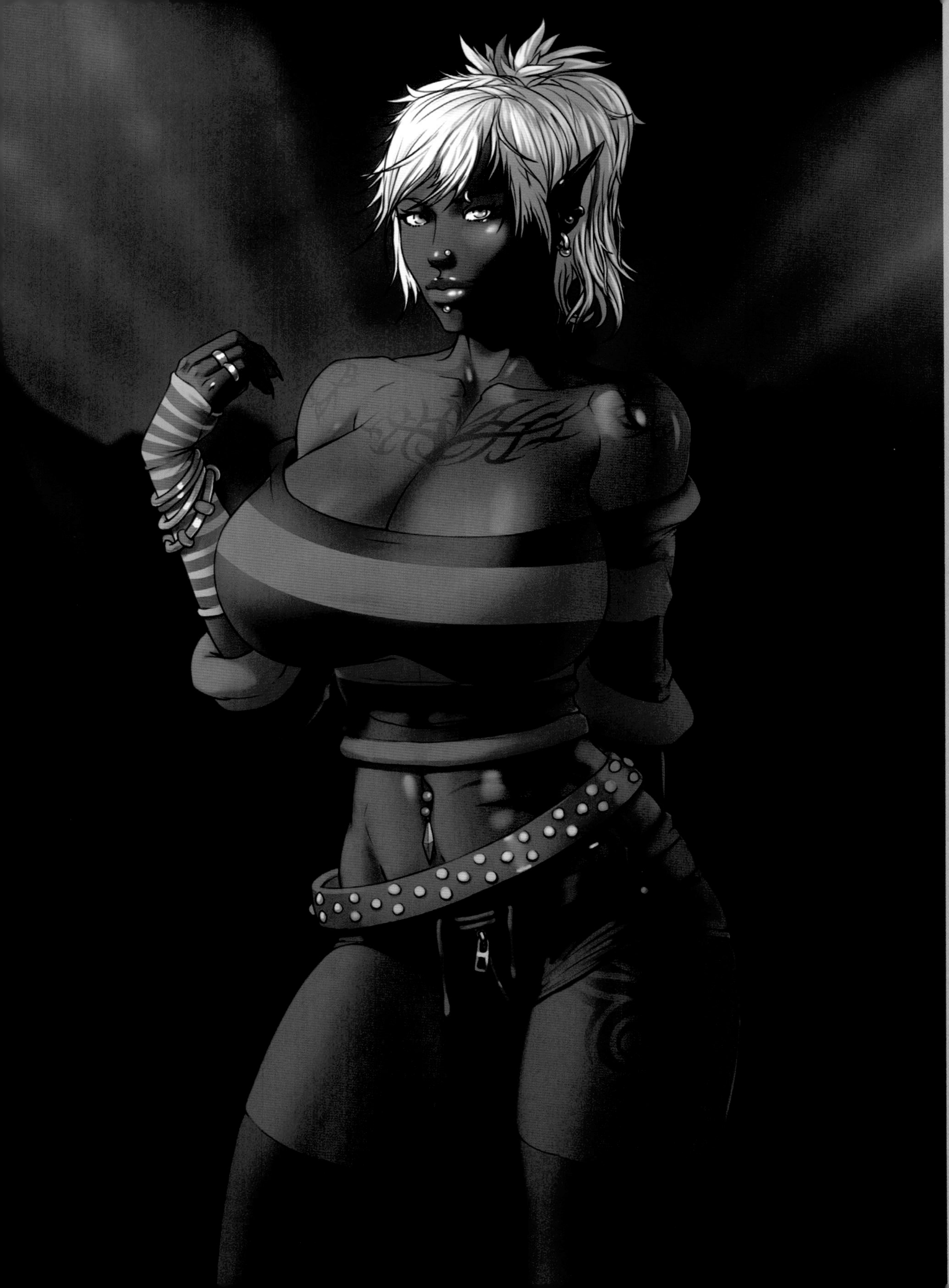

◄ **Clubbing Drow**
Dmitry Sergeev
Adobe Photoshop
http://dmitrys.deviantart.com

Sergeev's Clubbing Drow *gives a contemporary edge to the traditional fantasy character. "Dark elves, like any other, like to relax after a long working week. From the start, this scene was supposed to be very dark, so I paid a lot of attention to the lighting."*

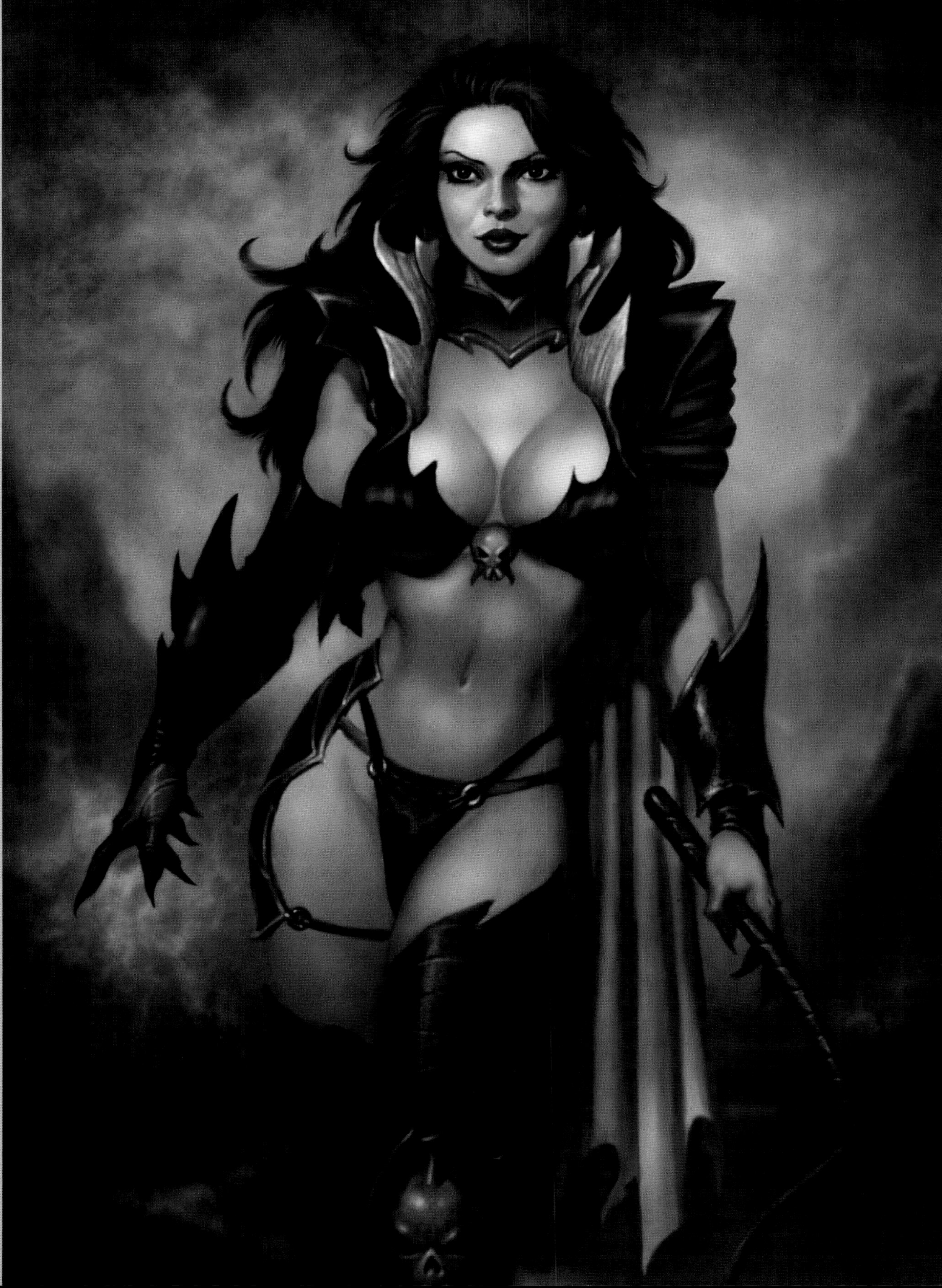

Black Queen
Paul Abrams
Pencil, marker, Prismacolor Pen, Adobe Photoshop, and Corel Painter
www.paulabrams.com

"I was looking over some drawing commissions I had recently completed, when I came across one of the Black Queen. The costume she wore seemed too traditional, so I began designing a new one. Using a standard pose so I could focus on the design, I worked it out with a mixture of pencils and markers, and a black prismacolor pen. The artwork was then scanned and worked on in Photoshop and Painter. I wanted an environment that would enhance the mood, and completed the piece using standard and custom brushes."

▶ **Mucha Girl**
Nacho Molina
Adobe Photoshop
and PaintTool SAI
www.nachomolina.deviantart.com
www.nachomolinablog.blogspot.com

"I wanted to give a comical look to this illustration, making a free interpretation of one of Alphonse Mucha's nymphs that he used in his fantastic art noveau advertisings, but giving her a modern Gil Elvgren-like pinup look with the spicy touch of Adam Hughes. I started in Photoshop, with a rough but accurate drawing of the figure and the composition. After that, using PaintTool SAI, I traced all the line work of the figure, the hair, and the background. Finally, again in Photoshop, I continued painting the illustration until it was complete. I wanted to mix elements that had volume with other plain elements to avoid loosing the lithography feel of the original."

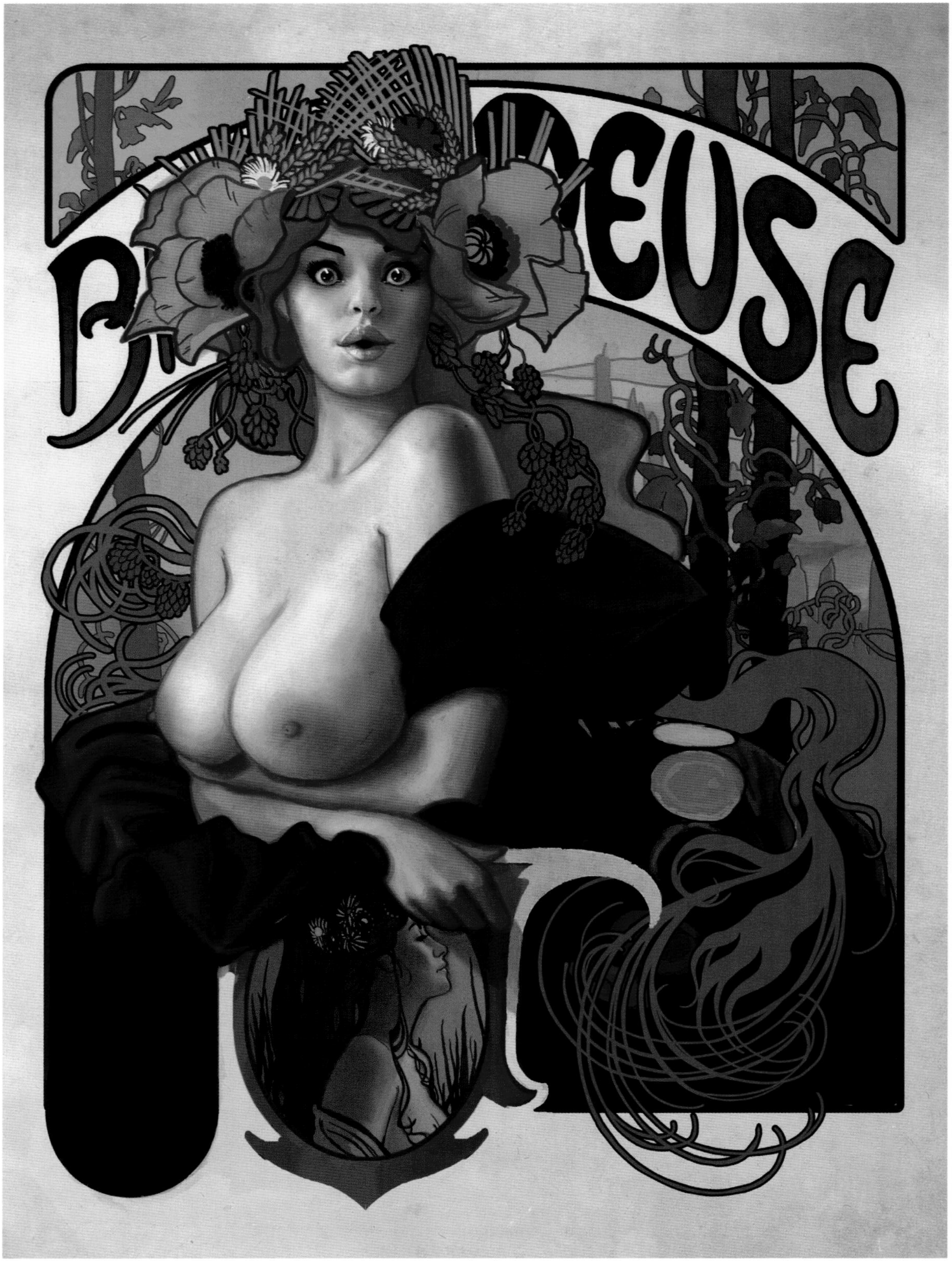

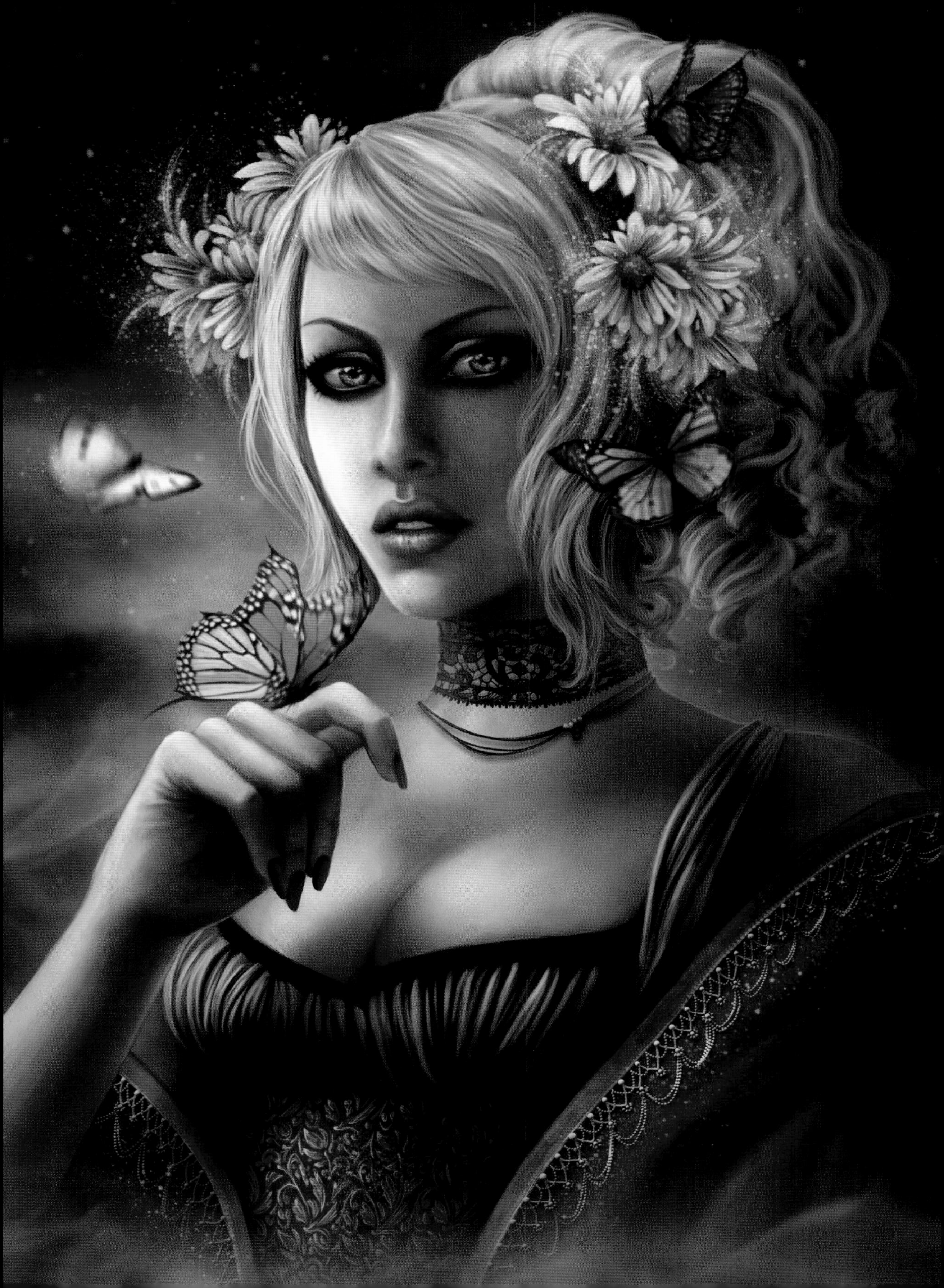

▶ **After Dusk**
Gracjana Zielinska
Pencil, Adobe Photoshop, and Corel Painter
www.vinegaria.com

"A sensual woman, surrounded by curious butterflies that reflect her unearthly gaze. Warm mood but with a subtle hint of danger —that was the idea. I used a reference for her hand (my own, in the mirror) and studied photos of butterflies to get those little creatures right. The butterflies create an interesting contrast —being a symbol of innocence and sensuality at the same time."

Dark Queen

Lorenzo Di Mauro
Pencil, Adobe Photoshop,
and Corel Painter
www.lorenzodimauro.com
http://llorenzoart.blogspot.com

"For this painting I had in mind a sort of haughty, seductive queen of darkness. Looking for references, I was inspired by a great photo of a model and used only this. Often it is not so simple, and when making my pieces, to get what I want, I take parts from several photo references. This time I fell in love with the sensuality of the pose, the sexy outfit, and great lights, which I tried to recreate, integrating them with the other fantastical elements of her regal clothing that are based on my fantasy."

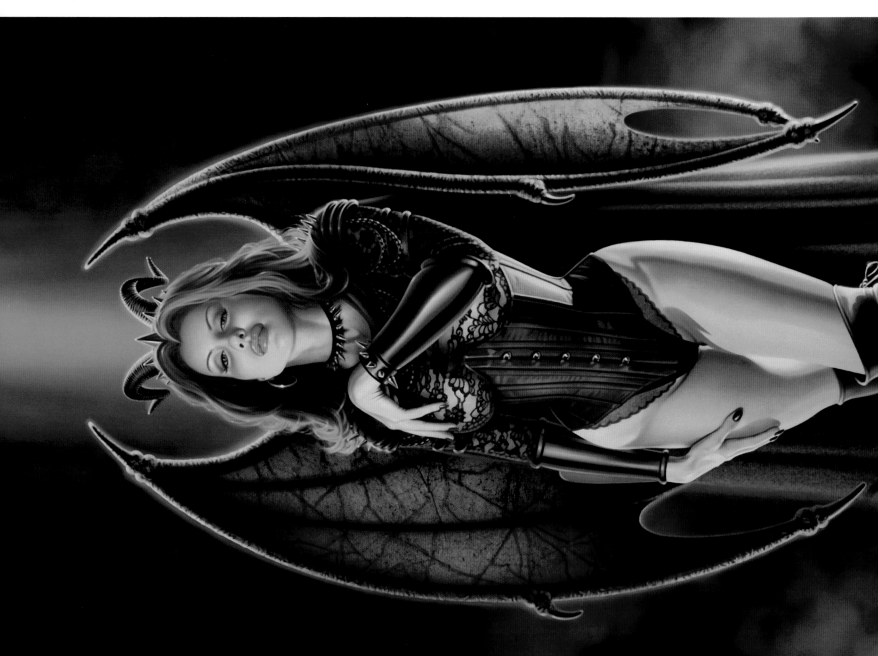

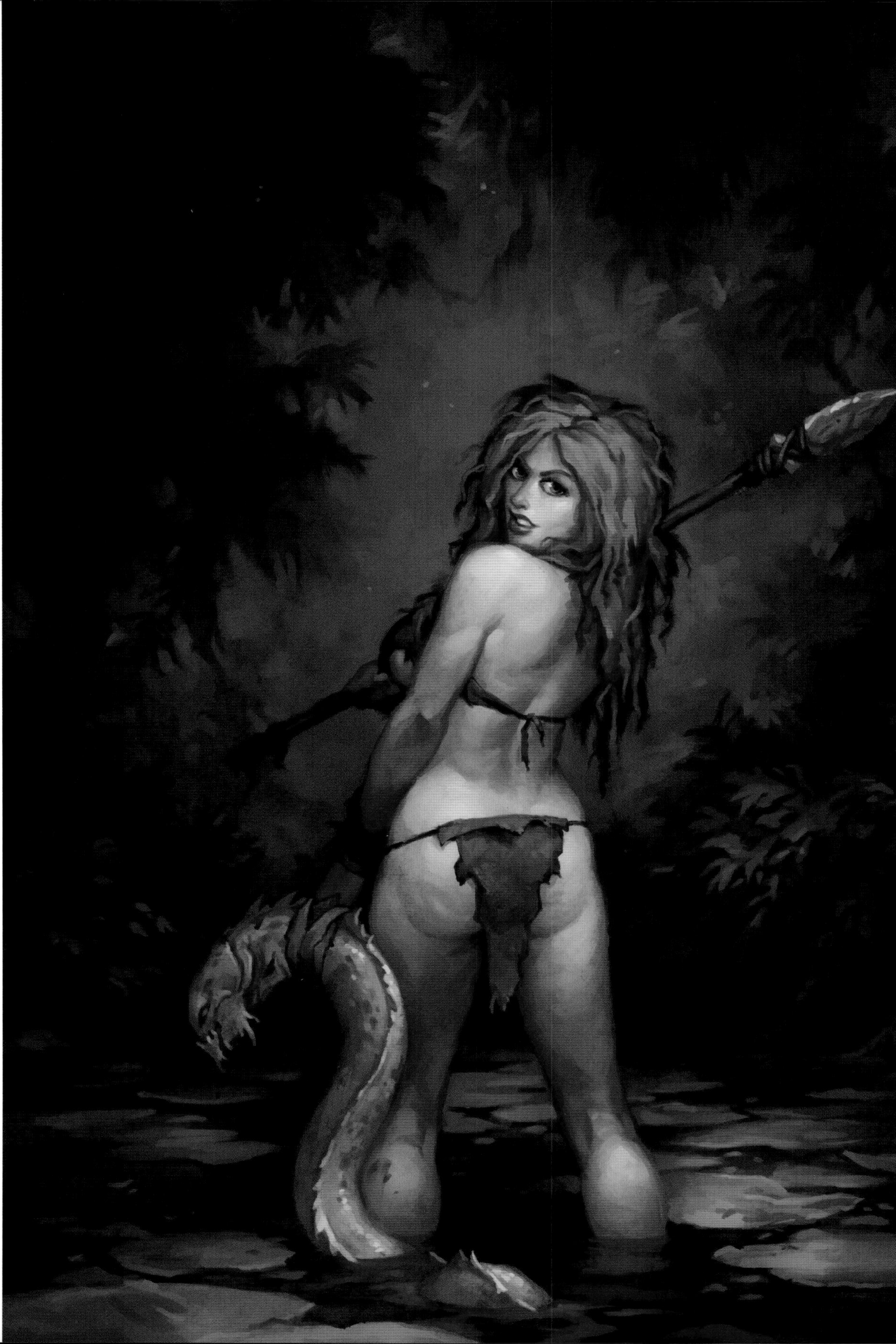

Gone Fishin'
Matt Dixon
Adobe Photoshop
www.mattdixon.co.uk

"A sense of confidence, power, and capability is equally as attractive as the most dangerous set of womanly curves. This amazonian huntress is clearly a match for her treacherous environment, the dangerous creatures which inhabit it, and no doubt any males that may cross her path."

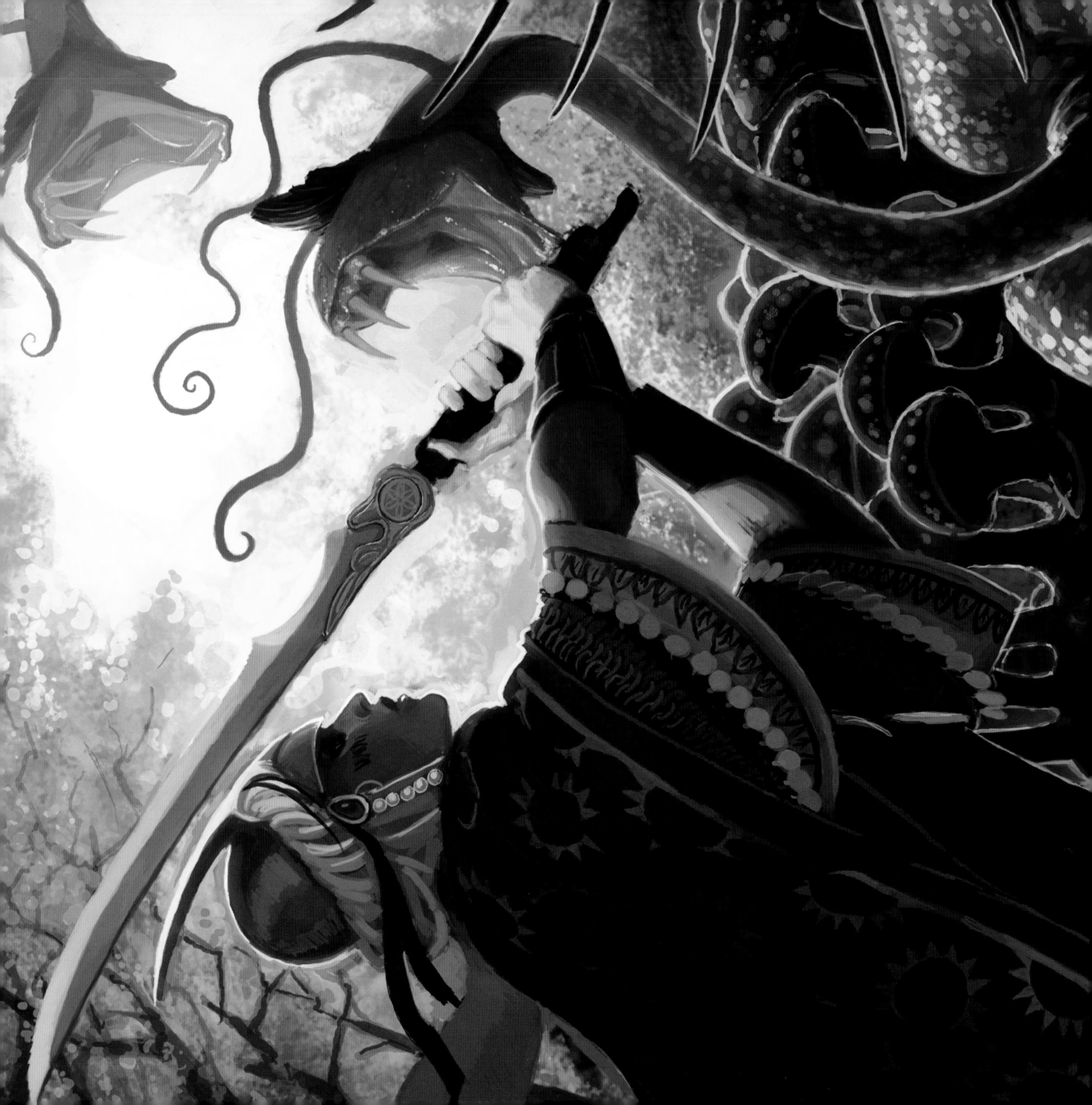

CHAPTER 7

ENCHANTING MAGIC

▼ **Pathfinder 10**
Francisco Rico Torres
For Paizo Publishing, LLC
Adobe Photoshop
and Corel Painter
www.pacorico.blogspot.com

"This is an illustration I did fo
Pathfinder Adventure Pat
#36: Sound of a Thousand
Screams. *The client asked m*
to paint Kyra fighting a stran
sneaky green woman in a wei
overgrown garden. This was f
to paint because they gave me
lot of freedom to design the pla
and the woman. To add some
contrast to the image I gave t
character a weird sexual feel a
a deadly poisonous look at the
same time. The plants are a m
between a flower, a snake, and
something else. The righteous Ky
(originally designed by Wayne
Reynolds) brings a bit of sanit
to the image."

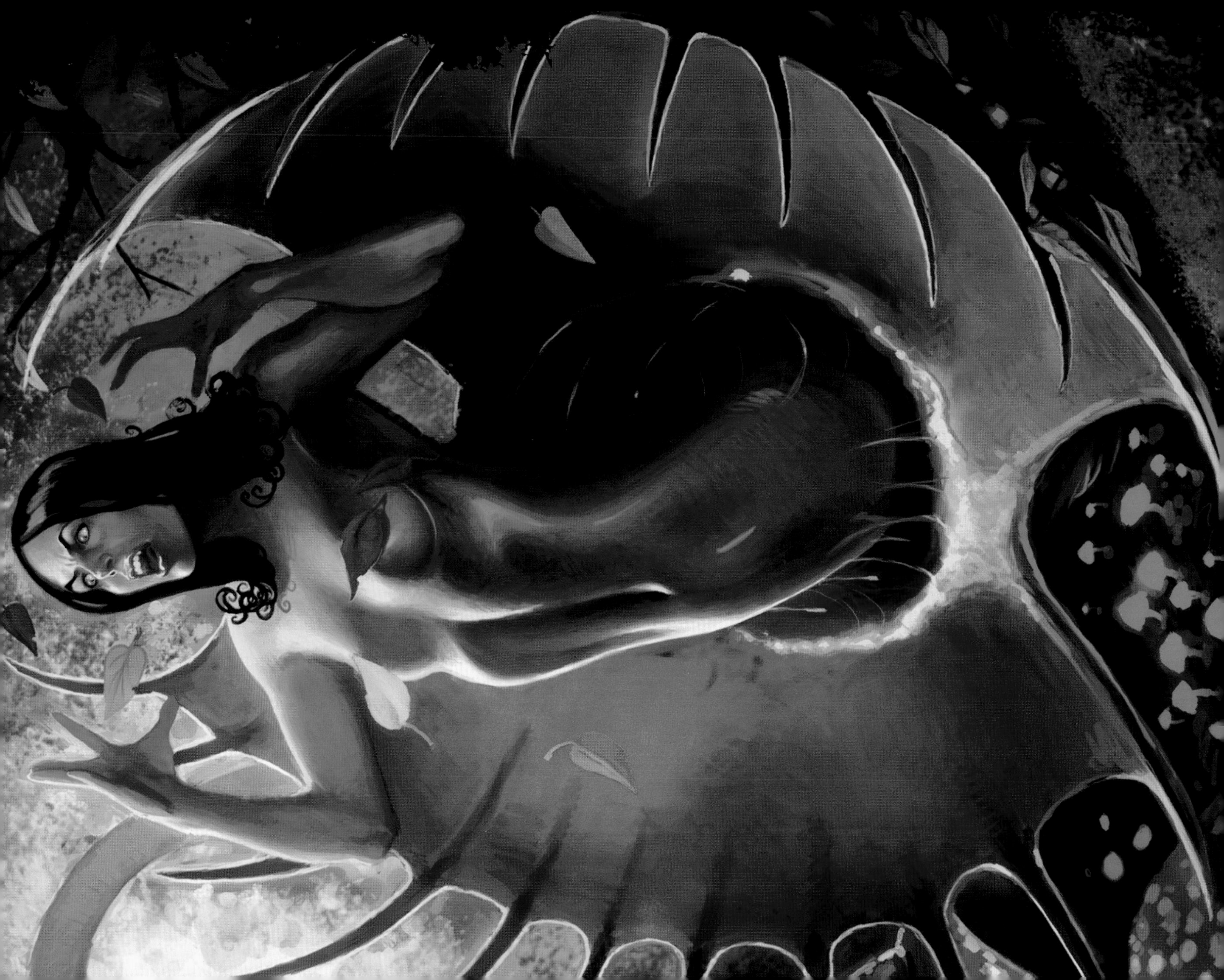

The Apprentice
RGUS
Poser Pro

"This piece was influenced by Middle-earth themes and the Jedi apprentices from Star Wars. The costume was added to bit by bit until a feel of darkness and fantasy was created. Selecting a dark and heavy skin texture added the right amount of congruity with the surrounding scene. I felt it lacked a certain focus without a dash of color, so I placed a fire ball at the end of her staff so that the eye moves upwards along her slender body to the intricacies of her headgear and strewn hair. The atmosphere was rendered in Poser Pro to give that extra feel of mysticism and magic. The image was made completely in Poser Pro, there was no additional postwork on the image in Photoshop."

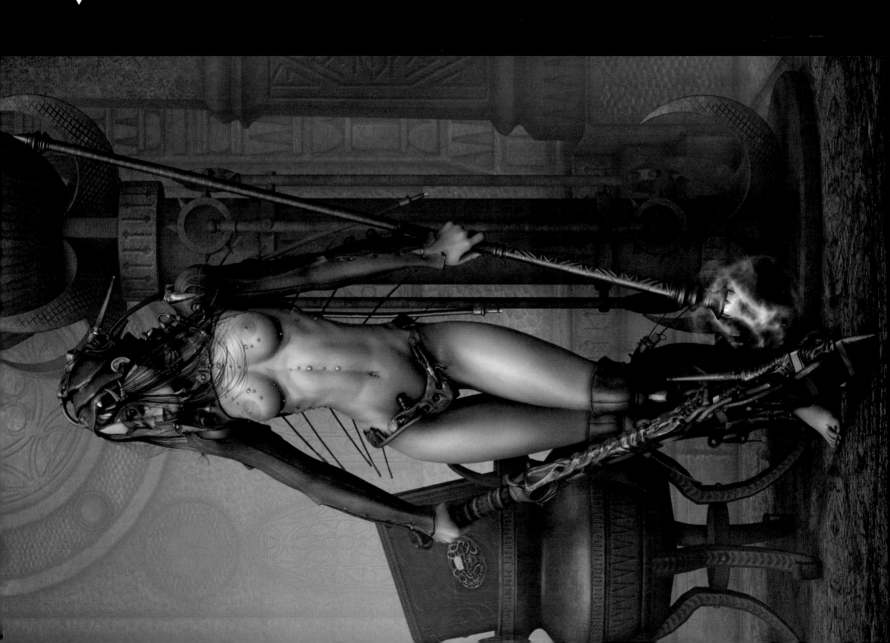

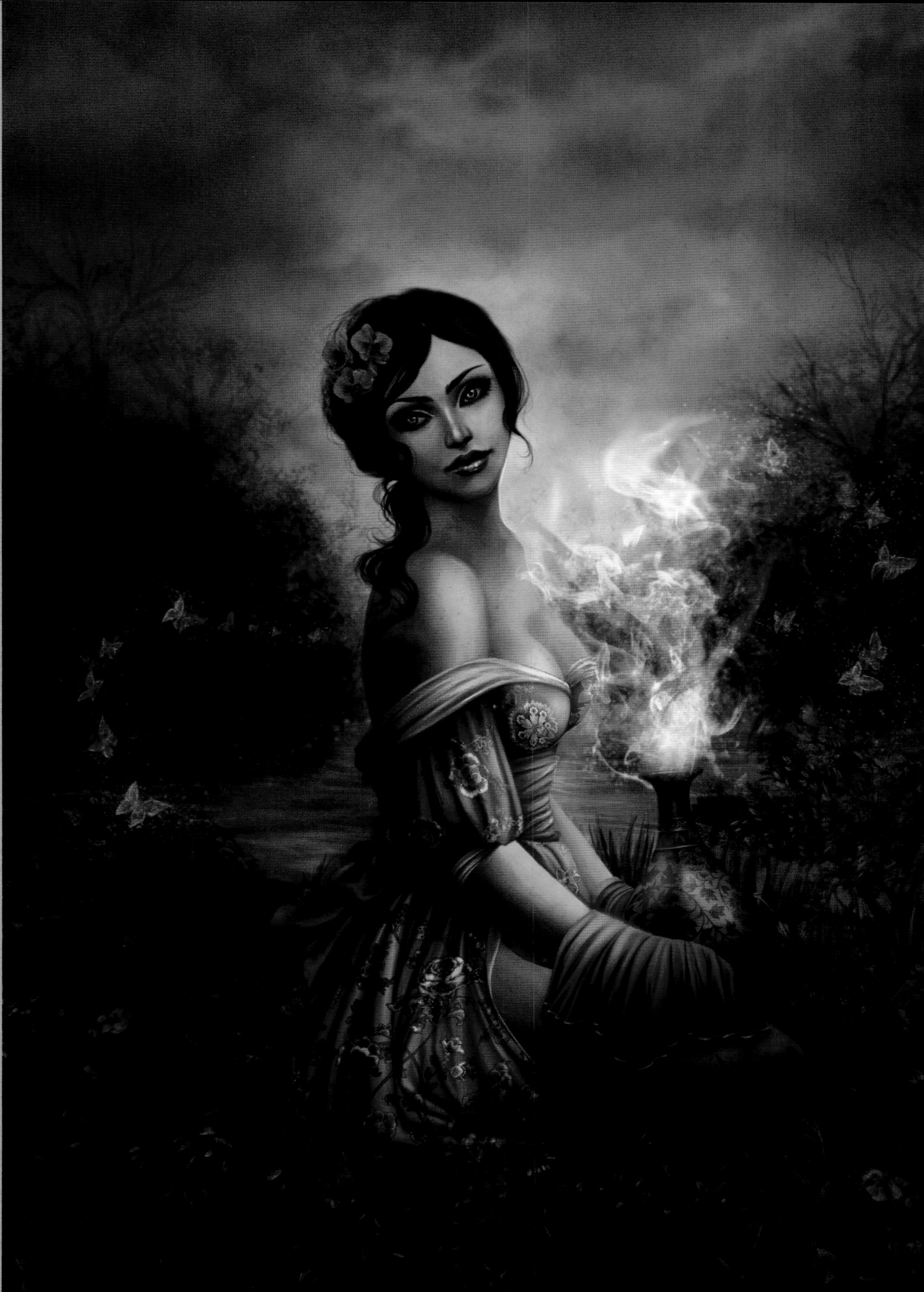

Sensual Dream
Gracjana Zielinska
Pencil, Adobe Photoshop, and Corel Painter
www.vinegaria.com

"I wanted to depict a sensual mood that was warm and a bit magical at the same time. So, this depicts a hot, late summer evening and a girl with a charming gaze bathed in the light of the setting sun and some magic. I didn't use any visual references, I treated this picture as an exercise in lighting and creating the right atmosphere. Red was the most used color here, even if added only lightly in a few places, as it usually is seen as a symbol of sensuality."

▶ **The Sword of Light**
Felipe Machado Franco
Pencil and Adobe Photoshop
http://finalfrontier.thunderblast.net

"This artwork started with the basic idea of a female character holding a sword. As I was creating the character, I thought about how I keep forgetting that space in any artwork is as important as the characters within it. So I created a basic element out of a trivial plane shape and gave it a stone-like texture. Out of that single action, I created the background's crazy-looking walls, the floor, the spots of light in it, the sword, and the armor on the character's arms. I did this by changing the size, form, and direction of the basic starting shape. But if you look closely at the illustration, you'll notice the element or shape is all around. I call this technique: SUTMTD or 'Speeding Up to Make the Deadline.'"

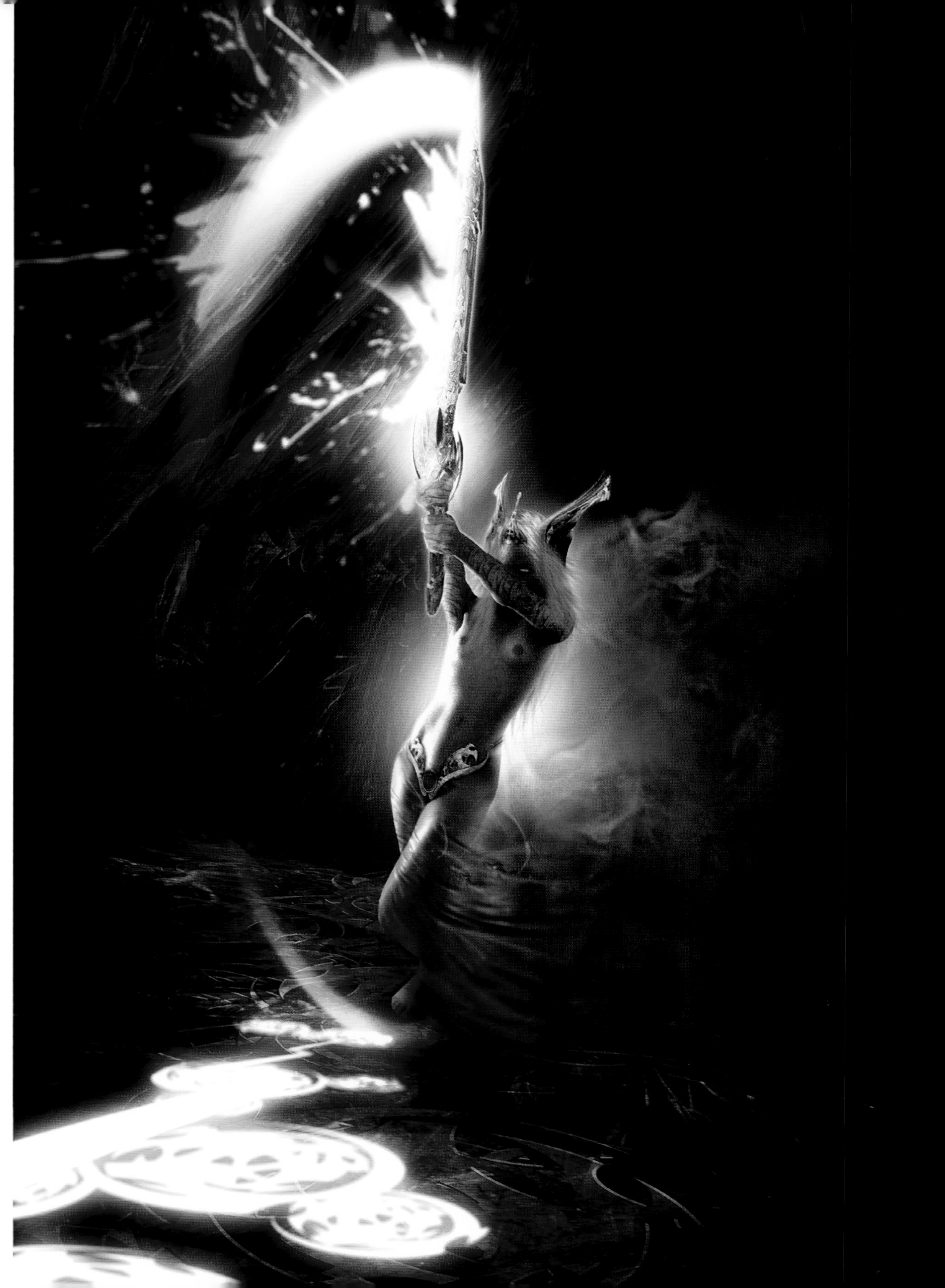

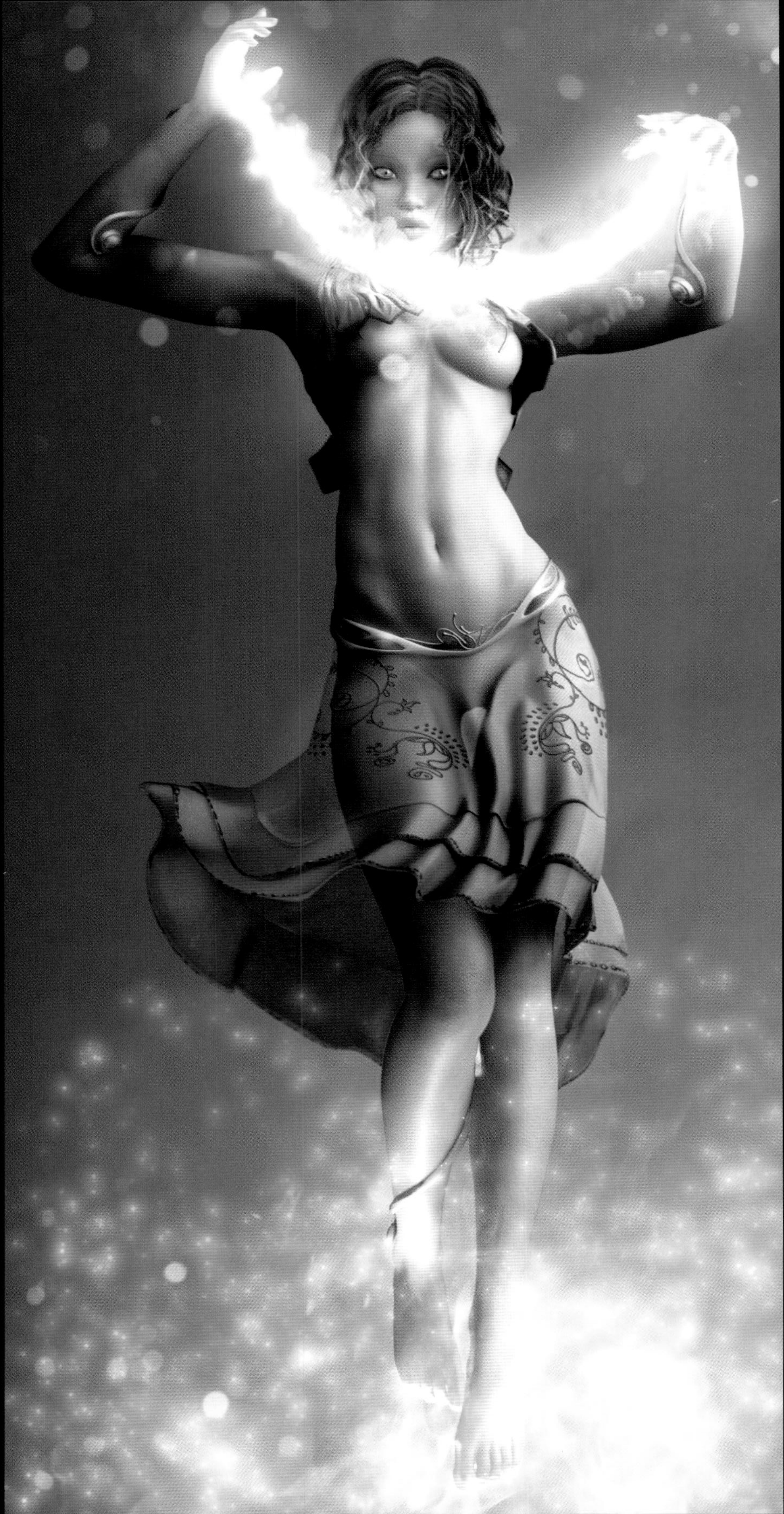

The Fate in your Hands
As Shanim & Siliphiel of Aery Soul
Maya, ZBrush, Adobe Photoshop, and Poser Pro
www.aerysoul.deviantart.com

"The setup for this image was done in Poser Pro where I put the clothes, hair, and textures on the female model, posed her, and adjusted the clothes to match her pose. I then imported her into Maya using the Poser Fusion plug-in. As the materials between the two tools do not translate well, I had to edit or recreate them in Maya, especially the skin. I then used Maya particles to create the 'magical' effects and rendered it with a IBL portal light and spotlight lighting setup. I opened it in Photoshop and added some sparkle effects using brushes, adjusted the color and contrast, and saved it. Alice's character, skin, hair, clothes, and poses were all created by us at Aery Soul."

Dragons Whisper
E.Crellin aka DarkElegance
Poser and Adobe Photoshop
http://art-of-darkelegance.daportfolio.com

"The inspiration for this was born from a concept of an opium den and
an exotic 'dragon woman,' with a slightly hallucinogen-induced waft
coming from her. A seductress with the narcotic enticement of opium.
I wanted to give a slightly surreal atmosphere to the lovely lady. This
piece took time, as it uses dynamic cloth simulation to get the drapes
of the robe. It is also an example of postwork, where you take your image
into a graphics editing program and add to it, correct flaws, anything."

Spirit of the Crow
Oliver Wetter
Adobe Photoshop
http://fantasio.info

"In ancient mythology the crow is the guardian of ceremonial magic and healing. Crows are the bringers of messages from the spiritual world, which otherwise would have to dwell beyond the realms of time and space. 'One who has the honor of having a crow fly by her side, is an individual who has the role of carrying souls lost in pain, denial, bitterness or ill intent, into the light of forgiveness and self-awareness.' My goal was to achieve an art nouveau piece combined with erotic fantasy that creates the feeling of motion within a static frame."

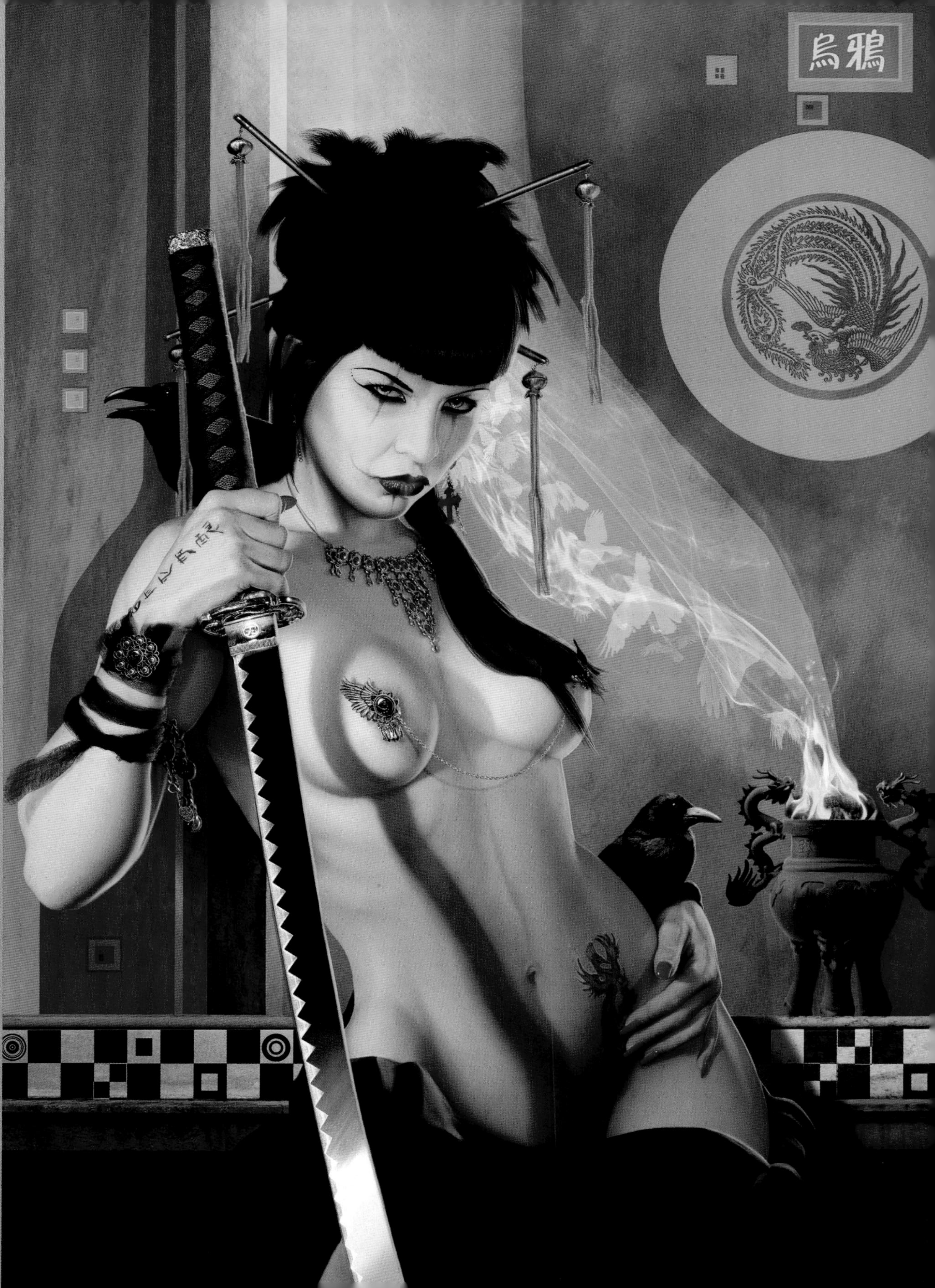
烏鴉

▶ **Autumn**
Anne Cain
Graphite and Adobe Photoshop
www.annecain-art.com

"This illustration was originally created for a personal commission in October, the perfect time of year to be inspired by the richness of the color in the landscape and the seasonal change. I have fond memories of gathering leaves as a child, captivated by the bold reds and crisp golds in the foliage, and these recollections set the palette for Autumn. *The pose and use of a male figure as an allegory for the season is based on the classical tradition in Greek and Roman art, and it complements wonderfully the idea that fall is the time of harvest, change, and a celebration of life."*

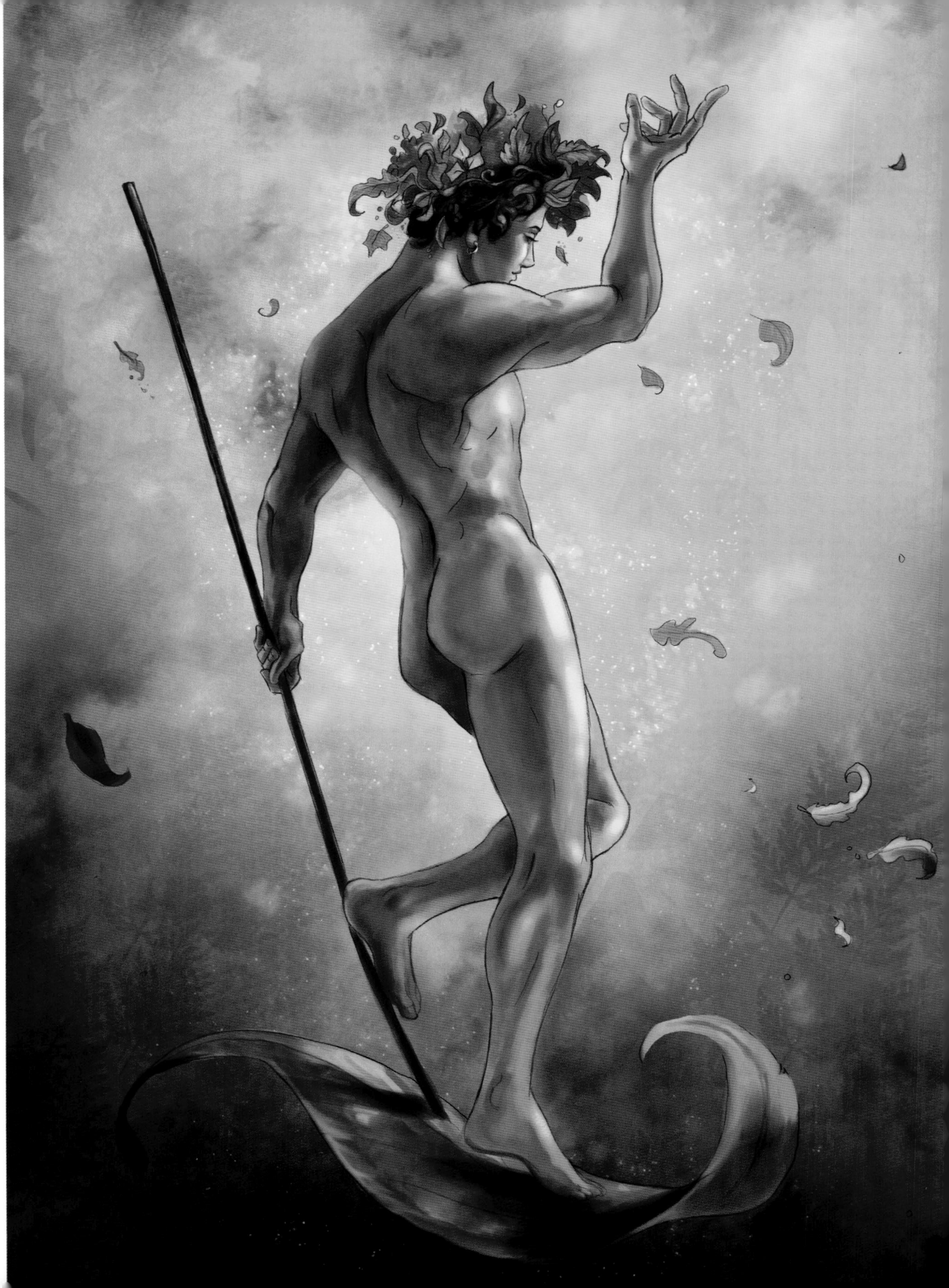

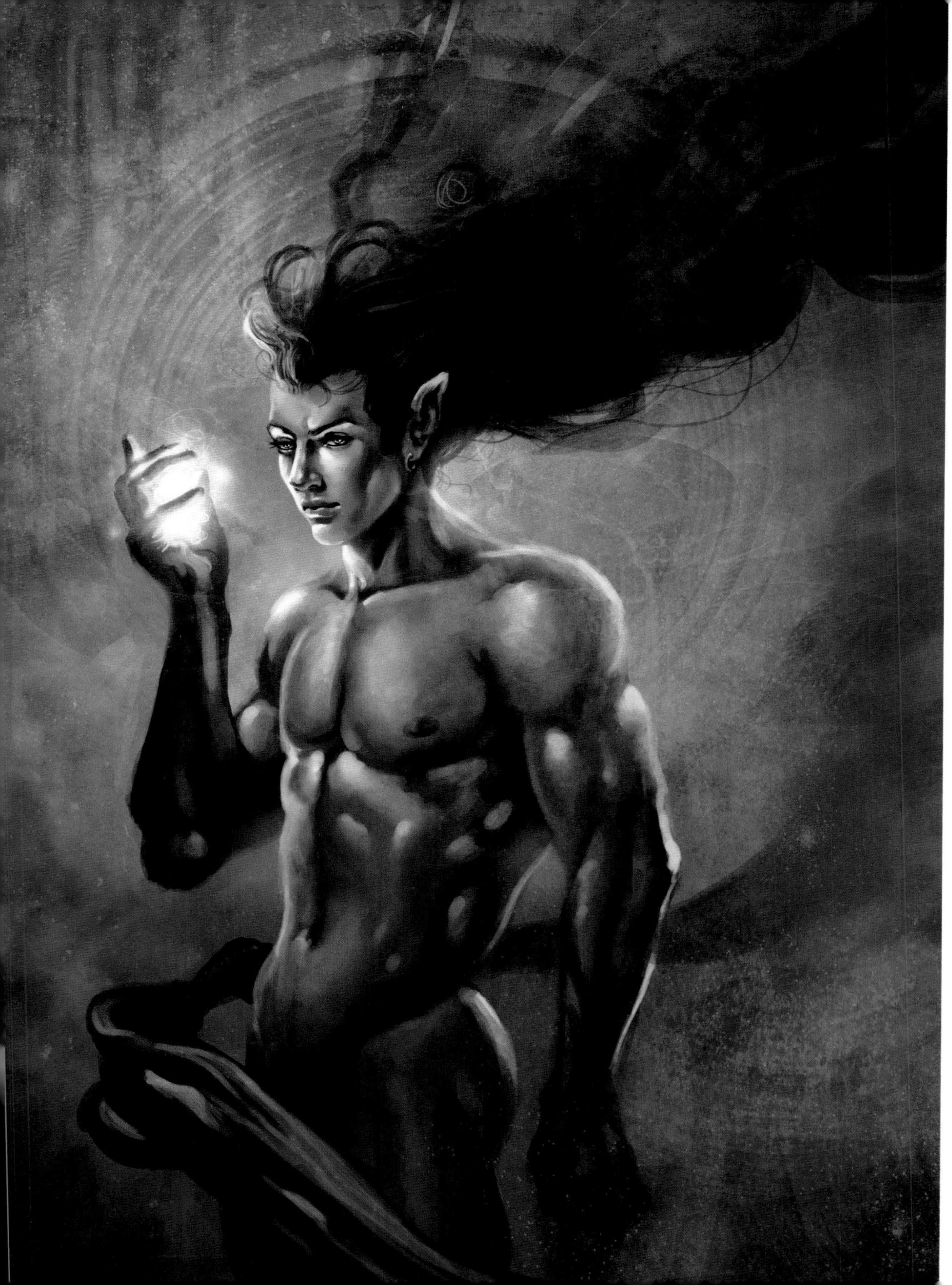

◀ **Dark Magik**
Anne Cain
Graphite and Adobe Photoshop
www.annecain-art.com

"The allure of magic and the sensuality of the elven race — these are incredibly fertile sources of artistic inspiration. They ignite the imagination in a unique way that no other muse can, and I use these themes in much of my artwork, bringing to life the worlds of sorcery and fantasy that exist in my mind's eye. Dark Magik *explores these themes of the supernatural and the immortal, with an undercurrent of sensuality in the beauty of the male form. He is an elven lord of magic, the power that courses through him stems from his life-force and sexuality."*

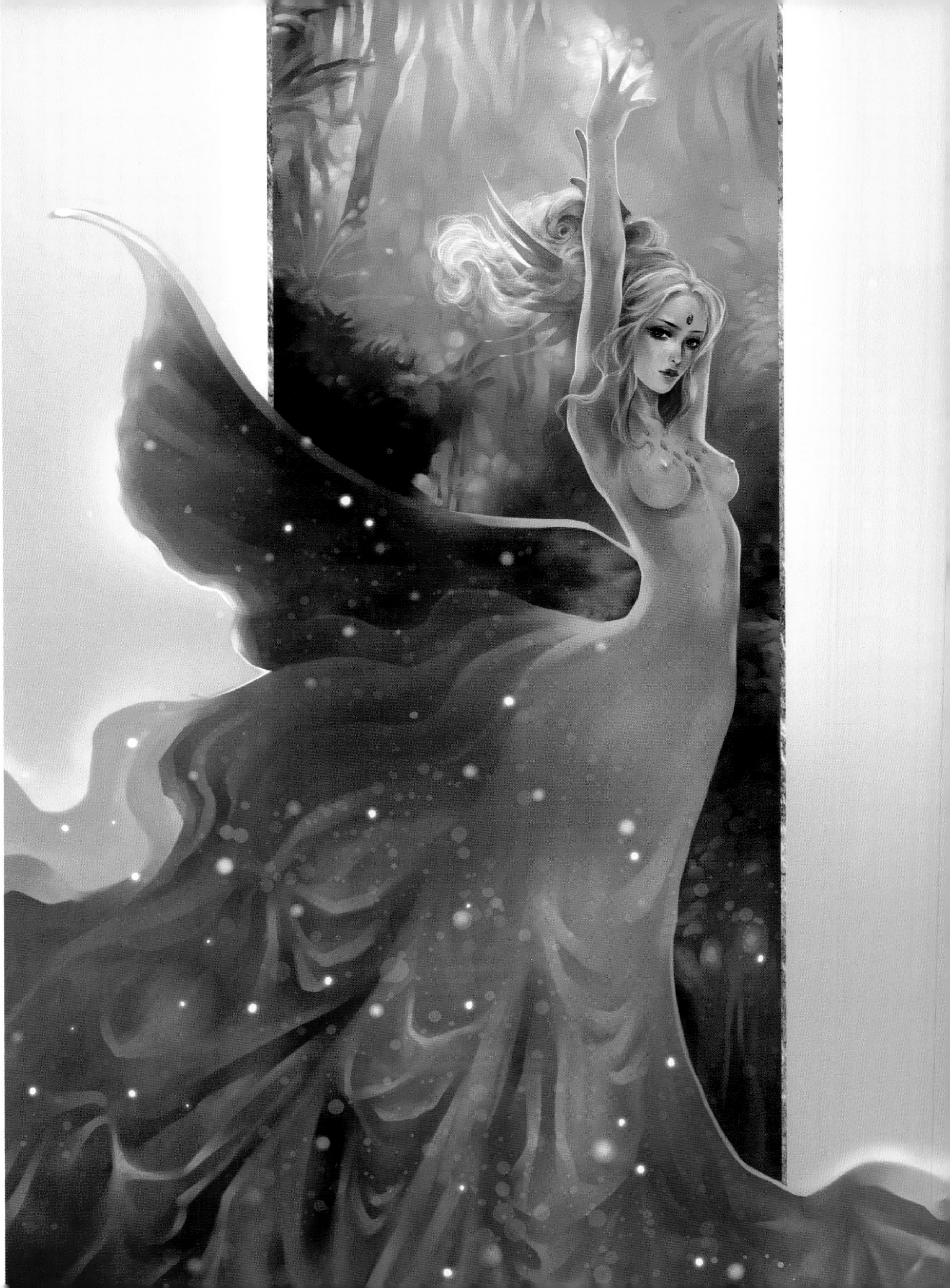

▶ **The Summoning**
Schin Loong
Adobe Photoshop
and Corel Painter
http://lucioleloong.com

"For this piece I envisioned a guardian of a forest with a dress of water just passing by. It took a while to settle on a color scheme before I decided on something subdued and gentle. A lot of thought was put into the composition as well, but eventually I went back to my original idea and decided it was the best."

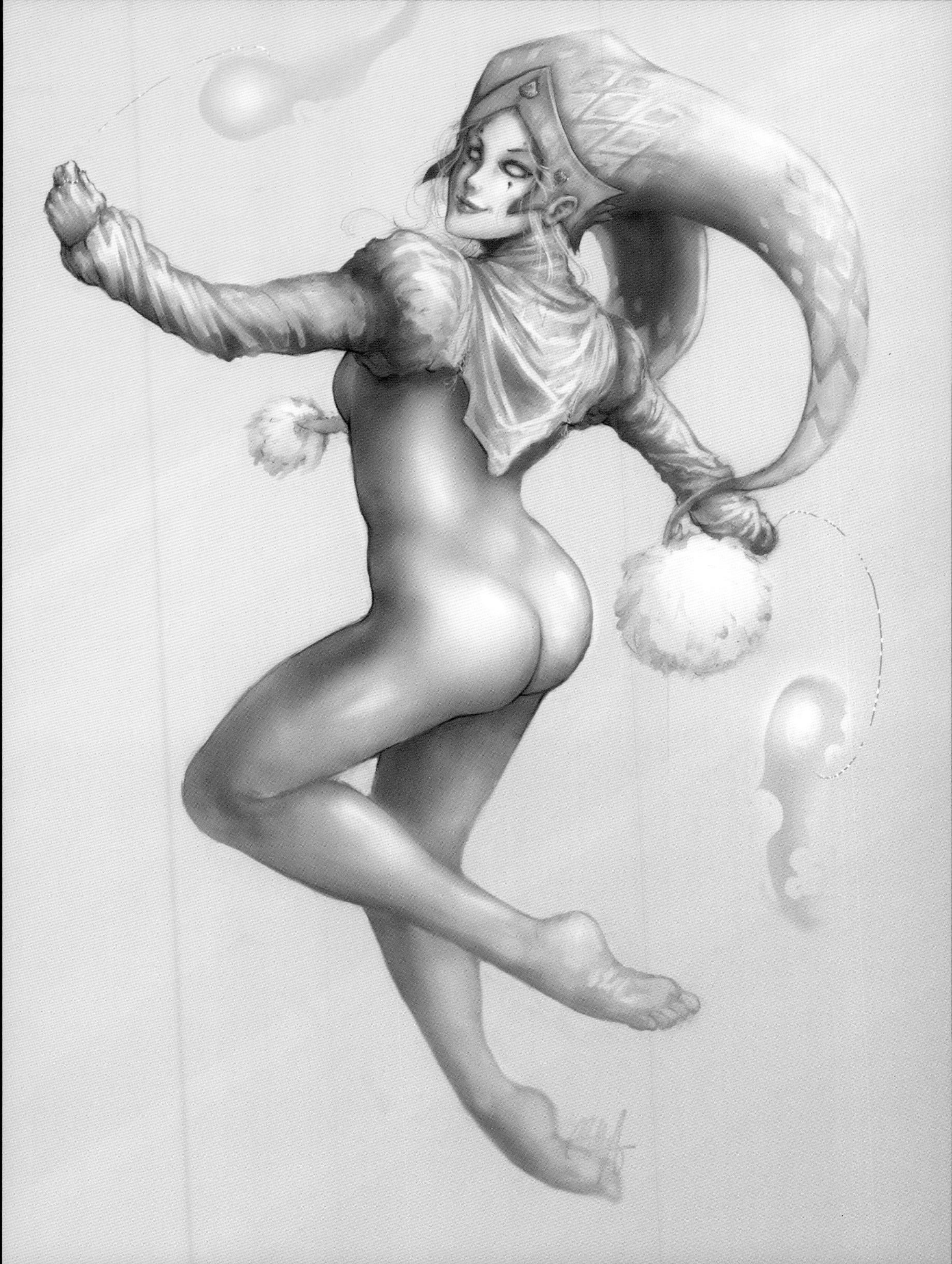

Barely
K. Wainwright
Pencil and openCanvas
http://yilamstation.com

"I got the idea for this piece from a variety of sources. I had just started teaching myself to poi —lots of fun, highly recommend it, but don't do what I did and start by practicing with a lime in a sock, if it hits you in the face it will really hurt. Further inspiration came from one of the clown dolls I have sitting on my shelf and my love for the blushing porcelain Pierrot. As for the jester here, considerably more graceful than me, I imagine she loves to perform. The title refers to her bare feet, seeming to barely touch the cold marble floor of the court as she cavorts for the entertainment of the gathered bourgeoisie."

▶ **Sorceress of the Autumn**
Frank Granados
Corel Painter
www.granados602.deviantart.com

Granados has said how he aims to draw central attention to the face and the eyes of his figures, which is evident here. The artist's works have an ethereal quality to them. "Most of my work is from my own imagination and dreams I've had. I don't work from photographs, that's why there are a lot of imperfections."

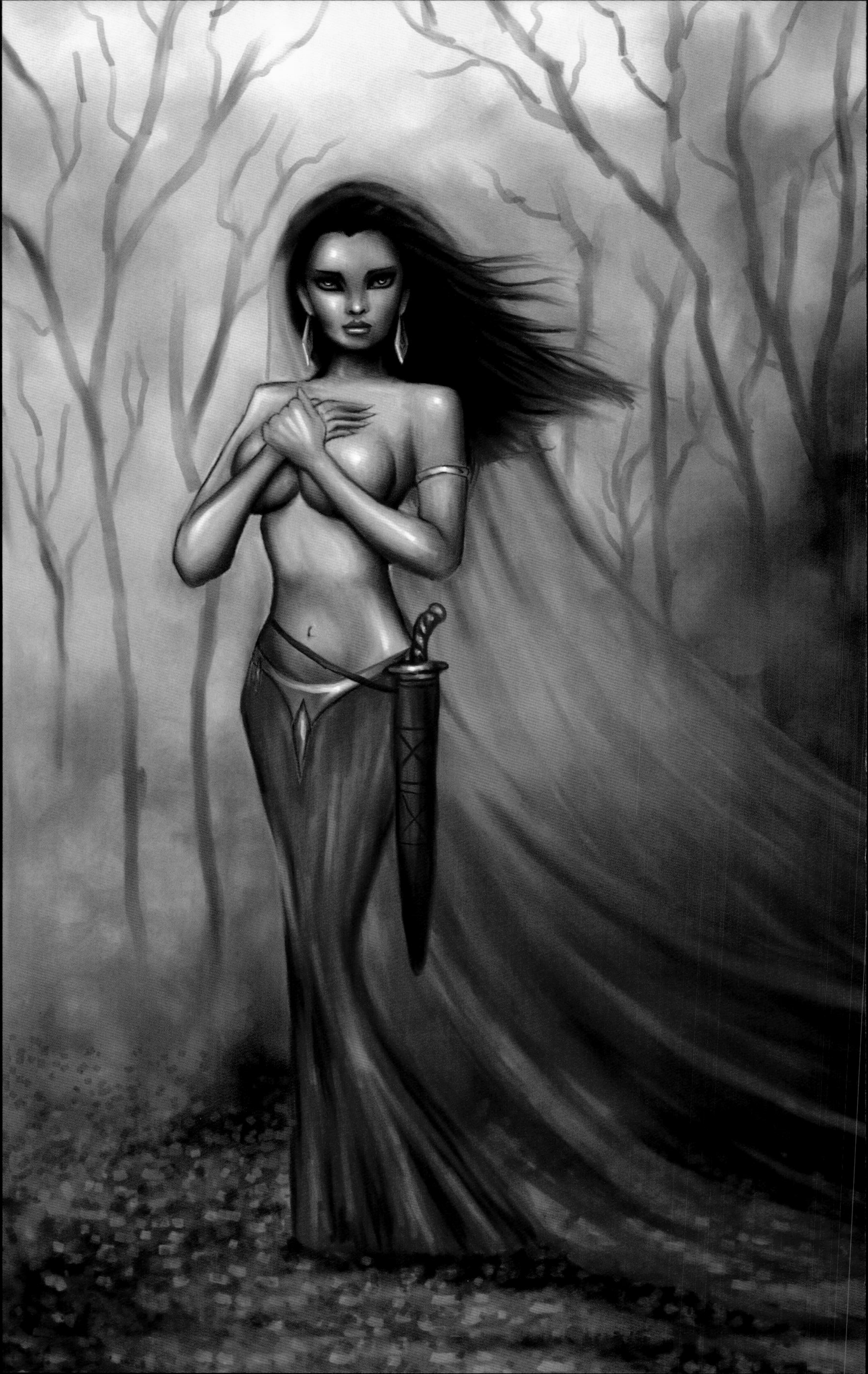

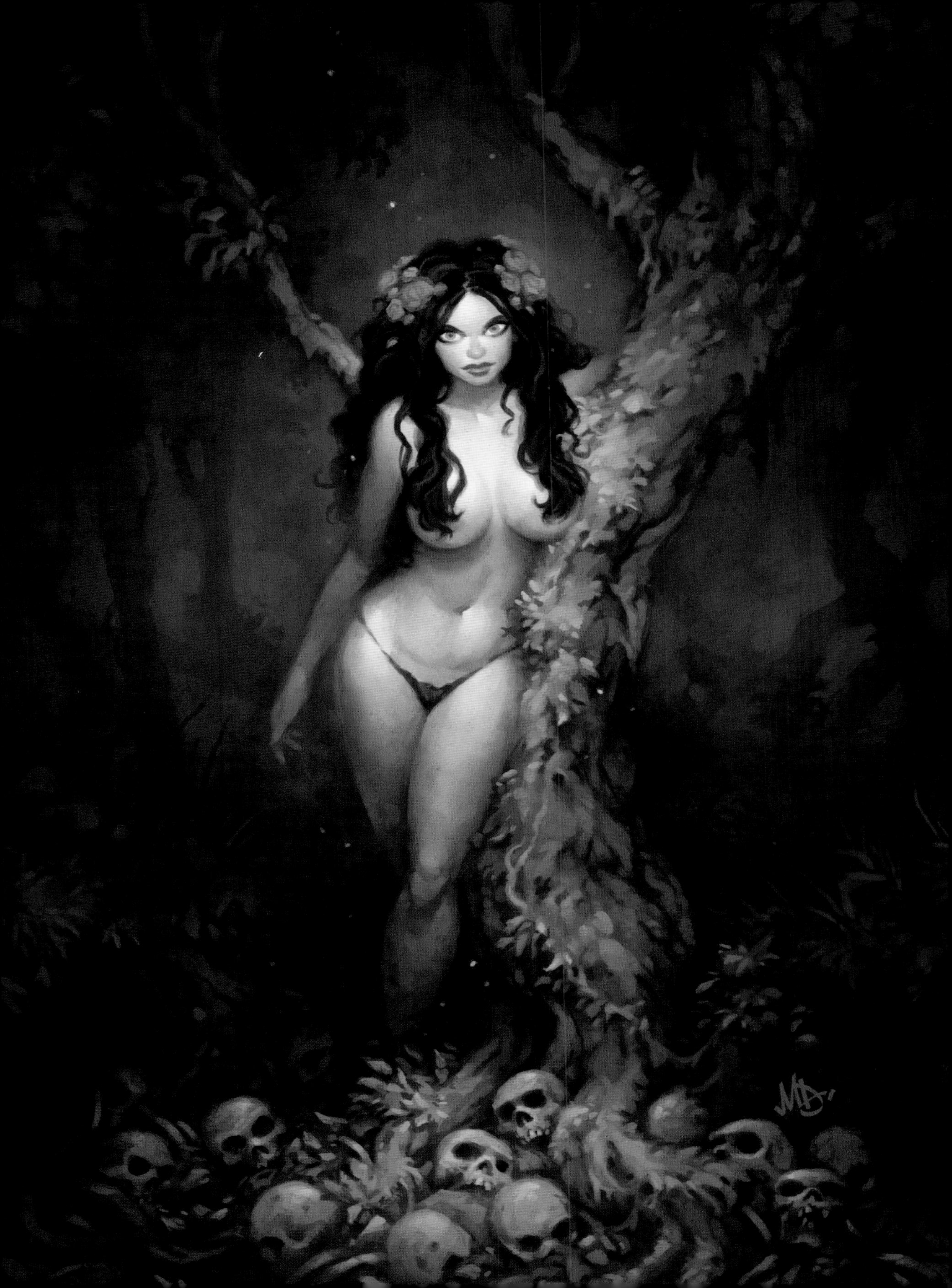

▶ **Dryad**
Matt Dixon
Adobe Photoshop
www.mattdixon.co.uk

"A dryad is a tree nymph and is often seen portrayed as a playful, fairy-like being. I prefer the idea of a nature spirit that embodies both the beautiful and the wild, sometimes frightening, aspects of the natural world, and that's what I've attempted to portray here."

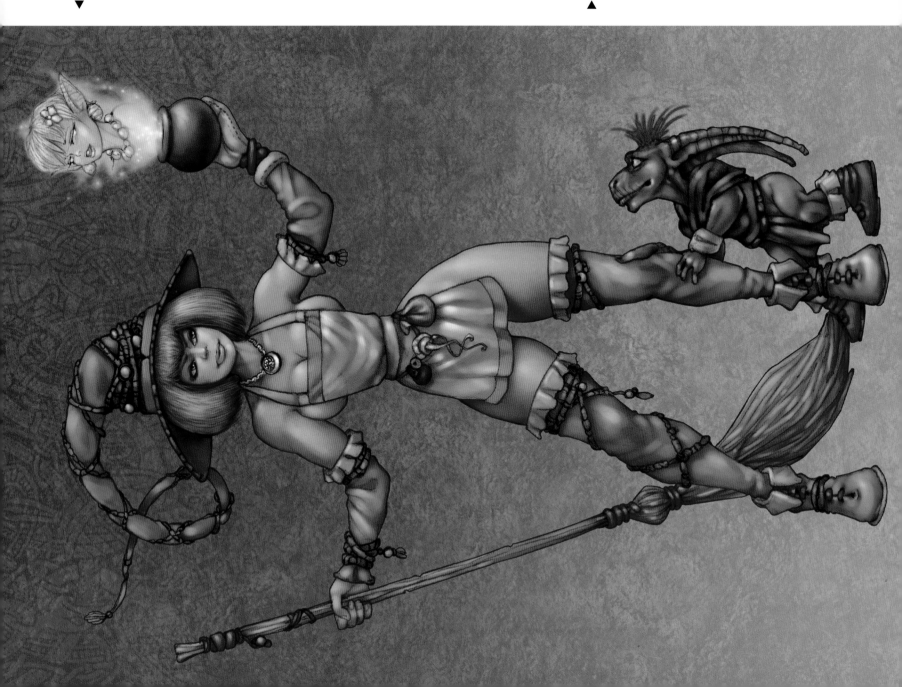

Early Halloween
Alejandro Gutiérrez Franco
Adobe Photoshop
http://maidencomics.20m.com

"I love to draw and paint witches all year, so this image is not just another Halloween season sample. She is depicted as more of a Celtic or pagan sorceress, rather than an evil or wicked one, so the overall look gives us a natural earth-toned impression. The long-eared little guy belongs to a goblin race that I have been drawing for a long time. As for the painting techniques, I got the oil-like finish of the girl's skin and clothes with a mix of soft and hard-edged Photoshop brushes. The hair was done with a hairy brush."

Witch / Groundwelling
Ricardo Landell
Adobe Photoshop
and Corel Painter
www.hardinkgirls.com

"This was inspired by Halloween as well as Night of the Witch. This witch summons young girls as slaves through her magic to satisfy her lust for power and erotic pleasure. After sketching it in Photoshop, the image was transfered to Painter for inking by retracing the sketch. The clean line work was then transferred back to Photoshop for coloring with the Pen tool, Lasso tool, and Paint Bucket."

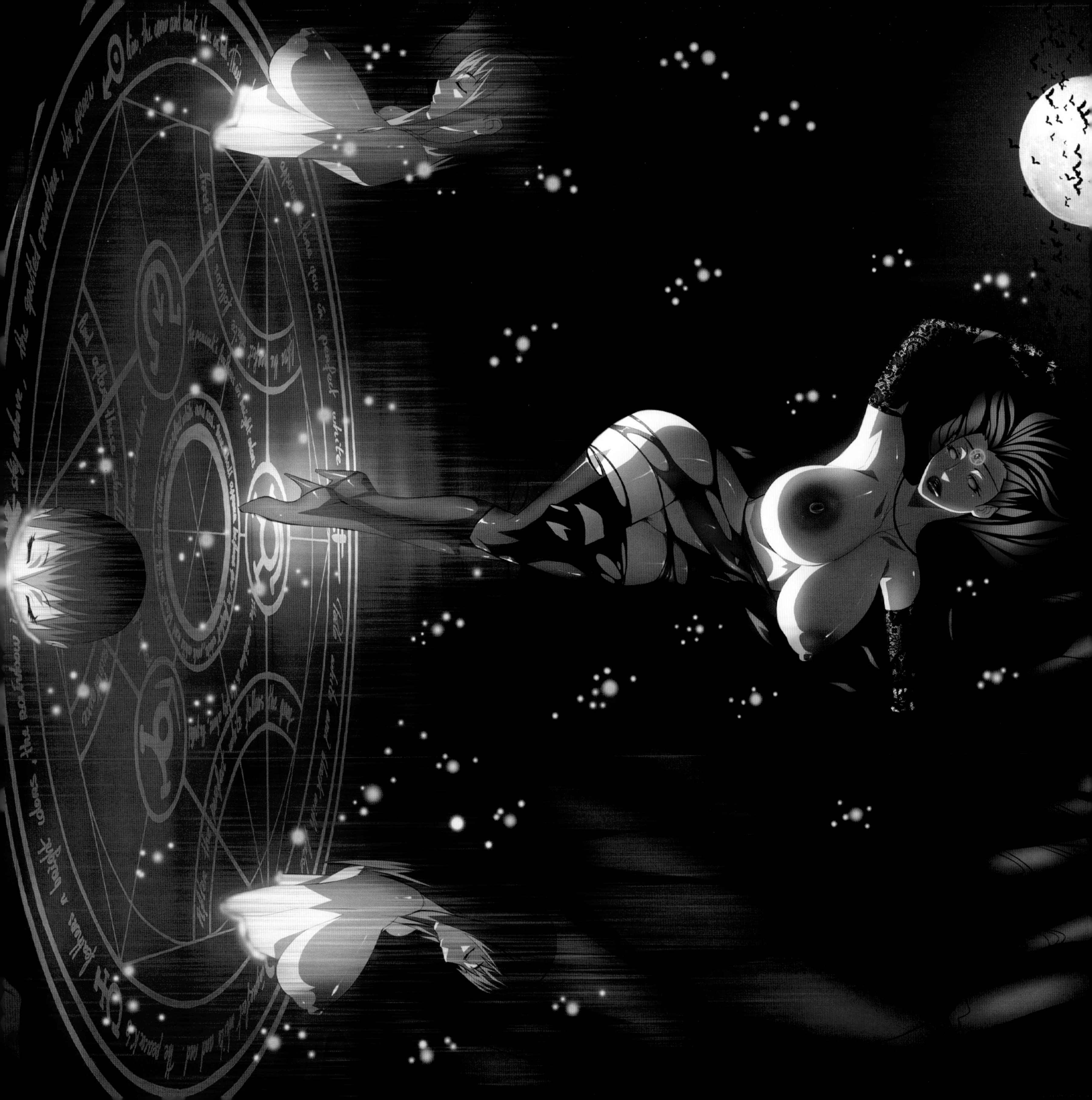

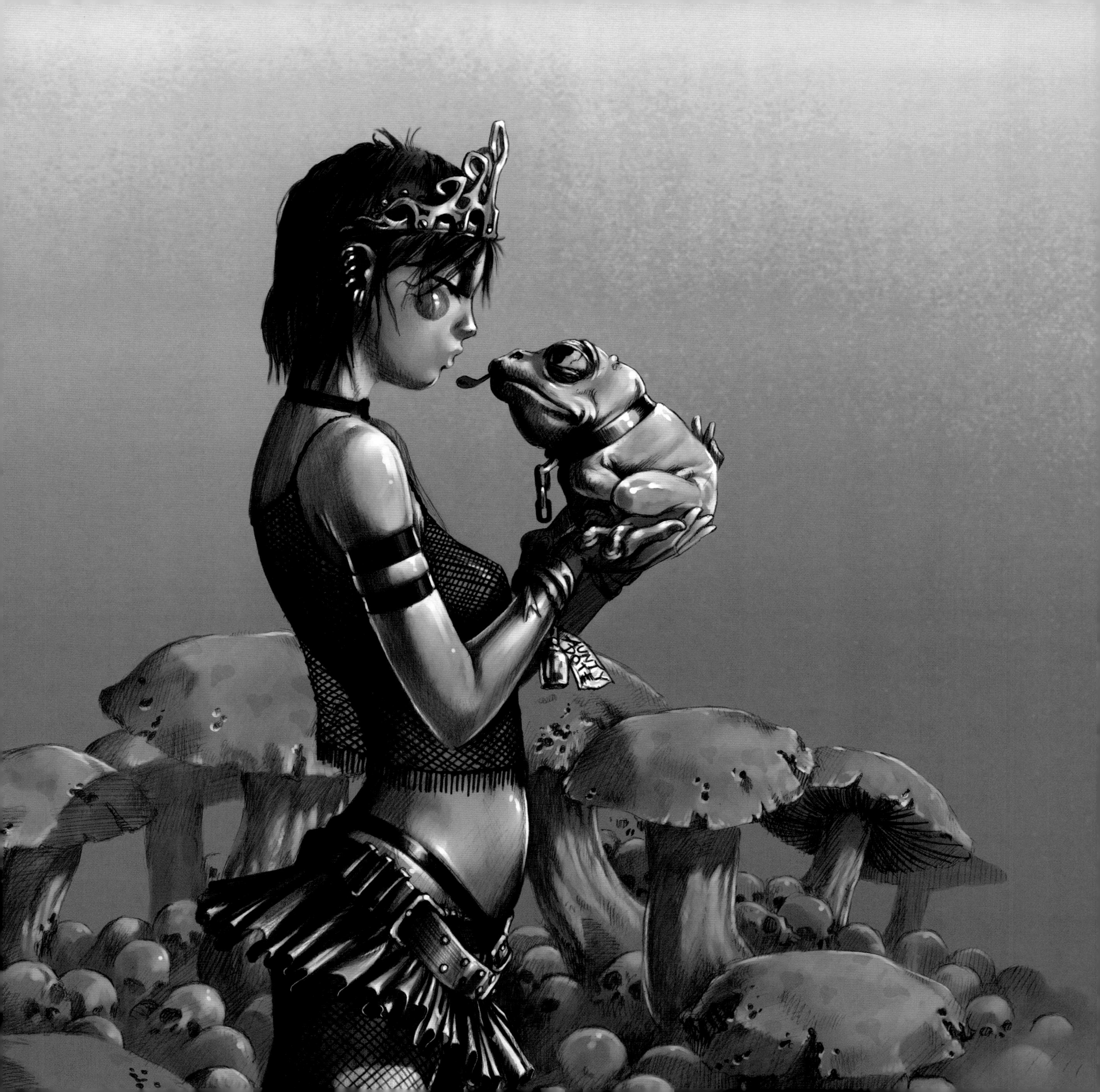
AUNTY DOTE

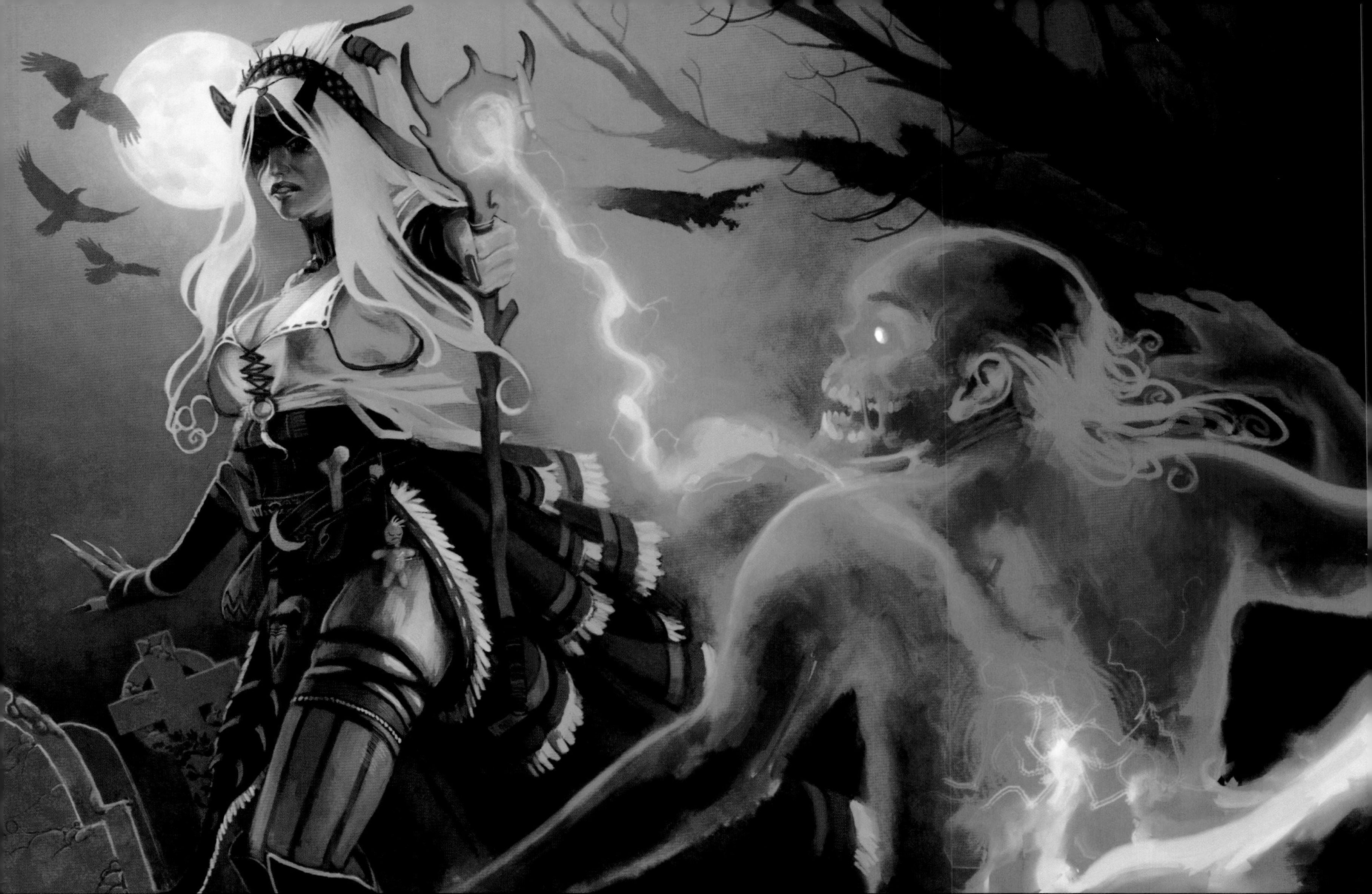

◀ **Love's Dream**
Andy Hepworth
For White Wolf
Pencil and Corel Painter
http://andyhepworth.blogspot.com

"I loved working on Changeling, *the pen-and-paper RPG by White Wolf. It allowed me have a lot of fun with subject matter and themes that are close to my heart, and a sense of the odd was positively encouraged by the art director, Aileen Miles. This image was a little twist on the frog prince tale, seen through a gothic looking gloss and cast into our own modern times as the setting dictated."*

▲ **Pathfinder 7**
Francisco Rico Torres
For Paizo Publishing, LLC
Adobe Photoshop and Corel Painter
www.pacorico.blogspot.com

"This was for Pathfinder RPG: Advanced Player's Guide. *I was commissioned to paint Feiya (a witch) fighting a zombie ghost. Feiya's look was designed by the great illustrator Wayne Reynolds. I tried to give Feiya a sexy look, but since she is a witch, I also wanted to give her skin a sick, pale-gray look. Painting the zombie ghost was interesting—the Blender tools in Painter are really useful for the translucent undead."*

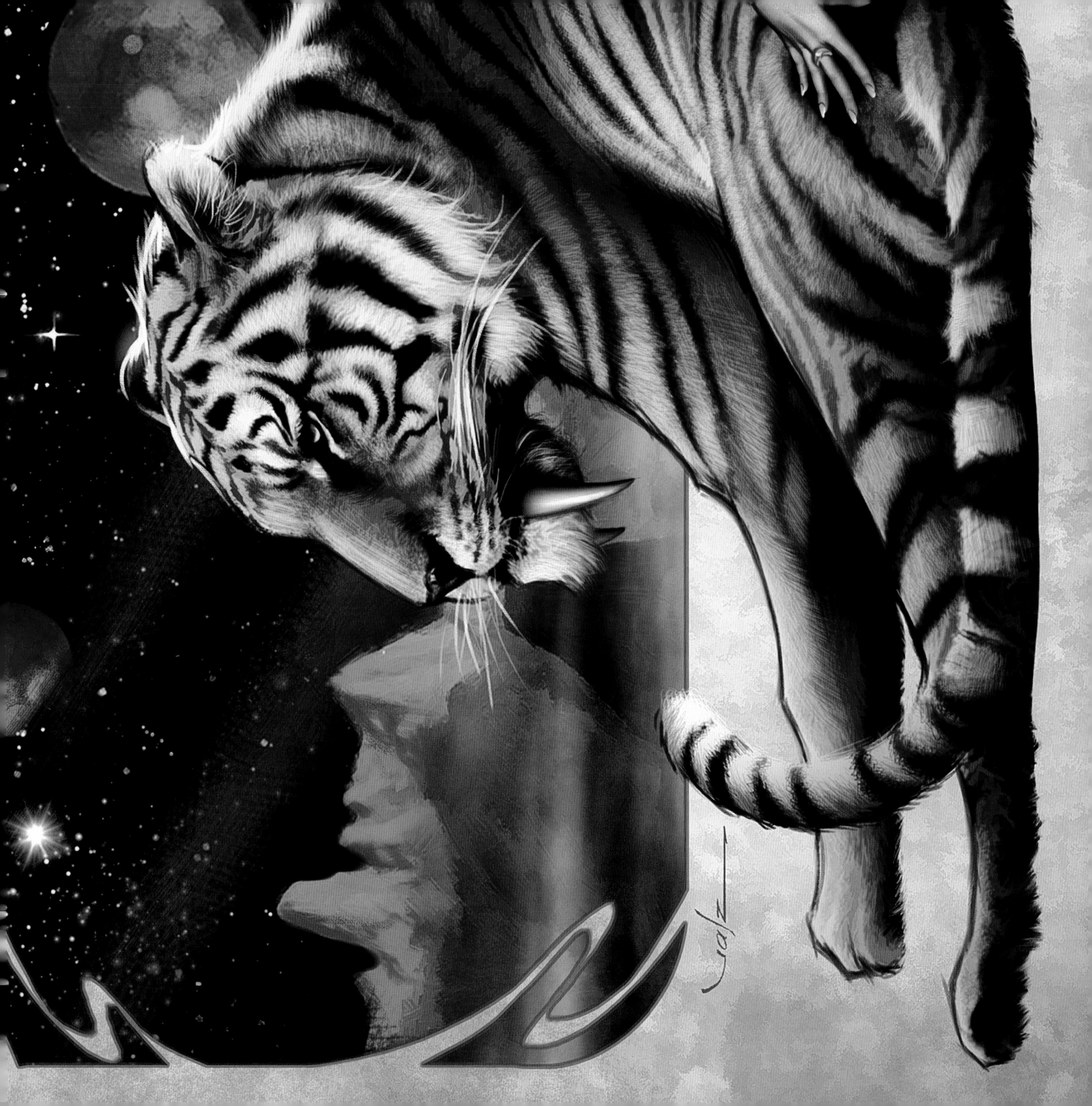

CHAPTER 8

SCI-FI AND CYBER GALS

▼ **Martian Princess**
Carlos Valenzuela
Adobe Photoshop and ArtRage
http://valzonline.deviantart.com

"The beautiful and sexy Dejah Thoris (from the book A Princess Of Mars *by Edgar Rice Burroughs). When I paint just for me, the works always tend to have a retro/nostalgic feel. I'm some sort of old-fashioned artist using technology to make art, always trying to avoid the digital look in my pieces, going for a more 'traditional' tone. I achieve this with the help of some very nice custom brushes, plus the use of the fantastic ArtRage, an affordable software that manages 'traditional tools' very convincingly."*

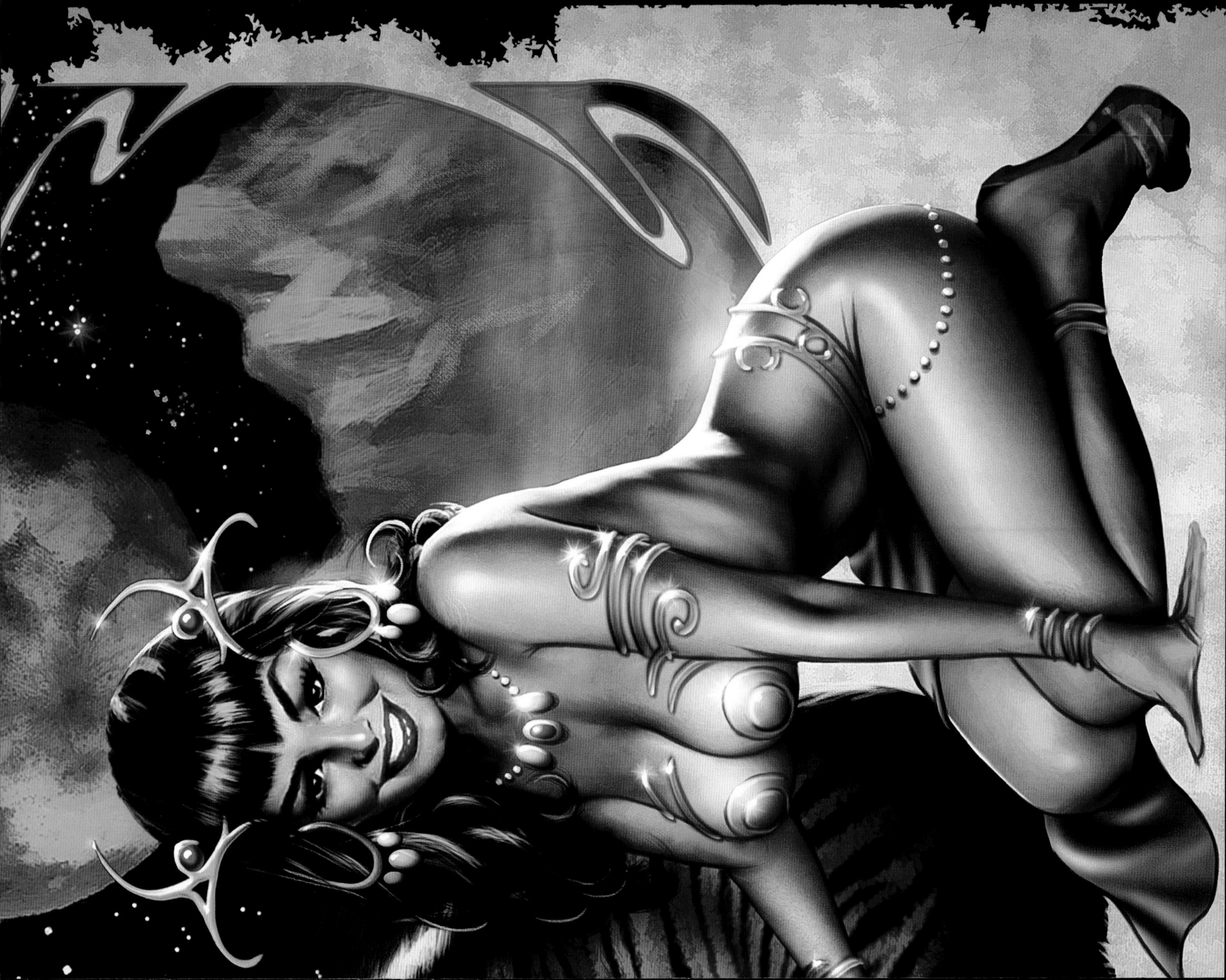

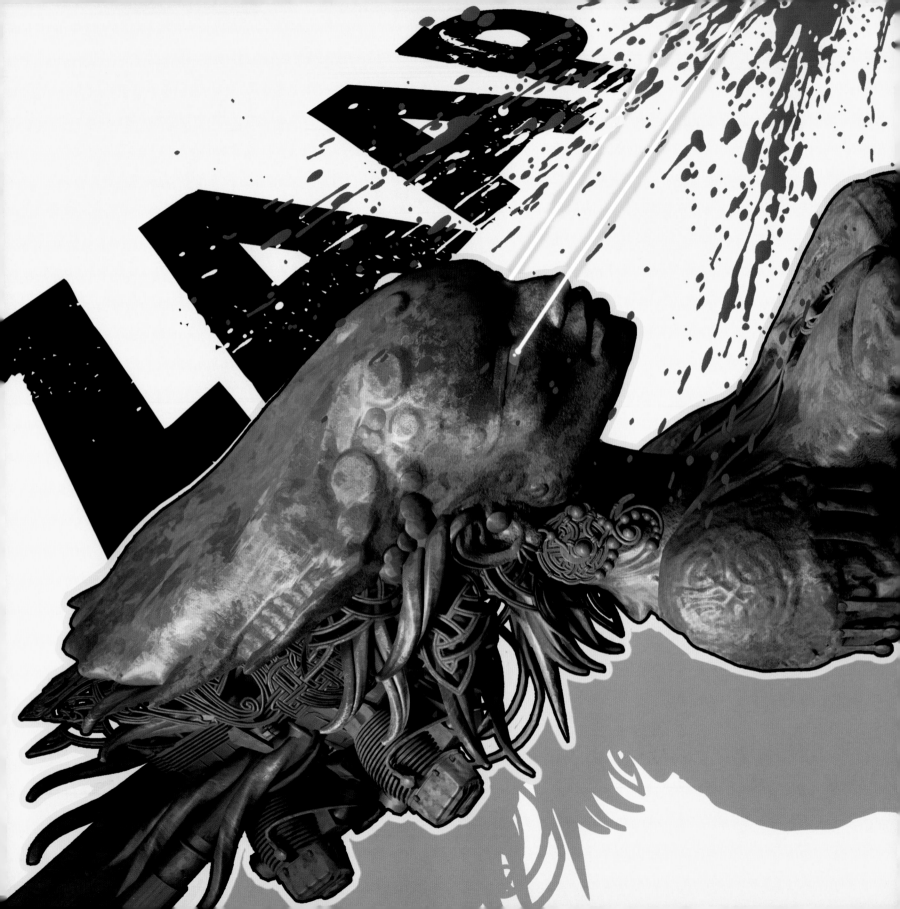

Zapp
Pascal Blanche
Adobe Photoshop,
3ds Max, and ZBrush
www.3dluvr.com/pascalb

"I wanted to play around with the idea of a mechanical and living sculpture gal, some kind of sphinx with a sci-fi touch. I created the main bust with ZBrush and added some mechanical pieces to the back of the head. Then I came up with the idea of the two lasers and the splat of blood to give the whole picture a more dynamic vibe."

Lorna
Nacho Molina
Adobe Photoshop
www.nachomolina.deviantart.com
www.nachomolinablog.blogspot.com

"Girls and guns in outer space, what else can I say? I tried to paint this beauty in the seat of her spaceship, basing it on the work of Alfonso Azpiri. The sexy look was central to the character, so I tried to give to the illustration a strong, shiny pink and purple atmosphere using blured layers in Soft Light and Overlay modes in Adobe Photoshop. It was interesting to depict different kinds of materials like skin, hair, and leather using more rough or softer brush stokes on different surfaces."

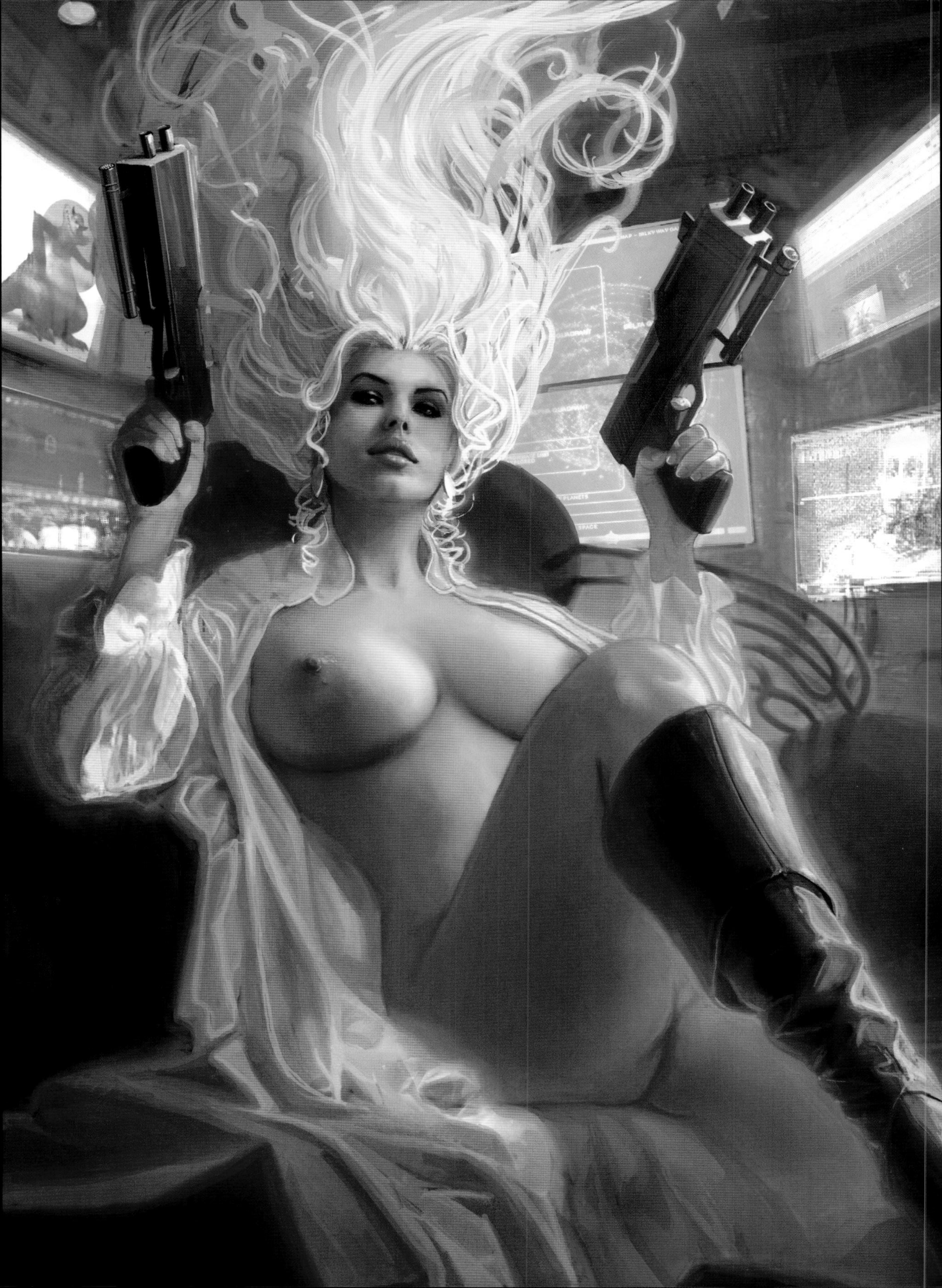

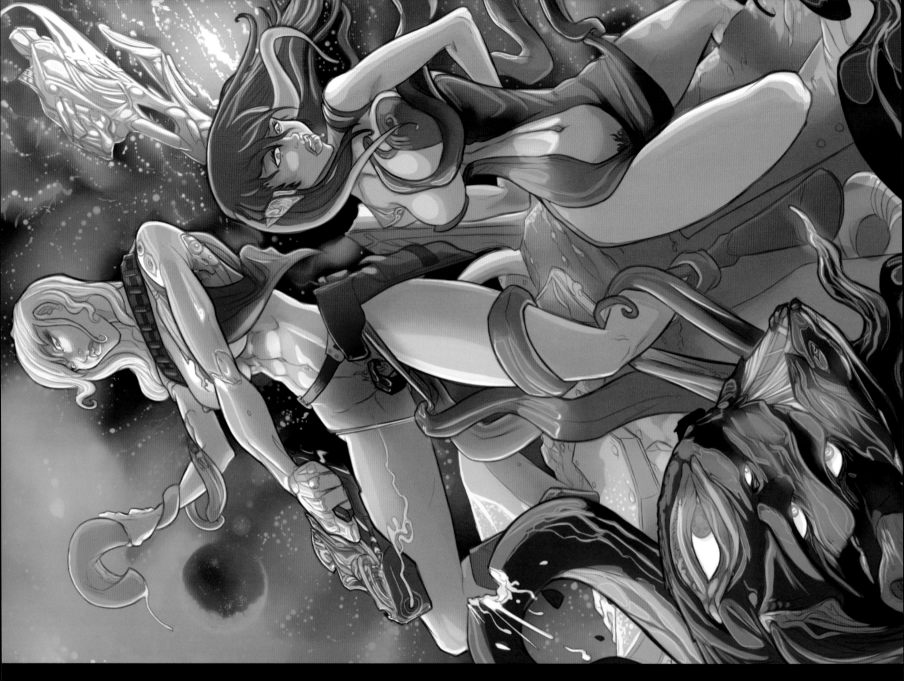

▲ **Lovasion**
Frederic Bodo
PaintTool SAI
www.holydamned.deviantart.com

"I work solely with a computer and pen tablet. It offers me great flexibility. It's also because it's futuristic — I love sci-fi so much that my art must have a little touch of high-tech. I wanted to make a sexy tribute to the heroes of my childhood. But I replaced the traditional virile space captain rescuing sexy alien princesses with a sapphic fearless bounty huntress. For the background, I used a black mask and put each star on it one by one to form a red supernova and blue nebula for contrast. It's important not to place the stars in the same way to create a more credible star field and I googled 'nebula' for reference pictures. As for the tentacles . . . tentacles have been famously used in a lot of erotic Japanese art."

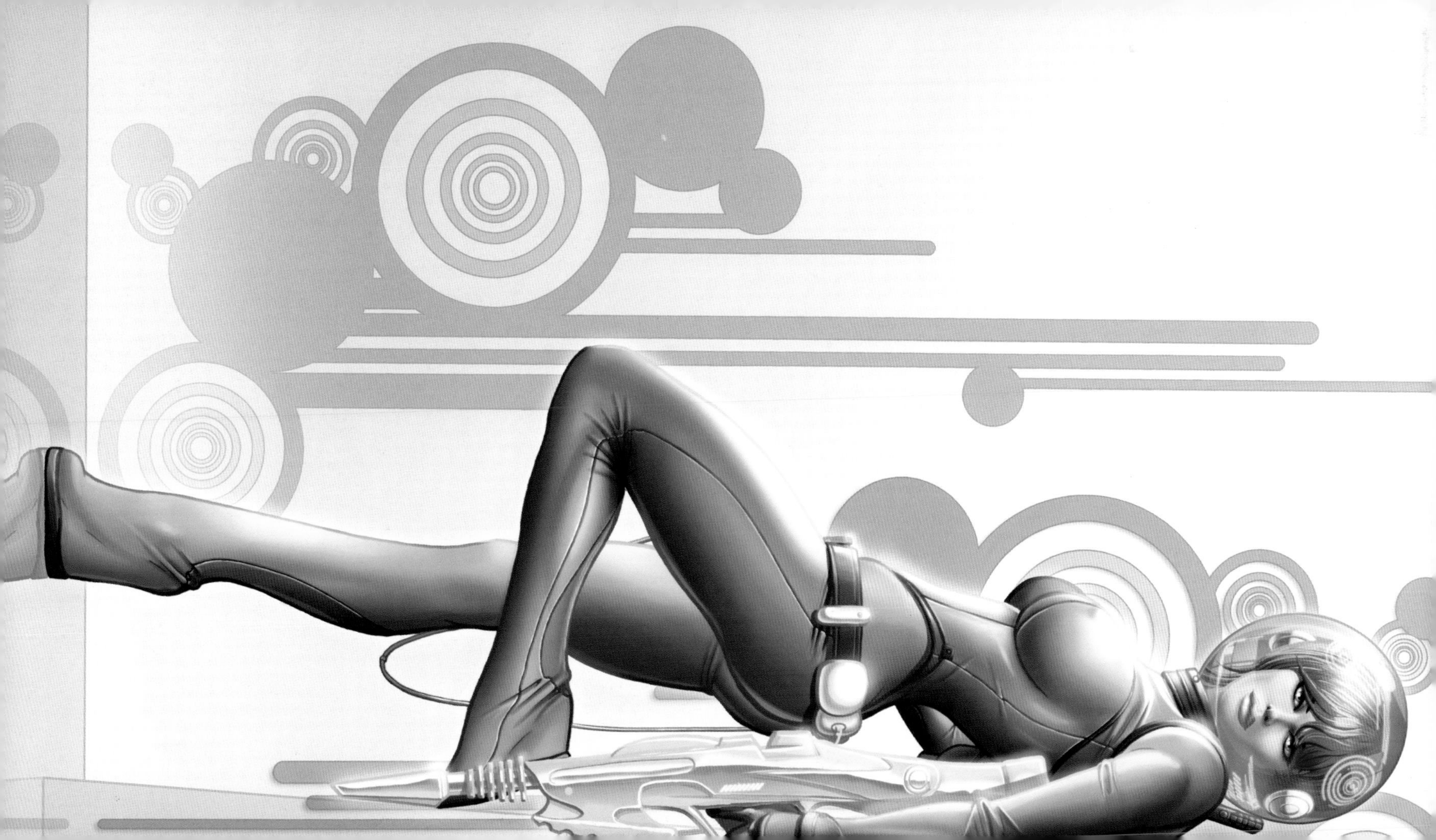

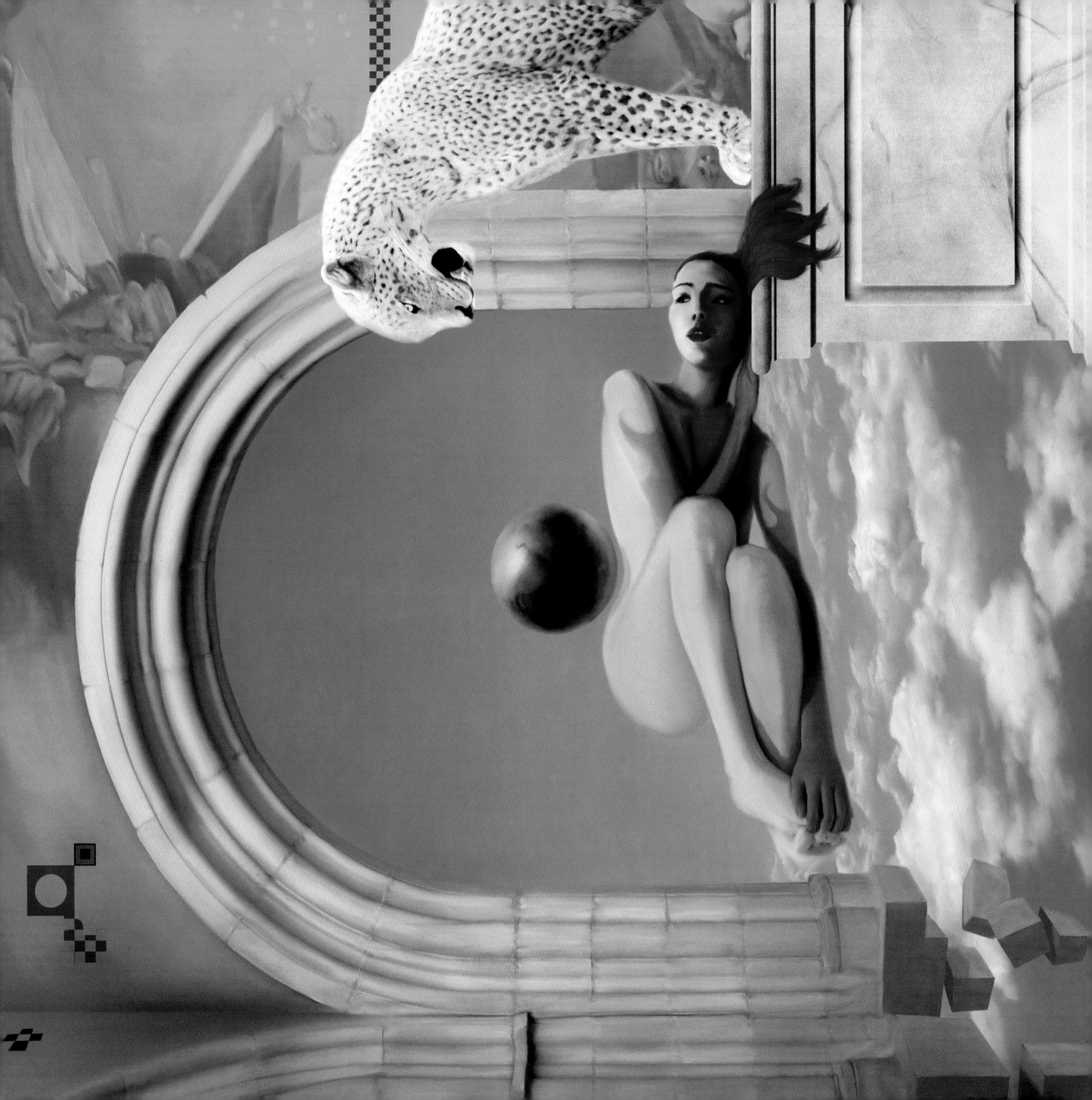

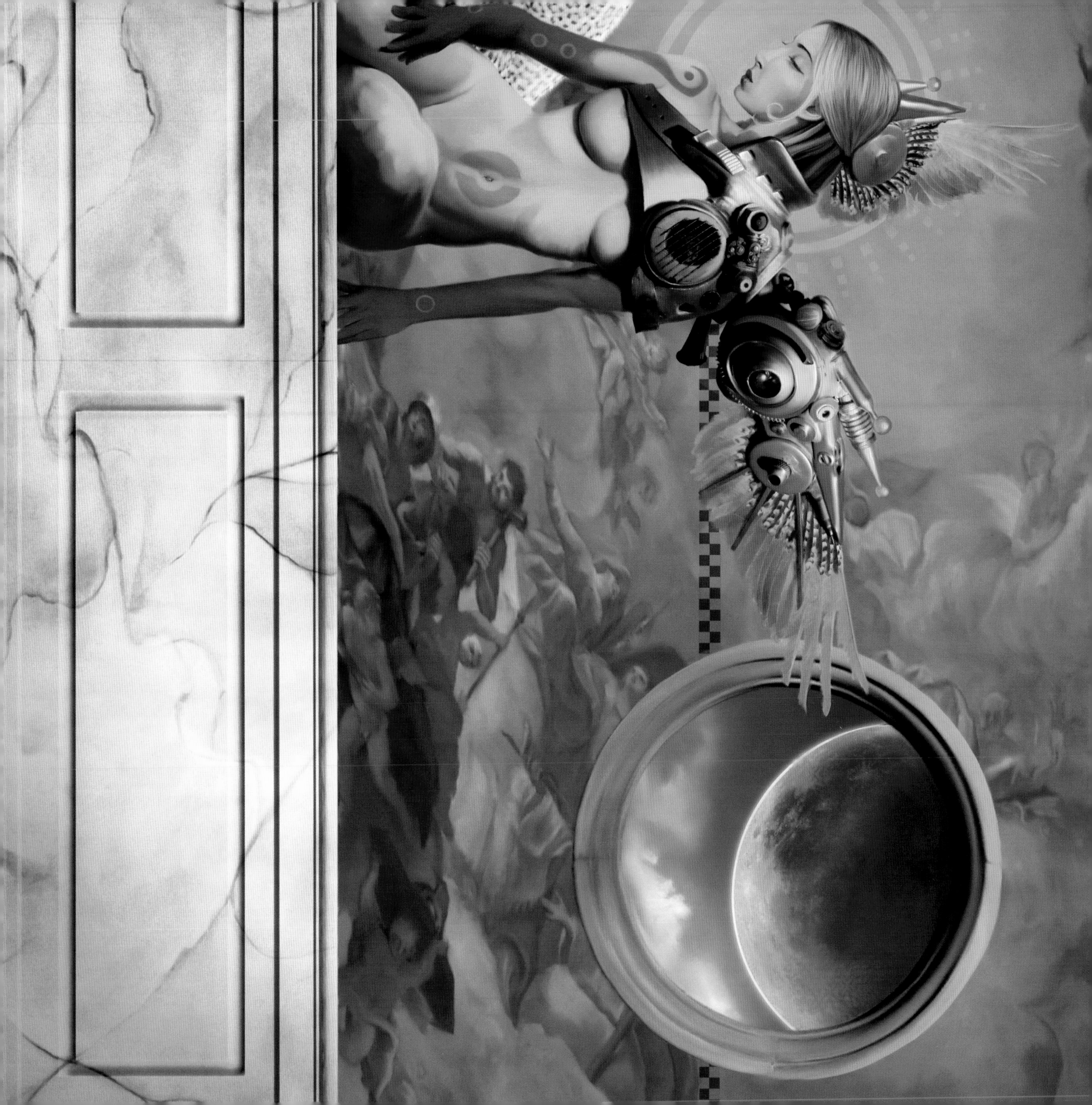

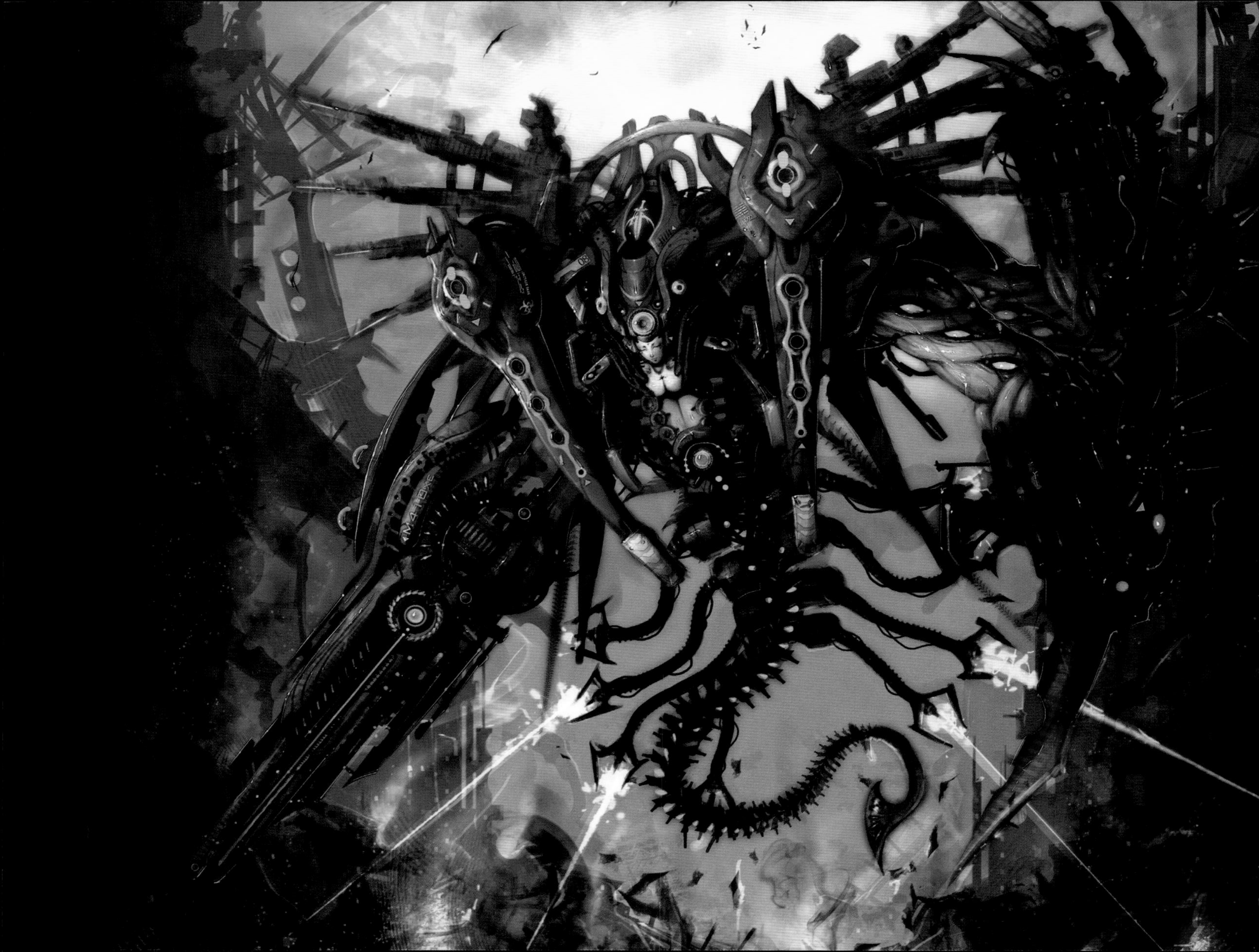

◀ **The Disquisition**
Oliver Wetter
Adobe Photoshop
http://fantasio.info

"This is a tribute to art nouveau and artists like Pascal Blanché and Michael Parkes. Parts of this painting are miniature models that were created using plaster, findings, and a physical airbrush, like the technical parts that hold the wings for example. I love to play with graphic elements and composition. Like some other pieces of mine, this one was also created with architectural precision."

▲ **DWIV: M410XE Cyborg**
Chung Yee-Ling
Adobe Photoshop
http://syncmax.deviantart.com

"This piece was created for an international game character design challenge called Dominance War IV. This work won 19th place, within the Top 20. The idea was to create a powerful game character to dominate the universe. The M410XE cyborg was an intelligent human combined with powerful war machinary technology, making it a fearsome force to fight with."

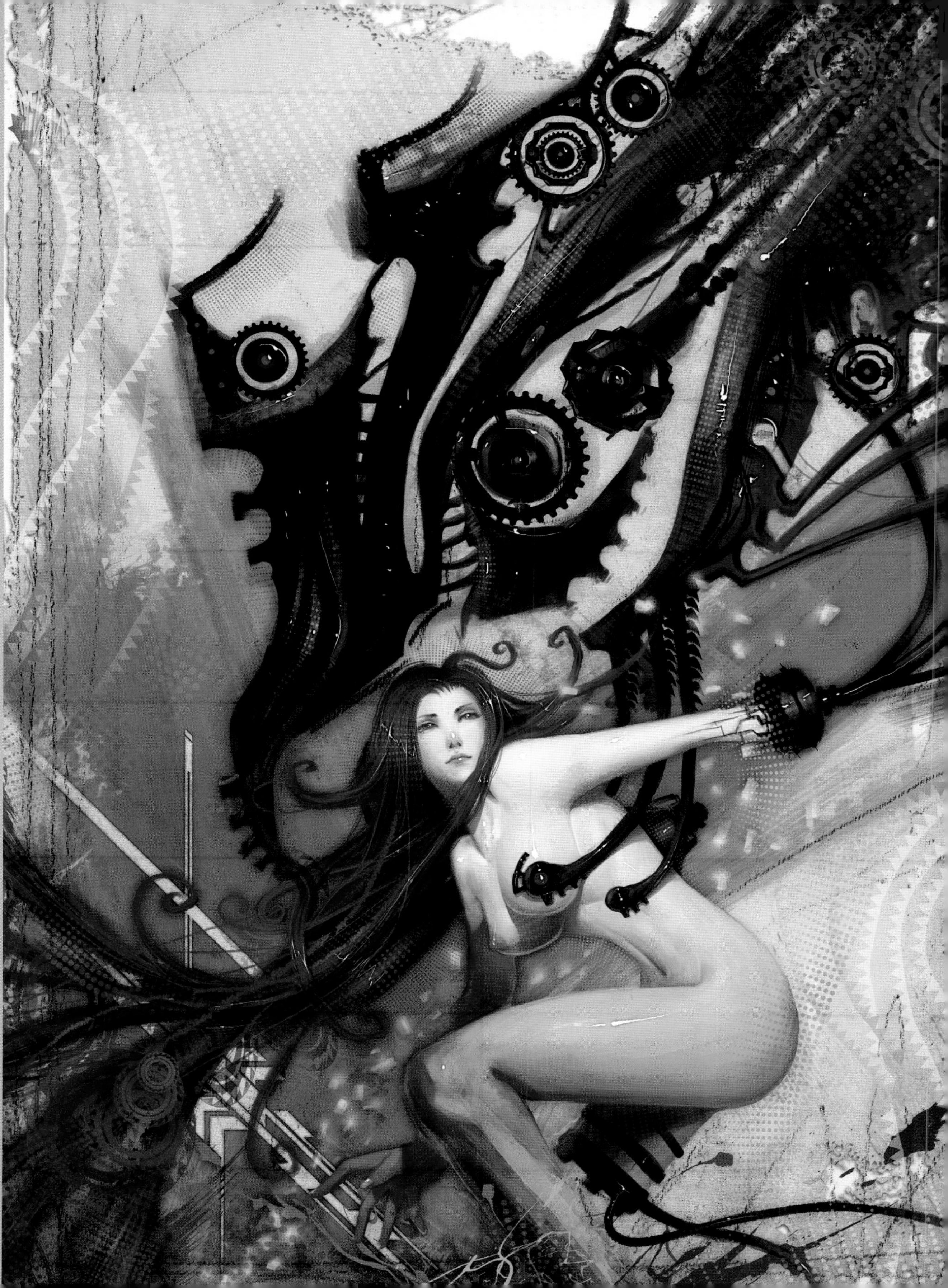

Anna
Chung Yee-Ling
Adobe Photoshop
http://syncmax.deviantart.com

"This piece was inspired by a Swedish Eurodance song called Boten Anna *by Basshunter. It's about an IRC user [which stands for Internet Relay Chat – a form of real-time online messaging] who has administrative capabilities to take care of the IRC channel. She does her tasks so quickly and powerfully that she is mistaken for a computer bot."*

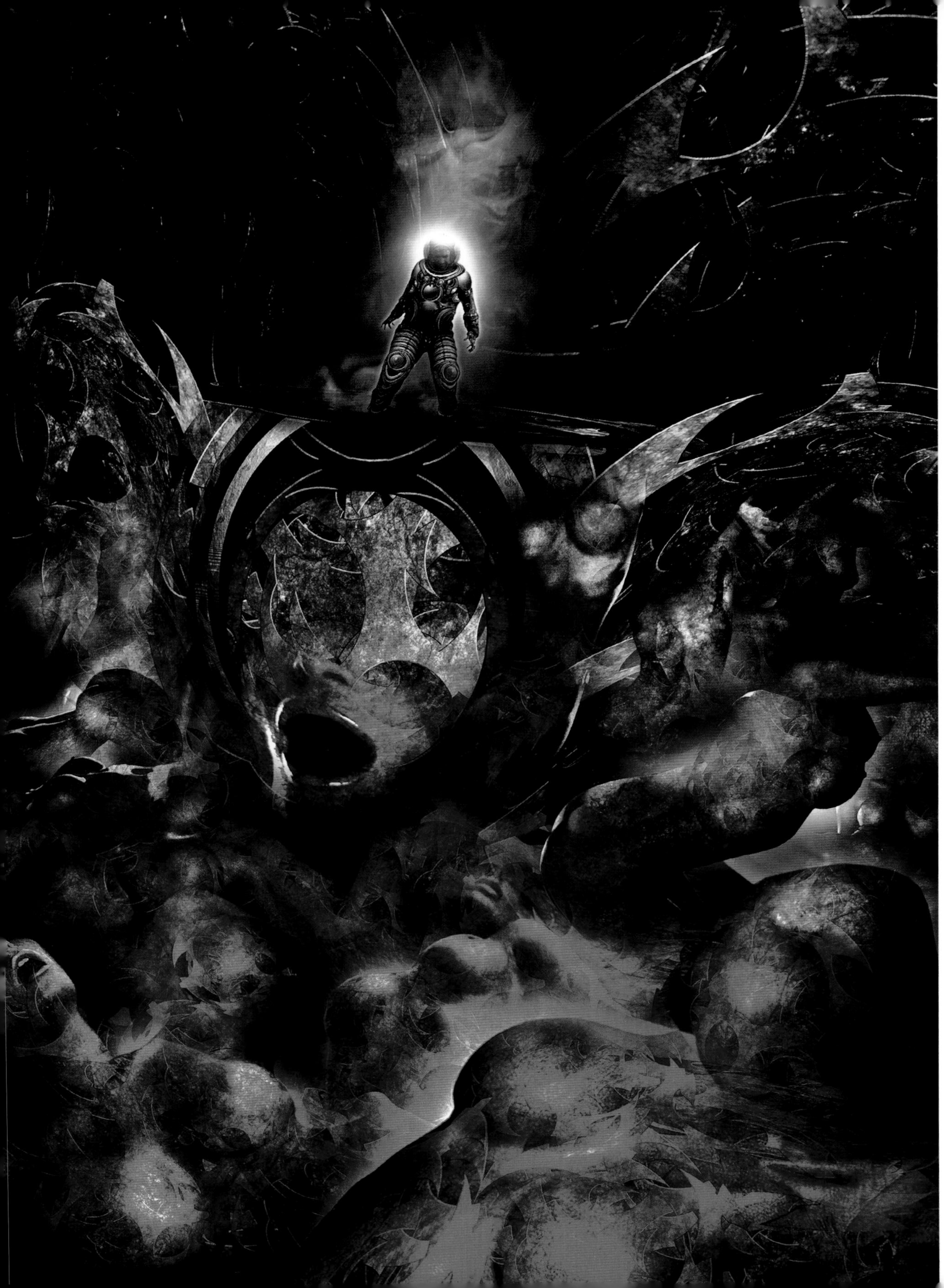

◀ **The Stone Harem**
Felipe Machado Franco
Adobe Photoshop
http://finalfrontier.thunderblast.net

"I started thinking about how eroticism is always depicted by an action or a female character . . . but what if eroticism was a place? A place in our minds or a utopian land? I had this idea of a land where shapes somehow resembled the female form or the interaction of bodies. I created many stone-texture shapes of models and started composing a web of body parts. For me it was important to have a character discover this land, so I created a sort of astronaut looking at the edge of this erotic valley. I like to have a library of different shapes or elements for organizing and transforming into characters or places. Up close they look abstract, but inside the space or character they give them imperfections that for me make an illustration more interesting."

▶ **We Only Infect the Willing**
I.L. Jackson
DAZ Studio 3 Advanced and GIMP
http://darklorddc.deviantart.com

"I was inspired to do this piece by the modern desire to romanticize our monsters before allowing lust and seduction to take place. In ages gone by, this was not the case. Vampires, for example, were horrible creatures with bad breath, but women fell for them anyway. They were a lesson about the perils of lust, which can lead you into the arms of a vicious monster. A lesson all too many of us learn the hard way in the real world. So when I did this piece I wanted her in the arms of an unabashedly horrid creature, with drool and slime running into her mouth, her hair, and her face . . . all the places we'd wipe such stuff away."

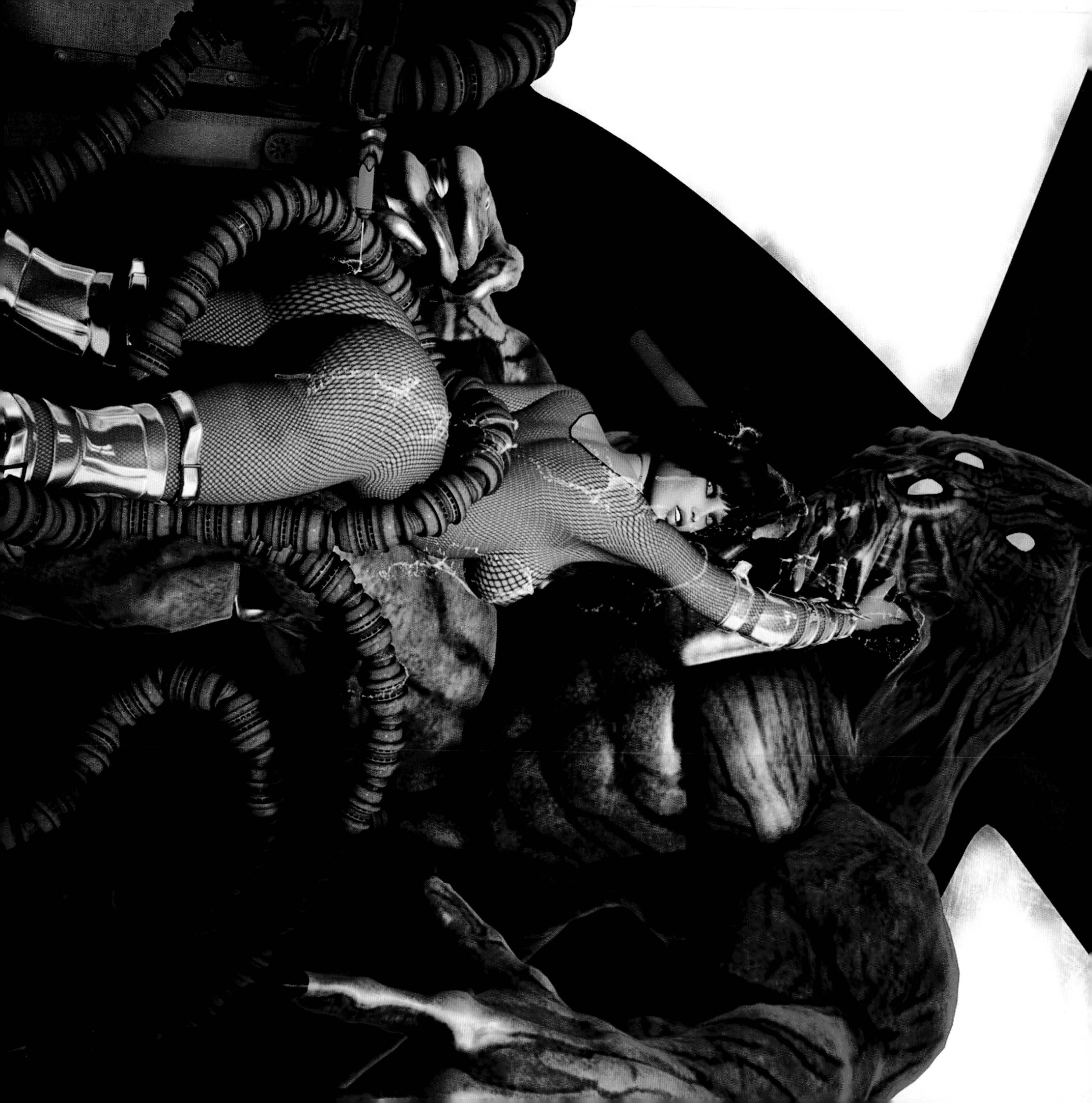

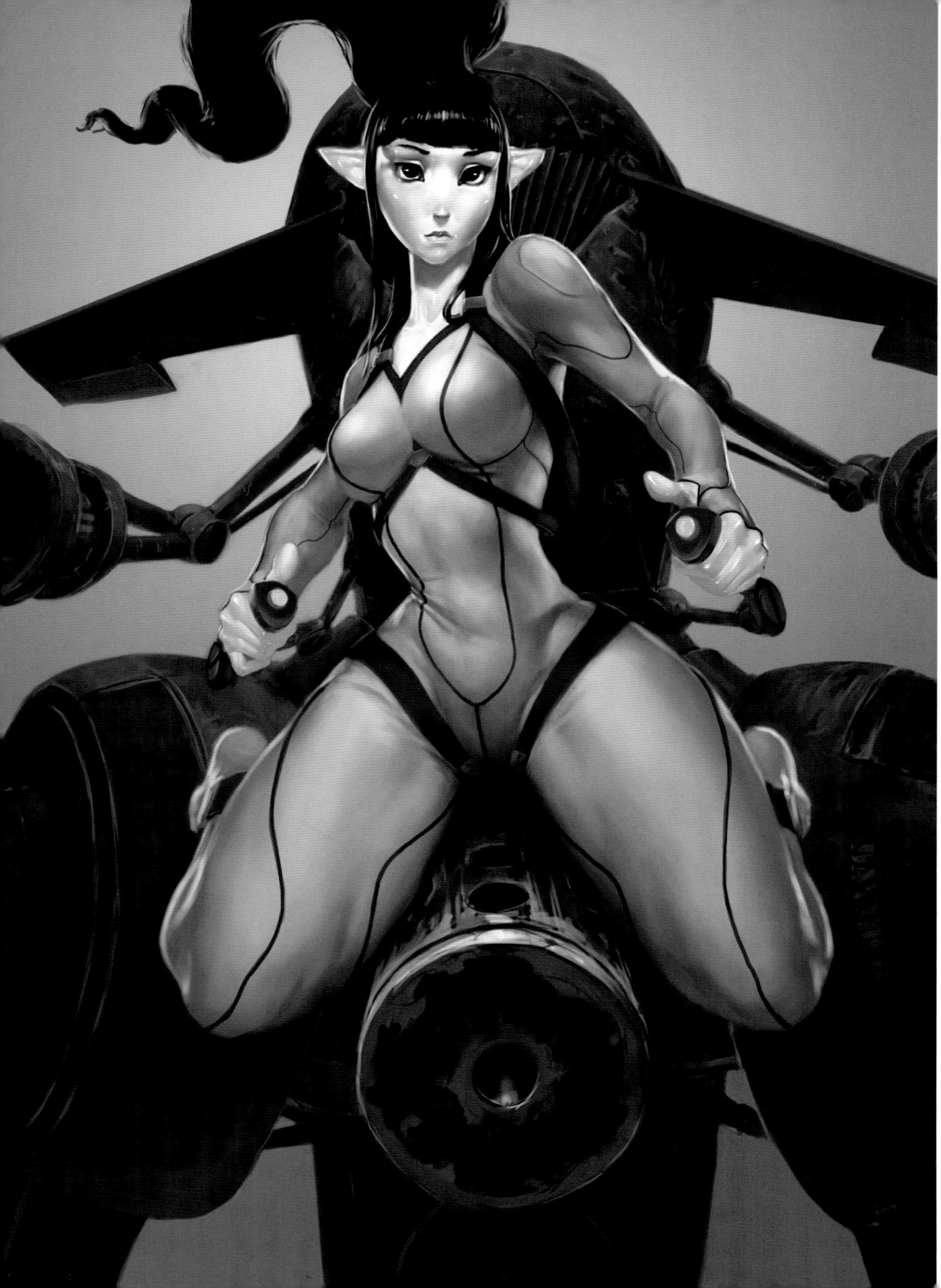

◀ **Wrong! But Sexy**
David Smit
Adobe Photoshop
www.davidsmit.com

"To be honest, this image was an accident. It was one of those days where I felt I really needed a break from what I'd been doing for a while, and just wanted to make something else. Something different, something sexy! So as I was sketching, I thought of what would be the most unlikely things for me to draw combined. This resulted in an elf girl with a porcelain face, in a tight spandex suit, sitting on the massive gun of a robot. Logical yes!? I had a lot of fun creating this one."

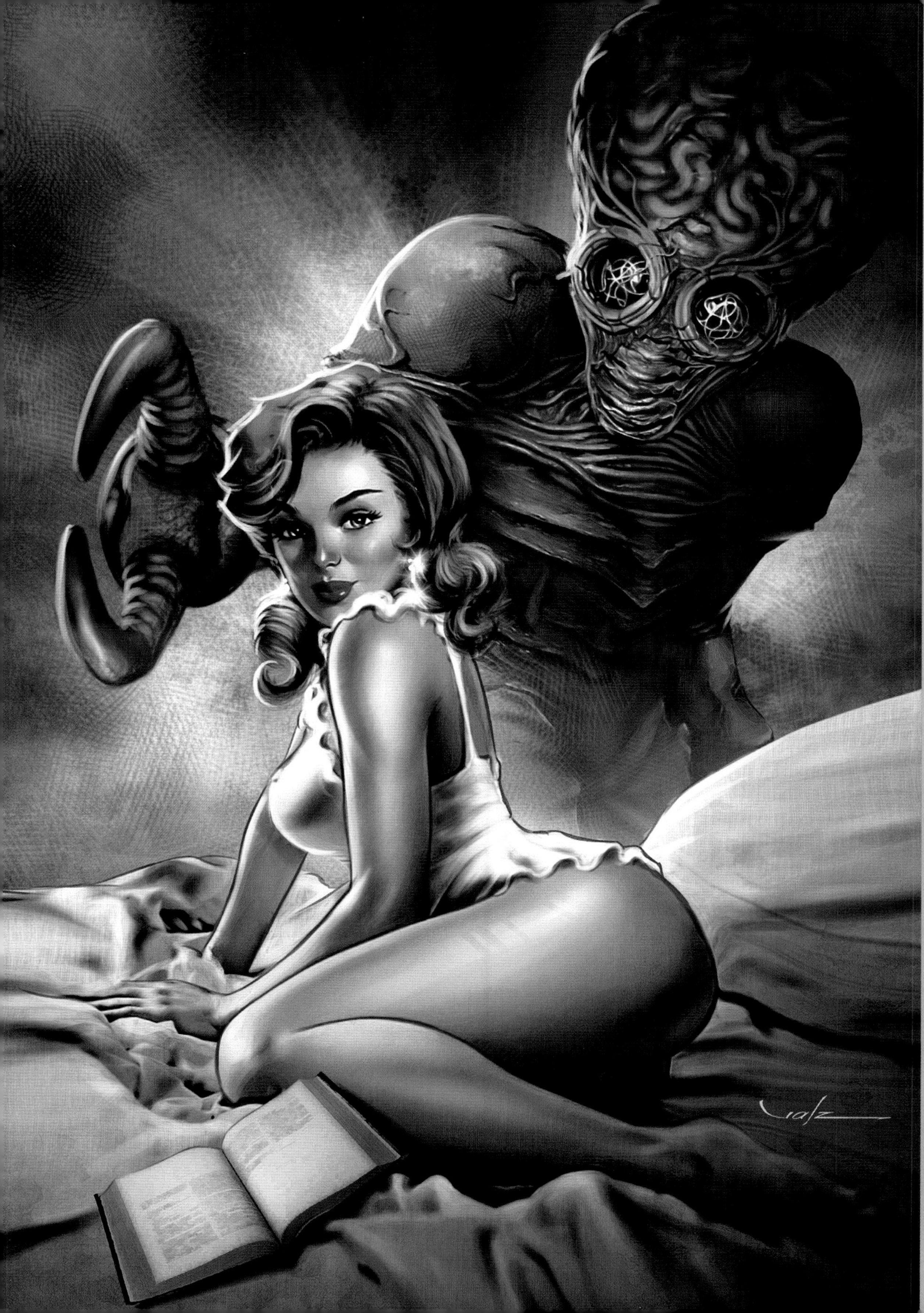
valz

◄ **The Visitor**
Carlos Valenzuela
Adobe Photoshop
http://valzonline.deviantart.com

"Let's see, I love pinup art from the 40s and the 50s. Also, I'm a BIG fan of the classic sci-fi movies from the 50s. I love to paint beautiful women, but also I really enjoy painting monsters and strange creatures. So, here is the result of all these ingredients! This piece helped me to get a lot of exposure, and was the first in a series of retro pinup horror pieces that I did, along with some really cool private commissions with a similar subject. The creature is a Metaluna mutant from the classic sci-fi cult movie This Island Earth."

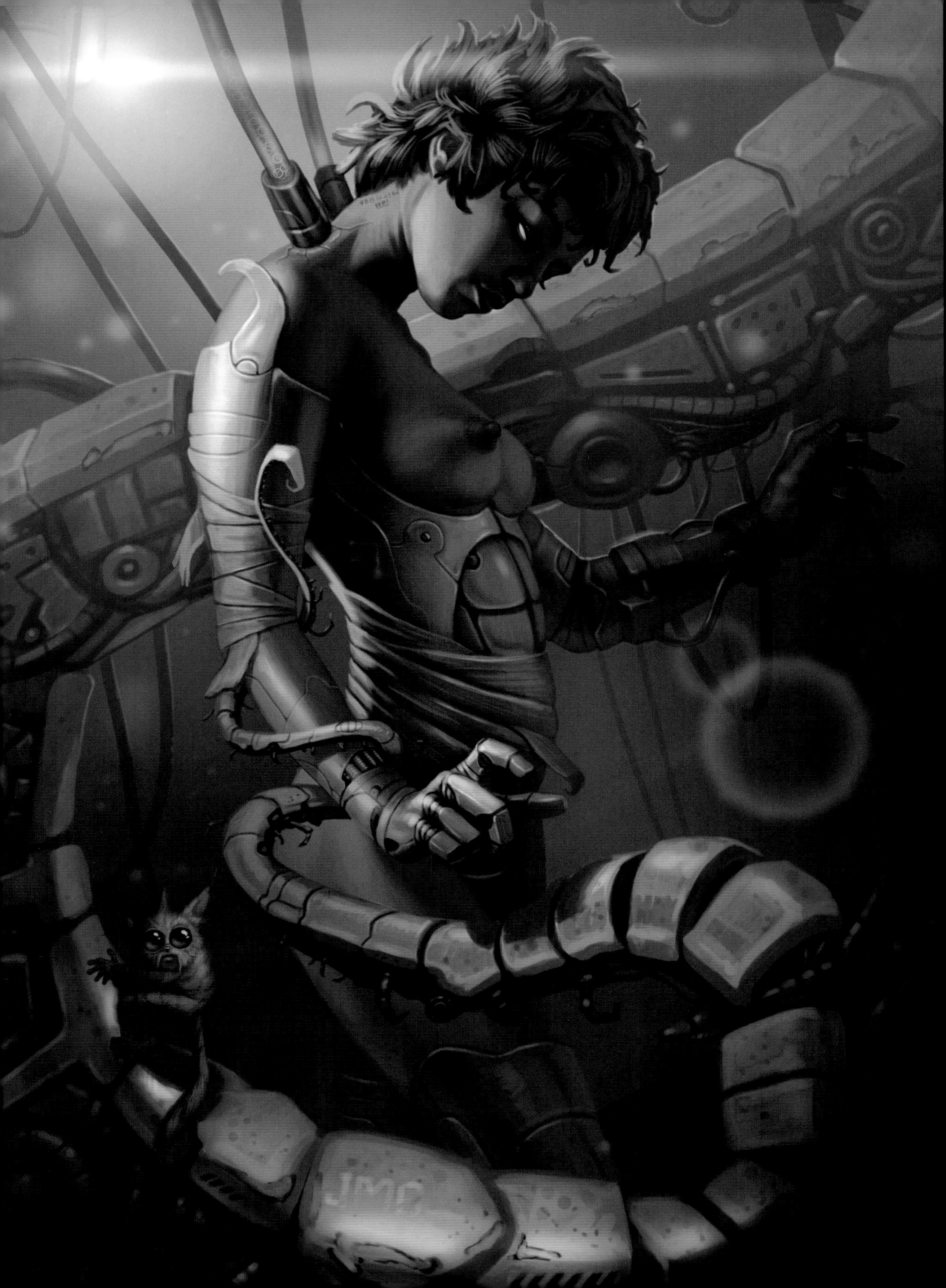

◄ **Petting the Damned**
Jhoneil Centeno
Adobe Photoshop
www.jhoneil.com

"This is my modern take on the Frankenstein legend. The creator is off-screen but controlling the various machinery and chemicals to give life to the 'creature.' The mechanical tentacle wrapping itself around her arm represents the creator as he marvels at his creation. The bandages are a nod to the old Hollywood Frankenstein movies."

► **Apple**
Yigit Koroglu
Adobe Photoshop
www.yigitkoroglu.com

"I wanted to portray an oriental desert rider in a sci-fi universe. She is blind and rides with the aid of the swoop's GPS. Whenever I look at this picture, it reminds me of an apple, hence the colors of her outfit and the title."

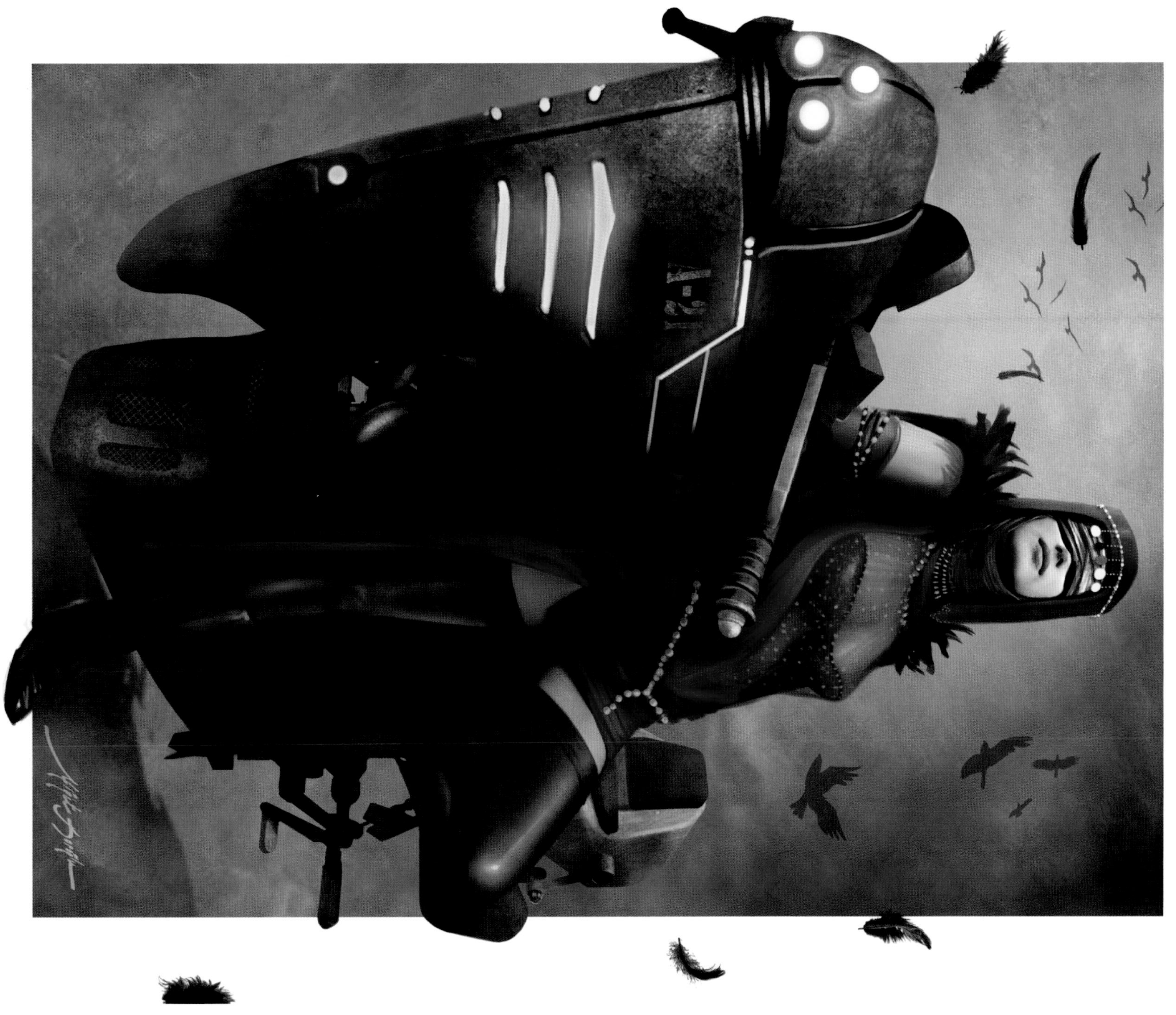

▶ **Insect**
Raúl Cruz Figueroa
Watercolor and acrylics
www.racrufi.com

"For this piece, I tried focusing on the constrast between the smoothness of the female skin and the roughness of old, rusty metal. To make the contrast more evident, I painted a mechanical creature in the shape of a worm that drips blood on the beautiful girl's chest. This was complemented with a glove in the shape of a claw with Aztec details, and a backdrop of an old and dirty place."

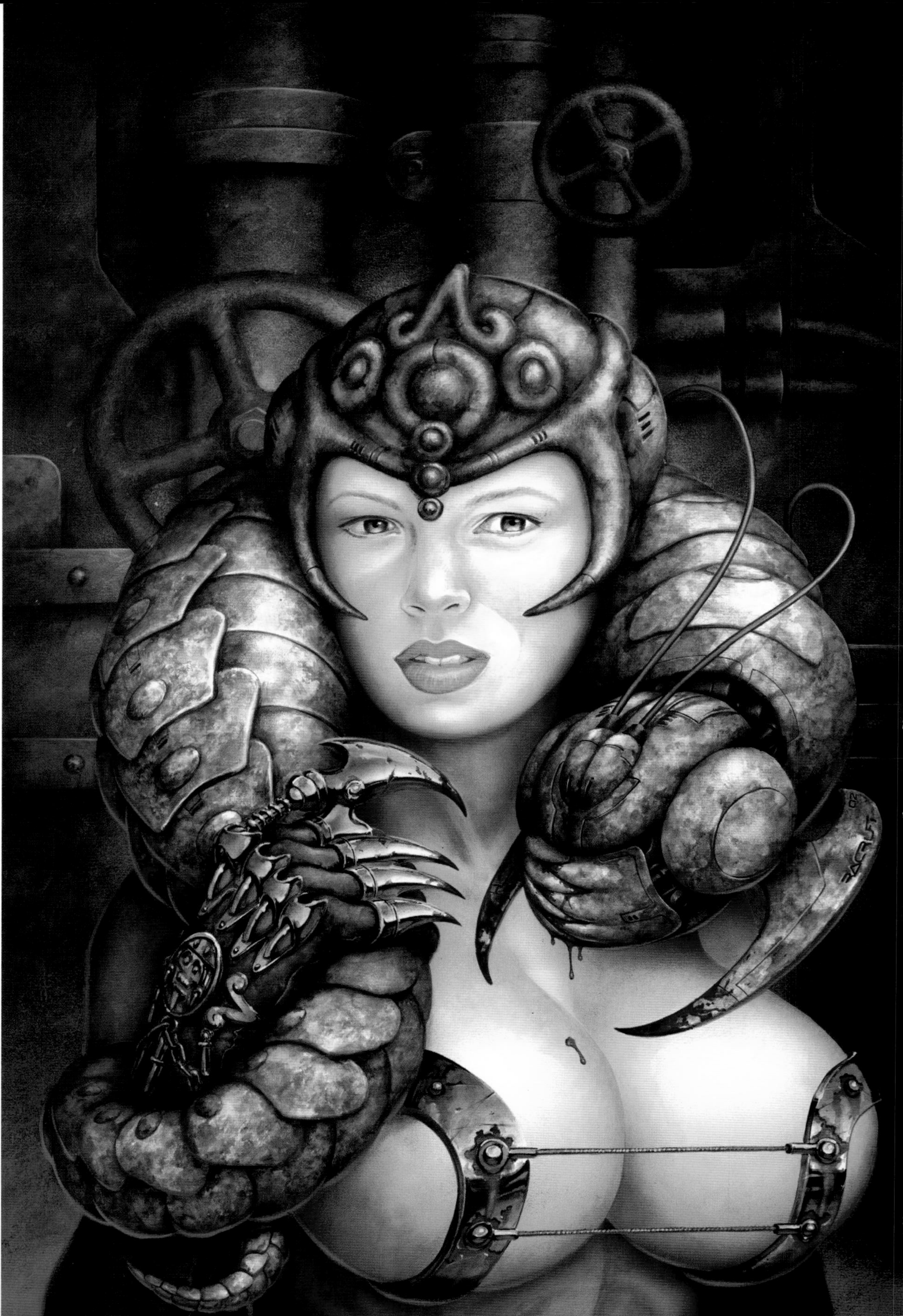

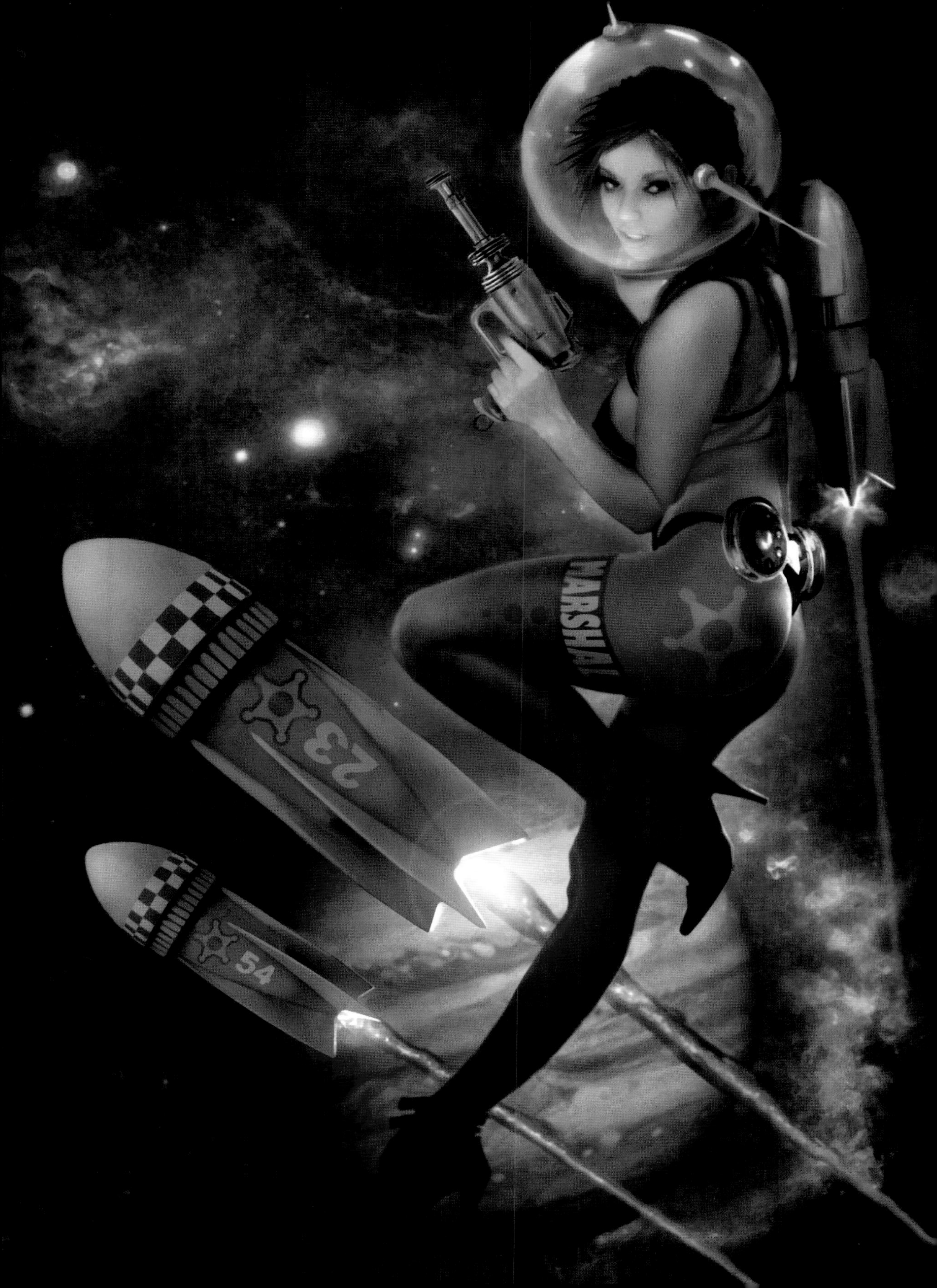

23
54
MARSHALL

▶ **Marshall**
John Blumen
Adobe Photoshop
www.johnblumenillustration.com

"Marshall is based on an earlier time in sci-fi when the ships and equipment of Buck Rogers and Flash Gordon didn't bother with the practical demands of space travel, they just looked good and futuristic. Being a fan of that retro aesthetic, I enjoy including it in my work where I can. Combining that look with a traditional pinup seemed to be a natural fit—add in a little western flavor and Marshall took flight."

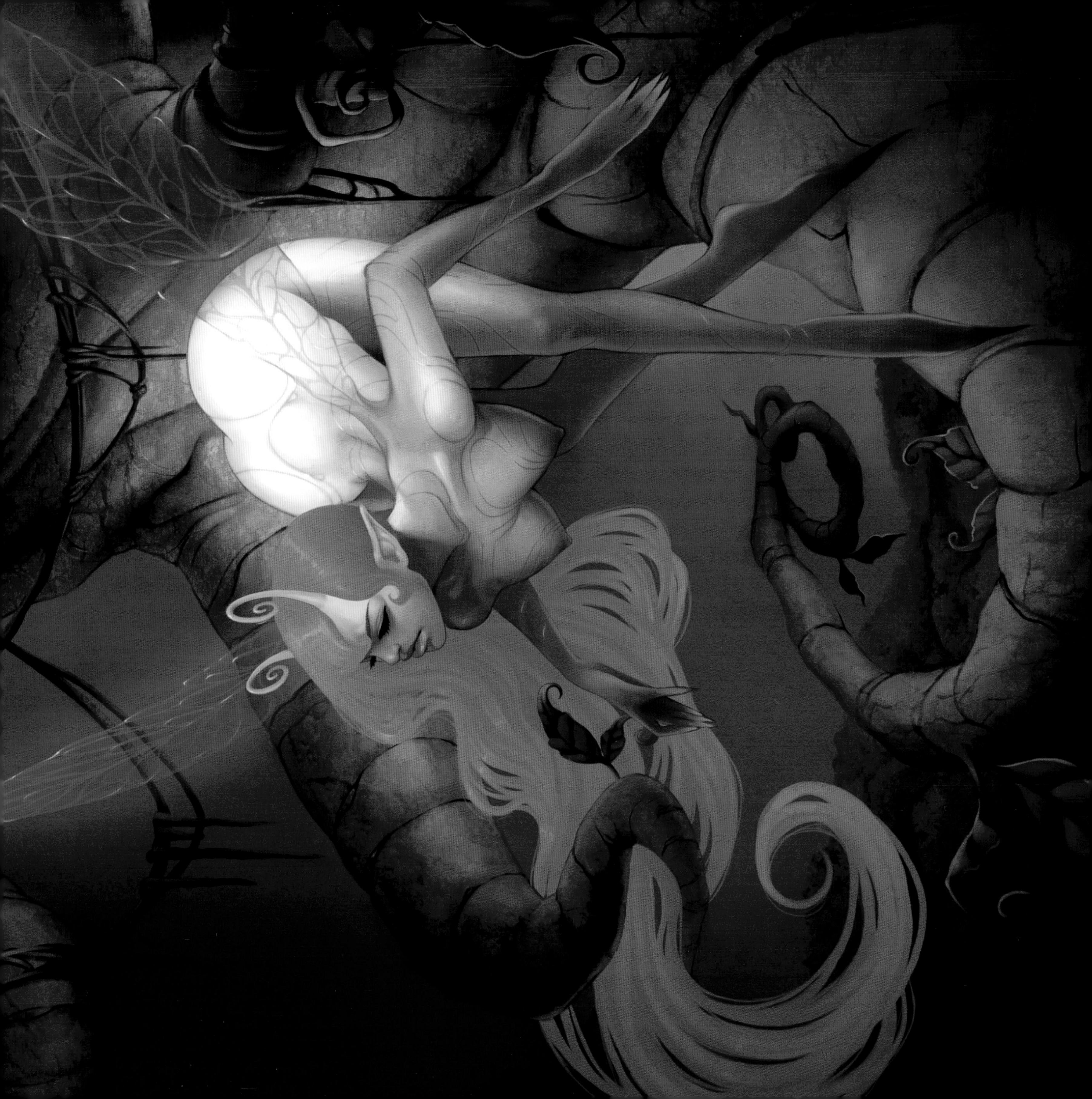

CHAPTER 9

ANGELS AND FAIRIES

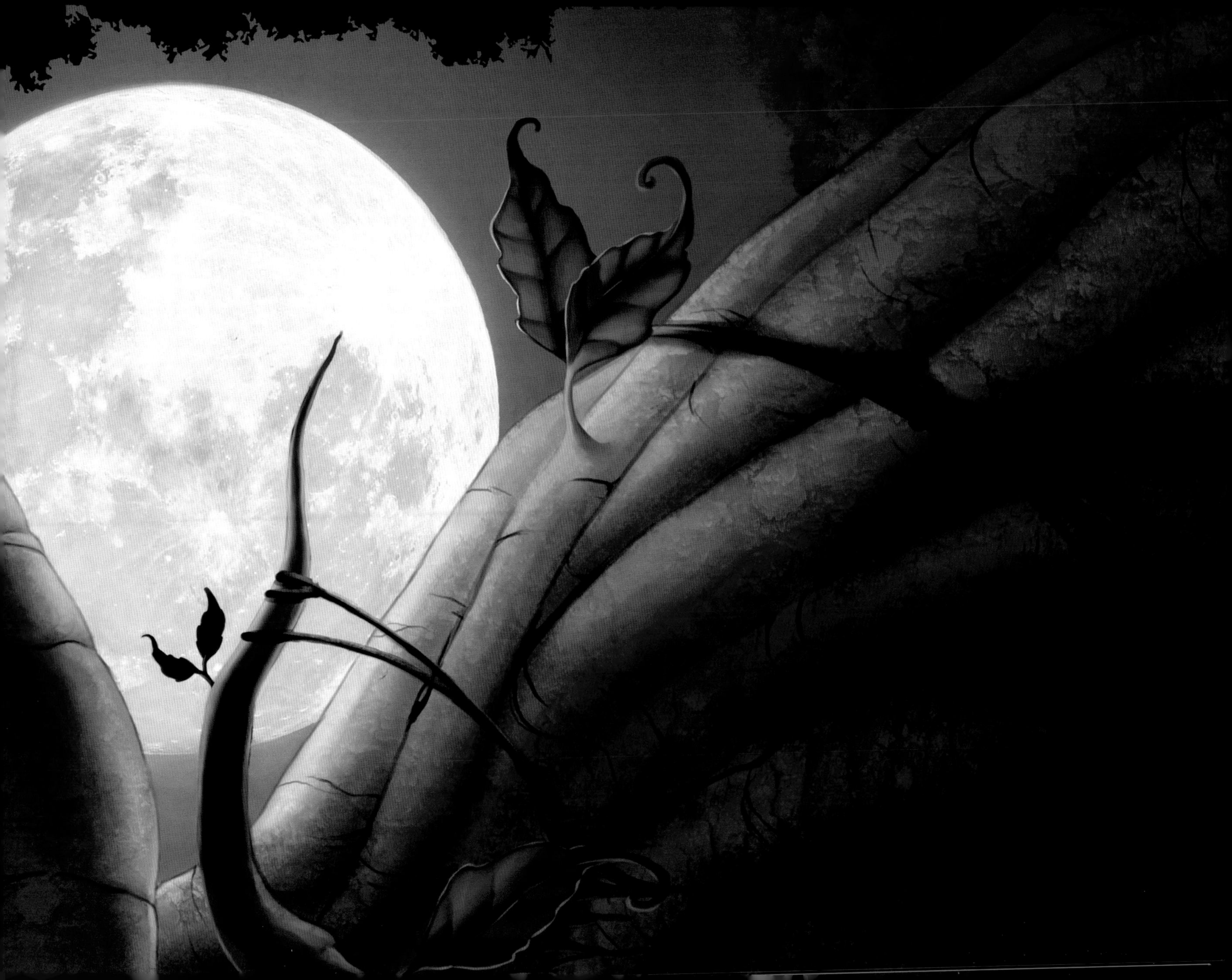

▲ **The Tree**
Daniela Uhlig
Pencil and Adobe Photoshop
www.du-artwork.de

"I drew the sketch for this painting a long time ago, and I finally finished it years later. It was done in an A4 format, but was nothing like the composition here. And up till then the firefly did not have long hair. It's not often that I find the time to create a picture with characters and background. I wanted to create a nice, romantic but dark and somehow kitschy mood. So I decided on the color combination of purple, blue, and pink. I like to imagine that the firefly is a kind of keeper of the tree. On hearing a sound, she slowly slides from her branch to check out what's going on."

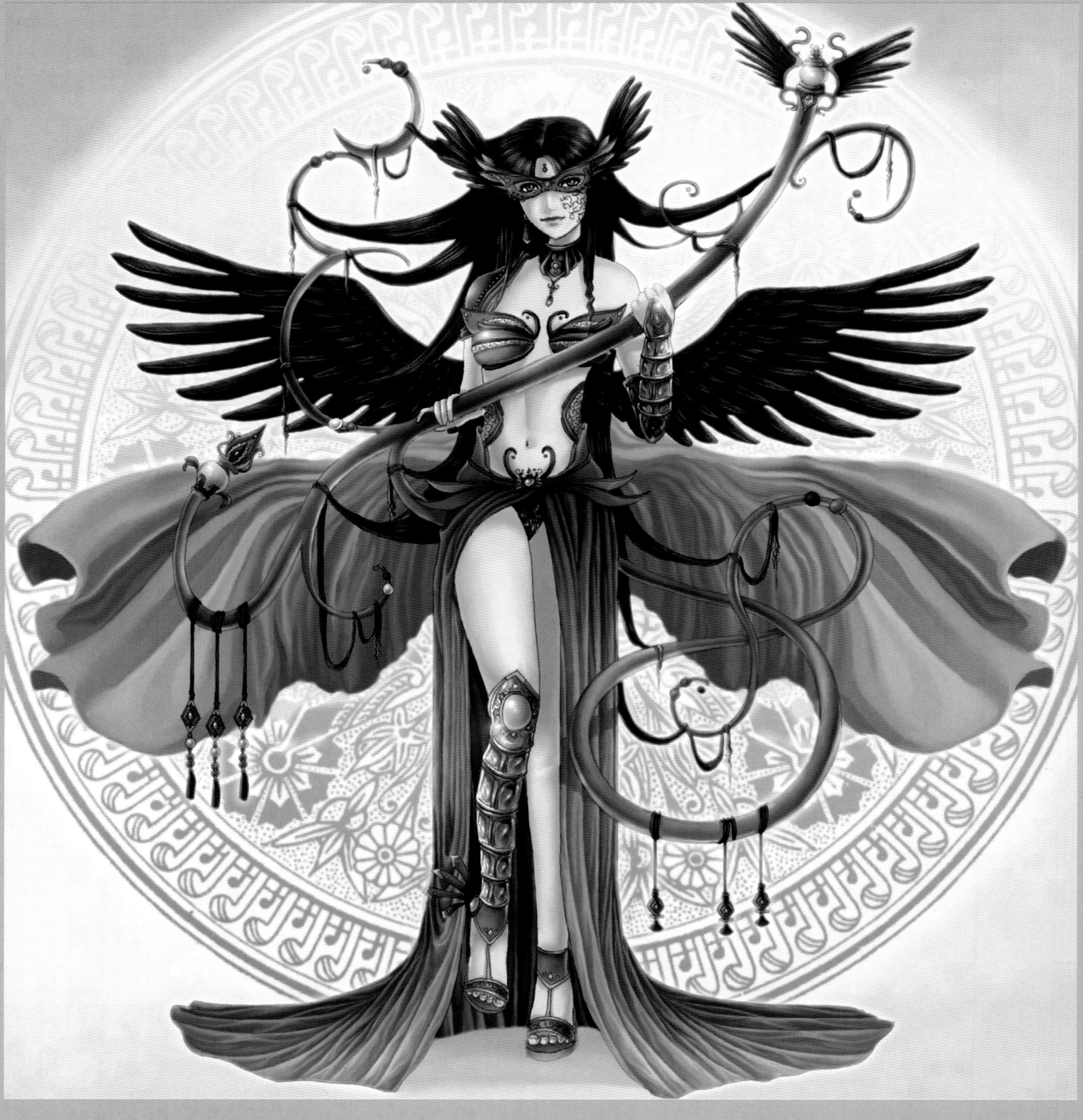

◀ **The Crook Goddess**
Vanette Kosman
Adobe Photoshop
www.vanettekosman.artworkfolio.com

"I remember that the first idea I had in mind for the creation of this drawing was to do something completely fanciful and full of ornaments. Thus, strokes started to flow to create this intense, oneiric, and full-of-life character. I named her Goddess for her extravagance and firm bearing, and included the crook in her depiction because it is her object of affection and support, and it certainly stands out in the drawing. I chose pastel colors and violet and lilac tones because I wanted to give the image a dreamy aspect, a place full of fantasy and extraordinary journeys."

▶ **My Sanctuary**
Vanette Kosman
Adobe Photoshop
www.vanettekosman.artworkfolio.com

"I've wanted to make a six-winged angel for a long time, and I finally accomplished it with this picture. These spread wings suggest peace and purity, and frame the picture perfectly. The character is sitting and yet there's nothing underneath to support her. This is what the fantasy of the work is about—the receiver decides if she is just floating or if it is her skirt that keeps her stable. The background is very simple and the title explains why. It is a sanctuary, a unique place for her where she is in touch with her emotions, isolated from the world. The colors of her clothes are in purple and blue tones to express tranquility and flow, like the water that is beneath her."

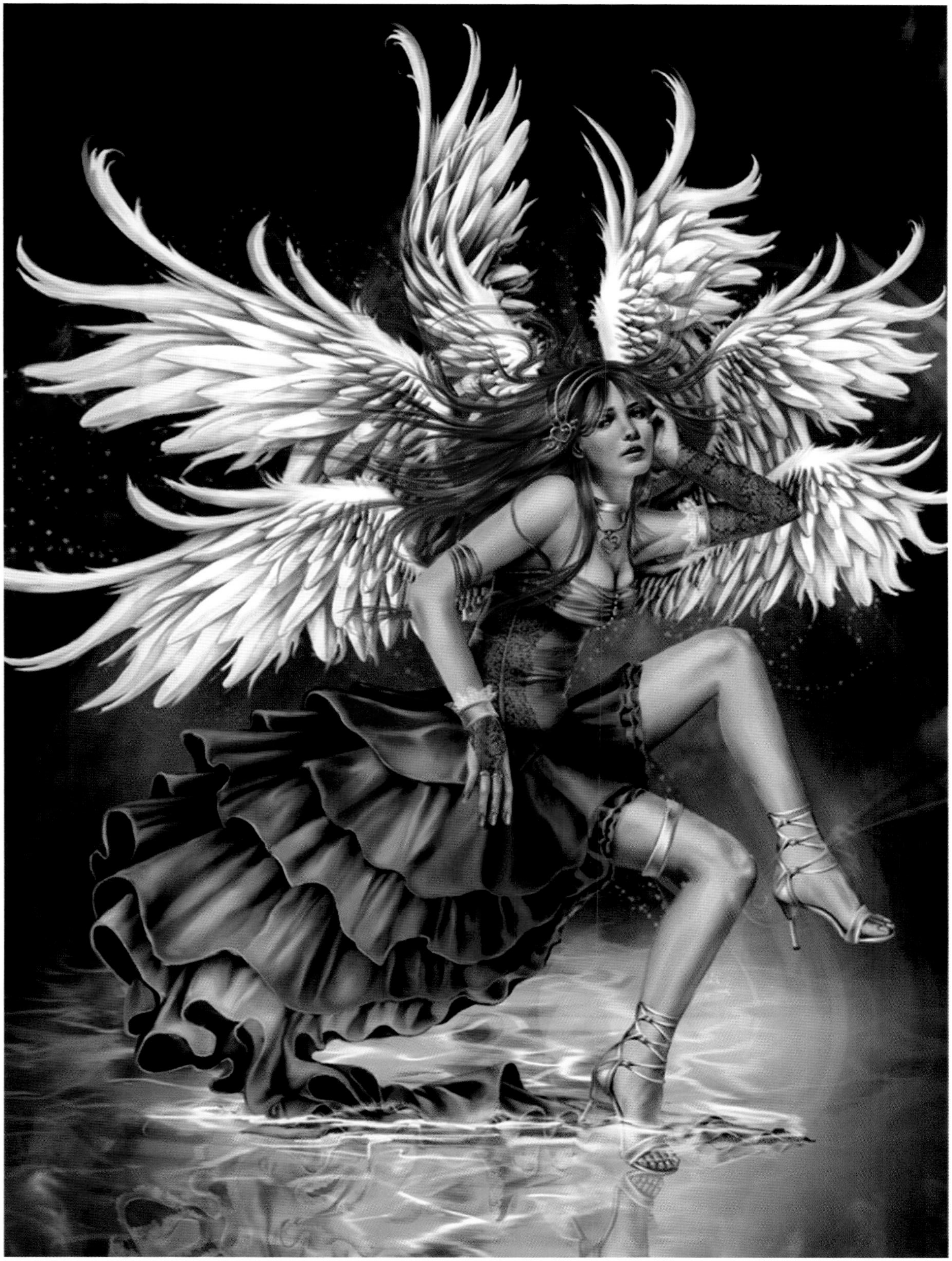

▶ **Dark Angel**
Guido Leber
Poser and Adobe Photoshop
www.goor.deviantart.com

"Most images of angels are peaceful. I felt that my angel should be dark, mysterious, and sexy. If we go to hell, I hope the angels there are dangerous and sexy. As with much of my digital art, the figure was created in Poser with the post-processing done in Photoshop."

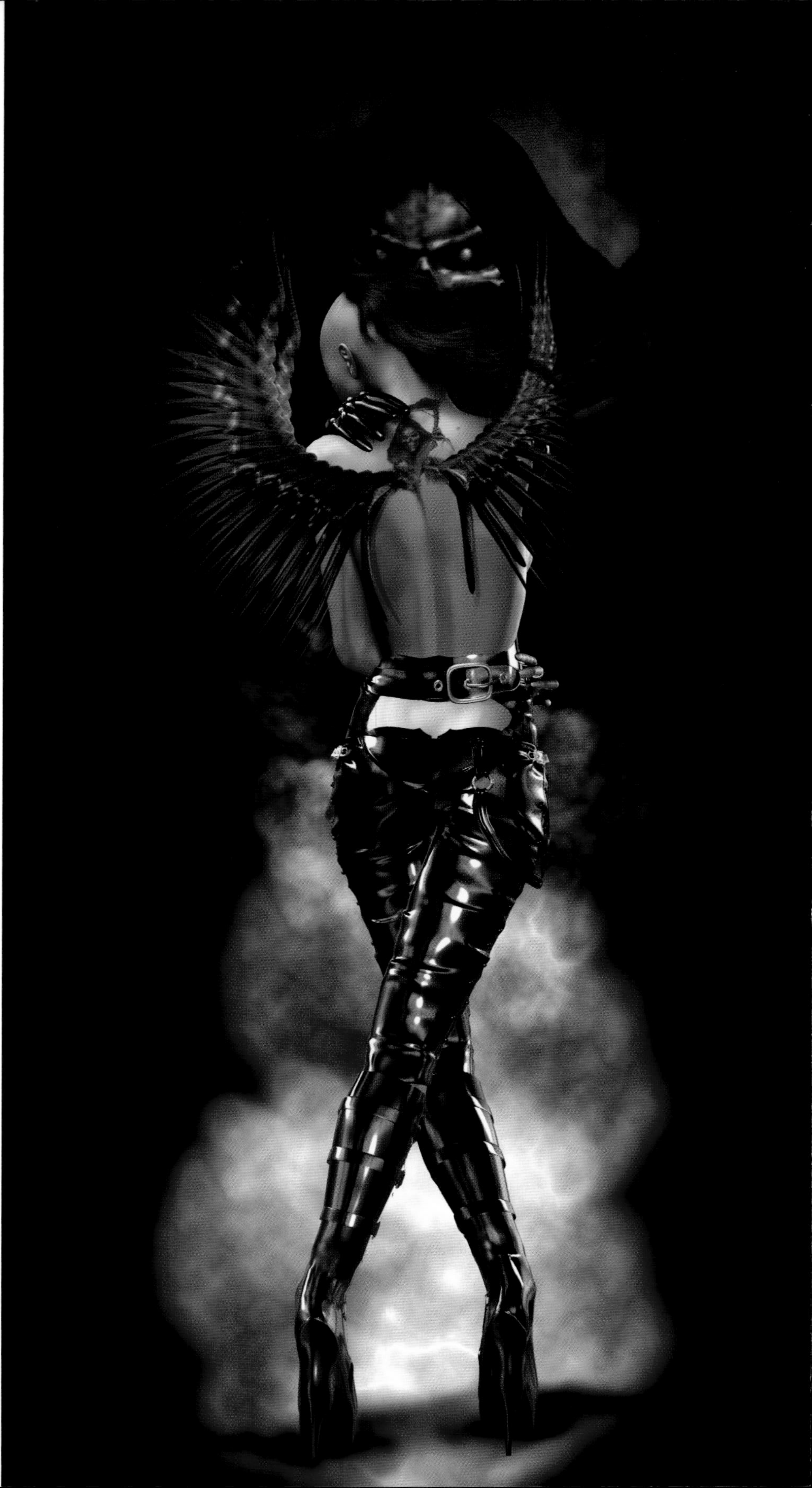

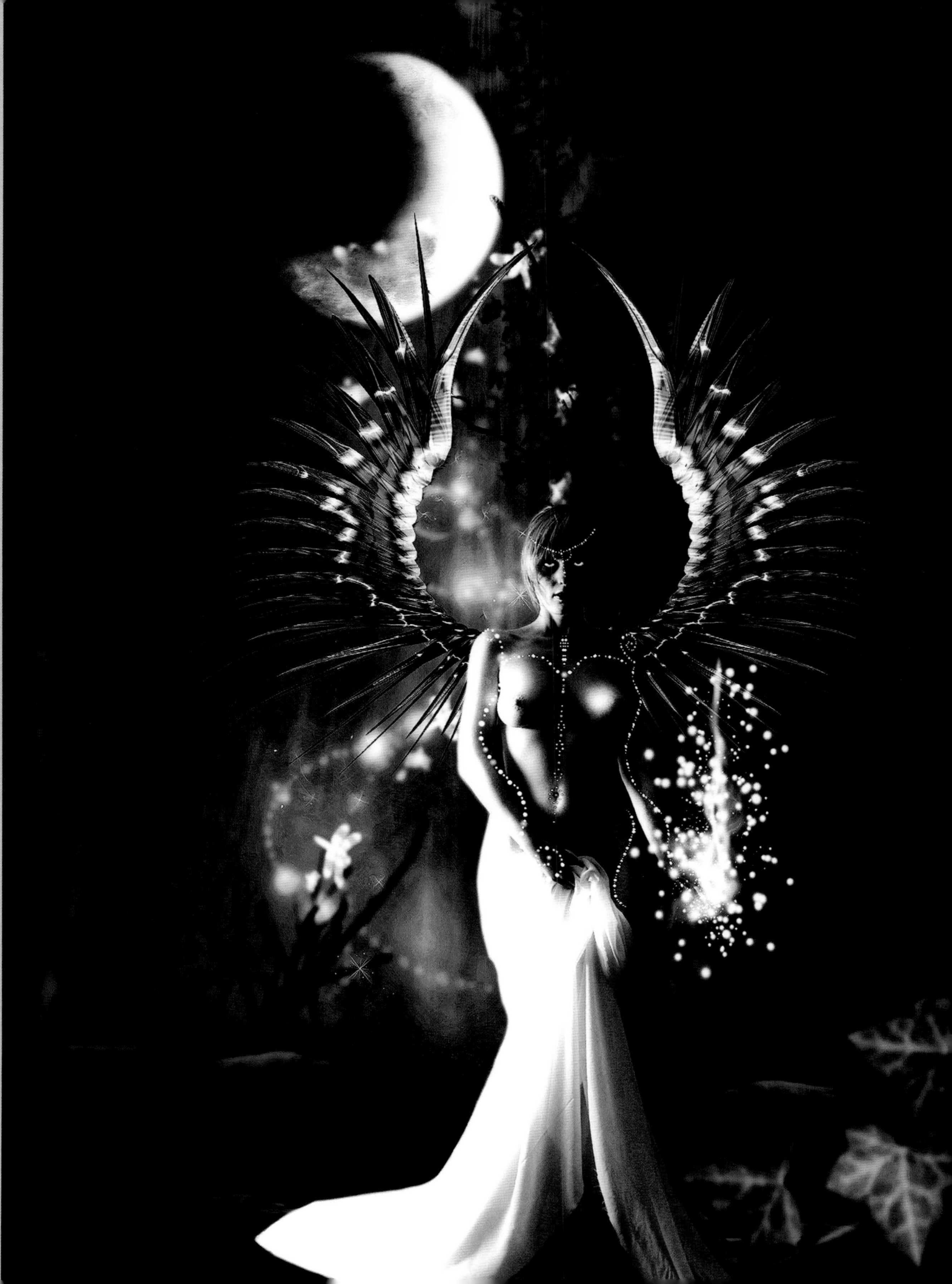

The Glow of Passion
Logan Knight
Adobe Photoshop
www.knightmanproductions.com

"My work tends to be dark and gothic or horror inspired, but from time to time I enjoy seeing lighter, softer ideas come from my creative mind. So, with this piece, I wanted to convey a feeling of passion and magical fantasy, yet have a tiny taste of mystery and a hint of darker undertones. I usually try and think of what it might be like if a creature like this existed in our world, and what a chance encounter with one of them might look like."

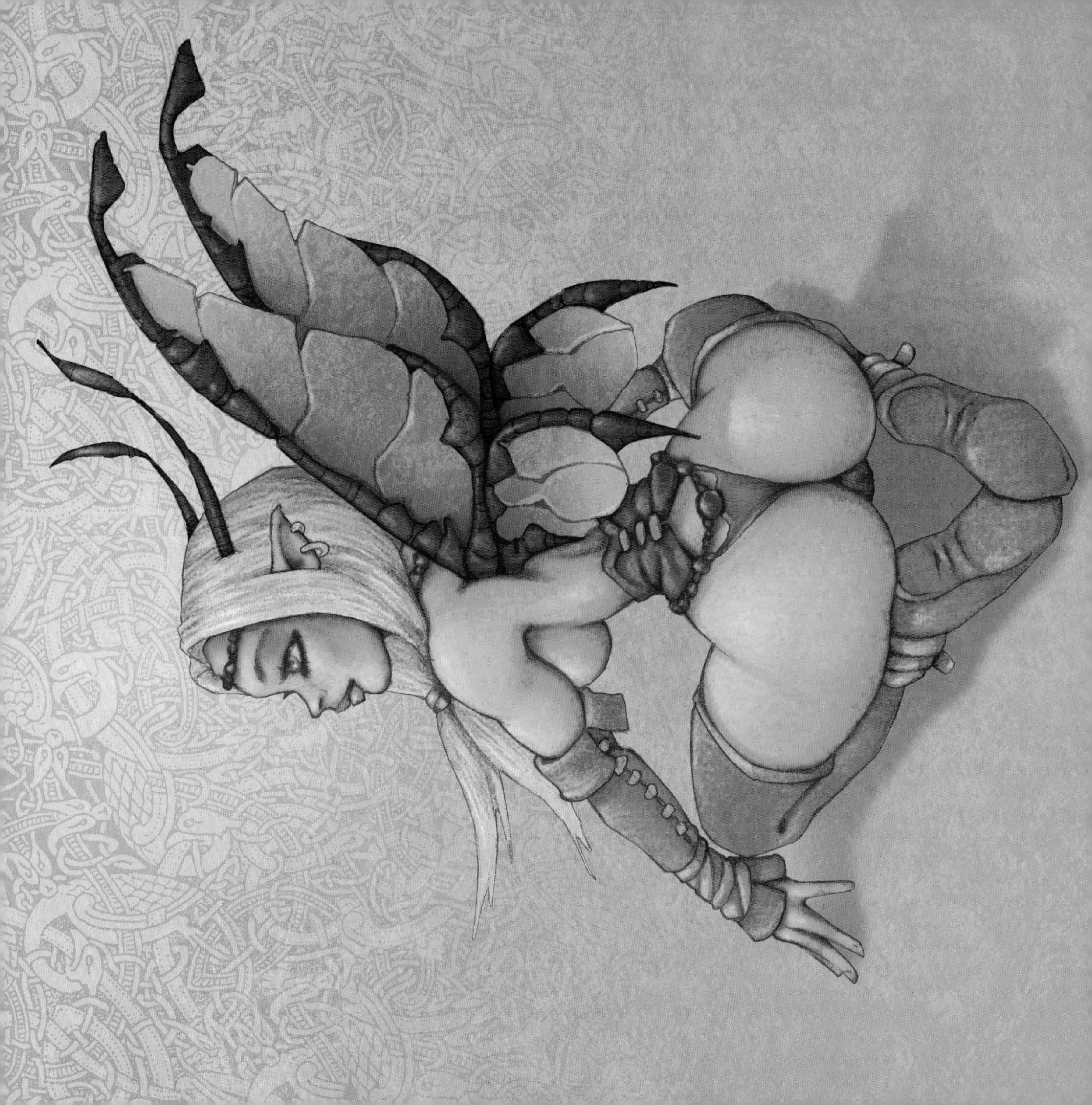

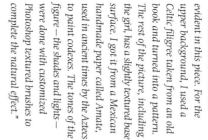

Light Fairy
Alejandro Gutiérrez Franco
Pencil and Adobe Photoshop
http://maidencomics.20m.com

"The scanned textures are evident in this piece. For the upper background, I used a Celtic filigree taken from an old book and turned into a pattern. The rest of the picture, including the girl, has a slightly textured base surface. I got it from a Mexican handmade paper called Amate, used in ancient times by the Aztecs to paint codexes. The tones of the figure—the shades and lights—were done with customized Photoshop textured brushes to complete the natural effect."

▼

Steampunk Fairy
Alejandro Gutiérrez Franco
Pencil and Adobe Photoshop
http://maidencomics.20m.com

"This pinup picture is a personal work. I wanted to add some manga influences to my own style, in a steampunk setting. The idea was to put a fairy, a traditional fantasy subject, in an unusual but plausible environment. I like to use natural paper textures for different surfaces. In this picture, even the metals were created from a scanned handmade paper. All elements — main character, background gears, round window — are in separate layers to get a desired atmospheric effect."

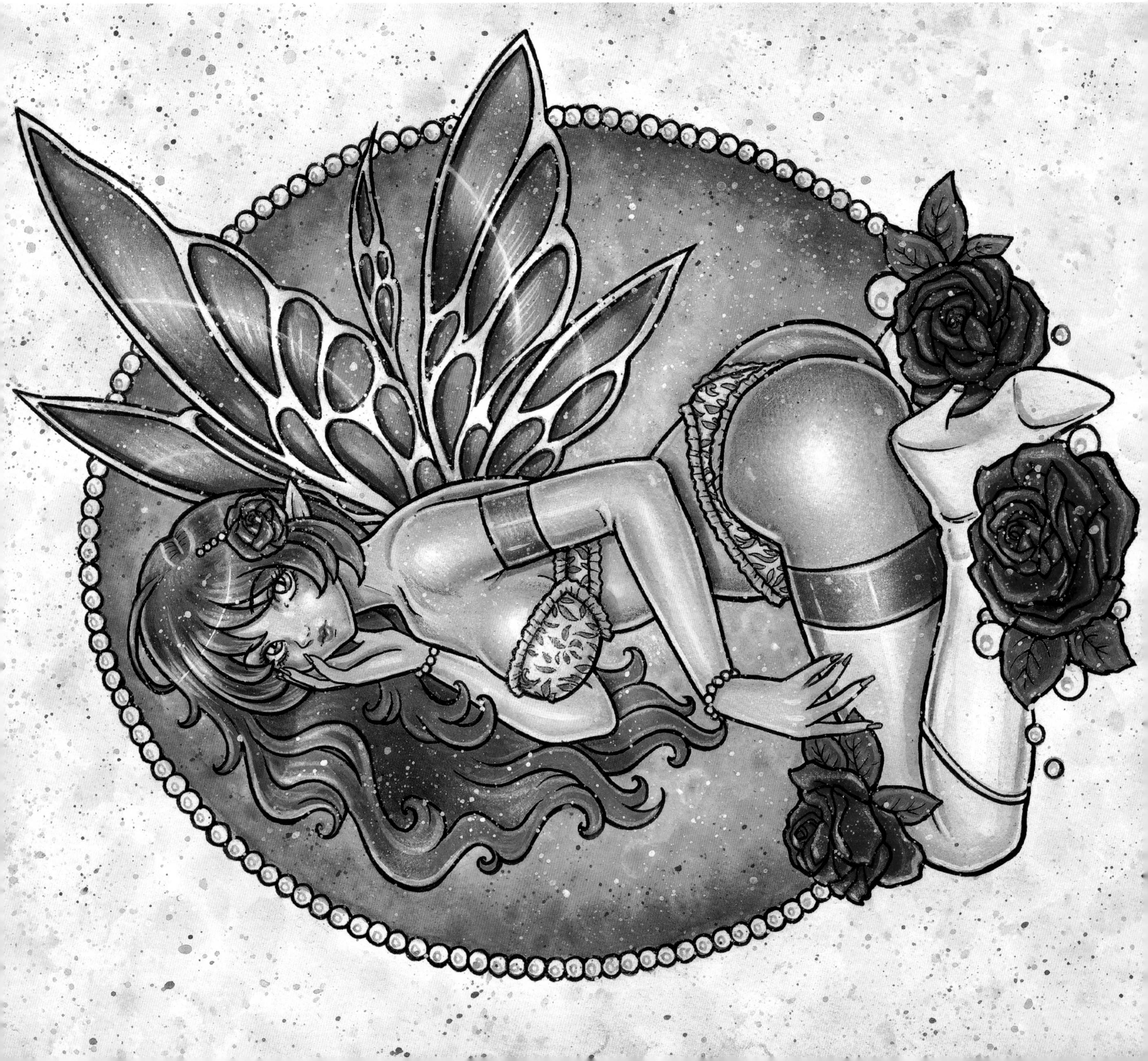

▲ Pearls and Roses
Delphine Lévesque Demers
Acrylics, ink, and marker
www.zerick.com

This piece was thoughtfully designed. The composition draws us to the fairy's face and hand, and her breast and her thigh. Demers explains: "Curves, pearls, roses, wings, and lingerie—as you can see, this one would entice anyone for a magical bedtime story. It's an image for those who are not so innocent when they dream!"

▼ Rebel Wings
Delphine Lévesque Demers
Acrylics, ink, and marker
www.zerick.com

This isn't your grandmother's fairy. Tattooed and smeared with makeup, he looks like he was created with some concoction of steampunk, not storybook, magic. Demers describes her motivations for the piece as a "tribute to the beauty of the male form." His moral ambivalence is deliberate: "This one I leave to the viewers to decide which side is more tempting, the good or the evil inside him?"

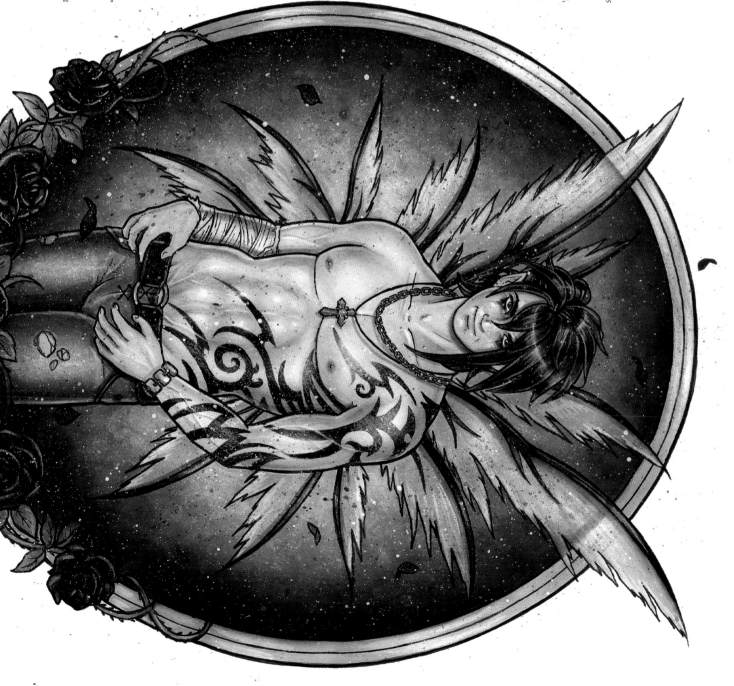

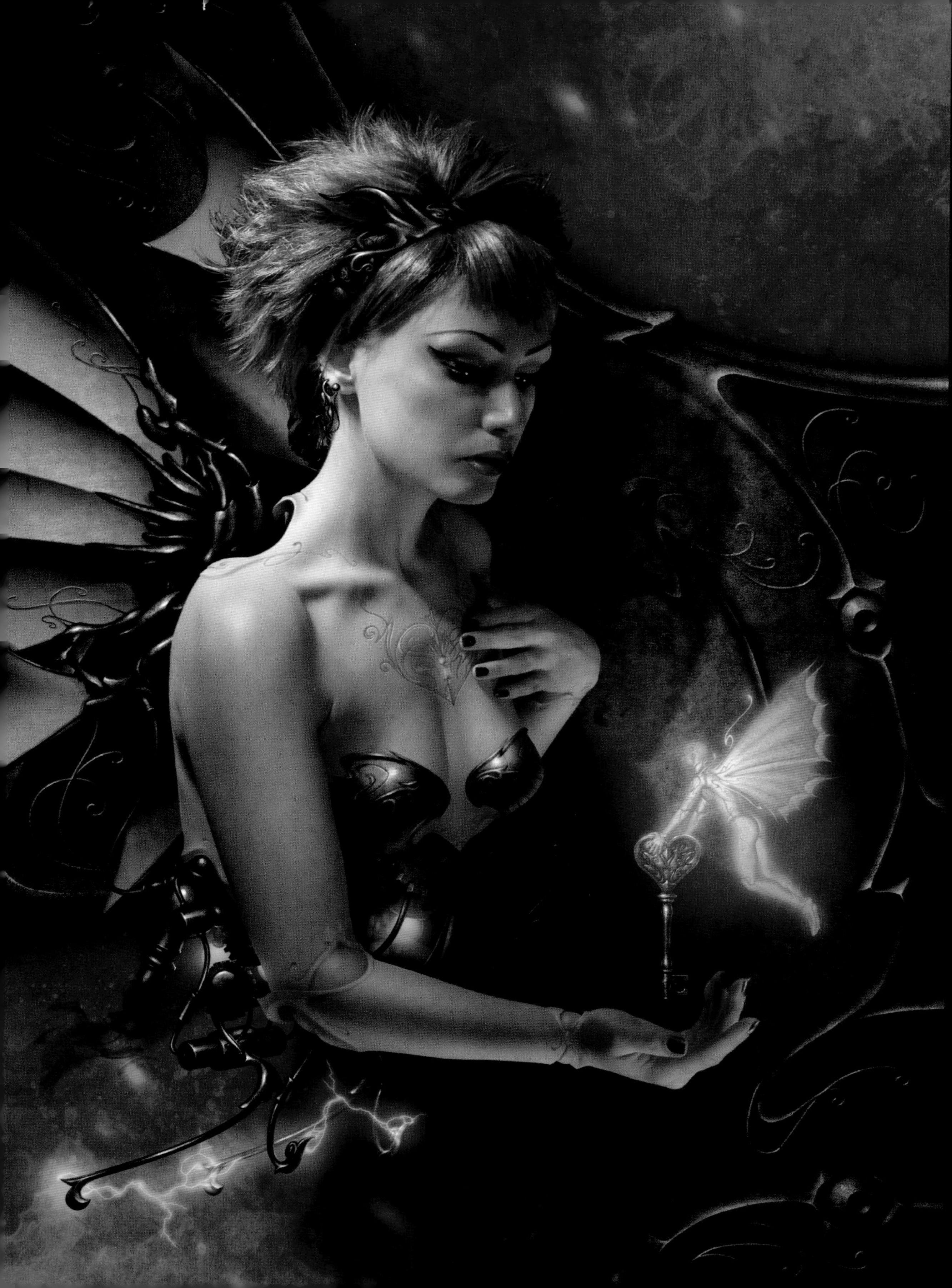

◀ **Faerie Queen**
Jason Juta
Photography
and Adobe Photoshop
www.jasonjuta.com

"I had a strong desire to start creating a series of fairy-themed images, while bringing my own dark aesthetic to them. I wanted a sort of magical, almost steampunk, technological element, and thought of the heart key idea. These are fairies who have evolved with changing times. All additional elements, besides the model herself, were painted in Photoshop."

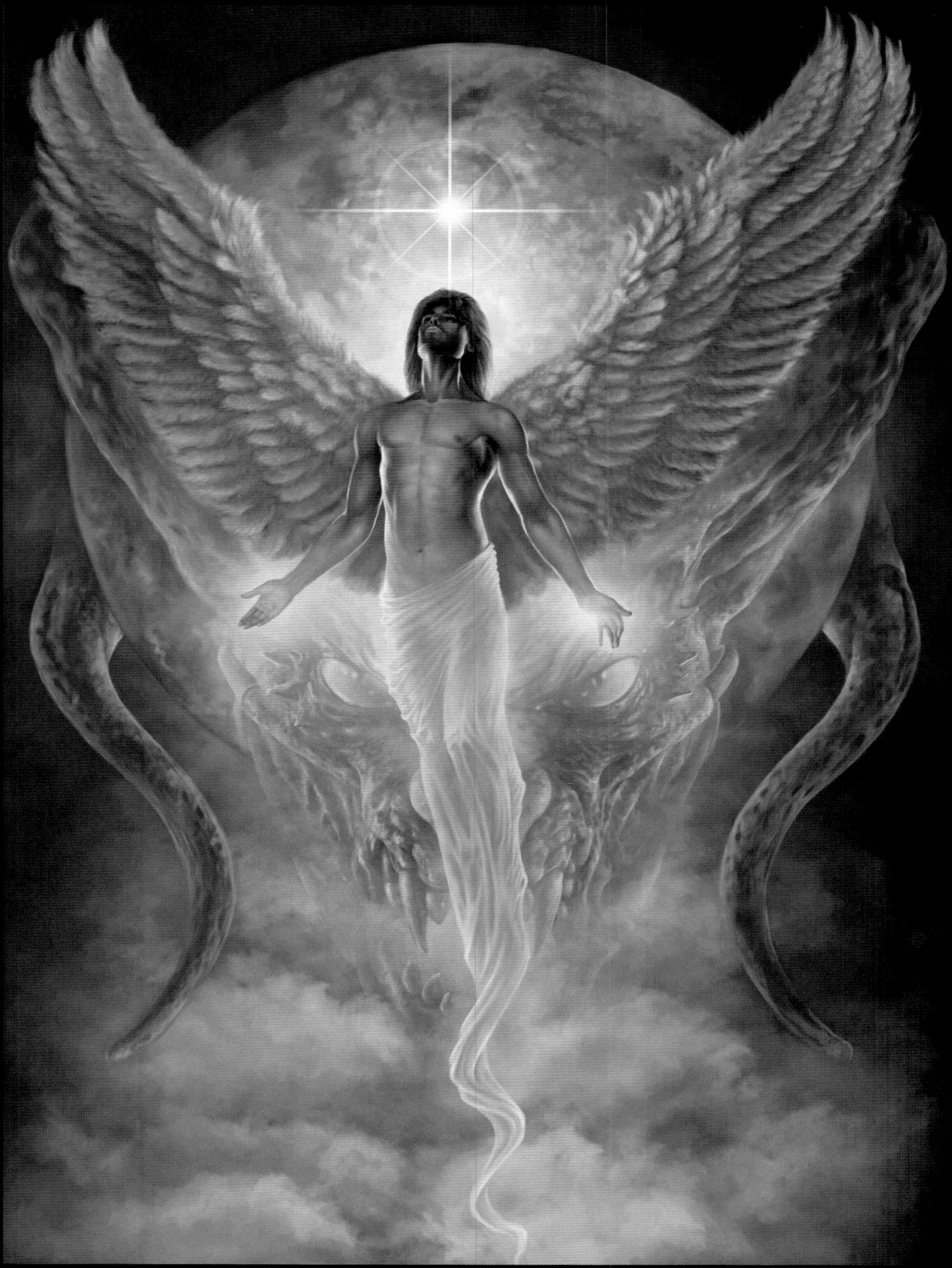

▶ **Bringer of Light**
Uwe Jarling
ZBrush, Corel Painter, and Adobe Photoshop
www.jarling-arts.com

"For a long time I've wanted to do a piece with the devil as the subject matter. The idea behind this piece was to show the devil before his fall as a beautiful angel, and after the fall as the ugly horned guy we all think of him as. I wanted the devil face in the back not to be too obvious, so that it takes a moment before one really notices it in the back. The evil face was 3-D-sculpted in ZBrush and over-painted in Painter and Photoshop to fit in with the rest of the painting."

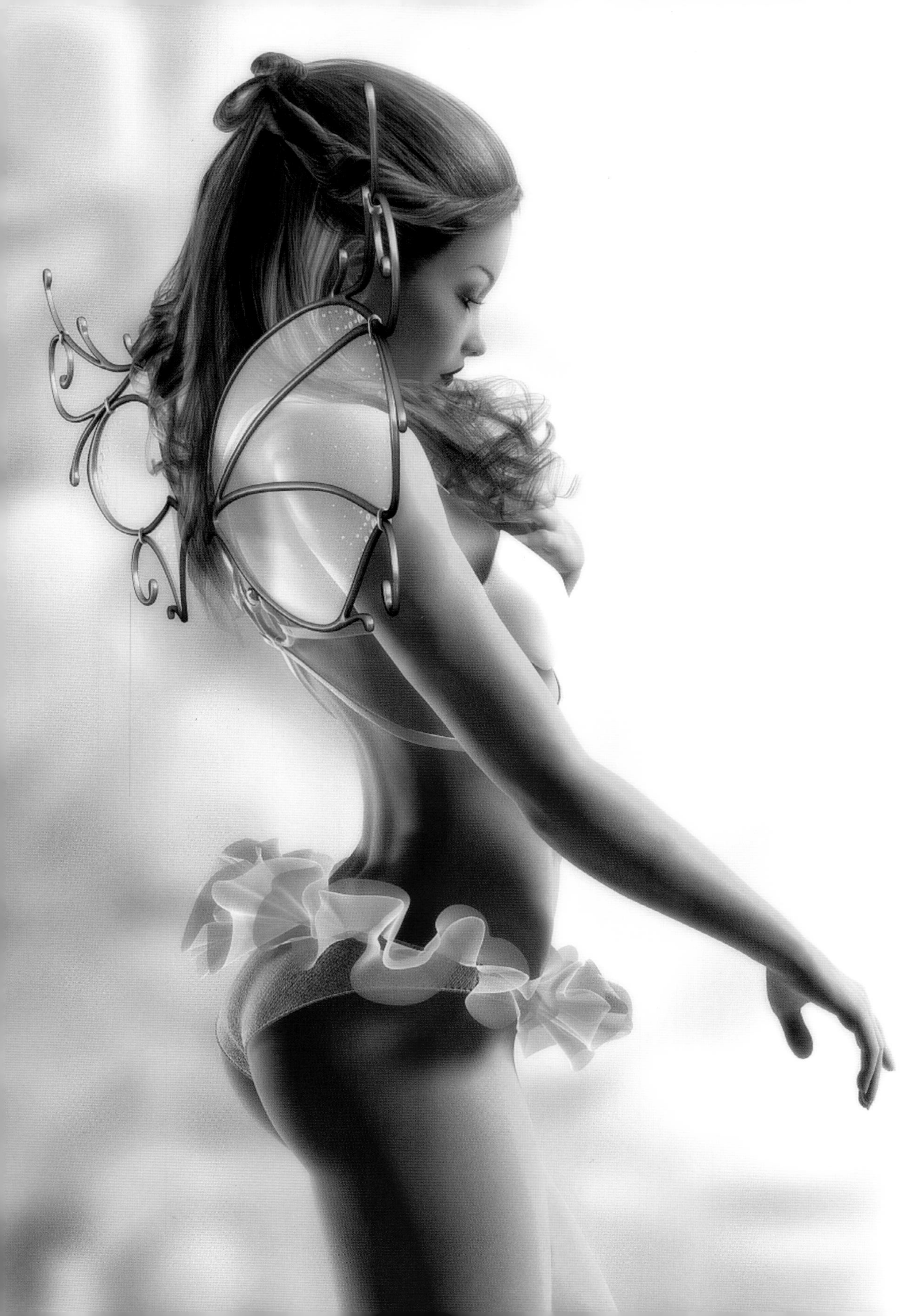

◄ **I Miss You**
RGUS
Poser Pro and Adobe Photoshop

"This piece really grew from a frontal portrait; the intention was to show well-rounded form. A curvaceous body shape was placed in a side profile pose and the elements of the outfit added one by one, rendered then appraised, discarded, or kept. The feeling of youth and delicateness soon emerged as the only possible conclusion to the image. To further emphasize the smooth, gentle and angelic feel to the image, faerie wings were a last addition, which I believe halts the eye from wandering off to the left and makes the mind wonder what she's pointing at. The title was something a friend suggested as being about an angel in heaven missing her loved one on Earth. Poser Pro was used for rendering the main figure and clothing. Photoshop was used to remove image noise and skin softening. The background was added in Photoshop and blurred, so as to not dominate the final scene."

Callipygian Angel
Lorenzo Di Mauro
Pencil, FreeHand, Adobe Photoshop, and Corel Painter
www.lorenzodimauro.com
http://lorenzoart.blogspot.com

"While drawing this cute angel based on the likeness of a pretty model, I started doing a vector line-art based on the original pencil sketch in Freehand. I then painted the colors, looking for the right color variations in the white wings and the background, mixing it with a scan of crumpled paper, which looked as though it were a sort of vellum texture. Here, skin tones are less carnal, more pale, to emphasize the ethereal nature of such an angelic creature."

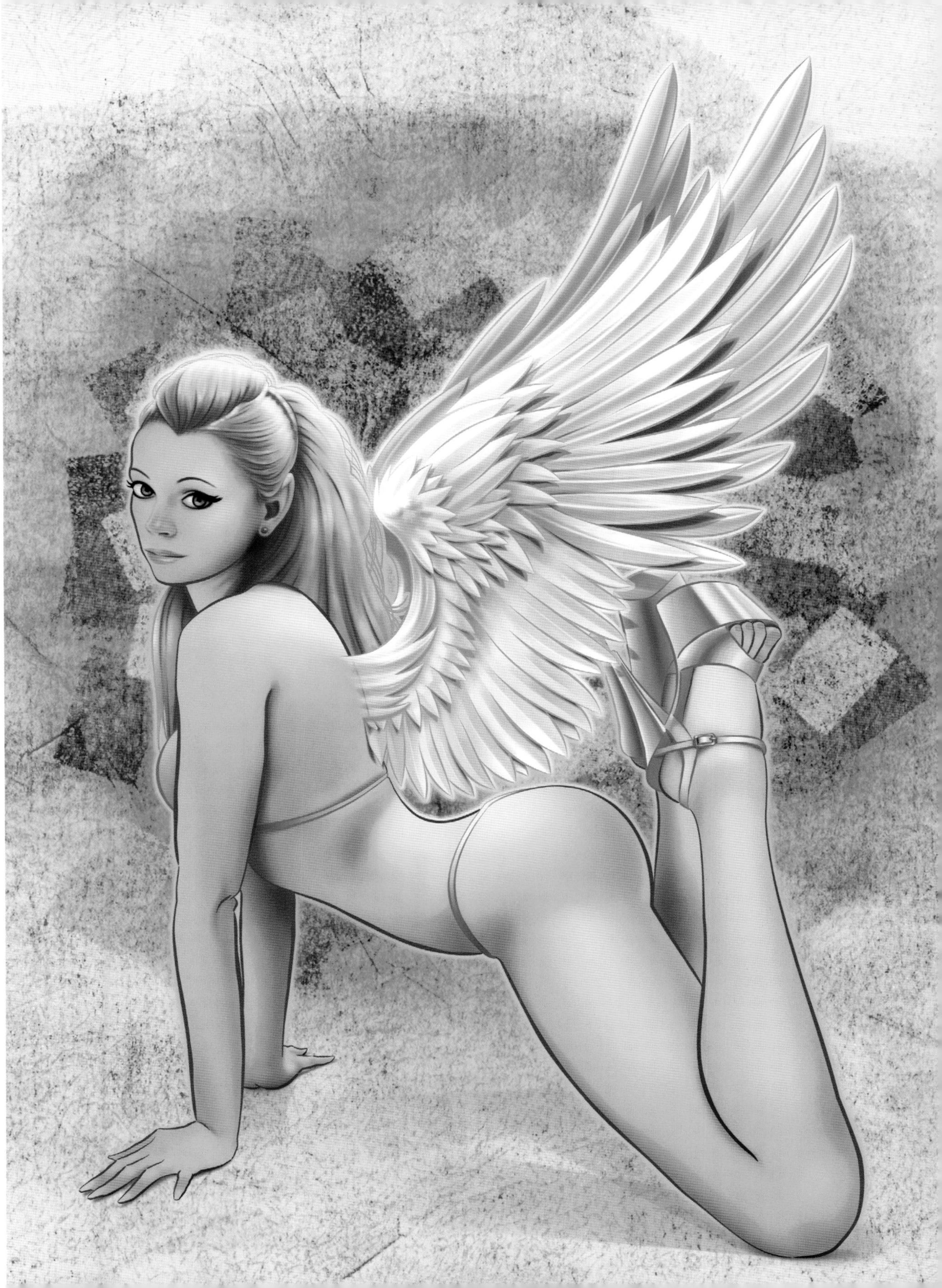

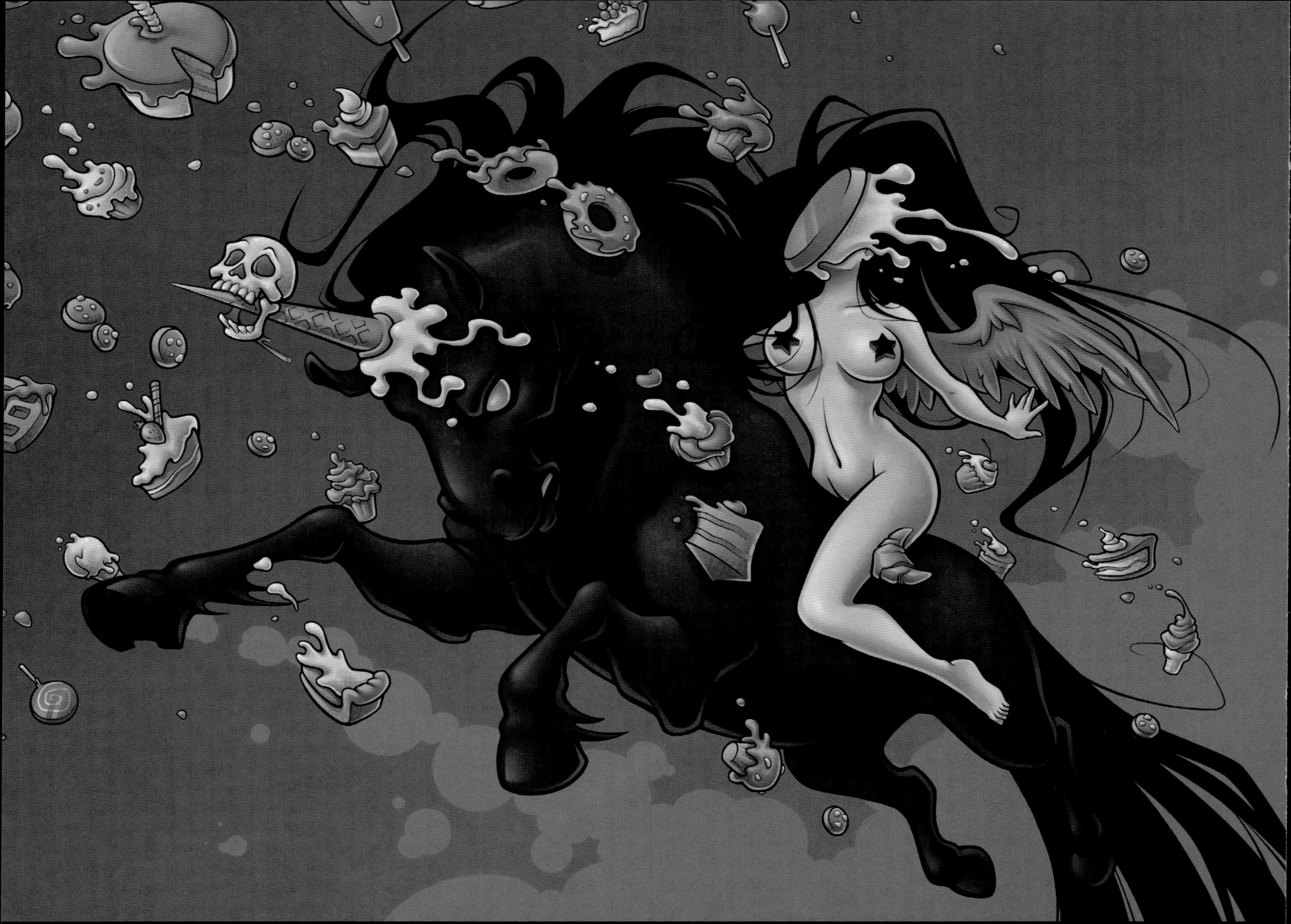

▲ **Unicorn**
Aleksandra Marchocka
Adobe Photoshop
www.olamarchocka.com

"A nude woman riding a horse is a theme that always reminds me of Władysław Podkowinski's symbolist painting Frenzy*, on which I loosely based the idea for this picture. My main goal was to make fun of classic fantasy motifs and turn them into something absurd, silly, and surreal. So the epicness of the unicorn galloping through a stormy sky and the eroticism of the rider is contrasted by the cuteness and childishness of the pink candy rain. As for the composition, I tried the diagonal view to make the image look more dynamic and capture the feeling of movement."*

Reincarnation
Chung Yee-Ling
Adobe Photoshop
http://syncmax.deviantart.com

"The idea behind this work was an elf trying to get away from the evil world in which she lived, as she regretted all the bad things she had done. However, her race disagreed with her decision and tried to use any and every method to stop her and lock her in their world. But she would not give up. Her efforts finally touched the god's heart, and she has been given the chance to be reborn as an angel."

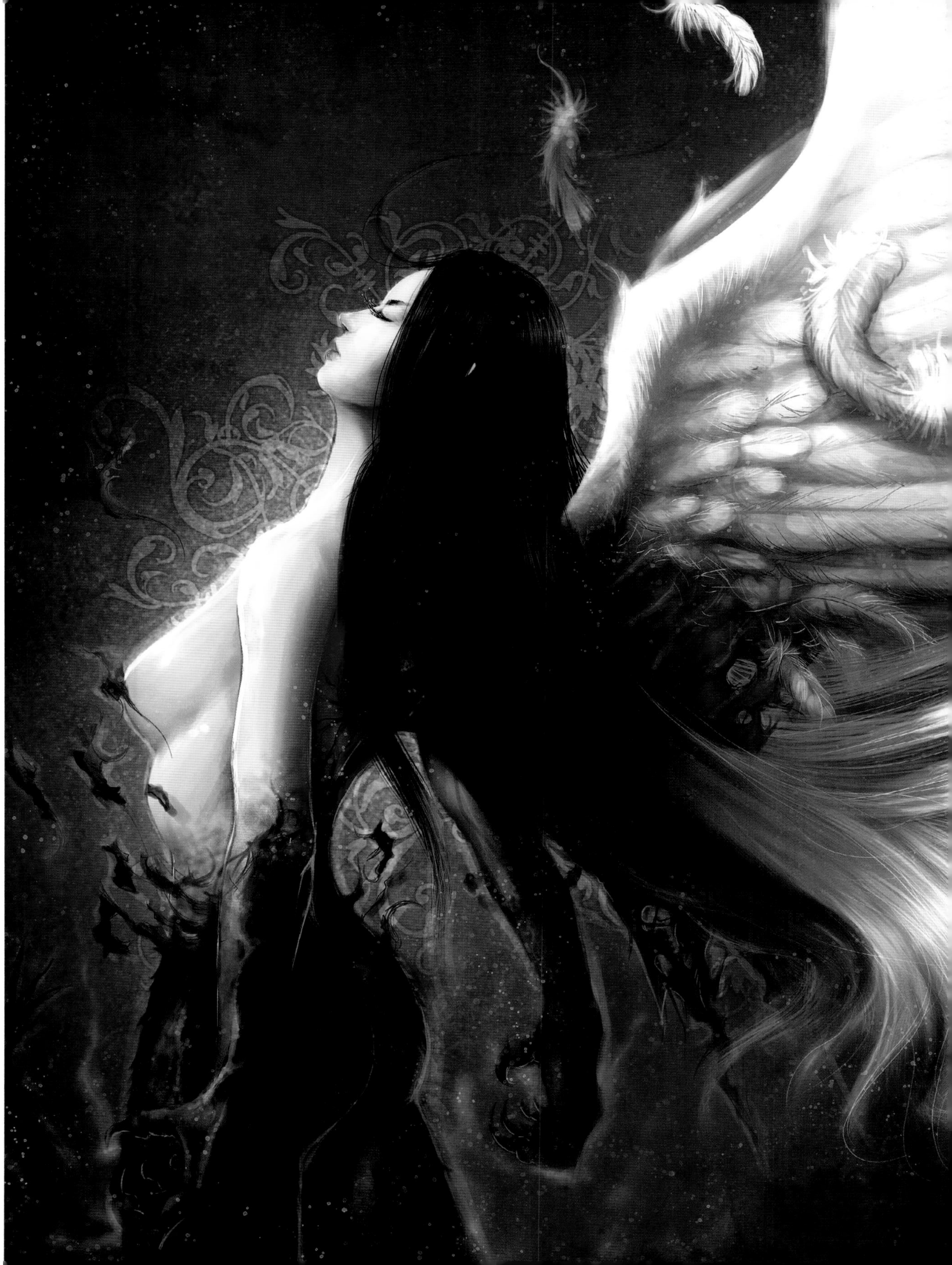

PAUL ABRAMS
www.paulabrams.com
obliviongrin@yahoo.com
Black Queen p133

CHRIS ACHILLÉOS
www.chrisachilleos.co.uk
Penthesilea p6
Fishgirl p8
First Lady p9

ARTEMIS (SHARYN YEE)
http://dragonfly3d.deviantart.com
sharyn_yee@yahoo.com
Taming the Wild p56
A Knowing Touch p59

JASMINE BECKET-GRIFFITH
www.strangeling.com
jasminetoad@aol.com
Absinthe Mermaid p34
Blue Butterflies p74

DANIEL BERNAL
http://imaginante.daportfolio.com
www.imaginante.deviantart.com
www.danielbernalportfolio.blogspot.com
imaginante@gmail.com
The Beauty of the Beast p110
The Head Collector p111

PASCAL BLANCHE
www.3dluvr.com/pascalb
lobo971@yahoo.com
Angelblues p55
Dinoblues p102
Zapp p158

JOHN BLUMEN
www.johnblumenillustration
john@johnblumenillustration.com
Lilly p89
Marshall p173

**FREDERIC BODO
(BODO2XZERO)**
www.holydamned.deviantart.com
bodo2xzero@gmail.com
Lovasion p160

DEVON CADY-LEE
www.gorrem.cghub.com
gorremhome@hotmail.com
Close Call p82
Sacred p83

ANNE CAIN
www.annecain-art.com
annecain.art@gmail.com
Lotus in the Wild p58
Dark Elves: Awakening p78
Autumn p146
Dark Magik p147

MICHAEL CALANDRA
www.calandrastudio.com
www.frameworksartandframe.com
www.zazzle.com/mcalandra
Awakening p65
Devil Girl p126

JHONEIL CENTENO
www.jhoneil.com
Flight and Roses p50
Bad, Barbarian, Marian p113
Petting the Damned p170

CHARLENE CHUA
www.charlenechua.com
charlene@charlenechua.com
Ninja Bunny p14
Drow p15
Vampyr p87

**ELISA CRELLIN
(DARKELEGANCE)**
http://art-of-darkelegance.daportfolio.com
http://eroticelegance.deviantart.com
emp71@msn.com
Heaven Sent p60
Latex Bound and Love p66
Deadly Seduction p73
Medusa's Lover p88
Dragons Whisper p144

JEANNEDARK (SETO KAIBA)
http://jeannethedark.daportfolio.com
fatalframefotography@yahoo.de
Biohazard Evolution p21

DARTHHELL
www.darthhell.deviantart.com
Burning Halo p42
Belial p109
Pay Homage p114

DCWJ
www.dcwj.deviantart.com
blurblurkia@yahoo.com
Red Knight p19
The Duel p105

DEEDEE DAVIES
www.seedydeedee.co.uk
deedee@seedydeedee.co.uk
Where Heaven and Hell Meet p61
Hunger p69
Tread Softly p116

DELPHINE LÉVESQUE DEMERS
www.zerick.com
delphine@zerick.com
Pearls and Roses p182
Rebel Wings p183

MATT DIXON
www.mattdixon.co.uk
mail@mattdixon.co.uk
Selkie p92
Gone Fishin' p137
Dryad p151

EAMON O' DONOGHUE
www.eamonart.com
eamon@eamonart.com
Space Girl p161

MR. ECCHI
www.cutepet.org
studiocutepet@gmail.com
Angel in Egypt p75

RAÚL CRUZ FIGUEROA
www.racrufi.com
raul@racrufi.com
Storm p70
Insect p172

ALEJANDRO GUTIÉRREZ FRANCO
http://maidencomics.20m.com
http://alexfrancoart.com
contact@alexfrancoart.com
Early Halloween p152
Light Fairy p180
Steampunk Fairy p181

FELIPE MACHADO FRANCO
http://finalfrontier.thunderblast.net
newdimensionart@yahoo.com
Zainib p10
The Sword of Light p142
The Stone Harem p166

FRANK GRANADOS
www.granados602.deviantart.com
www.granados602.cgsociety.org
granados602@gmail.com
Vixen Of Venus p131
Sorceress of the Autumn p150

ANDY HEPWORTH
www.andyhepworth.com
http://andyhep.deviantart.com
http://andyhepworth.blogspot.com
hepworthandrew@aol.com
Velvet Dreams p96
Love's Dream p154

ANDREW HUNTER
www.zarathul.deviantart.com
wormius@gmail.com
Pond Nymph p41
Tanys Defiant p91

CARMEN INDORATO
http://eroticsignature.ning.com/profile/
carmenindorato
www.modelmayhem.com/131010
http://shantetoo.deviantart.com
10plus7@cox.net
White Snake p67

I.L. JACKSON
www.darklorddc.deviantart.com
jacksonsdc@comcast.net
Cybervalkyrie p18
The Space Pirate p20
Trials of Valhalla p118
We Only Infect the Willing p167

UWE JARLING
www.jarling-arts.com
uwe@jarling-arts.com
About Elves and Steel p29
Dragon Pet p121
Domino Lady p124
Bringer of Light p185

JANE DAHL JENSEN
http://janedj.deviantart.com
jane@janedj.dk
Woman and Pirate p17
Woman or Beast p32
Shameless p39

JASON JUTA
www.jasonjuta.com
jason@jasonjuta.com
Centaur p38
Zombie p84
Faerie Queen p184

KASSIDI KEYS
www.theartofkkeys.com
www.afterburns.com
http://kassidikeys.deviantart.com
lizzieborden@gmail.com
The Naga Dancer p43
The Sea Witch p44
If I Had a Heart p51
The Unicorn Kiss p63

LOGAN KNIGHT.
www.knightmanproductions.com
knightflyte69@yahoo.com
Ever After p95
MultiVerse p112
The Glow of Passion p179

SUSANNE KORFF-KNOBLAUCH
www.kaanamoonshadow.deviantart.com
korffknoblauch@gmx.de
The Mage p104
Quality Time p106

YIGIT KOROGLU
www.yigitkoroglu.com
yigitkoroglu@gmail.com
Apple *p171*

VANETTE KOSMAN
www.vanettekosman.artworkfolio.com
vanu_5_coa@hotmail.com
Demonic Obsession *p128*
Succubus by the Sea *p129*
The Crook Goddess *p176*
My Sanctuary *p177*

SCOTT KOZNAR
http://weenie2.deviantart.com
www.gargirlscomics.com
gargirls002@yahoo.com
Erotic Thoughts *p16*

JOE KURZ
www.joes3dfantasyworlds.com
jk@joekurz.info
Worshipping the Moon *p120*

RICARDO LANDELL
www.hardinkgirls.com
cyberunique@msn.com
Leaden Wings *p31*
Vampire Bloodlust *p98*
Succubus Aflight *p99*
Witch / Groundwelling *p153*

GUIDO LEBER
www.goor.deviantart.com
go.or@hotmail.de
Blow *p64*
Shy *p127*
Dark Angel *p178*

SCHIN LOONG
http://schin-art.com
http://schin.etsy.com
schin@schin-art.com
Descendent *p47*
Persephone Destroys the Light *p62*
The Summoning *p148*

LUNARIIS (AARON BIRCH)
http://lunariis.deviantart.com
www.treeworx.org
lunariis@gmail.com
Cullie *p22*
Lunarix—Moonwell *p68*

MANON
www.artbymanon.com
artbymanon@gmail.com
Danae *p72*
The Lady of the Lake *p79*
Siren *p94*

ALEKSANDRA MARCHOCKA
www.olamarchocka.com
aleksandramarchocka@interia.pl
The Little Mermaid *p36*
Pink Tranquility p37
Ink Devil *p46*
Unicorn *p188*

LORENZO DI MAURO
www.lorenzodimauro.com
http://lorenzoart.blogspot.com
contact@lorenzodimauro.com
It's Time For Heroes *p24*
Dark Queen *p136*
Callipygian Angel *p187*

PAUL MCCAFFREY
www.coroflot.com/paul_mccaffrey
p-mac@tesco.net
Boom! *p26*
She's Alive! *p76*
Vampire Nouveau *p97*

DAN MENDOZA
www.toxiccandie.com
daninashell@aol.com
What Was Lost *p86*

NACHO MOLINA
www.nachomolina.deviantart.com
www.nachomolinablog.blogspot.com
lordnatxet@msn.com
Dungeon of Doom Girls *p28*
Mucha Girl *p134*
Lorna *p159*

VINCE NATALE
http://vincenatale.com
vnatale@hvc.rr.com
The Hunted *p4*

BEN NEWMAN
www.bennewmanart.blogspot.com
ben.newman.art@hotmail.co.uk
Promises *p90*

TARIQ RAHEEM
www.tariqart.net
tariqart12@googlemail.com
Maiden of War *p23*
The Witch Queen *p25*
Creatura *p48*

RGUS
rgus@xtra.co.nz
The Apprentice *p140*
I Miss You *p186*

STEVE SAMPSON
www.thedarkinker.com
sampson_art@zen.co.uk
Fallen Angel *p2*
Prey *p93*

DMITRY SERGEEV
http://dmitrys.deviantart.com
dmitrysart@gmail.com
Mage vs Warrior *p12*
Baba Yaga *p27*
Ork Amazon *p33*
Clubbing Drow *p132*

AL SEROV
www.alserov.com
oserov@sympatico.ca
Mage vs Warrior *p12*
The Mines of Barrad-Mishar *p108*
King's Favorite *p122*
In the Throne Room *p130*

AS SHANIM & SILIPHIEL (AERY SOUL)
www.aerysoul.com
www.aerysoul.deviantart.com
support@aerysoul.com
The Fate in your Hands *p143*

DAVID SMIT
www.davidsmit.com
david@davidsmit.com
Wrong! But Sexy *p168*

CHRIS SPOLLEN
www.illoz.com/spollen
cjspollen@aol.com
Lake Girl *p49*
May Flower *p100*
Night Watch *p101*

MAVROSH STRATIOTIS
www.mavrosh.deviantart.com,
mavroshstratiotis@web.de
Eyes Like Ice *p52*
The Hunter *p53*

NESTOR TAYLOR
www.nestortaylor.blogspot.com
nestortaylor@hotmail.com
Hotvalencia *front flap (Ilex edition)*
La Criatura Del Pantano *p45*
Amantes Marinas *p71*

LES TOIL
www.toilgirls.com
lestoil@comcast.net
Carrie *p30*

FRANCISCO RICO TORRES
www.pacorico.blogspot.com
guybrushthreephood@hotmail.com
Pathfinder 10 *p138*
Pathfinder 7 *p155*

DANIELA UHLIG
www.du-artwork.de
www.danielauhlig.blogspot.com
info@du-artwork.de
Melting *p40*
Red Ink II *p40*
The Tree *p174*
Oracle *p192*

CARLOS VALENZUELA
http://valzonline.deviantart.com
valzonline@gmail.com
The Huntress *p125*
Martian Princess *p156*
The Visitor *p169*

K. WAINWRIGHT
http://yilamstation.com
kswainwright1@googlemail.com
Mars In Furs *p80*
Cold Marble Floor *p81*
Barely *p149*

NICOLE WEST
www.pbase.com/nicolewest
wingdthing@gmail.com
Ice Crystal Mermaid *p54*

OLIVER WETTER
http://fantasio.info
fantasiox@googlemail.com
Spellbound II / Lady Blue *p85*
Spirit of the Crow *p145*
The Disquisition *p162*

CHUNG YEE-LING
http://syncmax.deviantart.com
syncmax_se@yahoo.com
Earth and Fire *p117*
DWIV: M410XE Cyborg *p164*
Anna *p165*
Reincarnation *p189*

GRACJANA ZIELINSKA
www.vinegaria.com
vinegaria@gmail.com
After Dusk *p135*
Sensual Dream *p141*

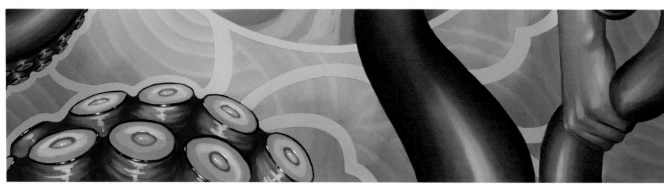

▶ **Oracle**
Daniela Uhlig
Adobe Photoshop
www.du-artwork.de
www.danielauhlig.blogspot.com

Acknowledgments

To my wife Yolanda, without whose help this book would never have happened; to Tim Pilcher and Brad Brooks for their support and advice; to the good folks at Ilex who worked with me on this project; and to all my friends who have taught me the value of passion: Thank you.